SPARC® ARCHITECTURE, ASSEMBLY LANGUAGE PROGRAMMING, AND C

SECOND EDITION

Richard P. Paul

Department of Computer and Information Science
University of Pennsylvania

Prentice Hall, Upper Saddle River, New Jersey 07458

Library of Congress Cataloging-in-Publication Data

Paul, Richard P.
    SPARC architecture, assembly language programming, and C /
Richard P. Paul. — 2nd ed.
    p. cm.
    Includes bibliography references.
    ISBN: 0-13-025596-3
    1. Reduced instruction set computers. 2. Assembler language
(Computer program language). 3. C (Computer program language)
I. Title
QA76.9.A73 p38   2000
005.265—dc21   99-32663
                                                    CIP

Acquisition editor: *Petra Recter*
Editorial assistant: *Sarah Burrows*
Editor-in-chief: *Marcia Horton*
Editorial director: *Tim Bozik*
Editorial/production supervision: *Barbara A. Till*
Assistant managing editor: *Eileen Clark*
Executive managing editor: *Vince O'Brien*
Manufacturing buyer: *Pat Brown*
Manufacturing manager: *Trudy Pisciotti*
Creative director: *Paul Belfanti*
Director of production and manufacturing: *David W. Riccardi*
Art director: *Jayne Conte*
Cover designer: *Kiwi Design*
Copy editor: *Barbara Zeiders*

The author and publisher of this book have used their best efforts in preparing this book. These efforts include the development, research, and testing of the theories and programs to determine their effectiveness. The author and publisher make no warranty of any kind, expressed or implied, with regard to these programs or the documentation contained in this book. The author and publisher shall not be liable in any event for incidental or consequential damages in connection with, or arising out of, the furnishing, performance, or use of these programs.

Printed in the United States of America

10 9 8 7 6 5 4 3 2 1

0-13-025596-3

Prentice-Hall International (UK) Limited, *London*
Prentice-Hall of Australia Pty. Limited, *Sydney*
Prentice-Hall Canada Inc., *Toronto*
Prentice-Hall Hispanoamericana, S.A., *Mexico*
Prentice-Hall of India Private Limited, *New Delhi*
Prentice-Hall of Japan, Inc., *Tokyo*
Prentice-Hall (Singapore) Pte. Ltd., *Singapore*
Editora Prentice-Hall do Brasil, Ltda., *Rio de Janeiro*

SPARC is a registered trademark of SPARC International
UNIX is a registered trademark of AT&T Bell Laboratories

Contents

Preface

Preface to the First Edition

This book is written as an introductory text in computer architecture for the SPARC[1] reduced instruction set architecture. It is assumed that readers have a working knowledge of C and UNIX.[2] The GNU compiler gcc and the gdb debugger are used.

Computer architecture is closely related to assembly language programming, as it is through assembly language programs that the architecture of a machine is made apparent. The presentation of the material breaks from the tradition of computer architecture texts in which assembly language programming was presented as a language in which one might write programs; with a knowledge of the computer architecture, there are, today, a number of high-level languages, such as C, which provide most of the capabilities of assembly language programming. The use of high-level languages results in much higher programmer efficiency and level of representation. It is, however, important to understand the machine at the assembly language level in order to write high-level programs intelligently: to decide between competing data and control structures, the use of global variables and function parameters, the use of recursion, nested procedures, etc. While many of these choices are influenced by high-level factors, the machine architecture has a profound effect on the computational efficiency of the resulting choice.

Although the machine language of a computer is easy to understand, its use results in vast quantities of numeric data that have little meaning. Related to the very heart of computer science is the use of symbol manipulation to simplify and to bring to a clear level of understanding the manipulation and generation of low-level numeric codes. Therefore, symbol manipulation is introduced in the first chapter in the form of the m4 macro processor. Throughout the remainder of the book macros are used to simplify and clarify what is being programmed. The generation of reams of assembly language code is discouraged in favor of the highest level of representation possible.

---

[1]SPARC is a registered trademark of SPARC International, Inc.
[2]UNIX is a registered trademark of AT&T Bell Laboratories.

The computer is introduced by way of the calculator, as most students are familiar with calculators. We make use of the Hewlett-Packard programmable calculator, which reveals many details of machine architectures. The HP calculators have a natural machine language. Assembly language programming is introduced to generate calculator programs making use of m4. A more formal introduction to the machine is presented in the latter half of the first chapter. Stack, accumulator, and load/store machine architectures are also introduced in the first chapter.

The second chapter introduces the SPARC architecture so that students may start programming as early as possible. Like swimming, assembly language programming is not learned in a library! Making use of the machine registers for variable storage, students may start writing short programs by the end of the chapter. The assembler, as, is introduced along with gdb, the debugger. Formatted output is deferred until very late in the book to prevent students from developing the "insert a print statement" mode of program debugging. Instead, gdb is introduced as a natural way to examine memory and registers, and to execute programs. The assembler, as, lacks a macro expansion capability, as it was only designed to be an efficient final pass for the compiler, which has its own macro facilities. In general, we will use the assembler as a second pass to m4, which provides a macro facility. Branching is introduced in the second chapter, as it is difficult to write very interesting programs without branches. Together with branching, pipelining is introduced with the resulting need for delay slot instructions. As the initial specification of the SPARC architecture did not have a multiplication or division instruction, calls to the system routines .mul and .div, etc., are introduced in the second chapter without discussing what happens when the call is made.

As each of the architectural features of the machine is introduced it is related as closely as possible to C language constructs so that students learn the relationship between C and the resulting machine language structures. In the second chapter the control structures of C are introduced in assembly language form. In general, algorithms are written in C and then hand-coded into assembly language. Frequently, optimizations are then seen and the assembly language code optimized. However, we then return to C to learn how the optimized code might have been generated directly from C or why it could not. In this way students learn the problems that compiler writers must face and the reasons why many programs are written the way they are.

Once students are able to write and execute simple assembly language programs, binary logic and arithmetic are introduced. Chapter 3 introduces binary storage devices and number systems: binary, octal, and hexadecimal and their conversions. Bitwise logic operations are introduced and the use of the register %g0, which always yields a zero when used as a source register, effectively increasing the instruction set of the machine. Chapter 4 introduces modulus arithmetic and binary multiplication and division. The treatment of multiplication is fairly extensive, as it is needed to understand the multiply-step instruction of the SPARC architecture. Signed and unsigned comparisons are discussed. The chapter concludes with extended precision arithmetic.

Chapter 5 introduces the stack for the storage of variables. Frames are introduced to provide local storage for functions. The definition of variable offsets is discussed and problems of memory alignment and the load and store instructions. Macros are made use of in the definition of stack offsets and the adjustment of the stack pointer to provide storage. Variables are addressed relative to the frame pointer, which is natural for this architecture. We defer the use of static data until Chapter 9, as their use is clumsy with the SPARC architecture and is not representative of current programming practice.

Chapter 6 introduces multidimensional arrays and structures. Problems of array bound checking and lower bounds differing from zero are discussed along with the problems of dynamic arrays so that students understand the reasons for array addressing restrictions in C. Multiplication by constants for array subscripting is introduced and macros for the automatic generation of multiplication sequences developed in Appendix C. The simplicity of structure addressing is presented so that students understand that arrays, while conceptually simple, are usually a poor choice when structures may be used in their place. Macros are developed for the definition of structure fields and storage allocation.

Functions are then introduced, with discussion of the following: register sets, subroutine linkage, arguments, and return values. Examples are given of simple function calls and of function calls with many arguments or that return aggregates. Finally, leaf routines are presented with their limited register usage.

Chapter 8 introduces the machine language of the SPARC architecture and presents the concepts of instruction decoding and operand access. The handling of 32-bit constants is presented together with program counter relative addressing.

In Chapter 9, global data, initialized data, and addressing methods are discussed. ASCII strings are introduced and formatted output discussed. The `switch` C statement's translation into assembly language is introduced in this chapter. The handling of C command line arguments is presented along with linking with other code.

Chapter 10 discusses input/output from character devices up through I/O processors. The chapter concludes with a section on system input/output using traps.

It is not until Chapter 11 that floating-point is introduced. Floating-point may be left out of a course without affecting the other material. The concept of additional processors with multiple functional units is discussed as well as the interlocking of the floating-point processor with the integer unit. Single, double, and extended precision number formats are described along with NaN's (not a number) and subnormal numbers.

Chapter 12 discusses supervisor mode, processor state registers, and traps. Register window saving by means of traps is discussed in detail. Interrupts are introduced together with hardware traps. This chapter may also be left out of a course without detracting from the other material.

Chapter 13 introduces sharing of the processor between many users and the mechanisms for so doing. Sharing memory is of primary importance and the SPARC virtual memory mapping, translation lookaside buffer, and cache memory system are presented. The chapter concludes with a discussion of context switching.

Chapter 14 presents some alternative architectures, the PDP-11 for historical interest, the VAX as an example of a CISC machine, and the MIPS RISC machine as a contemporary architecture. This chapter may also be left out of a course without detracting from the other material.

Appendices include the macro definitions used in the book, the use of macros to generate an open subroutine for integer multiplication by constants, the user mode instruction set, a table of powers of 2, and the description of `m4`.

In an introductory course for students, Chapters 1 through 9 would logically be followed in order. Additional material could then be selected by the instructor: system I/O, floating-point, traps, virtual memory, other architectures; each of these chapters is independent and may be covered in any order.

For the professional reader, Chapter 2 provides an introduction, followed by the discussion of multiplication on the SPARC at the end of Chapter 4. This should then be followed by Chapters 5 through 13. The appendices provide all the necessary reference material for those interested in user mode programming. The text should be supplemented by the SPARC architecture manual for the professional programmer[22].

The book was produced by the Latex document preparation system [13] and postscript files were generated by Textures [4]. Figures were drawn using the `xfig` program.

Mark Foster helped with `gdb` and the UNIX operating system and provided extensive proofreading corrections. Craig Sayers assisted with the interpretation of the architecture and with technical aspects of the presentation. Angela Lai corrected the Instruction Set Appendix. Doug Nelson provided almost instant responses to my many questions relating to Sun. Horst Hogenkamp assisted with a very careful proofreading and suggestions for clarifying the presentation. Carl Bredlau offered support and thoughtful comments, suggestions, and corrections. Rina Ramamurthy and John Turner assisted with careful reviews and comments. Mel Paul assisted with revisions and editorial changes. Raymond McKendall was extremely helpful with the formatting of the final version of the book. My thanks to all the above. I also wish to thank Tom McElwee, Bill Zobrist, and Jennifer Wenzel at Prentice Hall, who made publication of the book such a pleasant and straightforward matter. Appendix D, Appendix E, and Appendix H are printed with permission from Sun Microsystems, Inc.

Richard P. Paul

Preface to the Second Edition

Since the first edition of the book Sun has announced both a superscalar version of the architecture and an increase in the memory address size from 32 bits to 64 — the Ultra SPARC. The architecture remains binary compatible with the original, which is discussed in detail in the book. A new chapter has been added to describe the new Ultra SPARC architecture, its additional instructions, its compatibility with the existing architecture, and changes to the supervisor mode.

A number of other changes have been made throughout the book to keep it current. The description of the Burroughs B5000, as an example of a stack architecture, has been replaced by a description of a version of the Java virtual machine to support the integer bytecode instructions together with a simulator written in C. New tools are provided for debugging double-precision programs. An extended discussion and example of tagged arithmetic has been added. New exercises have been included. The description of pipelining has been rewritten with a more detailed example. The example of division has been brought into line with the description of multiplication.

A number of people have helped with the preparation of the second edition. Raymond McKendall provided vital Latex support. Jorgen Wahlsten, Dave Reed, and Kostas Daniilidis helped with errors in the book. Joe Bissell provides corrections and pointed out that m4 now includes bitwise operators. Petra Recter, Barbara Till, and Alan Apt of Prentice Hall made the publication of the second edition as straightforward as the first. I also wish to thank reviewers Carl Bredlau and Peter Jones for their helpful insights. Alex Malex helped with Unix system problems and Sean Sheridan with the Web pages. Mel Paul helped with revisions and editorial changes.

Richard P. Paul

Availability of Software

Latest updates to the book may be obtained from the following Web site:

`http://www.prenhall.com/paul`

At this site you will also find all the software to accompany this text, macro definition files, and all example programs in the text. The example programs and files may be downloaded together or accessed individually from the Web. To obtain an instructors manual, which includes the originals for all figures and tables suitable for making slides and solutions to exercises, you should contact your Prentice Hall sales representative.

List of Figures

Chapter 1

THE COMPUTER

1.1 Introduction

Computers are very simple machines, much simpler than the people who designed them and the students who study them. To understand computers we need to have a solid grasp of their capabilities; to do this we need to master a number of simple concepts. The approach we take is to introduce these concepts in a number of different ways: We start with the hand-programmable calculator, a device with which a number of people are familiar; we then introduce the fundamental definition of the computer and its basic cycle; finally, we describe three classic implementations of the computer leading up to the SPARC machine, which is the subject of the book.

Much of computer architecture involves the substitution of numeric codes for symbols. In fact, much of computer science involves the manipulation of symbols and their eventual translation into numbers. Manipulating symbols is facilitated by a **macro** processor, and in this chapter we introduce **m4**, the UNIX macro processor [27].

1.2 Calculators

The calculator has replaced most other forms of calculation, such as the slide rule, the mechanical calculator, pencil and paper, the abacus, and so on. It is appropriate for calculations that are performed only once, such as a discount, a total, or the evaluation of a simple expression. The calculator with which most people are familiar has a numeric keyboard and a few function keys, +, -, x, /. It has a single register, the **accumulator**, into which numbers may be entered or combined with other numbers using the function keys. The contents of the **accumulator** are displayed after each entry and operation. Such a calculator may be obtained cheaply.

1.2.1   Stack Calculators

If we wished to use such a simple calculator to evaluate the following expression for $x = 10$:

$$y = \frac{(x-1)(x-7)}{(x-11)} \tag{1.1}$$

we would also need a pencil and paper to write down the intermediate results $(10-1)$, $(10-7)$, and $(10-11)$, in order to combine them, following the usual rules of precedence in which the parenthesized expressions are evaluated first, as follows:

$$
\begin{align}
(10 - 1) &= 9 \tag{1.2}\\
(10 - 7) &= 3 \tag{1.3}\\
(9 * 3) &= 27 \tag{1.4}\\
(10 - 11) &= -1 \tag{1.5}\\
27/(-1) &= -27 \tag{1.6}
\end{align}
$$

A simple calculator provides only computational power, an **arithmetic logic unit (ALU)** capable of performing arithmetic operations such as addition, subtraction, multiplication, and so on. The piece of paper we used functions as **memory**, a place to store data for later retrieval.

The lack of memory is a rather severe limitation, as many expressions we might wish to evaluate have intermediate results that must be saved temporarily (we don't need the piece of paper in the example above once the calculation has been performed). Memory can be provided for the temporary results of expressions in the form of a stack. A stack is a first-in last-out data structure in which only the top stack elements are accessible [12]. If, in the previous example, a stack were available, the first result, $(10-1) = 9$, could be placed on the top of the stack when it had been computed. This could be followed by the result of $(10-7)$. These two results, now on the stack, could be removed from the stack, multiplied together, and their result once again placed onto the stack. Finally, the top element on the stack could be divided by the result of computing $(10-11)$ to yield the desired result. Placing data items on a stack is frequently referred to as *pushing* and removing items from the stack as *popping*.

The placing of results onto the stack can be combined with the computation of expression values if all arithmetic operations take place between the top two elements of the stack. That is, the operations of addition, subtraction, multiplication, and division remove the top two elements of the stack and then push the result of the arithmetic operation back onto the stack. If a 3 is then pushed onto the stack, followed by a 4, and the addition operation performed, the stack will hold only one element, 7.

Stack memory is very convenient, as it is used in a direct manner without the need to *name* or **address** the memory cells. Hewlett-Packard calculators are built to perform arithmetic by using a stack. When a number is typed, it is entered onto the top of the stack. When an arithmetic key is typed, the top two elements of the stack are removed and replaced with the result. If two numbers have to be entered without an arithmetic operation, the *enter* key is used to separate the two numbers. Such a calculator is shown in Figure 1.1 and described fully in [9]. The top of the stack is always displayed.

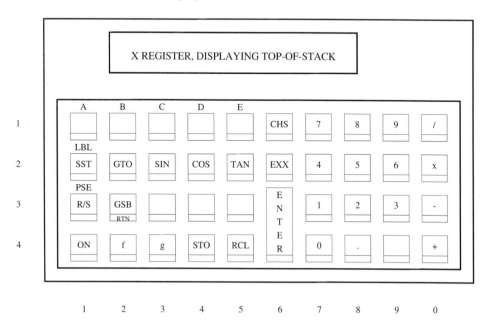

Figure 1.1: The HP-15C Programmable Calculator

In order to perform the expression above , evaluation for $x = 10$, we would enter the following key sequence:

10 enter	Push 10 onto the stack.
1 -	Push 1 and then subtract the top of the stack from the element immediately below it on the stack, leaving a 9 on the stack.
10 enter	Push 10 onto the stack again.
7 -	Push 7 and then subtract, leaving 3 above 9 on the stack.
*	Multiply the top two elements of the stack, leaving 27 on the stack.
10 enter	Push 10 onto the stack again.
11 -	Subtract 11, leaving a -1 above the 27.
/	Divide the top of the stack into the next element below it, leaving a -27 on the stack.

The subexpressions are evaluated in precedence order, with the results being naturally saved and used from the stack. *Naming* of the memory cells is not needed to store the temporary results.

As the calculation progresses, the state of the stack is as shown in Figure 1.2. Notice how the numbers are pushed onto the stack and then combined by the arithmetic function keys. When evaluating arithmetic operations, the top two elements of the stack are popped and the result pushed back onto the stack.

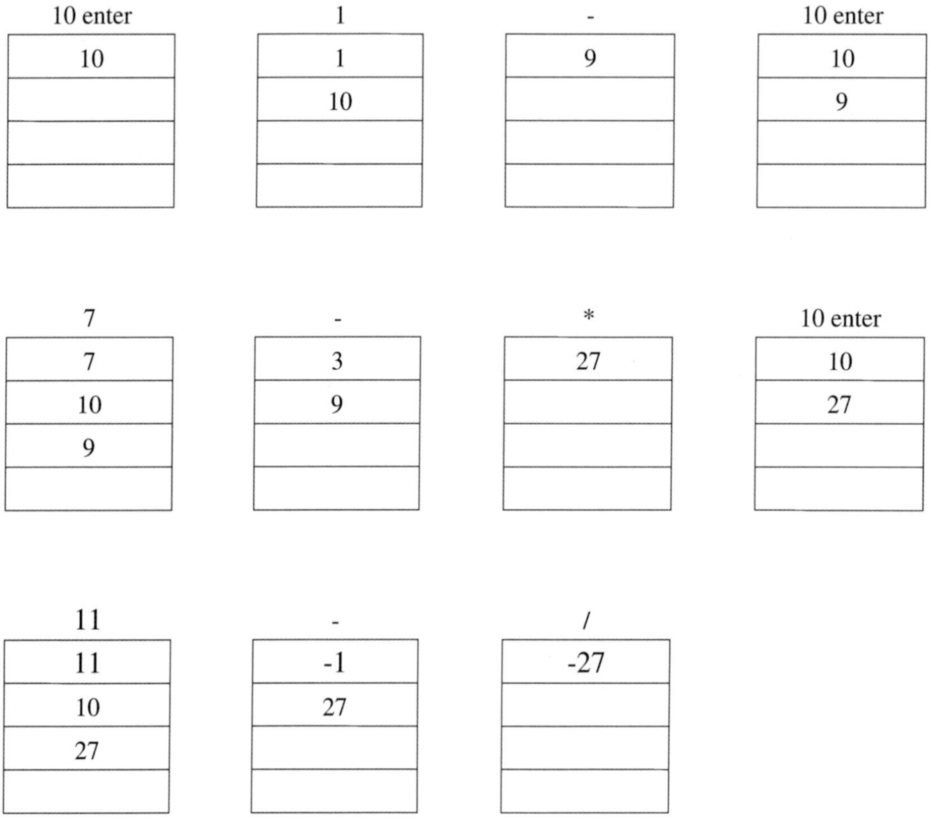

10 enter	1	-	10 enter
10	1	9	10
	10		9

7	-	*	10 enter
7	3	27	10
10	9		27
9			

11	-	/
11	-1	-27
10	27	
27		

Figure 1.2: The Evaluation of $y = (10 - 1)(10 - 7)/(10 - 11)$

1.2.2   The Use of Registers

If we wished to evaluate the expression for $x = 3.172843$, we could proceed as before but we would need to type in the number 3.172843 three times! As we continued to type in 3.172843, we would start to think that there must be a better way, and of course there is. Registers are provided to hold constants such as $x = 3.172843$. These registers are named by number, starting at 0, and approximately 10 are provided. Numbers may be stored into registers by first typing the number into the calculator followed by the key sequence sto and then the register name. This operation copies the number from the top of the stack into the register named. A number may be retrieved from a register to the top of the stack by typing rcl followed by the register name. Registers may also be used to hold intermediate results in evaluating expressions; however, unlike the stack, registers must be named by specifying their number. The use of registers to hold temporary results would make expression evaluation cumbersome, as we would have to remember the name of the register into which we placed each temporary result. The stack accepts and returns temporary results in the same order as an expression is naturally evaluated.

To evaluate the expression above, using the stack and a register, for $x = 3.172843$ we might enter the following key sequence:

3.172843 sto 0	Store the constant 3.172843 in register 0, leaving a copy of it on the top of the stack.
1 -	Push 1 and then subtract the top of the stack from the element immediately below it on the stack, leaving 2.172843 on the stack.
rcl 0	Copy the contents of register 0 onto the top of the stack, 3.172843.
7 -	Push 7 and then subtract leaving −3.827157 above 2.172843 on the stack.
*	Multiply the top two elements of the stack leaving -8.315811 on the stack.
rcl 0	Copy the contents of register 0 onto the top of the stack, 3.172843.
11 -	Subtract 11, leaving −7.827157 above −8.315811.
/	Divide the top of the stack into the next element below it, leaving a 1.062431 on the stack.

In this case we first store the constant 3.172843 into register 0 and then use it by recalling it to the top of the stack instead of entering it each time it is used, as we did in the first program.

Let us take stock of where we are. We have seen the use of an **arithmetic logic unit** to perform arithmetic operations. We have also seen the need for **memory** to facilitate expression evaluation, and to store constants. Memory was provided in two forms, a stack and registers. A stack is convenient for expression evaluation as memory **addresses** are not needed. **Registers** are useful when values enter into the computation in a less structured manner. However, to facilitate this less structured use, a *register name* must be specified. Registers may, however, be used in place of a stack.

1.2.3   Programmable Calculators

Now let us suppose that we wish to plot a graph of the function above for values of x such that $0 \leq x \leq 10$. We could proceed to store values of x into register 0 and then type the keys to evaluate the expression. It would be much simpler if we could just enter the value of x and then have the keystrokes automatically repeated. To do this we must **program** the calculator.

To program the calculator we first change the calculator into a program mode. When the calculator is in program mode, the keystrokes are not executed, but a code representing each key is stored into a memory that has both an **address** (a location in memory) and **data** (the keystroke entered).

We begin by storing the keystrokes into memory location zero. After each keystroke is entered, the memory address is incremented so that the next keystroke will be stored in the next memory location. How are keystrokes stored? The keys are stored as small numbers; the tens digit is the row number, and the units digit is the column number of the key. Rows and columns start numbering from the top left-hand corner of the keyboard. The top row is 1 and the bottom 4. The first column is 1 and the last 10. The tens digit is dropped from the column number, so that columns are stored as 1, 2, 3, 4, 5, 6, 7, 8, 9, 0. The only exception to this is for the number keys, in which case, the code stored is simply the digit. Thus, the key sequence 3, enter, 5, +, would be stored as 3, 36, 5, 40. Check these key codes by referring to Figure 1.1.

All keys have three designations:

- The principal designation, printed on the face of the key in white ink, is obtained simply by using the key.

- Above the key is a second designation printed in yellow; to obtain this function you must press the yellow **f** key followed by the function key.

- To obtain the designation on the lower face of the key, printed in blue, you must press the blue **g** key followed by the function key.

To indicate the end of the following program, the **rtn** key is entered after the blue prefix **g** (see Figure 1.1).

To evaluate the expression for a particular value of x, we will type the value of x into the calculator and then execute the stored program to compute y. The program will first store the last value entered into register 0, leaving a copy of it already on the stack, and will then proceed as before to evaluate the expression:

sto 0	Store the number entered in register 0, leaving a copy of it on the top of the stack.
1 -	Push 1 and then subtract the top of the stack from the element immediately below it on the stack.
rcl 0	Copy the contents of register 0 onto the top of the stack.
7 -	Push 7 and then subtract, leaving the result on the stack.
*	Multiply the top two elements of the stack.
rcl 0	Copy the contents of register 0 onto the top of the stack.
11 -	Subtract 11.
/	Divide the top of the stack into the next element below it, leaving the result on top of the stack.
g rtn	Return from the program to regular execution mode.

If we then type 3.172843 followed by R/S to execute the program, first "running" will appear in the display and then 1.062431, as before. We may now evaluate the expression for a number of values of x and plot the resulting y values.

We have now seen another use of memory, to store the program. Unlike the stack and the registers, this **memory** is **addressed**. Memory functions as a large array of numbers that may be indexed starting from zero. In the C programming language [11] we might declare such an array as

```
char memory[1024];
```

which would declare a 1024-byte memory array. The index of the array corresponds to the **address**. Like array indices, memory addresses, may be computed, unlike the registers, which are similar to a C structure and may be selected but not indexed:

```
struct registers {
  int r0, r1, r2, r3, r4,
      r5, r6, r7, r8, r9;
}
```

In the case of the calculator, the contents of the memory are the codes for the keystrokes. These codes are the **machine language** of the calculator. It is these codes that the **central processing unit (CPU)** executes. The codes are fetched one by one from memory, in sequence, and are executed. The address of the next keystroke to be executed is stored in a register called the **program counter (PC)**.

The contents of the calculator's memory after it has been programmed are shown in the following table. Check the key encodings with the key sequences by examining Figure 1.1.

Address	Machine Code	Keystrokes	Comment
000	44 0	sto 0	Store in register 0.
002	1	1	Enter 1.
003	30	−	Subtract.
004	45 0	rcl 0	Register 0 to stack.
006	7	7	Enter 7.
007	30	−	Subtract.
008	20	*	Multiply.
009	45 0	rcl 0	Register 0 to stack.
011	1	1	Enter 1.
012	1	1	Make it 11.
013	30	−	Subtract.
014	10	/	Divide.
015	43 32	g Rtn	Return to calculator mode.

1.2.4 Machine Language Programming

When functioning as a calculator, all the keyboard does is to send an appropriate numeric code, the **machine language**, to the **ALU**. When it is being programmed, the keyboard sends the appropriate numeric codes to **memory**. We could replace the function keyboard with a simple numeric keyboard if we were prepared to type the **machine language instructions** in place of using the calculator function keys.

Thus, to program the calculator to perform the expression evaluation above, we would need to type the numbers from the second column of the program shown above:

$$44\ 0\ 1\ 30\ 45\ 0\ 7\ 30\ 20\ 45\ 0\ 1\ 1\ 30\ 10\ 43\ 32$$

and we would have the calculator programmed. The keyboard, however, helps us to remember the **machine language** – the codes that the keys represent. If we were to write a **machine language** program, we would need a piece of paper with the key mnemonics and their corresponding **machine language instructions** written on it to remind us of the keys. For example, we might have the following list of symbols:

sto	44 0	rcl	45 0	div	10	mul	20
sub	30	add	40	ent	36	rtn	43 32

Making use of this list, we could translate the program, with symbols representing the keys:[1]

sto

1

---

[1]Here sto will generate the sequence sto 0 and rcl will generate the sequence rcl 0.

```
sub
rcl
7
sub
mul
rcl
1
1
sub
div
rtn
```

Inputting the program would now involve only looking up each mnemonic in the table and substituting the appropriate machine instruction. A program in the form shown above is known as an **assembly language** program. It is a program with symbols representing numeric values. Translating an **assembly language** program into a **machine language** program involves **looking up** the symbols and mnemonics in a **symbol table** (our piece of paper with the keys and their codes) and substituting the matching numeric value.

1.3 m4: The Macro Processor

There is a program, called **m4** [27], that may be used to translate symbols into numeric constants. **m4** is a macro processor and it basically copies its input to its output; however, as it does this, it checks all alphanumeric tokens in case they are macro definitions. An alphanumeric token is a string of letters or digits starting with a letter; the underbar character, _, is also considered an alphanumeric character. If m4 finds a macro token, it removes the token from the input and pushes the macro definition back into the input to be scanned.

Macros may be defined using the **define** macro. **define** takes two arguments, the macro token and the definition. For example, to define the machine instructions for the calculator, we would enter into a file the information we had earlier written on a piece of paper:

```
define(sto, 44 0)
define(rcl, 45 0)
define(div, 10)
define(mul, 20)
define(sub, 30)
define(add, 40)
define(ent, 36)
define(rtn, 43 32)
```

If these definitions were saved in a file, called, for example, **cal.m** along with the program:

```
sto
1
sub
rcl
7
sub
mul
rcl
1
1
sub
div
rtn
```

and **m4** run:

%m4 cal.m

the output would be a series of blank lines, one for each definition, followed by
the translated symbols, the **machine language**:

```
44   0
1
30
45   0
7
30
20
45   0
1
1
30
10
43   32
```

1.3.1   Macros with Arguments

Macros may have up to nine arguments. Arguments are specified in the macro
definition by $n, where n is a digit between 0 and 9. When scanning text, a macro
name followed *immediately* by an open parentheses "(" indicates the presence of
arguments. If there are arguments, enclosed in parentheses, each is evaluated before
being substituted into the macro definition in place of the matching $n formal
parameter. The entire macro text is pushed back into the input and rescanned.
The macro scanner expands everything it possibly can.

In collecting arguments, white space[2] before the argument is ignored, so that the definition of cat:

```
define(cat, $1$2$3$4$5$6$7$8$9)
```

and its call:

```
cat(  a, b, c,
d,    e, f,g,   h, i)
```

results in

```
abcdefghi
```

If we had fewer arguments than the nine specified, unsupplied arguments would be replaced by nulls, so that

```
cat(  a , b , c)
```

would result in

```
a b c
```

Notice that the trailing blank after each argument is not removed but becomes part of the argument string.

In our definition of mnemonics we defined `sto` and `rcl` always to store and retrieve register 0. There are, however, 10 registers. The register number should be an argument to `sto` and to `rcl`. We can redefine the macros to do this; instead of defining `sto` as `define(sto, 44 0)` we could define it as `define(sto,'44 $1')` and `rcl` as `define(rcl, '45 $1')` and enter the program as

```
sto(0)
1
sub
rcl(0)
7
sub
mul
rcl(0)
1
1
sub
div
rtn
```

---

[2]White space consists of spaces, tabs, and end-of-line characters.

which would produce the same machine code as before.

Why the single quotes in the definitions of `sto` and `rcl` above? `define` is a built-in macro and its arguments are evaluated as are all macro arguments. When making a macro definition we do not want the macro definition to be evaluated and may prevent this by enclosing the arguments in single quotes.[3] When a string enclosed by single quotes is encountered, the quotes are removed and the string is passed through without the evaluation of any macros that might be in the string.

One normally quotes all macro names being defined in case they were defined previously. Consider what happens when a macro is redefined:

```
define(N, 100)
N
define(N, 200)
N
```

The macro text above results in both evaluation of N as 100. This happens as a result of the evaluation process described above. The argument to the second **define**, N, is a macro name and is immediately expanded to its definition of 100. The second argument to the call to **define**, 200, is not a macro name and is not replaced. Thus, the input to the second **define** is `define(100, 200)`. This makes no sense and an error message is given.

One further refinement is to replace the numeric register argument with a symbolic argument. Instead of writing `sto(0)` we could write `sto(x_r)`. Why would we want to do this? If we had a program with a lot of variables stored in registers, we would have to remember into which register all the variables in the program were stored. We would, once again, need a piece of paper to keep track of the register assignments. We can, of course, use **m4** to do this for us. In the case of this simple program we could use a macro definition to define `x_r` to be 0. We can then use `x_r` as the argument to the sto and rcl macros. Notice that we have defined the register name holding the value of x to have the suffix `_r` to distinguish it from a symbol `x` defined to be the value of x. Our program then becomes

```
define(f, 42)
define(g, 43)
define(x_r, 0)
sto(x_r)
1
sub
```

---

[3]The `emacs` editor [23] may be changed to match single quotes, as it matches parentheses, by including the following two lines in the `.emacs` file in your home directory:

```
(modify-syntax-entry ?` "(’" text-mode-syntax-table)
(modify-syntax-entry ?’ ")`" text-mode-syntax-table)
```

The characters that syntactically represent the single quotes may also be changed by a macro `changequote` (see Appendix H).

```
rcl(x_r)
7
sub
mul
rcl(x_r)
1
1
sub
div
rtn
```

This also produces the identical machine code with everything now defined symbolically. This is good programming practice, as it makes programs clearer and much easier to understand.

1.3.2 Memory Location

We could also add the memory address of where in memory our instructions are stored. We do this by redefining all the macros as follows:

```
define(f, 42)
define(g, 43)
define(loc, 0)
define(sto, 'loc:        44 $1 define('loc', eval(loc + 2))')
define(rcl, 'loc:        45 $1 define('loc', eval(loc + 2))')
define(div, 'loc:        10 define('loc', eval(loc + 1))')
define(mul, 'loc:        20 define('loc', eval(loc + 1))')
define(sub, 'loc:        30 define('loc', eval(loc + 1))')
define(add, 'loc:        40 define('loc', eval(loc + 1))')
define(ent, 'loc:        36 define('loc', eval(loc + 1))')
define(rtn, 'loc:        g 32 define('loc', eval(loc + 2))')
define(digit, 'loc:      $1   define('loc', eval(loc + 1))')
```

Here we have first defined a symbol, loc, to have the value 0. This symbol will represent the **location counter**, the memory address of the instruction being assembled. Each macro definition has been changed first to print the current value of loc and then to redefine loc to be loc plus the memory locations needed to store the instruction.

The arguments to macros are characters and strings of characters, not numeric values. In redefining the value of loc we make use of another built-in macro **eval**.[4] **eval** takes its string argument to represent an arithmetic expression. **eval** evaluates this expression and returns its value in the form of a numeric character string. Redefining a macro in **m4** is the equivalent of the assignment operation in C. We

---

[4]The built in macros of m4 are listed in Appendix H.

have also defined a new macro `digit` to handle the input of numbers so that the location counter is also advanced.

When the macro definitions and program are run through **m4**, the following text results:

```
0:      44 0
2:      1
3:      30
4:      45 0
6:      7
7:      30
8:      20
9:      45 0
11:     1
12:     1
13:     30
14:     10
15:     43 32
```

Note the addresses of the machine instructions in the left-hand column.

1.3.3 Conditionals and Branching

Returning to our expression and graph generation, we may go one step further. If we wished to evaluate the expression for values of x, $0 \leq x \leq 10$, in increments of 1, we would still have a fair amount of typing just entering in the values of x. What we want to do is to execute the program, which evaluates the value of y given a value of x, a number of times for a sequence of values of x. We could do this if we could determine when we should stop evaluating the expression and change the address of the next instruction to be executed. These two capabilities are known as *testing* and *branching*.

In the HP15C calculator we may test if the current value of the top of the stack is zero. If it is not, the next instruction in line is skipped. Normally, the instruction following the test is a goto instruction, which will transfer control to some other point in the program. Targets of branches are labels. We will need three more macros to handle labels and branching:

```
define(label, 'define($1, loc)')
define(ifeq, 'loc      g 20 define('loc', eval(loc + 2)))')
define(gto, 'loc        22 $1 define('loc', eval(loc + 2)))')
```

The first of these macro definitions, `label`, defines its argument, in the case of the HP calculator, a letter, to have as value the current value of the location counter. If the label is later evaluated, it will have the value of the location of the next instruction to be executed. The second macro `ifeq` is the key code to test if the current value of the expression evaluation is zero. If it is zero, the next instruction is executed; otherwise, the next instruction is skipped. The third macro, `gto`, corresponds to the `gto` key. It has a label as argument. When it is executed, the **program counter** is assigned the value of the argument, which is the location of the target of the branch instruction. The next instruction to be executed will then be the labeled instruction, not the next instruction in line.

Finally, we will need to see the values of the expression evaluation. To do this with the calculator we would use the pause key `f pse`. This causes the calculator to pause and to display the current expression value:

```
define(pse, 'loc        f 31 define('loc', eval(loc + 2))')
```

We will use three labels in the program: A for the start of the program, B for the loop, and C for the return to calculator mode. The first piece of code is simply the labeled **rtn** statement. This code must appear first, as in **m4** all symbols have to be defined before they are used:

```
label(C)
rtn
```

Then follows the code to initialize the x register:

```
label(A)
digit(0)
sto(x_r)
```

The loop then follows: First the value of x is compared to 11 to see if the loop is to be executed; if it is to be executed, the value of y is computed and printed:

```
label(B)
rcl(x_r)
digit(1)
digit(1)
sub
ifeq
gto(C)
rcl(x_r)
digit(1)
sub
rcl(x_r)
digit(7)
sub
mul
rcl(x_r)
digit(1)
digit(1)
sub
div
pse
```

Finally, the value of x is incremented and the program branches back to the test:

```
rcl(x_r)
digit(1)
add
sto(x_r)
gto(B)
```

If the macro definitions are modified to compute the value of the location counter but not to print it out:

```
define(g, 43)
define(f, 42)
define(loc, 0)
define(sto, '   44 $1 define('loc', eval(loc + 2))')
define(rcl, '   45 $1 define('loc', eval(loc + 2))')
define(div, '   10 define('loc', eval(loc + 1))')
define(mul, '   20 define('loc', eval(loc + 1))')
define(sub, '   30 define('loc', eval(loc + 1))')
define(add, '   40 define('loc', eval(loc + 1))')
define(ent, '   36 define('loc', eval(loc + 1))')
define(rtn, '   g 32 define('loc', eval(loc + 2))')
define(digit, ' $1        define('loc', eval(loc + 1))')
define(label, 'define($1, loc)')
define(ifeq, ' g 20 define('loc', eval(loc + 2))')
define(gto, '   22 $1 define('loc', eval(loc + 2))')
define(pse, '   f 31 define('loc', eval(loc + 2))')
```

and the macro definitions and the program above are run through **m4**, the following **machine language** is generated:

```
43 32 0 44 0 45 0 1 1 30 43 20 22 0 45 0 1 30 45 0 7 30 20 45 0 1 1 30
10 42 31 45 0 1 40 44 0 22 5
```

If the program is then run, the following numbers are generated:

```
 -0.636364
  0.000000
  0.555556
  1.000000
  1.285714
  1.333333
  1.000000
  0.000000
 -2.333333
 -8.000000
-27.000000
```

1.4 The von Neumann Machine

The HP15C programmable calculator is a small computer and fits the definition of the stored program computer proposed by von Neumann in 1946 [3]. He had joined Eckert and Mauchly, who had designed and built the world's first electronic general-purpose computer, ENIAC, at the Moore School of the University of Pennsylvania [30]. ENIAC had twenty, 10-digit registers (each 2 feet long) and a total of 18,000 vacuum tubes; it took 200 microseconds[5] to perform an add operation. Programming of ENIAC was done by plugging cables and setting switches. Von Neumann helped to formulate the idea of a stored program computer in which the program was to be stored in the machine's memory as numbers together with the data. The first stored-program computer, EDSAC, was built at Cambridge University by Wilkes in 1949 [29].

The machine von Neumann helped to define consists of an addressable **memory**, capable of holding instructions and data, coupled with an **arithmetic logic unit**, capable of executing the instructions fetched from memory. The address of the next instruction to be executed was held in a register called the **program counter**. The cycle the von Neumann machine executed was

```
pc = 0;                 /* initialize the program counter */

do {
   instruction = memory[pc++];   /* fetch the instruction */
   decode(instruction);   /* decode the instruction */
   fetch (operands);      /* fetch the operands */
   execute;               /* execute the instruction */
   store (results);       /* store the results */
} while (instruction != halt);
```

Although it is clear that instructions were to be fetched from memory and executed, it is not clear how they were to be executed or how the operands were to be obtained. Let us look a little more closely at how the HP calculator fits the definition of a von Neumann machine.

1.5 The Stack Machine

In the HP calculator instructions such as **add** and **sub** are clearly fetched from memory. These instructions have no operands, as in a **stack** architecture the operands for arithmetic functions are always on the stack. The machine must decode the number representing the instruction it has fetched from memory in order to decide what operation is to be performed. This is done in the form of a hardware **switch** statement. The instruction is executed by first removing the operands from the

---

[5]The *micro* prefix implies 10^{-6}.

top of the stack, performing whatever operation is specified by the instruction, and storing the result, if any, back onto the top of the stack.

The test instruction `ifeq` has no operand. The `gto` instruction does have an operand, the new value of the program counter, the **pc**. The `digit` instruction is a little strange, as it simply stores a single digit of a number, fetched from memory, onto the stack. The HP calculator distinguishes between instructions and data based on the magnitude of the value fetched. If the instruction fetched is less than 10, it is a datum and is to be converted to a number and eventually pushed onto the stack. For example, `digit(1)` immediately followed by another `digit(1)` results in the constant 11 being pushed onto the stack. A constant stored in the program in this manner is called a **literal**.

An architecture such as the HP calculator is similar to a "stack" architecture; Burroughs developed the first such machine in 1963, the B5000 [1]. A stack architecture differs from the calculator in that it does not have a set of registers for holding constants and intermediate results. Thus, in our program, to compute the expression Eq. (1.1), we need to store the variables x and y in memory. To get these onto the stack, we introduce a new instruction, `load`, which has one operand, the memory address of where the data are stored in memory. To store the result away, we will define a `store` instruction, with operand the address in memory, where the top of the stack is to be stored. The stack architecture is shown in Figure 1.3. The machine has a program counter and an instruction decode register. Logic and arithmetic are performed by the arithmetic logic unit between the top two elements of a stack; the top two elements are popped from the stack and the result pushed back onto the stack. Memory is accessed by first loading an address into the memory address register, MAR; on a `pop` instruction, the top of the stack is popped into the memory data register, MDR, for storing into memory; on a `push` instruction, the MDR is loaded from memory and then pushed onto the top of the stack.

Stack architectures represent one of the simplest forms of machine orgainzation, specifying no registers, only a stack and an arithmetic logic unit. An abstract form of assembly language, called *abstract stack machine* code, is designed to be executed by such a simple machine. When programs are intended to be executed by many different computers, they are frequently represented as a modified form of abstract machine code and then executed by each different machine using a program called an *interpreter*. For example, Postscript printers are sent programs in stack machine code which come in the form of a file of characters. Upon receipt of the file, the characters are assembled into tokens, such as `add`, `sub`, and so on. and then the program is executed as it is read by the interpreter. This frees up the printer builder to use any computer he or she wishes, as long as it is programmed to interpret the stack code correctly.

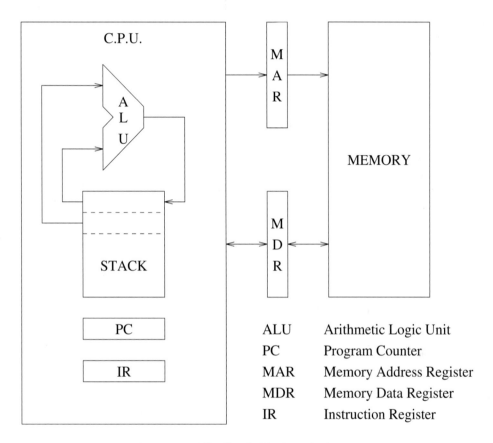

Figure 1.3: The Stack Machine Architecture

1.6   The Java Virtual Machine

More recently, interest in the ability to execute programs downloaded over the Web on any computer has resulted in a programming language called Java. Java, an object-oriented version of C, is compiled into bytecode. The bytecode may be downloaded and executed on any computer by a *Java virtual machine* [18], an interpreter designed to execute Java bytecode. Java bytecode is stack machine code in which the individual instructions are represented by numbers stored in a single byte. This gives the machine at most 256 instructions. The Java virtual machine can handle many data types and will perform arithmetic with real numbers as well as with integers. The Java integer arithmetic instructions are as follows:

Mnemonic	Code	Args	Operation
iconst_m1	2		Push -1 onto the stack.
iconst_0	3		Push constant 0 onto the stack.
iconst_1	4		Push constant 1 onto the stack.
iconst_2	5		Push constant 2 onto the stack.
iconst_3	6		Push constant 3 onto the stack.
iconst_4	7		Push constant 4 onto the stack.
iconst_5	8		Push constant 5 onto the stack.
bipush	16	n	Push signed byte n onto the stack.
iload_0	26		Push local variable 0 onto the stack.
iload_1	27		Push local variable 1 onto the stack.
iload-2	28		Push local variable 2 onto the stack.
iload_3	29		Push local variable 3 onto the stack.
iload	21	n	Push variable n onto the stack.
istore_0	59		Pop stack and store in local variable 0.
istore_1	60		Pop stack and store in local variable 1.
istore_2	61		Pop stack and store in local variable 2.
istore_3	62		Pop stack and store in local variable 3.
istore	54	n	Pop stack and store in local variable n.
pop	87		Pop stack.
swap	95		Exchange top two elements of stack.
dup	89		Duplicate top element of stack.
iadd	96		Pop elements, replace with sum.
isub	100		Pop elements, replace with diff.
imul	104		Pop elements, replace with product.
idiv	108		Pop elements, replace with quotient.
irem	112		Pop elements, replace with rem.
ineg	116		Negate top element of stack.
iinc	132	n d	Increment variable n, by d.

The first group of instructions pushes literals onto the stack. Notice that there are specific machine instructions to load each of the first few integers without need of an operand $-1 \leq \text{literal} \leq 5$. If you need a literal outside this range, you must use the `bipush` instruction, which has a byte following the instruction bytecode to store the integer value. The value is limited to $-128 \leq$ value ≤ 127.

The next set of instructions push the contents of Java's local variables onto the stack. Again, there are instructions for pushing the first few local variables onto the stack and a more general instruction which requires an operand following the code byte. This group of instructions is followed by instructions to pop the top of the stack and to store the value into a local variable.

Some stack manipulation instructions precede the integer arithmetic instructions. The last arithmetic instruction increments a local variable by an arbitrary value.

Let us define some macros to initialize memory of a Java virtual machine in the same manner as we did for the calculator so that we can write Java virtual machine code to perform computations.[6]

The first line of the following macro code is the `divert` macro, which will eliminate all the blank lines due to the macro definitions and comments enclosed in ' '. `divert(-1)` discards all input until a `divert` macro without an argument is encountered. The second line defines a `comment` macro whose argument is evaluated and then discarded, allowing us to comment our code after the final call to `divert`. The comment macro enables us to add comments to our program without affecting the machine code generated. The comment appears as the argument to the macro and should be enclosed in single quotes to assure that no macro names in a comment are evaluated when the arguments to `comment` are evaluated by m4.

```
divert(-1)
define(comment)
define(loc, 0) coment('location counter')
define(iconst_m1, 'loc: 2 define('loc', eval(loc + 1))') 'push -1'
define(iconst_0, 'loc:  3 define('loc', eval(loc + 1))') 'push 0'
define(iconst_1, 'loc:  4 define('loc', eval(loc + 1))') 'push 1'
define(iconst_2, 'loc:  5 define('loc', eval(loc + 1))') 'etc.'
define(iconst_3, 'loc:  6 define('loc', eval(loc + 1))')
define(iconst_4, 'loc:  7 define('loc', eval(loc + 1))')
define(iconst_5, 'loc:  8 define('loc', eval(loc + 1))')
'push signed byte arg following in instruction stream'
define(bipush, 'loc:   16 $1 define('loc', eval(loc + 2))')

define(iload_0, 'loc:   26 define('loc', eval(loc + 1))') 'push loc 0'
define(iload_1, 'loc:   27 define('loc', eval(loc + 1))') 'push loc 1'
define(iload_2, 'loc:   28 define('loc', eval(loc + 1))') 'etc.'
define(iload_3, 'loc:   29 define('loc', eval(loc + 1))')
'push variable stored in loc following in instruction stream'
define(iload, 'loc:   21 $1 define('loc', eval(loc + 2))')
```

---

[6]The Java virtual machine described fully in [18] includes a Java assembler, `jasmin`, which will assemble Java assembly language programs into class files that can be run on any Java virtual machine or viewed as applets.

```
define(istore_0, 'loc:   59 define('loc', eval(loc + 1))') 'pop> loc 0'
define(istore_1, 'loc:   60 define('loc', eval(loc + 1))') 'pop> loc 1'
define(istore_2, 'loc:   61 define('loc', eval(loc + 1))') 'etc.'
define(istore_3, 'loc:   62 define('loc', eval(loc + 1))')
'pop variable and store in loc following in instruction stream'
define(istore, 'loc:   54 $1 define('loc', eval(loc + 2))')

define(pop, 'loc:      87 define('loc', eval(loc + 1))') 'pop stack'
define(swap, 'loc:     95 define('loc', eval(loc + 1))') 'swap'
define(dup, 'loc:      89 define('loc', eval(loc + 1))') 'duplicate'

define(iadd, 'loc:      96 define('loc', eval(loc + 1))') '+'
define(isub, 'loc:     100 define('loc', eval(loc + 1))') '-'
define(imul, 'loc:     104 define('loc', eval(loc + 1))') '*'
define(idiv, 'loc:     108 define('loc', eval(loc + 1))') '/'
define(irem, 'loc:     112 define('loc', eval(loc + 1))') '%'
define(ineg, 'loc:     116 define('loc', eval(loc + 1))') 'negate'
'increment variable at loc, by const, args following in instr. stream'
define(iinc, 'loc:     132 $1 $2 define('loc', eval(loc + 3))')

'method call, index to name follows in instr. stream:
1 == print, 2 == println.  Variable number to print on stack'
define(invokevirtual, 'loc:     182 $1 define('loc', eval(loc + 2))')

define(return, 'loc:    177 define('loc', eval(loc + 1))')
define(label, 'define($1, loc)dnl')
divert
```

We have added the `invokevirtual` instruction, which in Java takes an index into a list of names of methods to be called, and have specialized it here to call either `print` or `println` to print out a local variable whose number is on the top of the stack. Print does not terminate the output line with a newline, whereas println does. The argument to the method is popped off the stack after execution. Finally, the `return` instruction ends execution.

A program to compute the expression Eq. (1.1) is as follows:

```
bipush(10)      comment('initialize x to 10, local_1')
istore_1
iload_1         comment('compute (x - 1)')
iconst_1
isub
iload_1         comment('compute (x - 7)')
bipush(7)
isub
imul            comment('(x - 1) * (x - 7)')
iload_1         comment('compute (x - 11)')
bipush(11)
```

```
isub
idiv            comment('(x - 1) * (x - 7) / (x - 11)')
istore_2        comment('store y in local_2')
iconst_1        comment('print(x), push variable number of x')
invokevirtual(1)comment('1 == print')
iconst_2        comment('println(y), push variable number of y')
invokevirtual(2)comment('2 == printn')
return
```

If this program is run through **m4**, the following output is generated:

```
0:        16 10
2:        60
3:        27
4:        4
5:        100
6:        27
7:        16 7
9:        100
10:       104
11:       27
12:       16 11
14:       100
15:       108
16:       61
17:       4
18:       182 1
20:       5
21:       182 2
23:       177
```

We may interpret this program by the following *Java virtual machine* written in C to interpret the integer instructions. The program first reads in the bytecode, storing the bytes in a char array **memory**. The program counter is then set to zero and the program interpreted by a single **switch** statement with a **case** for each instruction.

```
/* integer java virtual machine */
#include <stdio.h>

#define ICONST_M1 2     /* push -1 onto stack */
#define ICONST_0 3      /* push 0 onto stack */
#define ICONST_1 4      /* push 1 onto stack */
#define ICONST_2 5      /* push 2 onto stack */
#define ICONST_3 6      /* push 3 onto stack */
#define ICONST_4 7      /* push 4 onto stack */
```

```
#define ICONST_5 8      /* push 5 onto stack */
#define BIPUSH 16        /* bipush <value>, push <byte value> */

#define ILOAD_0 26       /* iload_0 push local variable 0 */
#define ILOAD_1 27       /* iload_1 push local variable 1 */
#define ILOAD_2 28       /* iload_2 push local variable 2 */
#define ILOAD_3 29       /* iload_3 push local variable 3 */
#define ILOAD 21         /* iload <varnum>, push <varnum> */

#define ISTORE_0 59      /* pop stack to local variable 0 */
#define ISTORE_1 60      /* pop stack to local variable 1 */
#define ISTORE_2 61      /* pop stack to local variable 2 */
#define ISTORE_3 62      /* pop stack to local variable 3 */
#define ISTORE 54        /* istore <varnum>, pop to <varnum> */

#define POP 87           /* discard top of stack */
#define SWAP 95          /* swap top two items of stack */
#define DUP 89           /* duplicate top of stack */

#define IADD 96          /* add */
#define ISUB 100         /* subtract */
#define IMUL 104         /* mul */
#define IDIV 108         /* div */
#define IREM 112         /* remainder */
#define INEG 116         /* negate */
#define IINC 132         /* iinc <varnum> <n>, add <n> to <varnum> */

#define IFEQ 153         /* ifeq <label>, if == 0, goto <label> */
#define IFGE 156         /* ifge <label>, if >= 0, goto <label> */
#define IFGT 157         /* ifgt <label>, if >  0, goto <label> */
#define IFLE 158         /* ifle <label>, if <= 0, goto <label> */
#define IFLT 155         /* iflt <label>, if <  0, goto <label> */
#define IFNE 154         /* ifne <label>, if != 0, goto <label> */
#define GOTO 167         /* goto <label> */

#define INVOKEVIRTUAL 182 /* method call specialized to call */
                          /* System.out.println with a local */
                          /* variable as argument */
#define PRINT 1          /* argument for System.out.print */
#define PRINTLN 2        /* argument for System.out.println */
#define RETURN 177       /* return from method */

#define MEMORY_SIZE 1000
#define STACK_SIZE 10
#define LOCAL_VARIABLE_SIZE 10

signed char memory[MEMORY_SIZE];/* program memory */
int pc;                        /* program counter */
```

```
int stack[STACK_SIZE];              /* the stack */
int locals[LOCAL_VARIABLE_SIZE];/* the stack */
int sp = -1;                /* stack pointer */

main() {
  int number;                       /* number argument */
  int run = 1;                      /* run flag */
  int sym;                          /* value read in */

  while (scanf("%d", &sym) != EOF)/* read in program */
    if (getchar() == ':') {
      if (sym != pc)
        printf("loader error, loc %d\n", pc), exit();
    }
    else
      memory[pc++] = sym;
  pc = 0;                   /* starting address */

  while (run)
    switch ((unsigned char) memory[pc++]) {
    case ICONST_M1:    /* push -1 onto stack */
      stack[++sp] = -1;
      break;
    case ICONST_0:     /* push 0 onto stack */
      stack[++sp] = 0;
      break;
    case ICONST_1:     /* push 1 onto stack */
      stack[++sp] = 1;
      break;
    case ICONST_2:     /* push 2 onto stack */
      stack[++sp] = 2;
      break;
    case ICONST_3:     /* push 3 onto stack */
      stack[++sp] = 3;
      break;
    case ICONST_4:     /* push 4 onto stack */
      stack[++sp] = 4;
      break;
    case ICONST_5:     /* push 5 onto stack */
      stack[++sp] = 5;
      break;
    case BIPUSH:       /* bipush <value>, push <byte value> */
      stack[++sp] = memory[pc++];
      break;
    case ILOAD_0:      /* iload_0 push local variable 0 */
      stack[++sp] = locals[0];
      break;
    case ILOAD_1:      /* iload_1 push local variable 1 */
```

```
      stack[++sp] = locals[1];
      break;
case ILOAD_2:          /* iload_2 push local variable 2 */
      stack[++sp] = locals[2];
      break;
case ILOAD_3:          /* iload_3 push local variable 3 */
      stack[++sp] = locals[3];
      break;
case ILOAD:            /* iload <varnum>, push <varnum> */
      stack[++sp] = locals[memory[pc++]];
      break;
case ISTORE_0:         /* pop stack to local variable 0 */
      locals[0] = stack[sp--];
      break;
case ISTORE_1:         /* pop stack to local variable 1 */
      locals[1] = stack[sp--];
      break;
case ISTORE_2:         /* pop stack to local variable 2 */
      locals[2] = stack[sp--];
      break;
case ISTORE_3:         /* pop stack to local variable 3 */
      locals[3] = stack[sp--];
      break;
case ISTORE:           /* istore <varnum>, pop to <varnum */
      locals[memory[pc++]] = stack[sp--];
      break;
case POP:              /* pop */
      --sp; break;
case SWAP:             /* swap top two items of stack */
      { int temp = stack[sp];
        stack[sp] = stack[sp -1];
        stack[sp - 1] = temp; }
      break;
case DUP:              /* copy */
      stack[sp + 1] = stack[sp];
      sp++; break;
case IADD:             /* add */
      stack[sp -1] = stack[sp - 1] + stack[sp];
      --sp; break;
case ISUB:             /* sub */
      stack[sp -1] = stack[sp - 1] - stack[sp];
      --sp; break;
case IMUL:             /* mul */
      stack[sp -1] = stack[sp - 1] * stack[sp];
      --sp; break;
case IDIV:             /* idiv */
      stack[sp - 1] = stack[sp - 1] / stack[sp];
      --sp; break;
```

```
case IREM:          /* mod */
  stack[sp -1] = stack[sp - 1] % stack[sp];
  --sp; break;
case INEG:          /* negate */
  stack[sp] = - stack[sp];
  break;
case IINC:  /* iinc <varnum> <n>, add <n> to <varnum> */
  locals[memory[pc++]] += memory[pc++];
  break;
case IFEQ:   /* be */
  if (stack[sp--] == 0)
    pc += memory[pc];
  else
    pc++;
  break;
case IFGE: /* bge */
  if (stack[sp--] >= 0)
    pc += memory[pc];
  else
    pc++;
  break;
case IFGT:          /* bg */
  if (stack[sp--] > 0)
    pc += memory[pc];
  else
    pc++;
  break;
case IFLE:          /* ble */
  if (stack[sp--] <= 0)
    pc += memory[pc];
  else
    pc++;
  break;
case IFLT:          /* bl */
  if (stack[sp--] < 0)
    pc += memory[pc];
  else
    pc++;
  break;
case IFNE:          /* bne */
  if (stack[sp--] != 0)
    pc += memory[pc];
  else
    pc++;
  break;
case GOTO:          /* goto */
  pc += memory[pc]; break;
case RETURN:        /* halt */
```

```
      run = 0; break;
  case INVOKEVIRTUAL: /* method call, one arg follows */
                    /* memory[pc] ==1, print; == 2 println. */
                    /* stack[sp] local variable number to */
    if (memory[pc] == 1)        /* print */
      printf("Local_%d: %d\t", stack[sp], locals[stack[sp]]);
    else if (memory[pc] == 2) /* println */
      printf("Local_%d: %d\n", stack[sp], locals[stack[sp]]);
    sp--, pc++;                 /* pop arg from stack */
    break;
  default:
    printf("instruction at memory[%d]: %d, bad, bad, bad\n",
          pc - 1, (unsigned char)memory[pc - 1]);
    exit(); break;
  }
 return 0;
}
```

The result of program interpretation is

```
Local_1: 10     Local_2: -27
```

Although the interpreter is long, it is a very simple program involving no more than array access, incrementing and decrementing variables, and the performance of arithmetic operations. You will also see some instructions that we did not mention: `ifeq`, `ifge`, `iflt`, and so on. These are testing instructions and test the contents of the top of the stack to see if it is **equal** to zero, **greater than or equal** to zero, **less than** to zero, and so on. These instructions pop the top of the stack, and if the condition is met, change the program counter so that the next instruction is fetched from the labeled instruction.

The macros that assemble these instructions are

```
('if ==, >=, >, <=, <, != and goto')
define(ifeq, 'loc:      153 eval($1 - (loc + 1)) define('loc',
                                     eval(loc + 2))')
define(ifge, 'loc:      156 eval($1 - (loc + 1)) define('loc',
                                     eval(loc + 2))')
define(ifgt, 'loc:      157 eval($1 - (loc + 1)) define('loc',
                                     eval(loc + 2))')
define(ifle, 'loc:      158 eval($1 - (loc + 1)) define('loc',
                                     eval(loc + 2))')
define(iflt, 'loc:      155 eval($1 - (loc + 1)) define('loc',
                                     eval(loc + 2))')
define(ifne, 'loc:      154 eval($1 - (loc + 1)) define('loc',
                                     eval(loc + 2))')
define(goto, 'loc:      167 eval($1 - (loc + 1)) define('loc',
                                     eval(loc + 2))')
```

Their argument is a label. The following program computes the value of y for values of x such that $0 \le x \le 10$.

```
iconst_0            comment('initialize x to zero, local_1')
istore_1
label(loop)
iload_1             comment('compute (x - 1)')
iconst_1
isub
iload_1             comment('compute (x - 7)')
bipush(7)
isub
imul                comment('(x - 1) * (x - 7)')
iload_1             comment('compute (x - 11)')
bipush(11)
isub
idiv                comment('(x - 1) * (x - 7) / (x - 11)')
istore_2            comment('store y in local_2')
iconst_1            comment('print(x), push variable number of x')
invokevirtual(1)comment('1 == print')
iconst_2            comment('println(y), push variable number of y')
invokevirtual(2)comment('2 == printn')
iinc(1, 1)          comment('local_1, x++')
bipush(10)
iload(1)
isub
ifge(loop)          comment('if >= 0 goto loop')
return
```

The output of the program execution is

```
Local_1: 0      Local_2: 0
Local_1: 1      Local_2: 0
Local_1: 2      Local_2: 0
Local_1: 3      Local_2: 1
Local_1: 4      Local_2: 1
Local_1: 5      Local_2: 1
Local_1: 6      Local_2: 1
Local_1: 7      Local_2: 0
Local_1: 8      Local_2: -2
Local_1: 9      Local_2: -8
Local_1: 10     Local_2: -27
```

1.7   Accumulator Machines

The stack architecture was not the first architecture developed. The architecture
of the EDSAC computer was an **accumulator** machine [29]. An **accumulator**
machine is like a very simple calculator. It has a single register, the accumulator,
whose contents are combined with a single operand, with the result of the operation
replacing the contents of the accumulator. For example, an add instruction has a
single operand, and the result of executing the instruction is

```
accumulator += operand;
```

To add two numbers together, we must first place one of the numbers into the
accumulator, then execute the add instruction, and finally, store the contents of
the accumulator back into memory. There are two instructions to load and store
the accumulator, both of which take a single operand:

```
load      operand
store     operand
```

The architecture of an accumulator machine is shown in Figure 1.4. Here you
will see that the input to the ALU is the accumulator, the ACC, and the memory
data register, MDR. The result of the arithmetic or logic operation is always placed
back into the ACC.

Accumulator machines do not have **registers** or a **stack** for storing temporary
results but make use of the main memory. The operand for all instructions is a
memory address. Thus, to add the contents of memory location 100 to the contents
of memory location 102, placing the result into memory location 300, we would
execute the following instructions:

```
load      100
add       102
store     300
```

A program to compute the expression in Eq. (1.1) for an accumulator machine
might be

$$\vdots$$

```
define(a2, 1)
define(a1, 7)
define(a0,11)
word(a2_m, a2)       comment('the polynomial coefficients')
word(a1_m, a1)
word(a0_m, a0)
word(x_m, 1)         comment('independent variable')
word(y_m, 0)         comment('dependent variable')
word(temp1_m, 0)  comment('needed for temporary results')
```

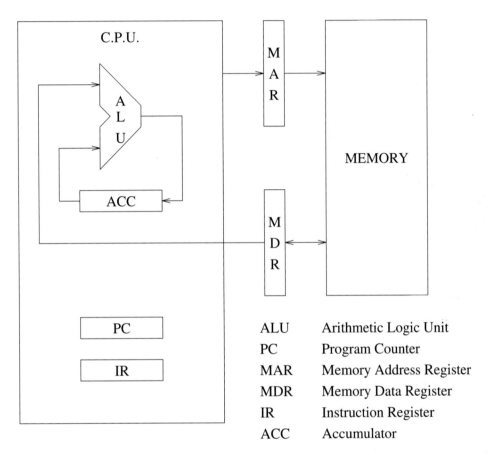

Figure 1.4: The Accumulator Machine Architecture

```
word(temp2_m, 0)

label(start)        comment('starting address')
load(x_m)           comment('temp1 = x - a0')
sub(a0_m)
store(temp1_m)      comment('the denominator')
load(x_m)           comment('temp2 = x - a2')
sub(a2_m)
store(temp2_m)
load(x_m)           comment('x - a1')
sub(a1_m)
mul(temp2_m)        comment('(x - a1) * (x - a2)')
div(temp1_m)        comment('x - a0')
store(y_m)
end(start)
```

In the program above we have labeled the starting address, but the machine does not know that we have done so. Historically, the starting address is always specified as the last number loaded into memory. That is, when memory is loaded, the last value loaded is also stored into the program counter, **PC**, and execution is started at that address. We follow this practice by defining a macro, **end**, to specify the starting address and also to signal the end of the program:

```
define(end,'     $1')
```

Notice how we first defined a2, a1, and a0 to have the values 1, 7, and 11, respectively. We then used these symbols as the values to be stored into memory. We defined the memory addresses to have a suffix _m to distinguish the address of the data from the data themselves, in the same manner as we added the suffix _r to indicate the name of a register to hold the value of a given variable.

Notice that in the program above we have had to make use of a memory location `temp1` and `temp2` to store intermediate results. If we were to define machine codes of 50 for load and 60 for store, the following equivalent machine language code would be generated:

```
0:      1
1:      7
2:      11
3:      1
4:      0
5:      0
6:      0


7:      50      3
9:      30      2
```

```
11:      60       5
13:      50       3
15:      30       0
17:      60       6
19:      50       3
21:      30       1
23:      20       6
25:      10       5
27:      60       4
          7
```

Compare the machine code for the two architectures, stack and accumulator, shown on pages 23 and 32. You will see that there are only 23 words of program for the stack machine, whereas the accumulator machine requires 28. However, the code for the accumulator machine is much more regular, as every instruction has one operand, an address. The accumulator architecture is also referred to as a single-address machine.

Although the program is shorter for the stack machine, the lack of regularity of the instructions might make decoding them more time consuming than for the accumulator machine. This is a fundamental question related to the design of computers – space versus time. That is, if we were to add more instructions with more operands to reduce the length of a program (space), decoding instructions and fetching operands might take more time and could lead to slower execution. Obviously, these questions have economic consequences, as one is interested in the fastest computer for the smallest cost. Although there was a debate related to the relative merits of accumulator architectures versus stack architectures, increasing memory size soon changed the debate to one related to the time required to access memory.

1.8   Load/Store Machines

Early machines had some hundreds of words of memory, and the time to access any particular memory location was the same for all addresses. Soon, however, memory size started to increase, due to the need for longer, more complex programs and with the development of technology to build much larger memories. With increasing memory size came another cost trade-off – cost versus access time. The faster a memory can be accessed, the greater its cost. As programs typically accessed a small number of variables much more frequently than others, it was natural to design machines with a memory hierarchy in which a small amount of high-speed memory was provided for frequently accessed variables and a much larger, slower memory was provided for the rest of the program and data. This high-speed memory frequently took the form of a **register file**. The machine would load and store these registers from memory and the arithmetic and logic instructions would then operate with registers, *not* main memory, for the location of operands [19].

The architecture for the load/store machine looks very similar to the architecture of the stack machine, with a register file replacing the stack. The main difference between the stack and the register file is that any of the registers may be selected with each instruction, whereas only the top two elements of the stack may be accessed at any time. The architecture for the load/store machine is shown in Figure 1.5.

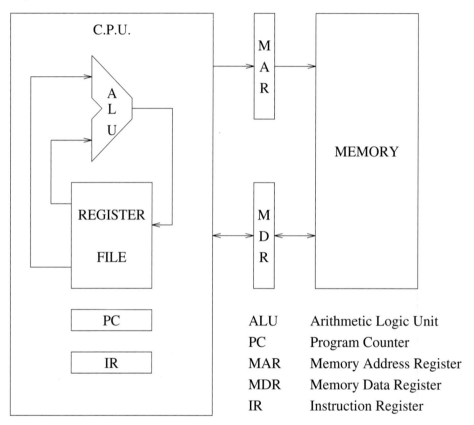

Figure 1.5: The Load/Store Machine Architecture

If the machine is addressing only a small number of registers, the instruction field to refer to a register will be short and there is no real limitation on the number of operands for each instruction; these machines frequently have instructions with three operands, two source operands and a destination operand; for example, the add instruction

        add   src1, src2, dest

will add the contents of register src1 to the contents of src2 and store the result into register dest. These machines are called *load/store machines* and the SPARC architecture, the subject of this book, is of this form.

We may define macros for a load/store machine as follows: The load and store instructions are like the load and store instructions for the accumulator machine except that they have an additional operand, the register, from which to load or to store:

```
define(load,
        'loc:        50      $1 $2 define('loc', eval(loc + 3))')
define(store,
        'loc:        60      $1 $2 define('loc', eval(loc + 3))')
```

The macros for the arithmetic instructions now take three operands each, two source operands and a destination operand:

```
define(div,
    'loc:        10      $1 $2 $3 define('loc', eval(loc + 4))')
define(mul,
    'loc:        20      $1 $2 $3 define('loc', eval(loc + 4))')
define(sub,
    'loc:        30      $1 $2 $3 define('loc', eval(loc + 4))')
define(add,
    'loc:        40      $1 $2 $3 define('loc', eval(loc + 4))')
```

We will need to define the machine code for the registers and will assume that in our machine we have eight registers:

```
define(r0, 0)
define(r1, 1)
define(r2, 2)
define(r3, 3)
define(r4, 4)
define(r5, 5)
define(r6, 6)
define(r7, 7)
```

With these definitions we can write the program to evaluate the expression given in Eq. (1.1):

```
define(loc,0)
define(word,
  'define($1,loc)loc: $2 define('loc', eval(loc + 1))')
define(label,'define($1, loc)')

define(div,
    'loc:        10      $1 $2 $3 define('loc', eval(loc + 4))')
define(mul,
    'loc:        20      $1 $2 $3 define('loc', eval(loc + 4))')
```

```
define(sub,
   'loc:       30       $1 $2 $3 define('loc', eval(loc + 4))')
define(add,
   'loc:       40       $1 $2 $3 define('loc', eval(loc + 4))')
define(load,
   'loc:       50       $1 $2 define('loc', eval(loc + 3))')
define(store,
   'loc:       60       $1 $2 define('loc', eval(loc + 3))')

define(end,'     $1')
define(comment)

define(r0, 0)    comment('the registers')
define(r1, 1)
define(r2, 2)
define(r3, 3)
define(r4, 4)
define(r5, 5)
define(r6, 6)

define(a2, 1)    comment('define the poly. coefficients')
define(a1, 7)
define(a0, 11)

word(a2_m, a2)   comment('define and initialize memory')
word(a1_m, a1)
word(a0_m, a0)
word(x_m, 1)     comment('independent variable')
word(y_m, 0)     comment('dependent variable')

label(start)     comment('starting address')
load(x_m, r1)    comment('load variables into registers')
load(a2_m, r2)
load(a1_m, r3)
load(a0_m, r4)
sub(r1, r2, r0)  comment('r0 = x - a2')
sub(r1, r3, r5)  comment('r5 = x - a1')
mul(r0, r5, r0)  comment('r0 = (x - a2) * (x - a1)')
sub(r1, r4, r5)  comment('r5 = x - a0')
div(r0, r5, r0)  comment('r0 = (x - a2)*(x - a1)/(x - a0)')
store(r0, y_m)   comment('store r0 into memory')
end(start)
```

The resulting machine code is

```
0:      1
1:      7
2:     11
3:      1
4:      0


5:     50      3 1
8:     50      0 2
11:    50      1 3
14:    50      2 4
17:    30      1 2 0
21:    30      1 3 5
25:    20      0 5 0
29:    30      1 4 5
33:    10      0 5 0
37:    60      0 4
        5
```

Comparison of the machine code for the load/store machine shown above with that for the stack and accumulator architectures shown on pages 23 and 32 might give the impression that the code for the load/store machine is much longer, 39 words versus 23 and 28. However, as the register addresses are very short (a single digit each in the case of the machine defined above), the register addresses are normally packed into a single word with the instruction code, the **opcode**.

Thus, by redefining the macros to take out the intervening space in the arithmetic instruction code as follows:

```
define(div,  'loc:     10$1$2$3 define('loc', eval(loc + 1))')
define(mul,  'loc:     20$1$2$3 define('loc', eval(loc + 1))')
define(sub,  'loc:     30$1$2$3 define('loc', eval(loc + 1))')
define(add,  'loc:     40$1$2$3 define('loc', eval(loc + 1))')
define(load, 'loc:     50$1$2 define('loc', eval(loc + 1))')
define(store, 'loc:    60$1$2 define('loc', eval(loc + 1))')
```

we would obtain the following machine code:

```
0:      1
1:      7
2:     11
3:      1
4:      0
```

```
 5:      5031
 6:      5002
 7:      5013
 8:      5024
 9:      30120
10:      30135
11:      20050
12:      30145
13:      10050
14:      6004
          5
```

In this case we would need only 15 words of memory. Of course, the decoding of instructions would now be more complicated, as the digits specifying the registers would have to be separated out from the instruction. A further complication is that the load and store instructions have only one register to be so obtained, whereas the arithmetic instructions have three. This means that the instruction type would have to be ascertained before the registers could be decoded.

If we look at the program above, the code is not very readable, and even more difficult to write, as we have to keep track of which register contains which variable. Once again, we need a piece of paper, and this is always an indication that we should be making some definitions. We can make these symbolic definitions when we assign registers to variables. We will add a suffix _r to name the register assigned to hold the value of a variable just as we added the suffix _m to indicate the memory address of the variable. If we do this, our program becomes

$$\vdots$$

```
define(a2, 1)    comment('define the poly. coefficients')
define(a1, 7)
define(a0, 11)

word(a2_m, a2)   comment('define and initialize memory')
word(a1_m, a1)
word(a0_m, a0)
word(x_m, 1)     comment('independent variable')
word(y_m, 0)     comment('dependent variable')

define(y_r, r0) comment('variable assignments to registers')
define(x_r, r1)
define(a2_r, r2)
define(a1_r, r3)
define(a0_r, r4)
define(temp_r, r5)
```

```
label(start)      comment('starting address')
load(x_m, x_r)  comment('load variables into registers')
load(a2_m, a2_r)
load(a1_m, a1_r)
load(a0_m, a0_r)
sub(x_r, a2_r, y_r)      comment('y_r = x - a2')
sub(x_r, a1_r, temp_r)  comment('temp_r = x - a1')
mul(y_r, temp_r, y_r)   comment('y_r = (x - a2)*(x - a1)')
sub(x_r, a0_r, temp_r)  comment('temp_r = x - a0')
div(y_r, temp_r, y_r)   comment('y_r = y_r / (x - a0)')
store(y_r, y_m)          comment('store y_r into memory')
end(start)
```

1.9 Assemblers

An **assembler** is a macro processor specialized for translating symbolic programs into machine language programs. This process is called *assembling* a program. The **assembler** does essentially what we have been using m4 to do, that is, to substitute one symbol for another, eventually translating all symbols into numbers. However, the assembler allows us to remove an important restriction – symbols may be used before they are defined. Careful examination of all our uses of m4 will reveal that we have arranged always to define a symbol before it is used. If we had not, the translation would not take place. An assembler effectively reads a file twice, once to determine all the symbol definitions and the second time to apply those definitions and thus translate the symbolic text into numeric instructions and data.

For example, in an assembler we could have written the load/store program with the variables moved to the end of the program:

$$\vdots$$

```
comment('variable assignments to registers')
define(y_r, r0)
define(x_r, r1)
define(a2_r, r2)
define(a1_r, r3)
define(a0_r, r4)
define(temp_r, r5)

label(start)                comment('starting address')
comment('load variables into registers')
load(x_m, x_r)
load(a2_m, a2_r)
```

```
load(a1_m, a1_r)
load(a0_m, a0_r)
sub(x_r, a2_r, y_r)      comment('y_r = x - a2')
sub(x_r, a1_r, temp_r)   comment('temp_r = x - a1')
mul(y_r, temp_r, y_r)    comment('y_r = (x - a2)*(x - a1)')
sub(x_r, a0_r, temp_r)   comment('temp_r = x - a0')
div(y_r, temp_r, y_r)    comment('y_r = y_r / (x - a0)')
store(y_r, y_m)          comment('store y_r into memory')
end(start)

comment('variable assignments to memory')
word(a2_m, a2)
word(a1_m, a1)
word(a0_m, a0)
word(x_m, 1)
word(y_m, 0)
```

If the program above were processed by m4, the symbols defining the memory locations, a2_m, a1_m, ... y_m would not be translated into addresses. We could handle this problem of forward references in m4 by first defining the macros for the load/store machine to update the location counter as the program is read, defining the values of labels but generating no code. This is the first pass of the assembler. The macros are then redefined for the second pass and the program read a second time. During the second pass the code is generated. The location counter is not updated during the second pass as all symbols were defined in the first pass.

As the code has to be read twice, it is best placed into a separate file, which we might call source.m:

```
comment('variable assignments to registers')
define('y_r', r0)
define('x_r', r1)
define('a2_r', r2)
define('a1_r', r3)
define('a0_r', r4)
define('temp_r', r5)


label(start)             comment('starting address')
comment('load variables into registers')
load(x_m, x_r)
load(a2_m, a2_r)
load(a1_m, a1_r)
load(a0_m, a0_r)
sub(x_r, a2_r, y_r)      comment('y_r = x - a2')
```

```
sub(x_r, a1_r, temp_r)   comment('temp_r = x - a1')
mul(y_r, temp_r, y_r)    comment('y_r = (x - a2)*(x - a1)')
sub(x_r, a0_r, temp_r)   comment('temp_r = x - a0')
div(y_r, temp_r, y_r)    comment('y_r = y_r / (x - a0)')
store(y_r, y_m)          comment('store y_r into memory')
halt

word(a2_m, 1)            comment('the polynomial coefficients')
word(a1_m, 7)
word(a0_m, 11)
word(x_m, 1)             comment('independent variable')
word(y_m, 0)             comment('dependent variable')

end(start)
```

We will place the macro definitions for the two passes into a file `assembler.m`. Note that all the opcodes are redefined before the second pass; note also the use of ' and ' to force redefinition of the opcode macros. Notice that the source file is read twice by the two `include(source)` macro calls, which has the effect of inserting the contents of the file, specified as the argument to `include`

```
divert(-1)
define(loc,0)
define(word,'define($1,eval(loc))define('loc', eval(loc + 1))')
define(label,'define($1,eval(loc))')
define(halt, 'define('loc', eval(loc + 1))dnl')
define(div, 'define('loc', eval(loc + 4))dnl')
define(mul, 'define('loc', eval(loc + 4))dnl')
define(sub, 'define('loc', eval(loc + 4))dnl')
define(add, 'define('loc', eval(loc + 4))dnl')
define(load, 'define('loc', eval(loc + 3))dnl')
define(store, 'define('loc', eval(loc + 3))dnl')
define(print, 'define('loc', eval(loc + 2))dnl')
define(end,'dnl')
define(comment)
include(source.m)
define('loc',0)
define('word',' $2')
define('label','')
define('halt', ' 0')
define('div', ' 10 $1 $2 $3')
define('mul', ' 20 $1 $2 $3')
define('sub', ' 30 $1 $2 $3')
define('add', ' 40 $1 $2 $3')
define('load', ' 50 $1 $2')
```

```
define('store', ' 60 $1 $2')
define('print', ' 90 $1')
define('end',' $1')
define(r0, 0)
define(r1, 1)
define(r2, 2)
define(r3, 3)
define(r4, 4)
define(r5, 5)
define(r6, 6)
divert
include(source.m)
```

The effect of the first pass is to generate **defines** for all labels with the appropriate values of the location counter.

When the assembler is run:

```
%m4 assembler.m
```

the following output is generated:

```
        50          39 1
        50          36 2
        50        ' 37 3
        50          38 4
        30          1 2 0
        30          1 3 5
        20          0 5 0
        30          1 4 5
        10          0 5 0
        60          0 40
        0
        1
        7
        11
        1
        0

        0
```

Another important difference between an assembler and m4 is the definition of location counter values. Many of our macros involve saving, defining, or using location counter values; word, for example, defines a symbol to have the value of the location counter and generates a word consisting of its second argument. Similarly, label macro defines a symbol to have as its value the current value of the location counter. In an assembler, a symbol immediately followed by a colon (:) defines the symbol to have as its value the current value of the location counter. Making use of this feature we could further rewrite our program:

$$\vdots$$

```
comment('variable assignments to registers')
define(y_r, r0)
define(x_r, r1)
define(a2_r, r2)
define(a1_r, r3)
define(a0_r, r4)
define(temp_r, r5)

comment('load variables into registers')
start:
  load(x_m, x_r)
  load(a2_m, a2_r)
  load(a1_m, a1_r)
  load(a0_m, a0_r)
  sub(x_r, a2_r, y_r)      comment('y_r = x - a2')
  sub(x_r, a1_r, temp_r)   comment('temp_r = x - a1')
  mul(y_r, temp_r, y_r)    comment('y_r = (x - a2)*(x - a1)')
  sub(x_r, a0_r, temp_r)   comment('temp_r = x - a0')
  div(y_r, temp_r, y_r)    comment('y_r = y_r / (x - a0)')
  store(y_r, y_m)          comment('store y_r into memory')
  end(start)

comment('variable assignments to memory')
a2_m:   1
a1_m:   7
a0_m:   11
x_m:    1
y_m:    0
```

An identifier followed by a colon is called a *label*. Labels are the arguments for goto instructions. Assemblers improve the syntax of programs, eliminating many of the parentheses, and perform some checks, such as ensuring that register symbols are used when register symbols are needed. We will be using the UNIX assembler **as** [25] with **m4** (to perform some preprocessing of our programs) to write programs for SPARC. For example, **as** will not handle the redefinition of register names but m4 will allow us to do this. In the **as** assembler, register names are preceded by a % character. The assembler also allows us to terminate lines with comments beginning with an exclamation point (!). The exclamation point and remaining text on the line are ignored. Our program, written for **m4** and **as**, is

```
define(y_r, r0)              !variable assignments to registers
define(x_r, r1)
define(a2_r, r2)
define(a1_r, r3)
define(a0_r, r4)
define(temp_r, r5)


start:   mov     0, %x_r          !load variables into registers
         mov     a2, %a2_r
         mov     a1, %a1_r
         mov     a0, %a0_r
         sub     %x_r, %a2_r, %y_r     !y = x - a2
         sub     %x_r, %a1_r, %temp_r !temp = x - a1
         mul     %y_r, %temp_r, %y_r   !y = (x - a2) * (x - a1)
         sub     %x_r, %a0_r, %temp_r !temp = x - a0
         div     %y_r, %temp_r, %y_r   !y = (x - a2) * (x - %a1)
```

If the program is first processed by **m4**, the symbolic register definitions are processed to yield a program suitable for **as**:

```
start:   mov     0, %r1           !load variables into registers
         mov     a2, %r2
         mov     a1, %r3
         mov     a0, %r4
         sub     %r1, %r2, %r0    !y = x - a2
         sub     %r1, %r3, %r5    !temp = x - a1
         mul     %r0, %r5, %r0    !y = (x - a2) * (x - a1)
         sub     %r1, %r4, %r5    !temp = x - a0
         div     %r0, %r5, %r0    !y = (x - a2) * (x - %a1)
                                  ! / (x - a0)
```

In these programs we have avoided using memory for the variables by employing literals instead. Remember that a literal is a constant appearing directly in a machine instruction instead of its address. The `mov` instruction will load a constant directly into a register instead of fetching the constant from memory. Similarly, we have left the computed value for y in `y_r` instead of storing it back into memory. We leave accessing memory for variables for a later chapter.

1.10   Summary

We first introduced the computer by way of the programmable calculator. Although the computer predates the calculator, everyone is now familiar with the calculator, although probably not in its programmable form; the programmable calculator is, of course, a computer. The simplest calculator has only an arithmetic logic unit.

With the calculator we also introduced postfix notation for arithmetic expressions. Expressions given in postfix notation are simply computed using a stack. We introduced the need for registers, to store frequently occurring constants, and for memory, to store key sequences so that computations could be repeated.

Having introduced the calculator, we then dispensed with its keyboard by storing the machine code for key sequences directly into memory. To translate symbolic programs into machine codes, we introduced the macro processor m4. With m4 we went on to define various computer architectures, a Java virtual machine, an accumulator machine, and finally a load/store machine. We introduced the assembler and demonstrated how it simplifies the translation of symbolic programs into machine code.

Concepts defined in this chapter were:

Arithmetic Logic Unit (ALU): capable of performing arithmetic and logical operations on its inputs to produce an output.

Registers: provide for the storage of temporary results and constants. They may be named, but unlike memory, they have no address.

Memory: randomly accessible store of data. When read, the memory, presented with a numeric address, will return the data stored there; when written, the memory, presented with data and an address, will replace the contents of the addressed memory location with the new data.

Central Processing Unit (CPU): consists of an arithmetic logic unit and a control unit capable of fetching and executing instructions.

Machine Language: numeric values that represent the operations of a machine and the location of operands. The machine language is directly executable by the central processing unit.

Assembly Language: symbolic representation of the machine language of a computer.

Program Counter (PC): holds the address in memory of the next instruction to be executed.

von Neumann cycle:

```
pc = 0;                 /* initialize the program counter */

do {
  instruction = memory[pc++];/* fetch the instruction */
  decode(instruction);  /* decode the instruction */
  fetch (operands);     /* fetch the operands */
  execute;              /* execute the instruction */
  store (results);      /* store the results */
} while (instruction != halt);
```

Macro Processor: identifies macro tokens and arguments in its input stream and substitutes the macro definition in its place in the input stream to be rescanned.

`eval:` macro that considers its string argument as a numeric expression, returning a string that represents the evaluation of the expression.

`define:` macro that defines its first argument to be a macro token to be replaced, on evaluation, by its second argument.

Stack Machine: pushes operands onto the top of a stack from memory and pops results from the top of the stack back into memory. Arithmetic logic instructions operate between the top elements of the stack, popping all operands and pushing the result back onto the stack.

Java Virtual Machine: A computer program that interprets a Java program represented by its machine language in bytecode.

Accumulator Machine: combines an operand from memory with the contents of a single register, the accumulator, to produce a result that replaces the contents of the accumulator. The accumulator may be loaded from memory and its contents stored back into memory.

Load/Store Machine: performs all operations between the contents of a set of registers. The registers may be loaded from or stored into memory.

Assembler: program for translating between a symbolic representation of a program and its numeric machine language. An assembler allows for forward variable references by implementing a two-pass algorithm in which symbols are defined in its first pass to be used in the second pass.

Label: a symbol, whose value is the address where the instruction, or data, it references will be located in memory.

Symbol Table: table of symbol, value pairs.

Location Counter: variable, whose value is the address where the next instruction of data element will be assembled into memory.

1.11   Exercises

1–1 Define `assembly language` and `machine language`, clearly indicating the difference between them.

1–2 What is a `symbol table`, and what is it used for in an assembler?

1–3 Use `m4` to define all the constants in the following program symbolically:

```
for (i = 27; i < 305; i++)
  {
     a = i + 37;
     b[305 - i] = a;
  }
```

1–4 State how you would type arguments **h, o, w, n, o, w** to the macro **cat**, define(cat, $1$2$3$4$5$6$7$8$9) so that the printed result was

how now

1–5 What is the output of the following macro text? Interpret.

```
define(m, 4)
define( sum, 'incer($1) + $2')
define(incer, '$1 + 1')
sum( n, m)
sum('n', 'm')
sum(''n'', ''m'')
sum('''n''', '''m''')
sum(''''n'''', ''''m'''')
```

1–6 Define a macro **add_loc** with one argument, the number to add to the variable **loc**, to replace the lines of code in the example on page 21 such as

```
define(sto, 'loc        44 $1 define('loc', eval(loc + 2))')
```

with

```
define(sto, 'loc        44 $1 add_loc(2)')
```

1–7 Write a C program to simulate the HP15C calculator. Declare the following: a char array, **memory**, to hold the program; a double array, **stack**, for the calculations; a 20-element double array, **register_set**, for the register values. First read the output of a calculator program, processed by **m4**, into the char array. Then start fetching instructions from your calculator memory and executing them, printing the results.

1–8 If you have written a simulator for the HP15C calculator, use the macro definitions given for the HP15C calculator to write a program for the calculator to evaluate factorial 10.

1–9 Write a C program to simulate a single-address accumulator machine. Declare an int array, **memory**, to hold the program and an int for the accumulator. First read the output of a machine program, processed by **m4**, into the char array. Then start fetching instructions from your simulator's memory and executing them, printing the results. You should implement the following instructions: load, store, add, sub, mul, div, branch on greater than or zero result, branch always. You should also define an instruction that prints the value of a memory location. Then write a program to evaluate the maximum value of the expression

$$x^3 - 14x^2 + 56x - 64$$

with x in the range $-2 <= x <= 8$. Be careful that all your labels are defined before you use them as the target of a branch instruction.

1–10 Write a Java assembly language program to evaluate the maximum value of the expression described in Exercise 1-9.

1–11 Write a Java assembly language program to evaluate of the sum of powers of 4

$$y = 1^4 + 2^4 + 3^4 + 4^4 + \cdots + x^4$$

by the closed-form expression

$$y = (6x^4 + 15x^3 + 10x^2 - 1) * x/30$$

for $x = 10$. (If this is too easy, you might want to include looping to evaluate the series for $1 \leq x \leq 30$.) Be careful that all your labels are defined before you use them as the target of a branch instruction.

1–12 Write a C program to simulate a load/store machine. Declare an int array, **memory**, to hold the program and an array of eight integers for the registers. First read in the output of a machine program, processed by **m4**, into the char array. Then start fetching instructions from your simulator's memory and executing them, printing the results. You should implement the following instructions: load, store, add, sub, mul, div, branch on less, branch on greater than or zero, branch always. You should also define an instruction that prints the value of a memory location. Then write a program to evaluate of the sum of powers of 4 as described in Exercise 1-11.

1–13 Define macros for a two-pass assembler for a single-address machine that will handle references to addresses before they are defined.

1–14 What is the von Neumann machine cycle for a stack machine?

1–15 Describe exactly what happens when **word(a, 3)** is evaluated, if it were in the following macro definition file:

```
define(loc, 0)
define(word, 'define($1,loc)      $2 define('loc', eval(loc + 1))')
word(a, 3)
```

List each step in **m4**'s evaluation process and the results of all macro argument and macro evaluations.

1–16 Exactly what happens when **m4** is processing a file and encounters a token, which has been defined as a macro, followed immediately by an open parentheses "("?

Chapter 2

SPARC ARCHITECTURE

2.1 Introduction

The SPARC architecture is a load/store architecture [19]. The architecture is described in detail in the *SPARC Architecture Manual* [22]. All arithmetic and logical operations are carried out between operands located in registers. Load and store instructions are provided to load and store register contents from memory. The machine has 32 registers available to the programmer at any one time. It can address memory for a total of 2^{30}, or approximately 10^9, instructions or integers.

2.2 Registers

Registers provide for rapid, direct access in computation, and C register variables will in general be stored there. The Sun SPARC provides 32 registers for use by the programmer. These registers are logically divided into four sets: global, in, local, and out. The global registers are for global register data, data that have meaning to an entire program and are accessible from any function. The in registers contain calling function arguments and we describe their use in Chapter 7. The local registers are for local function variables and we will store our program variables in these registers. The out registers are for use as temporaries, passing arguments to functions, and obtaining returned values from functions. For the present, we will not make use of the in registers. The registers are referred to in the assembler as %g0 - %g7, %l0 - %l7, %o0 - %o7, and %i0 - %i7. Two of the out registers, %o6 and %o7, are reserved for a special use and you should not use them. The first of the global registers, %g0, is also a special register, always returning a zero when read and discarding whatever is written to it. All registers will store a signed integer n, $-2^{31} \leq n < 2^{31}$, or approximately $|n| < 10^9$.

Register	Synonyms	Usage
%g0	%r0	Always discards writes and returns zero
%g1	%r1	First of seven registers for data with
%g2	%r2	global context
%g3	%r3	
%g4	%r4	
%g5	%r5	
%g6	%r6	
%g7	%r7	
%o0	%r8	First of six registers for local data
%o1	%r9	and arguments to called subroutines
%o2	%r10	
%o3	%r11	
%o4	%r12	
%o5	%r13	
%sp	%r14, %o6	Stack pointer
%o7	%r15	Called subroutine return address
%l0	%r16	First of eight registers for local
%l1	%r17	variables
%l2	%r18	
%l3	%r19	
%l4	%r20	
%l5	%r21	
%l6	%r22	
%l7	%r23	
%i0	%r24	First of six registers for incoming
%i1	%r25	subroutine arguments
%i2	%r26	
%i3	%r27	
%i4	%r28	
%i5	%r29	
%fp	%r30, %i6	Frame pointer
%i7	%r31	Subroutine return address

2.3 SPARC Assembly Language Programming

We have already seen on page 43 is almost an assembly language program for the SPARC machine. In the form given there, it would not execute and we need to describe the assembler in more detail together with instructions on how to load the program into memory and execute it.

The SPARC assembler, **as** [25], is in effect a two-pass assembler. In the first pass the assembler updates the location counter as it processes machine statements, without paying attention to undefined labels that might be used as operands. Whenever it sees a label followed by a colon (:) it defines the label symbol to have the value of the location counter. The program is then read a second time; this time, however, all the symbols and labels have been defined, and whenever a label is encountered its value is substituted for the symbol. During the second pass, labels followed by a colon are ignored.

Assembly language programs are line based, with each statement typically specifying a single instruction or data element. Statements may be labeled; an identifier followed by a colon labels a statement. Labels start at the beginning of a line and the instruction or data specification one tab stop in. Operands follow a further tab stop in. Finally, comments start at about the center of the line, commencing with an exclamation point (!). C-style comments may also be used, opening with a /* and closing with a */. These comments may extend over many lines and are used for opening comments. Extensive commenting is required for assembly language programs, as they are far less readable than high-level language programs such as C. For example:

```
/*  instructions to add and to subtract the contents of
registers %o0 and %o1 storing the result into %l0 and %l1 */

start:  add     %o0, %o1, %l0         !l0 = o0 + o1
        sub     %o0, %o1, %l1         !l1 = o0 - o1
```

All machine instructions have mnemonics such as **add** and **sub**. There are other statements that do not generate machine instructions, such as data definitions and statements that provide the assembler information. These instructions, called *pseudo-ops*, generally start with a period. The **word** macro we defined in Chapter 1 to initialize a memory location, along with defining a symbol to have the value of the location counter, corresponds to the .word pseudo-op in **as**. Like any other statement, such a pseudo-op may be labeled. The .word pseudo-op has any number of arguments that are evaluated as integer expressions and the resulting values loaded into sequential memory locations. We will need the **.global** pseudo-op to define a label to be accessible outside the program in which it is defined. For example, to define the label **main** to be global, we would write

```
        .global main
main:
```

We will make use of the C compiler to call the assembler **as** and to load our program for us. As we know, all C programs have a ".c" file name extension. The C compiler will produce files of the same name but with an ".o" extension - the **object** file. These files are the machine code corresponding to the C code for each file. After the C compiler has produced all the ".o" files, it calls the linker to combine all the object files with library routines, such as the input/output functions, to make an executable program. This executable program is by default stored in a file called "a.out."

Compiling a C program is a two-step process; first, the compiler translates the C program into assembly language, placing the code in a file with a ".s" extension to indicate that it is assembly language. The compiler then calls **as** to assemble this file to produce the ".o" file. Most of these files disappear when the compilation process is completed but may be retained if we desire. If you would like to see the assembly language for one of your C programs, call the compiler with the "-S" switch and it will produce only the ".s" assembly language file, which you may then examine

```
%gcc -S program.c
```

If the compiler is given a file with an .s extension, it assumes that it is a file containing assembly language statements and simply calls **as** to assemble the file to produce the ".o" machine code. We will learn how to combine C programs with assembly language programs that we write, but to start with we will just assemble one assembly language program. For example, we might write the program to evaluate the expression, Eq. (1.1), in a file called **expr.s**. To have this assembled and made ready for execution, we would type

```
%gcc expr.s -o expr
```

This will assemble our program and place it in a file called **expr** ready for execution.

When we assemble and load our program we must also specify the starting address. In Chapter 1 we did this with the **end** macro. The C compiler expects to start execution at an address **main**.[1] This label must appear in our program at the first statement we want executed, and furthermore, it must be declared global by using the .global pseudo-op.

The first instruction to be executed should be

```
        .global main
main:   save    %sp, -96, %sp
```

The **save** instruction provides space to save our registers when the debugger is running. This instruction is explained fully in Chapter 7.

We will normally have macros to be expanded before we assemble our program, in which case we write our program in a file with a .m extension, indicating that **m4** must first be run to produce the .s file:

```
%m4 expr.m > expr.s
%gcc expr.s -o expr
```

---

[1]In the Berkeley version of UNIX all function names, variables, and labels are prepended by an _ to prevent name conflicts with those the compiler may generate. The starting address would appear as _main in Berkeley UNIX.

2.4 An Example

We can now begin to write a program to evaluate the expression in Chapter 1. We will use two of the local registers, %l0 and %l1, to store x and y respectively. We will use the polynomial coefficients directly as *literals*

```
/* This program computes the expression:
    y = (x - 1) * (x - 7) / (x - 11)
The polynomial coefficients are:
*/
        define(a2, 1)
        define(a1, 7)
        define(a0, 11)


/* Variables x and y are stored in %l0 and %l1 */

        define(x_r, 10)
        define(y_r, 11)


        .global main
main:   save    %sp, -96, %sp
```

We now need to describe a number of the SPARC instructions to evaluate the expression. Most SPARC instructions take three operands: two registers and a literal constant, or three registers:

   op reg_{rs1}, reg_or_imm, reg_{rd}

The contents of the first source register reg_{rs1} is combined with the literal or the contents of the second source register reg_{rs2} to produce a result that is stored in the destination register reg_{rd}. The contents of the source registers are unchanged. A literal constant, c, must have the range $-4096 \leq c < 4096$.

The first instruction we need is used to clear a register to zero:

   clr reg_{rd}

The second instruction we need is the mov instruction used to copy the contents of one register to another register, or to load a constant into a register:

   mov reg_or_imm, reg_{rd}

The add and subtract instructions combine the contents of the two source registers, or source register and literal, with the sum or difference going into the destination register. In the case of the sub instruction, the second operand is subtracted from the first, as follows:

   add reg_{rs1}, reg_or_imm, reg_{rd}
   sub reg_{rs1}, reg_or_imm, reg_{rd}

We are now in for an unpleasant surprise: The SPARC architecture does not have a multiply or divide instruction! The SPARC architecture is a *Reduced Instruction Set Computer* (RISC) [19]. These architectures are carefully designed in close cooperation with compiler writers to make sure that all the instructions are necessary and actually reduce the execution time of programs. By minimizing the number of instructions the machine may be made to run faster and its architecture easier to implement. RISC architectures endeavor to execute an instruction each clock cycle of the computer. Multiplication and division are complicated instructions and would be very hard to implement to execute in one cycle; it is more efficient to implement multiplication and division in the form of a small number of simpler instructions than to implement them as separate machine instructions. To multiply or divide, we place the two arguments into two of the out registers, %o0 and %o1 and then call for the multiply or division instructions to be executed. This is done with the `call` instruction, which is described fully in Chapter 7. The result of the multiplication or division is returned in %o0. Thus, to achieve

```
a = b * c
```

we would load b and c into %o0 and %o1 and then call the multiplication subroutine:

```
mov     b, %o0
mov     c, %o1
call    .mul
```

To divide

```
a = b / c
```

we would write

```
mov     b, %o0
mov     c, %o1
call    .div
```

Be careful, as a called function may use any of the first six out registers, %o0 through %o5, possibly changing their contents. These registers are for temporary results, and their contents are not preserved over function calls. One further complication remains before we are ready to write our program.

2.5   Pipelining

To achieve very fast execution, computers are *pipelined*. That is, the von Neumann cycle is broken up into its components parts. For a RISC architecture the components are:

Instruction fetch	Fetch and decode the instruction, obtain any operands from the register file.
Execute	Execute an arithmetic instruction, compute a branch target address; compute the memory address for a load or store instruction.
Memory access	Access memory for a load or store instruction; fetch the instruction at the target of a branch instruction.
Store results	Write the instruction results back to the register file.

Each component is then executed independently and concurrently. Thus, the instruction fetch component proceeds to fetch the next instruction immediately after it has finished fetching the current instruction. The instruction fetch component does not wait until the instruction it has just fetched has been executed, as this will be done in another component. This is illustrated in Figure 2.1.

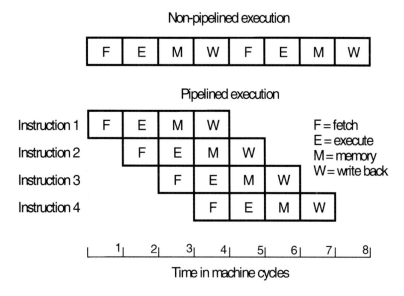

Figure 2.1: Pipelined Execution

On the top line of the figure you will see the normal sequential execution of the SPARC von Neumann cycle - instruction fetch, instruction execute, access memory, store results. If each component of the cycle takes one machine cycle, it will take four cycles to execute each instruction (in the figure, two instruction executions are shown). The lower part of the figure shows pipelined execution. There are four processes running together in parallel. As soon as each component finishes its work, which takes only one cycle, it starts work on the next instruction. The pipelined machine can execute one instruction every machine cycle, four times the rate of the nonpipelined machine. Note that the hardware does not have to run four times faster; instead, the hardware is broken into four parts and all parts run concurrently. This pipeline is four deep. In the nonpipelined architecture, each component remains idle 75% of the time.

Two problems occur when a machine is pipelined. The first relates to load instructions, the second to branches.

Coinsider the following code fragment:

```
load    [%o0], %o1
add     %o1, %o2, %o2
```

When a load instruction is executed (load   [%o0], %o1)the data is not obtained until the end of the M cycle. If the instruction (add   %o1, %o2, %o2) attempts to use this data, it will obtain the prior contents of the register! Fortunately, the machine detects this and waits a cycle to allow the data to be obtained (see Figure 2.2). If you can insert an instruction between the load and the next instruction which uses the result of the load, no cycles are wasted.

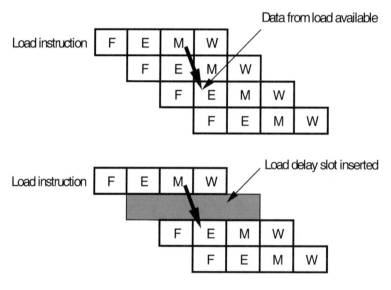

Figure 2.2: The Load Delay Slot

The second problem occurs when a branch instruction is encountered, as a branch instruction changes the program counter. Unfortunately, the branch target address is not available until after the execution of the branch instruction, and this is **not** until after the following instruction has been fetched (see Figure 2.3). Once again a cycle must be wasted. In this case, however, the machine does not insert a wait cycle but expects the programmer to insert some instruction that may be executed after the branch instruction. This is called a branch delay slot instruction.

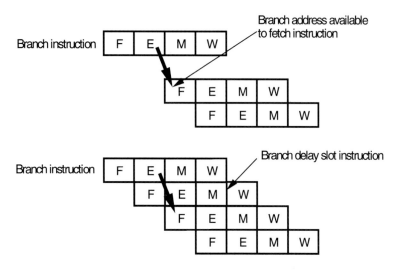

Figure 2.3: The Branch Delay Slot

Part of the concept of the new RISC architectures is to make these architectural features evident to the programmer.

It is frequently possible to place an instruction after the branch that can be usefully executed. The SPARC architecture allows the progammmer to make use of these instructions following a branch by maintaining two program counters, %pc and %npc, the program counter and the next program counter. In the SPARC architecture the machine executes the instruction to which the %pc is pointing while at the same time fetching the instruction to which the %npc is pointing. The instruction fetched is generally the one following the instruction being executed. When a branch occurs, the instruction following the branch has already been fetched and will be executed. A simplified SPARC machine cycle diagram is shown in Figure 2.4 to show how the program counters are updated.

The left half and right half of the diagram execute simultaneously, with time running down the page. The contents of the %npc are copied into the %pc after the first instruction has been executed. The dashed line labeled "next" is to indicate that what lies above it has to be executed before that which lies below it may be executed. If a branch is executed and is taken so that the next instruction fetched will be from the memory location of the branch address, the %npc is loaded with the branch address; otherwise, it is incremented to point to the next instruction in line. Note that, independent of what happens to the %npc, the instruction that was fetched before the branch instruction is *always* executed. When we **call** a function we are branching to another address in memory, and the instruction following the **call** instruction will be executed before the first instruction of the called function is executed.

The simplest thing to do following any branch instruction is to insert a **nop**

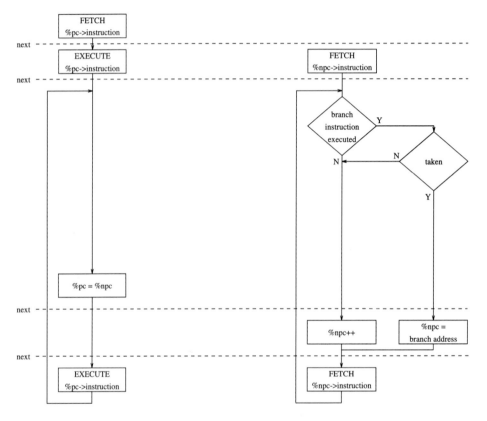

Figure 2.4: Simplified SPARC Machine Cycle

instruction. This is a mnemonic for "no operation" and is an instruction that does nothing to change the state of the machine:

```
nop
```

2.6   The Example Continued

We can now write our program to compute the expression for $x = 9$ given in Eq. (1.1):

```
/* This programs computes the expression:
   y = (x - 1) * (x - 7) / (x - 11) for x = 9
The polynomial coefficients are:
*/
        define(a2, 1)
        define(a1, 7)
        define(a0, 11)

/* Variables x and y are stored in %l0 and %l1 */

        define(x_r, l0)
        define(y_r, l1)

        .global main
main:
    save    %sp, -96, %sp
    mov     9, %x_r          !initialize x
    sub     %x_r, a2, %o0    !(x - a2) into %o0
    sub     %x_r, a1, %o1    !(x - a1) into %o1
    call    .mul
    nop                      !result in %o0
    sub     %x_r, a0, %o1    !(x - a0) into %o1, the divisor
    call    .div
    nop                      !result in %o0
    mov     %o0, %y_r        !store it in y

    mov     1, %g1           !exit request
    ta      0                !trap to system
```

The last two instructions in the program return us to the operating system. The trap instruction **ta** calls the operating system with the service request encoded into register %g1. A few of the traps are as follows:

%g1	Service Request
1	exit
2	fork
3	read
4	write
5	open
6	close
8	create

We discuss traps in more detail in Chapter 12, but for now the sequence

```
mov      1, %g1              !exit request
ta       0                   !trap to system
```

is a good way to get back to the system after executing a program.

The rest of the program should be fairly clear. The value 9 is first stored into %x_r and then the first two terms computed, storing the results into %o0 and %o1, where they are needed to be multiplied together. The result of the multiplication, conveniently, is in %o0, where we need it for the division. The third term is evaluated and stored into %o1, the divisor, and the division performed. The result of the division in %o0 is then stored into %y_r before trapping to the operating system.

If this program were saved in expr.m and run through **m4**:

```
%m4 expr.m > expr.s
```

with the output redirected into expr.s, the following assembly code would be produced:

```
    .global main
main:
    save     %sp, -96, %sp
    mov      9, %l0              !initialize x
    sub      %l0, 1, %o0        !(x - 1) into %o0
    sub      %l0, 7, %o1        !(x - 7) into %o1
    call     .mul
    nop                          !result in %o0
    sub      %l0, 11, %o1       !(x - 11) into %o1, the divisor
    call     .div
    nop                          !result in %o0
    mov      %o0, %l1           !store it in y

    mov      1, %g1             !trap dispatch
    ta       0                  !trap to system
```

This could then be assembled and the executable output put into a file expr by

```
%gcc expr.s -o expr
```

If the program is then executed:

```
%expr
%
```

2.7   The Debugger gdb

Having written a program, which apparently executed, we have no way of knowing what it did, as it produced no output. In fact, we do not even know if the program was correct. The technique of inserting **printf** statements into a program to verify correctness and to find bugs is a rather cumbersome process in assembly language, as arguments have to be placed in registers and `printf` called. If we are trying to debug a program that has other variables stored into the registers needed to call printf, real problems start to develop. The debugger **gdb** provides a way of printing out values without having to change the program in any way. The debugger **gdb** may also be used to execute a program, to stop execution at any point and to single-step execution. A detailed description of **gdb** is to be found in [24] or directly from http://www.cygnus.com/gdb/gdb_toc.html.

Having assembled the program, placing the output into **expr** as we did in the example above, **gdb** may be entered by typing

```
%gdb expr
```

gdb prints a disclaimer, some warnings which we may ignore, and waits for commands:

```
GDB is free software and you are welcome to distribute copies of it
  under certain conditions; type "show copying" to see the conditions.
There is absolutely no warranty for GDB; type ...
GDB 4.16 (sparc-sun-solaris2.5.1),
Copyright 1996 Free Software Foundation, Inc...(no debugging ...
(gdb)
```

To run the program in **gdb**, type "r":

```
(gdb) r
Starting program: /home/lou/book/sparc/ch02/a.out
warning: Unable to find dynamic linker breakpoint function.
warning: GDB will be unable to debug shared library initializers
warning: and track explicitly loaded dynamic code.
(no debugging symbols found)...(no debugging symbols found)...
Program exited with code 0370.
(gdb)
```

Apparently, the program executed, but we are not much further ahead than we were when we executed the program within the shell. We need to set a *breakpoint* in

the program. A breakpoint may be set at any address and whenever the computer
is about to execute the instruction at which the breakpoint was set, it stops and
returns to **gdb**, whereupon the program and its state of execution may be examined.
Typing "c" will tell **gdb** to continue execution from the breakpoint. To set a
breakpoint at a memory address, we need to type

```
(gdb)b *addr
```

where addr is the machine memory address. A good place to break our program
would be at the first instruction after the `save` instruction has been executed. To
do this in gdb, we type

```
(gdb) b main
Breakpoint 1 at 0x106a8
(gdb)
```

The command "b" followed by a label sets a breakpoint at the instruction following the labeled instruction; `gdb` assumes the labeled instruction to be a `save`
instruction.

If we then run the program

```
(gdb) r
Starting program: /home/lou/book/sparc/ch02/a.out
warning: Unable to find dynamic linker breakpoint function.
warning: GDB will be unable to debug shared library initializers
warning: and track explicitly loaded dynamic code.

Breakpoint 1, 0x106a8 in main ()
```

gdb issues some more warnings and then informs us that we are at breakpoint 1,
which should be the first instruction in our program. The program counter, `%pc`,
will have the address of the instruction 0x106a8.

We can examine memory by typing "x" followed by an address. In this case we
would like to use the contents of the `%pc` as the address. To do this, we type

```
(gdb) x/i $pc
0x106a8 <main+4>:        mov  9, %l0
(gdb)
```

The examining command "x" has to be followed by a format specified to tell **gdb**
how to print out the value stored in the memory location. The "i" format specifier
states that the contents of the memory location should be interpreted as a machine
instruction. In **gdb** all machine registers are referred to by a $ in place of the %
used in **as**.

By typing a return we repeat the last command but with the address incremented by the size of the last data element typed out:

```
(gdb)
0x106ac <main+8>:        sub   %10, 1, %o0
(gdb)
```

We may print the entire program by typing x/12i main, which will repeat the examine command 12 times:

```
(gdb) x/12i main
0x106a4 <main>: save    %sp, -96, %sp
0x106a8 <main+4>:        mov   9, %10
0x106ac <main+8>:        sub   %10, 1, %o0
0x106b0 <main+12>:       sub   %10, 7, %o1
0x106b4 <main+16>:       call  0x20870 <.mul>
0x106b8 <main+20>:       nop
0x106bc <main+24>:       sub   %10, 0xb, %o1
0x106c0 <main+28>:       call  0x2087c <.div>
0x106c4 <main+32>:       nop
0x106c8 <main+36>:       mov   %o0, %11
0x106cc <main+40>:       mov   1, %g1
0x106d0 <main+44>:       ta  0
```

If we want to see whether the program ran correctly, we can set another break-point at the **trap** instruction located at main+44. To obtain an address, given a label, we prepend an **&** much as we would do in C. Thus, to set a breakpoint at **main + 44**, we would type

```
(gdb) b *&main + 44
Breakpoint 2 at 0x106d0
(gdb)
```

While *& is an identity operation in C, it is not in **gdb**. We would then command **gdb** to continue execution by typing "c" (remember we are currently stopped at the first location in our program):

```
(gdb) c
Continuing.

Breakpoint 2, 0x106d0 in main ()
(gdb)
```

The program executes and stops at the last breakpoint we set. At this point the value should be stored in register %11. To print the contents of a register, we use the print command "p"

```
(gdb) p $11
$2 = -8
(gdb)
```

This tells us that the contents of register %l1 is −8, the correct value. The $2 =
is part of **gdb's** history feature. The value −8 has been saved in a history variable
$2 and may be used at any time by typing $2.

What would happen if our program were incorrect and did not compute the
correct value? We could single-step the program starting at the beginning by
typing "ni" for next machine instruction. To do this at this point we would need
to run the program again:

```
(gdb) r
The program being debugged has been started already.
Start it from the beginning? (y or n) y
Starting program: /home/lou/book/sparc/ch02/expr
warning: Unable to find dynamic linker breakpoint function.
warning: GDB will be unable to debug shared library initializers
warning: and track explicitly loaded dynamic code.

Breakpoint 1, 0x106a8 in main ()
(gdb)
```

We are executing the program, but it would be helpful to know what instructions
were being executed. We can discover this by examining the memory location the
%pc is pointing to:

```
(gdb) x/i $pc
0x106a8 <main+4>:        mov  9, %l0
(gdb)
```

and indeed we have just executed the first instruction and are about to execute the
second. If we execute the second instruction, by typing **ni**, %l0 should contain the
value 9:

```
(gdb) ni
0x106ac in main ()
(gdb) p $l0
$2 = 9
(gdb)
```

and indeed it does.

As we single-step our program we would probably like to have the instruction to
which the program counter is pointing printed out every time without our having
to type p $pc. We can do this with the "display" command, which prints its value
every time a command is executed:

```
(gdb) display/i $pc
1: x/i $pc  0x106ac <main+8>:    sub  %l0, 1, %o0
(gdb) ni
0x106b0 in main ()
```

```
1: x/i $pc  0x106b0 <main+12>:  sub  %l0, 7, %o1
(gdb)
```

Then when we execute the next command, the instruction about to be executed is printed out automatically. We are now about to execute the call to .mul:

```
(gdb) ni
0x106b4 in main ()
1: x/i $pc  0x106b4 <main+16>:  call  0x20870 <.mul>
(gdb)
0x106b8 in main ()
1: x/i $pc  0x106b8 <main+20>:  nop
(gdb)
0x106bc in main ()
1: x/i $pc  0x106bc <main+24>:  sub  %l0, 0xb, %o1
(gdb)
```

Note that the *delay slot instruction* is executed before the call to .mul. We have been typing "ni" for next instruction. We could have typed "si," but this would have stepped us through the .mul routine, a thing we probably don't want to do. Both "ni" and "si" execute single instructions, but "ni" does not single-step through any functions that are called. Note also that after typing "ni" the first time, we then typed only a carriage return; in **gdb** a carriage return repeats the last command.

These commands are not all the commands available to **gdb** but are enough to begin with and will enable you to write and to debug simple programs. One final command you must know is "q," to quit **gdb** and to return to the operating system:

```
(gdb) q
The program is running.  Quit anyway (and kill it)? (y or n) y
>
```

2.8 Filling Delay Slots

The call instruction is called a *delayed control transfer instruction*. A delayed transfer instruction changes the address from which future instructions will be fetched after the instruction following the delayed transfer instruction has been executed. The instruction following the delayed control transfer instruction is called the *delayed instruction* and it is located in the delay *slot*. Whenever a branch or call instruction is executed, it changes the contents of %npc, not the %pc. The instruction that follows the branching instruction will be executed **before** the branch or call happens. By filling the delay slot with a **nop** instruction we have not accomplished very much; the pipeline machine wastes an instruction execution every time it branches. However, as the delay instruction is executed before the first instruction at the branch address was executed, we may move the instruction prior to the branch instruction into the delay slot.

   In the following version of the program we have moved the **sub** instructions,
which compute the final argument to **.mul** and **.div** into the delay slots, thereby
eliminating the **nop** instructions. The resulting code does not lose any cycles at
all.

```
            .global main
main:
            save     %sp, -96, %sp
            mov      9, %l0              !initialize x
            sub      %l0, 1, %o0         !(x - 1) into %o0
            call     .mul
            sub      %l0, 7, %o1         !(x - 7) into %o1
            call     .div
            sub      %l0, 11, %o1        !(x - 11) into %o1, the divisor
            mov      %o0, %l1            !store it in y

            mov      1, %g1              !trap dispatch
            ta       0                   !trap to system
```

What is going on here? Let us assume that we are executing the mov 9, %l0
instruction while at the same time fetching the sub %l0, 1, %o0 instruction.

```
               .global main
main:
               save     %sp, -96, %sp
EXECUTE ->     mov      9, %l0              !initialize x
FETCH   ->     sub      %l0, 1, %o0         !(x - 1) into %o0
               call     .mul
               sub      %l0, 7, %o1         !(x - 7) into %o1
               call     .div
               sub      %l0, 11, %o1        !(x - 11) into %o1, the divisor
               mov      %o0, %l1            !store it in y

               mov      1, %g1              !trap dispatch
               ta       0                   !trap to system
```

Having fetched an instruction, we will execute it in the next cycle. As the instruction executed was not a branch instruction, the next instruction following will be
fetched.

```
               .global main
main:
               save     %sp, -96, %sp
               mov      9, %l0              !initialize x
EXECUTE ->     sub      %l0, 1, %o0         !(x - 1) into %o0
FETCH   ->     call     .mul
```

```
                sub      %l0, 7, %o1      !(x - 7) into %o1
                call     .div
                sub      %l0, 11, %o1     !(x - 11) into %o1, the divisor
                mov      %o0, %l1         !store it in y

                mov      1, %g1           !trap dispatch
                ta       0                !trap to system
```

Having fetched the `call` instruction, it will be executed in the next cycle. As the instruction executed `sub %l0, 1, %o0`, was not a branch instruction, the next instruction following will be fetched.

```
                .global main
main:
                save     %sp, -96, %sp
                mov      9, %l0           !initialize x
                sub      %l0, 1, %o0      !(x - 1) into %o0
EXECUTE ->      call     .mul
FETCH   ->      sub      %l0, 7, %o1      !(x - 7) into %o1
                call     .div
                sub      %l0, 11, %o1     !(x - 11) into %o1, the divisor
                mov      %o0, %l1         !store it in y

                mov      1, %g1           !trap dispatch
                ta       0                !trap to system
```

The execution of the `call` instruction will cause the next instruction to be fetched from the first location labelled by `.mul`. Having fetched the `sub %l0, 7, %o1` instruction, it will be executed. Note that its execution occurs before the first instruction from `.mul` has even been fetched.

```
                .global main
main:
                save     %sp, -96, %sp
                mov      9, %l0           !initialize x
                sub      %l0, 1, %o0      !(x - 1) into %o0
                call     .mul
EXECUTE ->      sub      %l0, 7, %o1      !(x - 7) into %o1
                call     .div
                sub      %l0, 11, %o1     !(x - 11) into %o1, the divisor
                mov      %o0, %l1         !store it in y

                mov      1, %g1           !trap dispatch
                ta       0                !trap to system
                . . .
.mul:
```

```
FETCH    ->  save . . .
             . . .
```

As the instruction executed, sub %l0, 7, %o1, was not a branching instruction, the next instruction following the instruction addressed by the %npc will be fetched while the instruction just fetched will be executed.

```
                .global main
main:
        save    %sp, -96, %sp
        mov     9, %l0          !initialize x
        sub     %l0, 1, %o0     !(x - 1) into %o0
        call    .mul
        sub     %l0, 7, %o1     !(x - 7) into %o1
        call    .div
        sub     %l0, 11, %o1    !(x - 11) into %o1, the divisor
        mov     %o0, %l1        !store it in y

        mov     1, %g1          !trap dispatch
        ta      0               !trap to system
        . . .
.mul:
EXECUTE ->  save . . .
FETCH    ->  . . .
```

Filling the delay slots in this manner makes reading the program more difficult, but by filling the delay slots the resulting execution is faster and the size of the program smaller. Care must be taken in filling delay slots to ensure that the algorithm is not changed. In general, when we write assembly language programs we will be expected to fill all possible delay slots.

2.9   Branching

We can now add, subtract, multiply, divide, and move data around. What we cannot yet do is to test and to branch. Without these capabilities we would not be able to write very interesting programs. Branching is used in conjunction with testing, which we discuss first.

2.9.1   Testing

In the HP calculator, the last number computed could be tested. For example, there was an instruction ifeq, which would skip the next instruction in line if the result last computed was zero. A similar technique is used in many computers, in which the state of the execution of each instruction may be tested. To do this, only information about the result need be kept, not the result itself. The state of execution is saved in terms of four variables:

- **Z** whether the result was zero

- **N** whether the result was negative

- **V** whether execution resulted in a number too large to store in the register

- **C** whether execution resulted in a number that generated a carry out of the register

This information is kept in four variables, the integer condition codes: Z, N, V, and C.

When we discussed pipelining it was shown that moving instructions around could eliminate empty delay slots. This causes a problem when we wish to conditionally branch, based on the result of a prior instruction execution, if the instruction was not immediately executed before the branch instruction. This problem is solved in the SPARC architecture by having a duplicate set of computational instructions, such as add and sub, which in addition to performing the arithmetic operation, set the condition codes. These instructions have "cc" appended to the mnemonic, which indicates that the instruction is to set the **condition codes** Z, N, V, and C to save the state of the instruction execution. We have so far encountered two instructions that have such equivalents, add and sub:

addcc	reg_{rs1}, reg_or_imm, reg_{rd}
subcc	reg_{rs1}, reg_or_imm, reg_{rd}

These two instructions are exactly the same as add and sub except that they also set the condition codes. The multiply and divide routines do not set the condition codes.

2.9.2 Branches

Like the call instruction, branch instructions have as their operand the label of the instruction to which they are to branch if the condition specified is met. Branch instructions are delayed control transfer instructions such that the following instruction will be executed before the effect of the branch takes place. Be careful, the delay slot of a conditional branch instruction may not be filled with another branching instruction. Branch instructions test the condition codes in order to determine if the branching condition exists:

b_{icc}   *label*

where b_{icc} stands for one of the branches testing the integer condition codes. There are a number of branches and we introduce only the signed number branches for the present:

Assembler Mnemonic	Unconditional Branches
ba	Branch always, goto
bn	Branch never

Assembler Mnemonic	Signed Arithmetic Branches
bl	Branch on less than zero
ble	Branch on less or equal to zero
be	Branch on equal to zero
bne	Branch on not equal to zero
bge	Branch on greater or equal to zero
bg	Branch on greater than zero

With these branch instructions we could extend our program to evaluate the expression for integer values of x from 0 up to 10 as we did in Chapter 1. Let us first write a C program to make clear what we are doing:

```
#define A2 1
#define A1 7
#define A0 11

main()
{
  int x, y;

  x = 0;
  do {
    y = ((x - A2) * (x - A1)) / (x - A0);
    x++;
  } while (x < 11);
}
```

The program is basically a **do** loop with some initialization.

When we translate this into assembly language a *branch less instruction* would be appropriate at the end of the loop. We will need to set a label at the beginning of the **do** loop for the target of the branch instruction:

```
/* This programs computes the expression:
   y = (x - 1) * (x - 7) / (x - 11) for x = 0, 1, ... 10
The polynomial coefficients are:
*/
  define(a2, 1)
  define(a1, 7)
  define(a0, 11)
```

```
/* Variables x and y are stored in %l0 and %l1 */

    define(x_r, 10)            !'%l0   x_r'
    define(y_r, 11)            !'%l1   y_r'

    .global main
main:
    save    %sp, -96, %sp

    clr     %x_r               !initialize x to zero

    .global loop
loop:                                  !the do loop
    sub     %x_r, a2, %o0      !(x - a2) into %o0
    call    .mul
    sub     %x_r, a1, %o1      !(x - a1) into %o1
    call    .div
    sub     %x_r, a0, %o1      !(x - a0) into %o1, the divisor
    mov     %o0, %y_r          !store it in y,

    add     %x_r, 1, %x_r      !x++

    subcc   %x_r, 11, %g0      !set condition codes
    bl      loop
    nop

    mov     1, %g1             !trap dispatch
    ta      0                  !trap to system
```

Note that the `bl` instruction is followed by a `nop` instruction in the delay slot. We cannot fill the delay slot as we did in the case of the `call` instruction simply by moving the instruction immediately before the branch into the slot, as this statement sets the condition codes to be evaluated by the `bl` instruction. If it is possible to rearrange the code before the conditional branch statement, so that the instruction immediately before the branch does not affect the condition codes set for the branch instruction, this instruction may be moved into the delay slot. We may rearrange the last few instruction as follows:

```
    add     %x_r, 1, %x_r      !x++
    subcc   %x_r, 11, %g0      !set condition codes
    mov     %o0, %y_r          !store it in y,
    bl      loop
    nop
```

We have moved the instruction that copies the contents of %o0 into %y_r to the end of the loop. Note that we could not move the `add` instruction, as it computes the value of x used in the subcc instruction. We are now free to move the mov instruction into the delay slot. The modified ".s" version of the program is as follows:

```
                         !%l0     x_r
                         !%l1     y_r

  .global main
main:
  save     %sp, -96, %sp
  clr      %l0               !initialize x to zero

  .global loop
loop:                                !the do loop
  sub      %l0, 1, %o0       !(x - 1) into %o0
  call     .mul
  sub      %l0, 7, %o1       !(x - 7) into %o1
  call     .div
  sub      %l0, 11, %o1      !(x - 11) into %o1, the divisor

  add      %l0, 1, %l0       !x++

  subcc    %l0, 11, %g0      !set condition codes
  bl       loop
  mov      %o0, %l1          !store result in y,

  mov      1, %g1            !trap dispatch
  ta       0                 !trap to system
```

The assembler recognizes

```
    cmp      reg_rs1, reg_or_imm
    for
    subcc    reg_rs1, reg_or_imm, %g0
```

so that we might have written

```
    add      %x_r, 1, %x_r    !x++
    cmp      %x_r, 11         !set condition codes
    bl       loop
    mov      %o0, %y_r        !store it in y,
```

and generated the same code.

When we execute the program we will need to set a breakpoint at loop to print out the value of y:

```
(gdb) b main
Breakpoint 1 at 0x106bc
(gdb) display/i $pc
(gdb) r
Starting program: /home/lou/book/sparc/ch02/a.out
warning: Unable to find dynamic linker breakpoint function.
warning: GDB will be unable to debug shared library initializers
warning: and track explicitly loaded dynamic code.
(no debugging symbols found)...(no debugging symbols found)...
Breakpoint 1, 0x106bc in main ()
1: x/i $pc  0x106bc <main>:      mov  %g0, %l0
(gdb) b loop
Breakpoint 2 at 0x106c0
(gdb) c
Continuing.

Breakpoint 2, 0x106c0 in loop ()
1: x/i $pc  0x106c0 <loop>:      sub  %l0, 1, %o0
(gdb) p $l1
$1 = -536872452
(gdb) c
Continuing.

Breakpoint 2, 0x106c0 in loop ()
1: x/i $pc  0x106c0 <loop>:      sub  %l0, 1, %o0
(gdb) p $l1
$2 = 0
(gdb) c
Continuing.

Breakpoint 2, 0x106c0 in loop ()
1: x/i $pc  0x106c0 <loop>:      sub  %l0, 1, %o0
(gdb) p $l1
$3 = 0
(gdb)
```

This works well but involves a lot of typing. We can program gdb to do this for us
with the commands instruction. This instruction specifies a number of commands
to be executed when the breakpoint is reached; its argument is the breakpoint at
which the commands are to be executed. In our case it is breakpoint 2 (the first
breakpoint is set at main).

```
(gdb) commands 2
Type commands for when Breakpoint 2 is hit, one per line.
End with a line saying just "end".
```

```
p $l1
c
end
(gdb)
```

This informs gdb that when it reaches breakpoint 2, it is to print out the contents
of register %l1 and then to continue. If we then run the program again:

```
(gdb) r
The program being debugged has been started already.
Start it from the beginning? (y or n) y
Starting program: /home/lou/book/sparc/ch02/a.out
warning: Unable to find dynamic linker breakpoint function.
warning: GDB will be unable to debug shared library initializers
warning: and track explicitly loaded dynamic code.

Breakpoint 1, 0x106bc in main ()
1: x/i $pc   0x106bc <main>:      mov   %g0, %l0
(gdb) c
Continuing.

Breakpoint 2, 0x106c0 in loop ()
1: x/i $pc   0x106c0 <loop>:      sub   %l0, 1, %o0
$4 = -536872452

Breakpoint 2, 0x106c0 in loop ()
1: x/i $pc   0x106c0 <loop>:      sub   %l0, 1, %o0
$5 = 0

Breakpoint 2, 0x106c0 in loop ()
1: x/i $pc   0x106c0 <loop>:      sub   %l0, 1, %o0
$6 = 0

Breakpoint 2, 0x106c0 in loop ()
1: x/i $pc   0x106c0 <loop>:      sub   %l0, 1, %o0
$7 = 0

Breakpoint 2, 0x106c0 in loop ()
1: x/i $pc   0x106c0 <loop>:      sub   %l0, 1, %o0
$8 = 1

Breakpoint 2, 0x106c0 in loop ()
1: x/i $pc   0x106c0 <loop>:      sub   %l0, 1, %o0
$9 = 1
```

```
Breakpoint 2, 0x106c0 in loop ()
1: x/i $pc   0x106c0 <loop>:      sub   %l0, 1, %o0
$10 = 1

Breakpoint 2, 0x106c0 in loop ()
1: x/i $pc   0x106c0 <loop>:      sub   %l0, 1, %o0
$11 = 1

Breakpoint 2, 0x106c0 in loop ()
1: x/i $pc   0x106c0 <loop>:      sub   %l0, 1, %o0
$12 = 0

Breakpoint 2, 0x106c0 in loop ()
1: x/i $pc   0x106c0 <loop>:      sub   %l0, 1, %o0
$13 = -2

Breakpoint 2, 0x106c0 in loop ()
1: x/i $pc   0x106c0 <loop>:      sub   %l0, 1, %o0
$14 = -8

Program exited with code 0345.
(gdb)
```

We see the values of y each time through the loop.

If you have a file .gdbinit in your current directory containing gdb commands, it will be executed first when you enter gdb. For example:

```
break main
display/i $pc
r
```

which are the commands to be executed before debugging the assembly language program.

2.10   Control Statements

When we write assembly language programs it is generally a good idea first to write the algorithm in a high-level language or at least in a pseudo-high-level language. In this way we can check the logic of the program, assign variable names, and so on. When we are satisfied with our algorithm it becomes a fairly direct process to translate the high-level program into assembly language. Of course, if we have already written our algorithm in a high-level language, we may use the compiler to translate the program. In many cases, this is what we will do, but as we are learning assembly language we need to know how to translate basic control structures into machine language and the architectural implications of that process.

We have already seen the representation of a C do loop in assembly language. The loop begins with a label, and at the end of the loop there is a conditional branch, which corresponds directly to the test specified in the while statement at the end of the loop. The branch is back to the beginning of the loop. This is the simplest form of loop and corresponds directly to the DO loop in Fortran, one of the first high-level programming languages. It is very efficient from an assembly language point of view, in that the branch is made at the end of the loop. As a consequence of this simple structure the body of a do statement is always executed once. This is fairly obvious in the C form but was never really obvious in its Fortran form, leading to much confusion.

2.10.1   While

The while loop is considered the most basic loop from a high-level-language point of view, but causes some problems in assembly language. Consider translating the following while statement into assembly language:

```
while ( a <= 17)
{
  a = a + b;
  c++;
}
```

The most obvious way to go is to perform the test, which must be performed before the loop is executed, execute the loop, and then branch back to the test:

```
test:
    cmp     %a_r, 17        !subtract 17 from a, setting the
                            !condition codes and discarding the
                            !result, i.e., storing it in %g0
    bg      done            !we have to reverse the logic of the
                            !test, as we need to branch over the
                            !loop when a > 17
    nop                     !the delay slot
    add     %a_r, %b_r, %a_r       !a = a + b
    add     %c_r, 1, %c_r   !c++
    ba      test            !branch back to the test
    nop                     !second delay slot
done:                       !whatever follows the while loop
```

The number of instructions to be executed initializing a loop is generally small compared to the number of instructions to be executed inside a loop, when multiplied by the number of times the loop will be executed. If we are interested in minimizing the number of instructions to be executed, we should concentrate on the instructions inside the loop. In the example above, there is a cmp, a conditional branch, two add instructions, a branch, and two nop instructions. The cmp and the two **add** instructions must be there with the conditional branch. However, the unconditional branch **ba test** might be removed, as may the two **nop** instructions.

By repeating the compare and test at the end of the loop we may eliminate the ba instruction:

```
test:
    cmp     %a_r, 17     !subtract 17 from a, setting the
                         !condition codes and discarding the
                         !result, i.e., storing it in %g0
    bg      done         !we have to reverse the logic of the
                         !test, as we need to branch over the
                         !loop when a > 17
    nop                  !the delay slot
loop:
    add     %a_r, %b_r, %a_r!a = a + b
    add     %c_r, 1, %c_r    !c++
    cmp     %a_r, 17         !test
    ble     loop     !branch back to the beginning of the loop
    nop              !second delay slot
done:                !whatever follows the while loop
```

Note that the loop is now two **add** instructions, the **cmp**, the conditional branch (all of which must be there), and a **nop** instruction - an improvement of two instructions! Notice also that the conditional branch inside the loop is the same logically as the condition in the **while** loop in C. We might also eliminate the code for the initial test, especially if the test is more complicated than that given in the example requiring many lines of code, by branching unconditionally to the test at the end of the loop:

```
    ba      test     !branch to test at end of loop to see
                     !if loop should be executed.
    nop              !the delay slot
loop:
    add     %a_r, %b_r, %a_r!a = a + b
    add     %c_r, 1, %c_r    !c++
test:
    cmp     %a_r, 17 !test
    ble     loop     !branch back to the beginning of the loop
    nop              !second delay slot
```

The **nop** following the conditional branch lies in the loop and is executed every iteration of the loop. We might be tempted to move the first instruction from the loop into the delay slot:

```
    ba      test     !branch to test at end of loop to see
                     !if loop should be executed.
```

```
        nop                 !the delay slot, first instruction of the test
loop:
        add     %c_r, 1, %c_r    !c++
test:
        cmp     %a_r, 17         !test
        ble     loop       !branch back to the beginning of the loop
        add     %a_r, %b_r, %a_r      !a = a + b
```

However, unlike the do loop, the condition of a while loop is to be evaluated before the loop is executed and, if the condition is not met, the loop, including the first instruction of the loop, is not to be executed. The first instruction of the loop, add, that we moved into the delay slot after the conditional branch instruction will be executed once every time we make the test, and it will, unfortunately, be executed even if the first test failed and the loop were not to be executed at all. If initially $a > 17$, the a = a + b; statement would still be executed once, which is, of course, not correct in a while loop.

From an architectural point of view it is very desirable to be able to conclude a loop with an conditional branch instruction back to the beginning of the loop, with its delay slot instruction filled with the first instruction of the loop. The SPARC architecture provides a way around this problem. All conditional branches may be **annulled**. If a conditional branch is **annulled**, the delay instruction is executed when the branch is taken (the usual case) but **not** if the branch is not taken (see Figure 2.5). That is, the instruction execution of the delayed instruction is annulled if the branch "falls through." Note that the delay slot instruction is still fetched; it is just that its execution is annulled, wasting a cycle, but as this happens only once, when the loop terminates, it is worthwhile.

To specify to the assembler that we want an annulled branch, we follow the branch mnemonic with **, a**.

```
        ba          test     !branch to test at end of loop to see
                             !if loop should be executed.
        nop                 !the delay slot, first instruction of the test
loop:
        add     %c_r, 1, %c_r    !c++
test:
        cmp     %a_r, 17         !test
        ble,a   loop       !branch back to the beginning of the loop
        add     %a_r, %b_r, %a_r      !a = a + b
```

The code segment above is now correct and the loop contains the minimum number of instructions: two adds, one compare, and a branch.

2.10.2   Do

Translating the code for a do loop is very direct and has been considered above. In the example the delay slot at the end of the loop was filled by moving an instruction

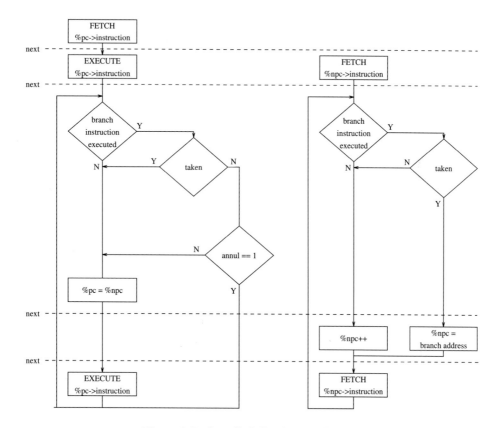

Figure 2.5: Annulled Conditional Branches

from the body of the loop. We had to be careful in doing this to avoid changing the code that evaluated the condition to be tested:

```
loop:                           !the do loop
    sub     %l0, 1, %o0         !(x - 1) into %o0
    call    .mul
    sub     %l0, 7, %o1         !(x - 7) into %o1
    call    .div
    sub     %l0, 11, %o1        !(x - 11) into %o1, the divisor

    add     %l0, 1, %l0         !x++

    cmp     %x_r, 11            !set condition codes
    bl      loop
    mov     %o0, %l1            !store result in y,
```

A simpler approach, making use of the annulled branch feature, is simply to repeat the first instruction of the loop in the delay slot, annul the branch, and change the target of the branch to the second instruction in the loop:

```
    sub     %l0, 1, %o0         !(x - 1) into %o0
loop:                           !the do loop
    call    .mul
    sub     %l0, 7, %o1         !(x - 7) into %o1
    call    .div
    sub     %l0, 11, %o1        !(x - 11) into %o1, the divisor
    mov     %o0, %l1            !store result in y,

    add     %l0, 1, %l0         !x++

    cmp     %x_r, 11            !set condition codes
    bl,a    loop
    sub     %l0, 1, %o0         !(x - 1) into %o0
```

This approach, although simple to implement, results in a program that is one instruction longer (generally not important) and wastes one machine cycle when the execution of the delay slot instruction is annulled (which happens only when the loop is finally exited).

2.10.3   For

A `for` statement is very simple to translate into assembly language if we follow the C definition of a `for`:

```
for ( ex1; ex2; ex3 ) st
```

as

```
ex1;
while ( ex2 ) {
  st
  ex3;
}
```

Thus, the translation of the following segment of C code:

```
for (a = 1; a <= b; a++)
  c *= a;
```

would be

```
    ba      test
    mov     1, %a_r          !a = 1;
loop:
    call    .mul
    mov     %c_r, %o1
    mov     %o0, %c_r
    add     %a_r, 1, %a_r
test:
    cmp     %a_r, %b_r
    ble,a   loop
    mov     %a_r, %o0        !first instruction of loop
```

2.10.4 If Then

Translating an `if` statement into SPARC assembly language is fairly straightforward. The statement following the relational expression is to be branched over if the condition is not true; to accomplish this we need to logically complement the sense of the branch, following the relational expression evaluation, before the code for the statement. The complements of the branches are as follows:

Condition	Complement
bl	bge
ble	bg
be	bne
bne	be
bge	bl
bg	ble

For example, to translate

```
d = a;
if ((a + b) > c) {
  a += b;
  c++;
}
a = c + d;
```

we would write, complementing the test into a `ble`:

```
    mov     %a_r, %d_r      !assignment statement before if
    add     %a_r, %b_r, %o0 !evaluate condition
    cmp     %o0, %c_r       !subtract and set condition codes
    ble     next            !branch over code if false
    nop
    add     %a_r, %b_r, %a_r!the then code
    add     %c_r, 1, %c_r   !incrementing c
next:
    add     %c_r, %d_r, %a_r!assignment statement following if
```

To fill the delay slot here we could move an instruction from before the `if` into the delay slot if the instruction had no effect on the `if` condition evaluation:

```
    add     %a_r, %b_r, %o0 !evaluate condition
    cmp     %o0, %c_r       !subtract and set condition codes
    ble     next            !branch over code if false
    mov     %a_r, %d_r      !assignment statement before if
    add     %a_r, %b_r, %a_r!the then code
    add     %c_r, 1, %c_r   !incrementing c
next:
    add     %c_r, %d_r, %a_r!assignment statement following if
```

If there is no such instruction, we could copy the instruction following the `if` into the delay slot, annul the branch, and change the target of the branch to skip over the copied instruction:

```
    mov     %a_r, %d_r      !assignment statement before if
    add     %a_r, %b_r, %o0 !evaluate condition
    cmp     %o0, %c_r       !subtract and set condition codes
    ble,a   next            !branch over code if false
    add     %c_r, %d_r, %a_r!assignment statement following if
    add     %a_r, %b_r, %a_r!the then code
    add     %c_r, 1, %c_r   !incrementing c
    add     %c_r, %d_r, %a_r!assignment statement following if
next:
```

Once again, the latter method is simpler but wastes an instruction and a cycle of execution if the branch is untaken.

2.10.5   If Else

An `if-else` statement allows us to do a little better with regard to filling the delay slot. Consider

```
if ((a + b) >= c) {
   a += b;
   c++;
} else {
   a -= b;
   c--;
}
c += 10;
```

We will complement the initial test to branch over the **then** code to the **else** code if the condition is false. Note that it is not considered good assembly language programming practice to exchange the **then** code with the **else** code to avoid complementing the test. One expects to read the code in the order in which it was written. After the **then** code, we will need an unconditional branch over the **else** code and then the **else** code itself:

```
        add     %a_r, %b_r, %o0 !compute condition
        cmp     %o0, %c_r       !compare it to c
        bl      else            !if less branch to less part
        nop
        add     %a_r, %b_r, %a_r!then code
        add     %c_r, 1, %c_r
        ba      next            !branch over else code
        nop
else:
        sub     %a_r, %b_r, %a_r!else code
        sub     %c_r, 1, %c_r
next:
        add     %c_r, 10, %c_r
```

We may eliminate the first **nop** instruction by replacing the **bl** instruction with an annulled **bl,a** instruction and moving the first instruction of the else part into the delay slot. If the else part is to be executed, the branch "takes" and the first instruction of the **else** part is executed in the delay slot. If the **then** part is executed, the branch is not "taken" and the first instruction of the **else** part is annulled:

```
        add     %a_r, %b_r, %o0 !compute condition
        cmp     %o0, %c_r       !compare it to c
        bl,a    else            !if less branch to less part
        sub     %a_r, %b_r, %a_r!first instruction of else code
```

```
        add     %a_r, %b_r, %a_r!then code
        add     %c_r, 1, %c_r
        ba      next            !branch over else code
        nop
else:
        sub     %c_r, 1, %c_r   !end of else code
next:
        add     %c_r, 10, %c_r
```

We can then deal with the nop after the unconditional branch instruction by moving one of the instructions from the end of the then part into the delay slot:

```
        add     %a_r, %b_r, %o0 !compute condition
        cmp     %o0, %c_r       !compare it to c
        bl,a    else            !if less branch to less part
        sub     %a_r, %b_r, %a_r!first instruction of else code
        add     %a_r, %b_r, %a_r!then code
        ba      next            !branch over else code
        add     %c_r, 1, %c_r   !last instruction of then code
else:
        sub     %c_r, 1, %c_r   !end of else code
next:
        add     %c_r, 10, %c_r
```

Or by copying the instruction following the if else into the delay slot following the ba instruction:

```
        add     %a_r, %b_r, %o0 !compute condition
        cmp     %o0, %c_r       !compare it to c
        bl,a    else            !if less branch to less part
        sub     %a_r, %b_r, %a_r!first instruction of else code
        add     %a_r, %b_r, %a_r!then code
        add     %c_r, 1, %c_r
        ba      next            !branch over else code
        add     %c_r, 10, %c_r
else:
        sub     %c_r, 1, %c_r   !end of else code
        add     %c_r, 10, %c_r
next:
```

Once again, we add an instruction to the length of the program, but in this case, do not add an additional cycle to the execution.

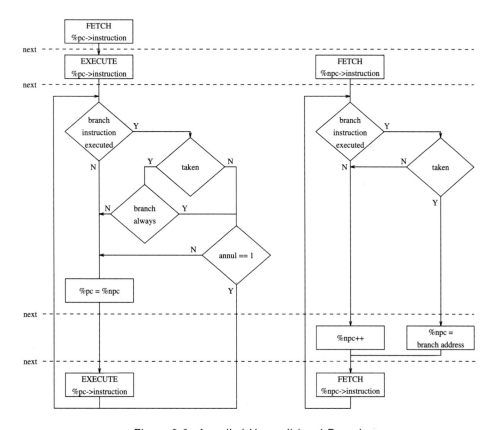

Figure 2.6: Annulled Unconditional Branches

2.11   Annulled Unconditional Branch

The `ba` unconditional branch instruction may also be annulled. Why would this be necessary, as an unconditional branch is always taken? Annulling an unconditional branch has been implemented to have the exact opposite effect of annulling a conditional branch; that is, if an unconditional branch is annulled, the delay slot instruction is *not* executed. An annulled unconditional branch provides a branch instruction that, in effect, has no delay slot and may be used to branch in a single instruction. Sometimes it is desirable to replace a single instruction with a branch to an emulation subroutine, and in this case an annulled unconditional branch may be used. However, annulling an unconditional branch instruction wastes a machine cycle, and it should not be used except when the branch must replace a single instruction.

The SPARC machine cycle is shown in Figure 2.6 to reflect execution of annulled branches. You will see that if a *branch always* instruction was executed in the previous cycle it was clearly taken, bringing the machine to the annul decision point. If the *branch always* instruction was not annulled then the delay slot instruction is selected for execution. If the *branch always* instruction was annulled, then the delay slot instruction is simply skipped.

2.12   Summary

The SPARC load/store architecture registers were described together with the arithmetic instructions, including calls to multiply and to divide, allowing for simple programs to be written. In conjunction with the `call` instruction, pipelining was described (pipelining makes it easier for a computer to execute one instruction every machine cycle). An extensive discussion of `gdb` followed so that the execution of a program could be monitored and the results examined. We then introduced the branching and testing instructions and used them to translate the C control structures into SPARC assembly language. In translating the C control structures, many of the features of the architecture were made apparent, including the annulled branch. A summary of `gdb` commands follows:

Command	Function
run args	Run file with command line args.
run	Run program with previous command line args.
break funct	Set breakpoint at function entry.
break *addr	Set breakpoint at address.
break ... if cond	Set breakpoint, break if conditions.
clear funct	Remove breakpoint at function entry.
delete bnum	Delete breakpoint bnum.
disable bnum	Disable breakpoint bnum.
enable bnum	Enable breakpoint bnum.
condition bnum	Set conditions for breakpoint bnum.
commands bnum	Set commands for breakpoint bnum.
cont	Continue execution from breakpoint.
step	Step next source level statement.
step**i**	Step next machine instruction.
next	Step next source level statement or function.
next**i**	Step next machine instruction or function call.
print expr	Print value of expression including $n for machine registers.
print/f expr	Print value of expression according to format specified by f: x hexadecimal, d decimal, u unsigned decimal, o octal, a address, c character, f single precision floating point.
x/sf addr	Examine memory of size s bytes in format f: s = b one byte, s = h halfword, s = w word, s = g double word; x hexadecimal, d decimal, u unsigned decimal, o octal, a address, c character, f single precision floating point, s ascii string, i machine instruction.
display/f expr	p/sf, print every gdb command.
display/sf addr	x/sf, examine every gdb command.
undisplay n	Remove item n from display list.
jump *addr	Execute next instruction at address addr.
printf string, exprs	Formatted output, similar to printf in C but without the parentheses surrounding the arguments.
info data	Information about break, display, registers, functions, variables

gdb reads commands from a file .gdbinit in your working directory before execution starts.

2.13   Exercises

2–1 Write an assembly language program to compute

$$y = (a + b) * (a - b)/c;$$

where: $a = 17$, $b = -3$, and $c = 3$.

Try to eliminate all **nop** instructions. Run the program using **gdb** to verify correctness.

2–2 Write an assembly language program to compute

$$y = 3x^4 + 5x^3 - 17x^2 + 33x - 15$$

when $x = 3$. Eliminate all **nop** instructions and run the program using **gdb** to verify correctness.

2–3 Write a program to find the maximum of

$$x^3 - 14x^2 + 56x - 64$$

in the range $-2 <= x <= 8$, by stepping one by one through the range.

2–4 Write a program to find the square root of a number $y = \sqrt{x}$, say for $x = 1000$, using the Newton-Raphson method outlined below:

```
pick y = x/2

do {
   old = y;
   dx = x - y * y;
   y = y + dx / 2y;
} while(y != old)
```

2–5 Assuming that all variables are in registers

```
define(a_r, 10)
define(b_r, 11)
define(c_r, 12)
define(x_r, 13)
```

translate the following C while loop into assembly language, minimizing the number of instructions, thus filling all delay slots with useful instructions:

```
while ((a + b) * c <= x)
{
    x = x - 10;
    c = (c * a) / b;
}
```

2–6 You are to find a zero of

$$y = 3x^4 - 17x^3 + 14x^2 - 23x + 15$$

by starting with $x = 10$ and decrementing x until you find the zero; that is, when $y = 0$. Your program should include a specific check so that x is not decremented below zero. You are to write a program in which constants and registers are symbolically defined using m4.

2–7 You are to write an assembly language program to compute the sum of sums for an argument n. The sum might be defined as

```
for ( sum = 0, i = 1; i <= n; i++)
    sum += i;
```

The sum of sums is the sum of these sums from 1 to n; for example, the sum of sums of 8 is 120. Your program should exit if the input is negative. Make sure your program works for all positive inputs, including zero, which do not result in an arithmetic overflow; you do not have to check for overflow. Do not perform any algebraic simplifications but rather, write the code as two nested loops. Use gdb to print out the result in the form

Sum of sums for 8 is 120

Make sure that you fill all delay slots and you have no wasted instructions!

2–8 The following program performs the addition of pounds, shilllings, and pence, an ancient form of currency used by the British in the days of the empire. There are 12 pence in a shilling and 20 shillings in a pound. Thus the sum of L 17/14/6 and L 53/5/7 would be L 71/0/1. The L is the nearest thing you can get to the funny symbol the British used to represent pounds, the equivalent of the $ sign. The "/"s separate the pounds from shillings and from pence.

The following program, which you should translate into assembly language, performs the addition by incrementing and decrementing. It does not use multiplication of division: sort of like the way one might write a recursive scheme function to perform the task, or like counting on your fingers.

You will see that the two numbers are "hard wired" into the program, you may wish to change them, but I would like to see the gdb output for the numbers given. You will need to set a couple of breakpoints with commands to handle the printf statements in gdb. You might turn in your assembly language program along with the appropriate .gdbinit file with the execution in gdb:

```
GDB is free software and you are welcome to distribute copies of it
 under certain conditions; type "show copying" to see the conditions.
There is absolutely no warranty for GDB; type "show warranty" for
details.
GDB 4.16 (sparc-sun-solaris2.5.1),
Copyright 1996 Free Software Foundation, Inc...(no debugging symbols
found)...
Breakpoint 1 at 0x10674
Breakpoint 2 at 0x106f0
(no debugging symbols found)...(no debugging symbols found)...
Breakpoint 1, 0x10674 in print ()
The sum of L 17/14/6 and L 53/5/7 is
Breakpoint 2, 0x106f0 in done ()
L 71/0/1

Program exited normally.
```

Translate the program as given without reorganizing the code in any way. Pay particular attention to the correct coding of the loops and of preincrement as opposed to postincrement. Needless to say all delay slot instructions must be filled and that no "ba" instruction are to appear inside loops. You will notice that the code is repetitious and is a good candidate for the use of macros. The body of my code is generated by three macro calls:

```
        carry(pence1, pence2, shillings2, 12)
        carry(shillings1, shillings2, pounds2, 20)
        add(pounds1, pounds2)
```

You might try your hand if you are feeling brave. If you do choose to use macros you might have trouble with labels. However, labels 0, 1, ... , 9 may appear many times in a program (and are thus good to use in macros), and branch instructions distinguish between which one of the labels is desired by appending a "b" of an "f" to the branch target. If "f" is appended, the branch is to the next statement labeled by the numeric label, whereas if the branch label is followed by a "b" the branch is to the last occurrence of the label before the branch. Keep the local variables in the local registers. */

```
main()
{
register int l1, s1, p1, l2, s2, p2;
register int t;

l1 = 17, s1 = 14, p1 = 6;
l2 = 53, s2 = 5,  p2 = 7;
```

```
printf("The sum of L %d/%d/%d and L %d/%d/%d is ", l1, s1, p1, l2,
      s2, p2);

t = p1;                              /* start with pence */
while (t--)                          /* p2 += p1 */
  p2++;

if (p2 >= 12)  {                     /* if p2 > 12 then increment */
  s2++;                              /* the shillings and subtract */
  t = 12;                            /* 12 from p2 */
  do
    p2--;
  while (--t);
}

t = s1;                              /* now shillings */
while (t--)
  s2++;

if (s2 >= 20)  {                     /* over 20? */
  l2++;                              /* better increment the pounds */
  t = 20;                            /* and subtract 20 from s2 */
  do
    s2--;
  while (--t);
}

t = l1;
while (t--)                          /* finally the pounds */
  l2++;
printf("L %d/%d/%d\n", l2, s2, p2);
exit(0);                             /* all's well that ends well */
}
```

2–9 Did you ever wonder how the date of Easter is figured out? Well from [12], we find the following algorithm due to the Neapolitan astronomer Aloysius Lilinus and the German Jesuit mathematician Christopher Clavius in the late sixteenth century, which is used by most Western churches to determine the date of Easter Sunday for any year after 1582. The first systematic algortihm for calculating the date of Easter was the canon paschalis due to Victorius of Aquitania (A.D. 457). There are many indications that the sole important application of arithmetic in Europe during the Middle Ages was the calculation of Easter date, and so such algorithms are historically significant. Here is the algorithm to translate into an assembly language program to compute the date of easter for the current year:

First compute the golden number G for the year Y for which the date of Easter is desired:

```
G = (Y mod 19) + 1;
```

G is the so-called *golden number* of the year in the 19-year Metonic cycle.

Compute the century C as

```
C = (Y / 100) + 1;
```

When Y is not a multiple of 100, C is the century number (i.e., 1988 is the twentieth century).

Compute two corrections:

```
X = (3 C / 4) - 12;
Z = [(8 C + 5) / 25] - 5;
```

X is the number of years, such as 1900, in which leap year was dropped in order to keep in step with the sun. Z is a special correction designed to synchronize Easter with the moon's orbit.

Find Sunday:

```
D = (5 Y / 4) - X - 10;
```

Find the "epact" E:

```
E = (11 G + 20 + Z - X) mod 30;
If E = 25 and the golden number G is greater than 11, or if
E = 24, then increase E by one. (E is the so-called "epact"
which specifies when a full moon occurs.)
```

Find full moon:

```
N = 44 - E;
If N < 21, then add 30 to N. (Easter is supposedly the "first
Sunday following the first full moon which occurs on or after
March 21." Actually, perturbations in the moon's orbit do not
make this strictly true, but we are concerned here with the
"calendar moon" rather than the actual moon.  The Nth of March
is a calendar full moon.)
```

Advance to Sunday:

```
N = N + 7 - ((D + N) mod 7);
```

Get month:

> If N > 31, the month M is 4 and the day N is (N - 31)
> otherwise the month M is 3 and the day is N.

Use the local registers, %l0–%l7, and the in registers, %i0–%i5, for local variables. Use m4 to define all registers, except for the out registers, symbolically.

Division a / b is obtained by the function call

```
mov     a, %o0
call    .div
mov     b, %o1
```

with the result appearing in %o0. The mod operator is the remainder: a mod b:

```
mov     a, %o0
call    .rem
mov     b, %o1
```

Finally, create a .gdbinit file in your working directory to set two breakpoints at the same place in your program to print out the result. The first breakpoint is conditional on the month being 3 and the second on the month being 4. Both breakpoints should have commands to include a printf statement. For example, if these are the second and third breakpoints specified in the .gdbinit file at location "out" then

```
b out if $l7 == 3
commands 2
printf "Easter Sunday is on March %d,  %d\n",  $l6, $l0
end
b out if $l7 == 4
commands 3
printf "Easter Sunday is on April %d, %d\n",  $l6, $l0
end
```

```
Creates output is the following form for the year 1998:
```

```
Breakpoint 3, 0x107d8 in out ()
1: x/i $pc  0x107d8 <out>:      st  %l6, [ %fp + -32 ]
Easter Sunday is on April 12, 1998
(gdb)
```

Chapter 3

DIGITAL LOGIC AND BINARY NUMBERS

3.1 Binary Hardware Devices

Bistable devices are easy to design and build. These are devices that are either on or off: they have two states. On the other hand, analog devices, such as amplifiers, throttles, variable-speed drives, etc. are difficult to design, as they must provide for a continuous output-related functionally to the input. Analog devices employ negative feedback to maintain an accurate functional relationship between input and output which slows down the response of the system; bistable devices, on the other hand, employ positive feedback to maintain the state of the device, which speeds up the response of the system. If one needs a system based on large numbers of devices, the choice of bistable devices leads to a more reliable and faster design. Computers are such systems, involving millions of devices, all of which must function correctly if the computer is to function as a whole.

Bistable devices have two states, which might be called:

- on/off
- yes/no
- true/false
- 1/0

The last representation uses two digits, 0 and 1, to represent the two states. This is called a binary digit, or *bit*. A single bit can represent two states, 0 and 1, or on and off.

Bit_0	State
0	1
1	2

Two such bits could represent four states:

Bit_1	Bit_0	State
0	0	1
0	1	2
1	0	3
1	1	4

depending on whether the bits were on or off, taking all possible combinations. Three bits would have eight states:

Bit_2	Bit_1	Bit_0	State
0	0	0	1
0	0	1	2
0	1	0	3
0	1	1	4
1	0	0	5
1	0	1	6
1	1	0	7
1	1	1	8

How many states can n bits represent? Clearly, 2^n states.

If we have such devices, how should we store decimal numbers? Three bits would be insufficient, as three bits can only represent eight states, and with decimal numbers we have 10 states. We would need four bits to represent the 10 digits:

Bit_3	Bit_2	Bit_1	Bit_0	Decimal Digit
0	0	0	0	0
0	0	0	1	1
0	0	1	0	2
0	0	1	1	3
0	1	0	0	4
0	1	0	1	5
0	1	1	0	6
0	1	1	1	7
1	0	0	0	8
1	0	0	1	9

Unfortunately, we have six states left over that are not used. On some machines this four-bit representation is used to represent decimal digits together with the plus (+) and minus (−) signs.

Bit_3	Bit_2	Bit_1	Bit_0	Decimal Digit
0	0	0	0	0
0	0	0	1	1
0	0	1	0	2
0	0	1	1	3
0	1	0	0	4
0	1	0	1	5
0	1	1	0	6
0	1	1	1	7
1	0	0	0	8
1	0	0	1	9
1	1	0	0	+
1	1	0	1	−

Note that the representation for 12 is used to represent "+" and 13 to represent "−." Such a group of four bits is called a *nibble* and a group of such nibbles is used to represent a decimal number, called *packed decimal*, or *BCD* (binary coded decimal). Apart from business applications of computers, packed decimal representation is seldom used. Instead, a representation that makes use of all the possible states is used to represent numbers. For bistable devices the representation is a base 2 number system. Decimal numbers, with which we are familiar, are base 10. That is, each digit represents some multiple of a power of 10. In base 2 numbers each digit represents a power of 2. There are only two digits in a base 2 number representation, 0 and 1, and the binary digits are the bits we have described above.

3.2   Decimal and Binary Number Systems

If we use a binary number system, we can store the number representations directly in a bistable memory using one bistable device for each bit. For example, the number 14 may be represented in binary as 1110. The number 14, 1110, could be stored in a four-bit memory device.

Using positional notation an n-digit number may be represented by an optional sign and a sequence of digits $S d_{n-1} d_{n-2} ... d_2 d_1 d_0$ where S is a sign. The interpretation of such a representation is

$$N = S(d_{n-1}R^{n-1} + d_{n-2}R^{n-2} + \cdots + d_2 R^2 + d_1 R^1 + d_0)$$

where

R is the number system base, 10 for decimal numbers
N is the number in base R
S is the sign, + or −
n is the number of digits

Note that digits are in the range $0 <= d_i <= (R-1)$. For decimal numbers the digits are in the range 0 to 9, and for binary numbers they are in the range 0 to

1. When one is using numbers in different bases, a trailing subscript indicating the base is frequently used:

$$14_{10} = 1110_2$$

When storing an n-bit binary number, n bistable devices are needed and all possible 2^n states are used. This is the most efficient storage system, allowing for the largest range of numbers to be stored in the smallest number of bistable devices.

Numbers in computers are stored in memory. If we are using bistable devices and storing binary numbers, we need a sequence of addressable n-bit binary memory cells. Each memory cell will have an address. Memory addresses also need to be stored and manipulated, as do the contents of the memory. Clearly, the arguments we made for a binary number representation for data would apply equally to memory addresses. That is, memory addresses should also be binary numbers. By using binary addresses a given number of bits of address will address the largest number of memory cells. Another factor in favor of binary addressable memory relates to the decoding of memory addresses in which one or another path is selected based on the state of each bit of the address in turn. If memory addresses are binary, memory sizes will be powers of 2. Thus, what is referred to as a 1K memory (k = kilo = thousand) is actually 1024 words of memory and needs 10 bits of address. $2^{10} = 1024$ (see Appendix G).

On actual machines memory addresses are typically much larger; 32 bits are quite popular, resulting in $2^{32} = 4,294,967,296$ memory cells. If we try to write down such large numbers in binary, we will have trouble keeping track of all the zeros and ones. To compare such numbers would require careful bit-by-bit comparisons. Although binary numbers might be good for computers, they are difficult for humans, who would rather make use of a larger vocabulary of symbols and have fewer digits. Octal and hexadecimal number systems provide us with a larger vocabulary of symbols and bear a very simple relationship to binary numbers.

3.2.1   Octal and Hexadecimal Numbers

By grouping the bits of a binary number into threes starting from the right, or least significant bit (LSB), we obtain

$$N = S(...(d_8 2^8 + d_7 2^7 + d_6 2^6) + (d_5 2^5 + d_4 2^4 + d_3 2^3) + (d_2 2^2 + d_1 2^1 + d_0))$$

or

$$N = S(...(d_8 2^2 + d_7 2^1 + d_6)2^{2*3} + (d_5 2^2 + d_4 2^1 + d_3)2^3 + (d_2 2^2 + d_1 2^1 + d_0))$$

but in the form above, the parenthesized expressions $(d_8 2^2 + d_7 2^1 + d_6)$ are the coefficients of base 8 digits, $N = S(d_2 8^2 + d_1 * 8 + d_0)$. By grouping binary digits into threes, we obtain the octal equivalent of the number. The translation of the groups of three bits is as described before:

Bit_2	Bit_1	Bit_0	Octal Digit
0	0	0	0
0	0	1	1
0	1	0	2
0	1	1	3
1	0	0	4
1	0	1	5
1	1	0	6
1	1	1	7

Note that there are eight octal digits. We may thus group the binary number $01101011011 0_2$ into sets of three bits, $011, 010, 110, 110_2$, and then write it as 3266_8. Octal numbers are normally used by programmers to write down binary numbers and to do arithmetic. In C, octal numbers are indicated by writing the number with a leading 0, and we would write 03266 if we wanted the constant 3266_8.

Some time ago registers were standardized into sizes of multiples of eight bits called bytes. A byte can represent $2^8 = 256$ possible states and is suitable for representing small numbers and character fonts, when each character in a font is represented by a small number. Translating an eight-bit number into octal creates a problem, as we have two groups of three and one group of two bits. Grouping the bits into groups of four would be a better match to register sizes, which are multiples of eight bits. This would result in a base 16 number system. If we do this, however, we have to invent additional symbols to represent the digits beyond the 9. The standard approach to this is to use the first six letters of the alphabet for the digits beyond 9 to represent the 16 digits:

```
0123456789abcdef
```

Such a number system is called *hexadecimal*. To translate $01101011011 0_2$ into hexadecimal, we first group the bits, starting from the right, into sets of four: $0110, 1011, 0110_2$. These groups of four bits may then be translated according to the following table:

Bit_3	Bit_2	Bit_1	Bit_0	Hexadecimal Digit
0	0	0	0	0
0	0	0	1	1
0	0	1	0	2
0	0	1	1	3
0	1	0	0	4
0	1	0	1	5
0	1	1	0	6
0	1	1	1	7
1	0	0	0	8
1	0	0	1	9
1	0	1	0	a
1	0	1	1	b
1	1	0	0	c
1	1	0	1	d
1	1	1	0	e
1	1	1	1	f

Thus, our number $0110, 1011, 0110_2 = $ 6b6$_{16}$. In C, hexadecimal numbers are designated by a leading 0x so that 0x6b6 would be interpreted by the compiler as 6b6$_{16}$ and stored in the computer as 011010110110.

3.2.2   Converting from Decimal to Binary

The conversion of numbers from decimal to binary is as follows. Consider the positional representation of a binary number where the left-hand side is the decimal number we wish to convert:

$$N_{10} = S(d_{n-1}2^{n-1} + d_{n-2}2^{n-2} + \cdots + d_2 2^2 + d_1 2^1 + d_0)$$

and the d_i are the binary bits that we wish to determine. By dividing both sides of the equation by the base 2, we obtain

$$N_{10}/2 = S(d_{n-1}2^{n-2} + d_{n-2}2^{n-3} + \cdots + d_2 2^1 + d_1)$$

plus a remainder, d_0, the least significant bit (LSB). Dividing again, we obtain, as remainder, the next least significant bit, d_1:

$$(N_{10}/2)/2 = S(d_{n-1}2^{n-3} + d_{n-2}2^{n-4} + \cdots + d_2)$$

For example, to convert 374_{10} to binary, we continue to divide by 2 until the quotient is zero. The remainders are the binary digits, LSB first:

$$
\begin{array}{c|ccc}
2 & 374 & & \\
2 & 187 & + & 0 \\
2 & 93 & + & 1 \\
2 & 46 & + & 1 \\
2 & 23 & + & 0 \\
2 & 11 & + & 1 \\
2 & 5 & + & 1 \\
2 & 2 & + & 1 \\
2 & 1 & + & 0 \\
2 & 0 & + & 1 \\
\end{array}
$$

The resulting number is 101110110.

Although this process is correct, handling all the divisions by 2 is error-prone. Conversion to base 8 requires fewer divisions and is less-error prone. To convert to octal, we divide repeatedly by 8, with the remainders the octal digits, least significant digit first. Repeating our example, converting 374 first to octal and then to binary:

$$
\begin{array}{c|ccc}
8 & 374 & & \\
8 & 46 & + & 6 \\
8 & 5 & + & 6 \\
8 & 0 & + & 5 \\
\end{array}
$$

yields the number 566_8. This number may then be converted to binary by translating each octal digit into the three-bit equivalent:

$$
\begin{array}{ccc|ccc|ccc|}
 & 5 & & & 6 & & & 6 & \\
1 & 0 & 1 & 1 & 1 & 0 & 1 & 1 & 0 \\
\end{array}
$$

If we are working in hexadecimal, we might wish to convert from decimal. This would involve dividing repeatedly by 16, which is difficult. A simpler approach is to convert first to octal (which is easy), then to binary (also easy), and then, finally, to group the binary bits into fours, from the right, translating each group into a hexadecimal digit. Following the example above, if we were requested to convert 374_{10} into hexadecimal, we would first convert to octal, shown above, to obtain 566_8 and then to binary, also shown above, to obtain 101110110_2. These bits can then be grouped in fours to obtain

$$
\begin{array}{cccc|cccc|cccc|}
0 & 0 & 0 & 1 & 0 & 1 & 1 & 1 & 0 & 1 & 1 & 0 \\
 & & & 1 & & & & 7 & & & & 6 \\
\end{array}
$$

or 176_{16}.

3.2.3   Converting from Binary to Decimal

If we need to convert from binary, octal, or hexadecimal to decimal, we first convert the representations to octal. That is, we convert binary to octal and hexadecimal to binary and then to octal. We are then left with the problem of converting from octal to decimal. Let us consider the conversion of $3ab_{16}$ to decimal. The conversion to binary is

$$\begin{array}{ccccccccccc}
3 & & & | & & a & & | & & b & & | \\
0 & 0 & 1 & 1 & 1 & 0 & 1 & 0 & 1 & 0 & 1 & 1
\end{array}$$

From binary we convert to octal, or if we were starting with a binary number, we would start here:

$$\begin{array}{cccccccccccc}
0 & 0 & 1 & 1 & 1 & 0 & 1 & 0 & 1 & 0 & 1 & 1 \\
& 1 & & | & 6 & & | & 5 & & | & 3 & & |
\end{array}$$

The conversion from octal to decimal is the evaluation of the equation defining positional notation:

$$N_{10} = S(d_{n-1}8^{n-1} + d_{n-2}8^{n-2} + \cdots + d_2 8^2 + d_1 8^1 + d_0)$$

or as

$$N_{10} = S((...(d_{n-1}8 + d_{n-2})8 + 2^{n-2})8 + \cdots + +d_2)8 + d_1)8 + d_0)$$

and might be mechanized as follows. The number is first written down in a column, most significant digit first:

```
1
6
5
3
```

Then the polynomial is evaluated:

```
          1  =    1
  1 * 8 + 6  =   14
 14 * 8 + 5  =  117
117 * 8 + 3  =  939
```

yielding the result of 939_{10}.

The debugger gdb may be used to convert numbers between bases by specifying the print format. For example:

```
(gdb) p/d 0x3ab
$1 = 939
(gdb) p/d 01653
$2 = 939
(gdb) p/x 939
$3 = 0x3ab
(gdb)
```

3.3 ASCII Representation of Characters

The printable character set, including carriage control and tab characters, is represented in memory as small integers. The characters are usually represented as hexadecimal numbers. The mapping between characters, as defined in C, and the ASCII[1] hexadecimal code are given in Table 3.1.

Constants to represent the ASCII character set are conveniently stored in the byte data type. When these constants are needed in an assembly language program, they may be represented by their hexadecimal code or by placing the single character in single quotes ('). Unfortunately, the use of single quotes is frequently used by m4 and their use to signify ASCII character constants would lead to confusion. The as assembler allows us to use double quotes (") to delimit characters. For example, to move the character representing the lowercase "a" into register %r1, one may write either:

```
mov     0x61, %r1
```

or:

```
mov     'a', %r1
```

or:

```
mov     "a", %r1
```

3.4 Bitwise Logical Operations

The complement of a binary variable is simply its opposite state; that is, the complement of 1 is 0 and the complement of 0 is 1. This is similar to a unary minus operator in arithmetic expressions and might similarly be referred to as the "not" operator. Thus, if a binary variable "a" had value 1, "not a" would have value 0.

Binary variables representing the two states 0 and 1 may be combined in boolean expressions. Consider the "and" function of two boolean variables: It is true only when both its arguments are true; otherwise, it is false. By considering 1 to represent truth and 0 to represent falsity, we may write a truth table for the **and** function as follows:

---

[1]ASCII, American Standard Code for Information Interchange.

Char.	Hex.	Char.	Hex.	Char.	Hex.	Char.	Hex.
\0	0x0					\a	0x7
\b	0x8	\t	0x9	\n	0xa	\v	0xb
\f	0xc	\r	0xd				
␣	0x20	!	0x21	"	0x22	#	0x23
$	0x24	%	0x25	&	0x26	'	0x27
(	0x28	)	0x29	*	0x2a	+	0x2b
,	0x2c	-	0x2d	.	0x2e	/	0x2f
0	0x30	1	0x31	2	0x32	3	0x33
4	0x34	5	0x35	6	0x36	7	0x37
8	0x38	9	0x39	:	0x3a	;	0x3b
<	0x3c	=	0x3d	>	0x3e	?	0x3f
@	0x40	A	0x41	B	0x42	C	0x43
D	0x44	E	0x45	F	0x46	G	0x47
H	0x48	I	0x49	J	0x4a	K	0x4b
L	0x4c	M	0x4d	N	0x4e	O	0x4f
P	0x50	Q	0x51	R	0x52	S	0x53
T	0x54	U	0x55	V	0x56	W	0x57
X	0x58	Y	0x59	Z	0x5a	[	0x5b
\	0x5c	]	0x5d	^	0x5e	_	0x5f
`	0x60	a	0x61	b	0x62	c	0x63
d	0x64	e	0x65	f	0x66	g	0x67
h	0x68	i	0x69	j	0x6a	k	0x6b
l	0x6c	m	0x6d	n	0x6e	o	0x6f
p	0x70	q	0x71	r	0x72	s	0x73
t	0x74	u	0x75	v	0x76	w	0x77
x	0x78	y	0x79	z	0x7a	{	0x7b
|	0x7c	}	0x7d	~	0x7e		

Table 3.1: The ASCII Character Code

a	b	and
0	0	0
0	1	0
1	0	0
1	1	1

Similarly for the **or** function, which is true when either or both its arguments are true:

a	b	or
0	0	0
0	1	1
1	0	1
1	1	1

Another function used frequently is the exclusive or function **xor**, which is true only when one of its inputs is different, one true and one false:

a	b	xor
0	0	0
0	1	1
1	0	1
1	1	0

Two other functions have been named, as they relate to the boolean operation of two very simple electrical circuits: **nand**, the logical complement of **and**:

a	b	nand
0	0	1
0	1	1
1	0	1
1	1	0

and **nor** the logical complement of **or**:

a	b	nor
0	0	1
0	1	0
1	0	0
1	1	0

Neither of these functions has any particular merit computationally.

A single boolean variable has two possible states, and for each of these two possible states there are four possible functions:

a	0	1	Logical Operation
0	0	false
0	1	a
1	0	not a
1	1	true

With the exception of **not a**, all the other functions are trivial. With two variables there are four possible states, and for each of these four possible states there are 16 possible boolean functions:

	a	0	0	1	1	Logical	Sparc	With
	b	0	1	0	1	Operation	Instruction	%r0
1		0	0	0	0	false		
2		0	0	0	1	a and b	and	
3		0	0	1	0	a and (not b)	andn	
4		0	0	1	1	a		
5		0	1	0	0	b and (not a)		
6		0	1	0	1	b		
7		0	1	1	0	a xor b	xor	
8		0	1	1	1	a or b	or	
9		1	0	0	0	a nor b		
10		1	0	0	1	a xor (not b)	xnor	not(a) or not(b)
11		1	0	1	0	not b		
12		1	0	1	1	a or (not b)	orn	
13		1	1	0	0	not a		
14		1	1	0	1	b or (not a)		
15		1	1	1	0	a nand b		
16		1	1	1	1	true		

We have numbered these functions in the left-hand column. Of the 16 the first and last are trivial, as are 4, a, and 6, b. Two pairs of functions are symmetric, with only the arguments reversed: 3 and 5, 12 and 14. Two functions are functions of only one variable: 11 and 13, not a and not b. If we eliminate these we have left:

	a	0	0	1	1	Logical	Sparc	With
	b	0	1	0	1	Operation	Instruction	%r0
2		0	0	0	1	a and b	and	
3		0	0	1	0	a and (not b)	andn	
7		0	1	1	0	a xor b	xor	
8		0	1	1	1	a or b	or	
9		1	0	0	0	a nor b		
10		1	0	0	1	a xor (not b)	xnor	not(a) or not(b)
12		1	0	1	1	a or (not b)	orn	
15		1	1	1	0	a nand b		

Of these remaining functions, **nor** and **nand** may be obtained by first performing an **and** or **or** operation followed by a **not** operation and are not included as instructions. The remaining functions are implemented in SPARC as machine instructions [22]. Note that the **not** operation may be obtained by using the **xnor** instruction with either source operand 0. Thus, the bitwise logic instructions provided in the SPARC architecture are

and	reg_{rs1}, reg_or_imm, reg_{rd}
andn	reg_{rs1}, reg_or_imm, reg_{rd}
xor	reg_{rs1}, reg_or_imm, reg_{rd}
or	reg_{rs1}, reg_or_imm, reg_{rd}
xnor	reg_{rs1}, reg_or_imm, reg_{rd}
orn	reg_{rs1}, reg_or_imm, reg_{rd}

Instructions that perform the operation and set the condition codes are also provided:

andcc	reg_{rs1}, reg_or_imm, reg_{rd}
andncc	reg_{rs1}, reg_or_imm, reg_{rd}
xorcc	reg_{rs1}, reg_or_imm, reg_{rd}
orcc	reg_{rs1}, reg_or_imm, reg_{rd}
xnorcc	reg_{rs1}, reg_or_imm, reg_{rd}
orncc	reg_{rs1}, reg_or_imm, reg_{rd}

The assembler recognizes

not	reg_{rs1}, reg_{rd}
not	reg_{rd}

as

xnor	reg_{rs1}, %**g0**, reg_{rd}
xnor	reg_{rd}, %**g0**, reg_{rd}

thus, in effect, providing a **not** instruction.

All these instructions combine their 32-bit operands bitwise in pairs to produce a 32-bit result, in which each bit represents the logical combination of the bits occupying the same position in the operands. In C, these operations correspond to the bitwise logical operations: & **and**, | **or**, ^ **xor**, ~ **not**.

3.4.1 Synthetic Instructions Using %g0

The SPARC architecture frequently makes use of the fact that the %r0, or %g0, always discards anything written to it and always has a value of zero. The **mov** instruction is actually an **or** instruction, since **mov** is recognized by the assembler as

or	%**g0**, reg_or_imm, reg_{rd}

These alternative forms of instructions, or instructions with one operand always %g0, are called *synthetic instructions*.

Another synthetic instruction we have used is `clr`, which the assembler recognizes for

$$\text{or} \qquad \textbf{\%g0, \%g0, } reg_{rd}$$

We have already discussed the synthetic `cmp` instruction. A similar synthetic instruction is `tst`, provided for the following situation:

```
if (a > 0)
   b++;
```

It is unnecessary to translate this into assembly language specifying a second operand of zero:

```
        cmp     %a_r, 0
        ble     next
        nop
        add     %b_r, 1, %b_r
next:
```

which will become, on expanding the macro for `cmp`:

```
        subcc   %a_r, %g0, %g0
        ble     next
        nop
        add     %b_r, 1, %b_r
next:
```

Instead, we may write

```
        tst     %a_r
        ble     next
        nop
        add     %b_r, 1, %b_r
next:
```

which will expand into

```
        orcc    %a_r, %g0, %g0
        ble     next
        nop
        add     %b_r, 1, %b_r
next:
```

The `orcc` instruction or's zero with the contents of register `%a_r`, which does not change the contents of the destination register but does set the condition codes. The assembler recognizes

```
    tst         reg_rs1
```

for

```
    orcc        reg_rs1, %g0, %g0
```

3.4.2 Flags

Individual bits are frequently used to represent boolean flags, and a word may contain 32 such flags. Operations on flags typically involve setting, clearing, and toggling. The following mnemonics are recognized by the assembler for setting, clearing, and toggling flags, making use of the logical instructions:

bset	or	bit set
bclr	andn	bit clear
btog	xor	bit toggle

Thirty-two flags may be operated in parallel using these instructions. Note the use of the **andn** instruction to clear flags, which is why it is normally included in an instruction set.

A synthetic instruction, **btst**, is provided to test if any or no flags are set:

```
    btst        reg_or_imm, reg_rs1
```

which the assembler expands to

```
    andcc       reg_rs1, reg_or_imm, %g0
```

For example, to test if either flags 0x10 or 0x8 are set in register **%a_r**, we would write:

```
    btst        0x18, %a_r
    be          clear
    nop
set:
clear:
```

Notice that in this synthetic instruction the order of the operands is reversed to allow us to place the constant in the first operand and the flag register in the second.

3.5 Summary

Bistable devices were introduced together with the binary number system. Positional notation was defined as

$$N = S(d_{n-1}R^{n-1} + d_{n-2}R^{n-2} + \cdots + d_2R^2 + d_1R^1 + d_0)$$

where

R is the number system base, 10 for decimal numbers
N is the the number in base R
S is the sign, $+$ or $-$
n is the number of digits

Octal and hexadecimal number systems were then introduced to represent and to manipulate binary numbers. Conversion between numbers in different bases was presented using pencil-and-paper methods. The ASCII encoding of characters was given, allowing characters to be stored in memory and compared as numbers. The logic instructions of the SPARC architecture were introduced together with versions that set their condition codes. The use of instructions in conjunction with register %g0 extended the instruction set without increasing the number of instructions to be decoded or increasing the time to execute these instructions. Finally, flags were described together with the SPARC instructions to set, clear, and toggle them.

3.6   Exercises

3–1 Write a program in assembly language to assemble the ASCII characters for the number 1365 into a register, the ASCII code for 1 in the most significant eight bits, the code for 3 in the next eight bits, and so on. Then write a program that selects each digit by using logical instructions and shifts to convert each digit to binary. Accumulate the number in binary by multiplying the number accumulated so far by 10, by shifting and adding, and adding in subsequent digits.

3–2 Write a program in assembly language to generate each of the 16 possible states shown in the table on page 108, using one or two machine instructions, each with operands 0011 and 0101. For example, the second line might be generated by

```
        and     %o1, %o2, %o0
```

where %o1 would contain 3, %o2, 5, and the result, 1, would go into register %o0.

3–3 Write a program to extract a field from register %l0. The position of the least significant bit is to be specified in register %l2 and the number of bits in the field in register %l3. The result of executing your program is to extract the field specified from register %l0, storing the field in %l1.

3–4 How many states can a 10-bit binary number represent?

3–5 Convert 6709_{10} to hexadecimal. Show all your work.

3–6 Evaluate $01651_8 - 00735_8$ using either two's complement or eight's complement arithmetic. Show all your work.

3–7 In addition to binary devices, tristate digital devices are also possible, a circuit may either be on positively, off, or on negatively. Such devices would naturally employ a base three number system.

Solve the following problem using base three numbers and three's complement arithmetic:

$$372 - 281$$

Perform the arithmetic in base three and then convert the result back into decimal. Check you result in decimal. Show all work.

3–8 What range of decimal numbers may be represented in three's complement arithmetic using two base three digits? List the base three numbers and their decimal equivalents.

Chapter 4

BINARY ARITHMETIC

4.1   Introduction

Bistable devices may be used to represent numbers in base two. It is possible to convert between base two numbers and decimal and it is possible to perform logic with such a representation. We will now consider arithmetic: addition, subtraction, multiplication, and division. The use of two's complement arithmetic allows us to reduce subtraction to addition. Multiplication is also reduced to addition, and division is reduced to addition and subtraction. Base two arithmetic is much simpler than decimal arithmetic. See [20] for an extensive discussion of computer number systems and arithmetic.

4.2   Binary Numbers and Addition

When two decimal digits are added, a sum and carry are produced. For example, if we add 7 to 5, we obtain a sum of 2 and a carry of 1. If we add 3 to 4, the sum is 7 and the carry 0. The procedure for adding multidigit numbers is to add the digits in pairs, starting from the right, producing both a sum and a carry for each digit. Then as we shift to the left, the carry is added to the next more significant pair of digits to produce a sum and a carry. For example, to add 377 to 419, we first add the 9 to the 7, producing a sum of 6 and a carry of 1:

$$
\begin{array}{rrr}
3 & 7 & 7 \\
4 & 1 & 9 \quad + \\
\hline
\end{array}
$$

Sum		6
Carry		1

The carry of 1, left-shifted, is then added to the 1 and 7, producing a sum of 9 and a carry of 0.

$$\begin{array}{ccc} 3 & 7 & 7 \\ 4 & 1 & 9 \quad + \\ \hline & 9 & 6 \\ & 0 & \end{array}$$

	3	7	7
	4	1	9 +
Sum		9	6
Carry		0	

The carry, left-shifted, is added to the 3 and 4 to produce a final sum of 7 with again a 0 carry and the process is complete.

	3	7	7
	4	1	9 +
Sum	7	9	6

If we were to add 1 to 99,999, then a carry of 1 would ripple left, turning all the 9's into 0's. This is called a *ripple carry*.

Turning our attention to binary numbers, the addition of a single bit is very simple, a sum and carry are produced, but in the binary case these may be only one or zero. There are four possible outcomes from the addition of two bits:

a	b	**Sum**
0	0	0
0	1	1
1	0	1
1	1	0

a	b	**Carry**
0	0	0
0	1	0
1	0	0
1	1	1

but comparison of the **xor** and **and** truth tables given earlier will reveal that the sum bit of the addition of two bits is the exclusive **or** and that the carry is simply the **and** of the two bits.

The process of addition may be represented in a C function as

```
add (int a, int b)  /* addition using logical operations */
{
  int s;                /*sum*/
  int c;                /*carry*/

  s = a ^ b;                /*sum is the xor*/
  while (c = (a & b) << 1) /*carry is the and of inputs*/
    {
      a = s;
      b = c;
      s = a ^ b;
    }
  return (s);
}
```

For example, adding 13 to 11 by the algorithm above, we have

$$
\begin{array}{rll}
\text{Add} & 001101 & = 13 \\
& 001011 & = 11 \\
\\
\text{sum} & 000110 & \\
\text{carry} & 001001 & \\
\\
\text{sum} & 000110 & \\
\text{carry} \texttt{<<} 1 & 01001 & \\
\\
\text{sum} & 010100 & \\
\text{carry} & 000010 & \\
\\
\text{sum} & 010100 & \\
\text{carry} \texttt{<<} 1 & 00010 & \\
\\
\text{sum} & 010000 & \\
\text{carry} & 000100 & \\
\\
\text{sum} & 010000 & \\
\text{carry} \texttt{<<} 1 & 00100 & \\
\\
\text{sum} & 011000 & \\
\text{carry} & 000000 & \\
\end{array}
$$

and the sum is $11000_2 = 24_{10}$.

4.3 Half and Full Adders

The generation of the sum and carry bits may be performed by very simple electronic circuits. These circuits are available in chip form to perform the logical functions described above and are called *gates*. The generation of the sum and carry requires an **and** gate and an **xor** gate. These may be obtained together in a circuit called a *half adder* (see Figure 4.1). Two half adders may then be combined together with an **or** gate to add two inputs, A and B, with a carry in, to produce a sum and a carry out. Such a circuit is called a *full adder* (see Figure 4.2). See [15] for a full discussion of digital logic.

4.4 Modulus Arithmetic

Modulus arithmetic considers only numbers in the range $0 <= n < M$, where M is the modulus. A modulus operator % in C will force a number to be in the appropriate range by performing an integer division by M and keeping the remainder. A car odometer is another, possibly more familiar, example of modulus

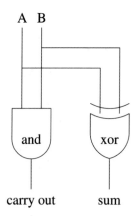

Figure 4.1: Half Adder

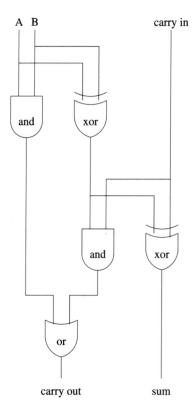

Figure 4.2: Full Adder

arithmetic. The odometer counts up until it reaches 99999, whereupon it returns to 0. Computers normally perform modulus arithmetic, as they have registers of fixed size, like the car odometer. If we have an n-bit register and count up from 0, then when the number reaches $2^n - 1$ (represented by all ones), the next increment returns the register to all zeros. A carry out of the MSB (most significant bit) has been lost.

Consider a computer with four-bit registers: The largest number will be $2^n - 1 = 2^4 - 1 = 15 = 1111_2$. Consider the addition of $3 + 2$:

$$
\begin{array}{rcl}
3 = & 0011 & \\
2 = & 0010 & + \\
\hline
5 = & 0101 &
\end{array}
$$

Further addition of 6 results in 11:

$$
\begin{array}{rcl}
5 = & 0101 & \\
6 = & 0110 & + \\
\hline
11 = & 1011 &
\end{array}
$$

If we add 7, we obtain $(11 + 7) \% 16 = 2$:

$$
\begin{array}{rcl}
11 = & 1011 & \\
7 = & 0111 & + \\
\hline
2 = & 0010 &
\end{array}
$$

The carry of 1 out of the MSB is lost.

4.5 Subtraction

Whereas addition is fairly simple, subtraction requires borrowing if the digit you are subtracting exceeds the digit from which it is to be subtracted. However, a neat hack can avoid these borrowing problems. Consider the following expression with arithmetic performed modulus r^n, where r is the base and n the number of digits:

$$
a - b = a + (r^n - 1 - b) + 1
$$

In the expression above the addition of r^n does not affect the result of the calculation, as the arithmetic is performed modulus r^n. The subtraction of b from $r^n - 1$ is particularly simple and *involves no borrowing*.

Consider the following example in decimal arithmetic with $r = 10$ and two-digit registers and thus $n = 2$:

$$
\begin{array}{rcl}
23 - 07 & = & 23 + (10^2 - 1 - 07) + 1 \\
& = & 23 + (99 - 07) + 1 \\
& = & 23 + 92 + 1 \\
& = & 23 + 93 \\
& = & 16
\end{array}
$$

What about $07 - 23$?

$$
\begin{aligned}
07 - 23 &= 07 + (99 - 23) + 1 \\
&= 07 + 76 + 1 \\
&= 07 + 77 = 84
\end{aligned}
$$

What does 84 represent? Let us look at $00 - 16$.

$$
\begin{aligned}
00 - 16 &= 00 + (99 - 16) + 1 \\
&= 00 + (83) + 1 \\
&= 84
\end{aligned}
$$

84 is negative 16. What then is -1?

$$
\begin{aligned}
00 - 01 &= 00 + (99 - 01) + 1 \\
&= 00 + 98 + 1 \\
&= 99
\end{aligned}
$$

Let us, using some intuition, list numbers around zero:

3	03
2	02
1	01
0	00
-1	99
-2	98
-3	97

Let us go further and look at the midrange, -49:

$$
\begin{aligned}
00 - 49 &= 00 + (99 - 49) + 1 \\
&= 00 + 50 + 1 \\
&= 51
\end{aligned}
$$

What is -50?

$$
\begin{aligned}
-50 &= 00 + (99 - 50) + 1 \\
&= 00 + 49 + 1 \\
&= 50
\end{aligned}
$$

Fifty is its own complement. Let us summarize our findings:

49	49	largest positive number
48	48	
... 3	3	
2	2	
1	1	
0	0	
-1	99	negative
-2	98	
... -48	52	
-49	51	
-50	50	largest negative number

This is called *complement arithmetic* and the representations of the negative numbers have names:

$$r^n - 1 - b \qquad \text{diminished radix complement} \qquad \text{nine's complement}$$
$$r^n - 1 - b + 1 \qquad \text{radix complement} \qquad \text{ten's complement}$$

Radix complement arithmetic has zero, positive, and negative numbers. In radix complement arithmetic the largest negative digit is its own complement and thus has no positive equivalent. Furthermore, for decimal numbers, if the most significant digit (MSD) ≥ 5, the number is negative. Subtraction may then be performed by the addition of the negative of the number that is to be subtracted.

Considering now binary numbers, we will see that complementing is even simpler than for decimal numbers. Let us consider four-bit arithmetic with $n = 4$. We will first subtract 2 from 4:

$$4 - 2 \;=\; 4 + (-2)$$

$$\begin{aligned} 4 &= 0100 \\ 2 &= 0010 \end{aligned}$$

$$\begin{aligned} 2^4 &= 10000 \\ 2^4 - 1 &= 1111 \\ 2^4 - 1 - 2 &= 1101 \\ 2^4 - 1 - 2 + 1 &= 1110 \end{aligned}$$

$$\begin{array}{r} 0100 \\ 1110 \quad + \\ \hline 0010 \quad = 2 \end{array}$$

$2^4 - 1 - 2 = 1101$ is called the *one's complement*, as the subtraction of a binary number from all ones is the logical complement. All ones are replaced by zeros and all zeros are replaced by ones. $2^4 - 1 - 2 + 1 = 1110$ is called the *two's complement*, and it is no more than the one's complement plus one.

Consider $2 - 4$:

$$\begin{aligned} 2 &= 0010 \\ 4 &= 0100 \\ \text{one's complement 1's} &= 1011 \\ \text{two's complement 2's} &= 1100 \end{aligned}$$

$$\begin{array}{r} 0010 \\ 1100 \quad + \\ \hline 1110 \end{array}$$

1110 must be a negative number, so let us complement it:

$$\begin{array}{ll} & 1110 \\ \text{1's} & 0001 \\ \text{2's} & 0010 \quad -2 \end{array}$$

Let us use some intuition and list all the four-bit two's complement numbers:

$$
\begin{array}{lll}
0111 & 7 & \\
0110 & 6 & \\
0101 & 5 & \\
0100 & 4 & \\
0011 & 3 & \\
0010 & 2 & \\
0001 & 1 & \\
0000 & 0 & \\
1111 & -1 & 0000 + 1 = 0001 \\
1110 & -2 & \\
1101 & -3 & \\
1100 & -4 & \\
1011 & -5 & \\
1010 & -6 & \\
1001 & -7 & \\
1000 & -8 & \text{its own complement } 1000 \\
\end{array}
$$

If the most significant bit, the sign bit, is a one, we know that the number is negative.

A signed number has a range of $[-2^{n-1}, 2^{n-1} - 1]$ and an unsigned number has a range of $[0, 2^n - 1]$. The two's complement system is an interpretation of numbers in registers; the hardware always performs binary addition. If we wish to subtract, we first form the two's complement of the number and then add; there is then no need for a hardware subtractor as well as a hardware adder. We will still, however, frequently consider numbers to be unsigned, considering the sign bit only as the most significant bit of the number; pointers are always unsigned numbers, as they refer to memory addresses.

4.6   Two's Complement Number Branching Conditions

In Chapter 2 we introduced signed arithmetic branches; these are the appropriate branches when we are interpreting the numbers in the machine as two's complement. Branching conditions are based on the setting of the N (negative), Z (zero), and V (overflow) bits. The Z bit is set when all the bits of the result are zero. The N bit is set when the most significant bit is 1. The overflow V bit is set when the register is not long enough to hold the true representation of the number. On subtraction, the V bit is set when the signs of the minuend and the subtrahend are different and the sign of the difference is the same as the subtrahend (difference = minuend − subtrahend).

When we compare two two's complement numbers, we subtract one from the other; overflow can frequently occur when this happens. Consider subtracting any positive number from the largest negative number.

The conditions for signed branches are:

Assembler Mnemonic	Signed Arithmetic Branches	Condition Codes
bl	Branch on less	(N xor V) = 1
ble	Branch on less or equal	Z or (N xor V) = 1
be	Branch on equal	Z = 1
bne	Branch on not equal	Z = 0
bge	Branch on greater or equal	(N xor V) = 0
bg	Branch on greater	Z or (N xor V) = 0

When overflow occurs, the sign is complemented. On integer addition the overflow bit is set when the sign of the addends is the same but the sign of the result is different.

4.6.1 Shifting

Three shift instructions are provided in the SPARC architecture to compute the contents of a register shifted left or right by a number of shifts. There are two shifts, arithmetic and logical. In the case of an arithmetic shift, the sign bit is copied into the most significant bit position on right shifts. In the case of a logical right shift, zeros are copied into the most significant bit position. Left shifts are identical in both cases with zeros shifted in from the right (see Figure 4.3).

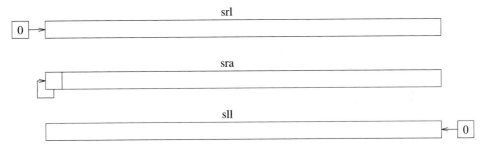

Figure 4.3: Shift Instructions

The shift count is the low five bits of reg_{rs2} or the low five bits of the immediate. These five bits are interpreted as a positive number, and thus the largest shift possible is $2^5 - 1$, or 31.

The shift instructions are as follows:

sll	reg_{rs1}, reg_or_imm, reg_{rd}	shift left logical
sra	reg_{rs1}, reg_or_imm, reg_{rd}	shift right arithmetic
srl	reg_{rs1}, reg_or_imm, reg_{rd}	shift right logical

Shifting a number left corresponds to multiplication by 2; shifting right arithmetic corresponds to division by 2.

4.7   Unsigned Arithmetic

In addition to signed arithmetic there is a need to perform unsigned arithmetic. In unsigned arithmetic, number representations are always considered positive and numbers have a range of $[0, 2^n - 1]$, twice that of signed numbers. In C, the declaration **unsigned** informs the compiler that the variable is to be interpreted as an unsigned number. Hardware operations on signed and unsigned numbers are identical.

There is no problem with addition, with a carry out of the most significant bit (C = 1), now indicating overflow. A carry out of the most significant bit occurs when the most significant bit of both operands is set but the most significant bit of the result is a zero, or when the most significant bit of either operand is set but the most significant bit of the result is zero.

It is also still possible to subtract unsigned numbers by imagining that there is an extra bit in the register to the left of the most significant bit. Then, by first forming the two's complement of the subtrahend and adding, we would expect a carry out of the most significant bit to be added to the imaginary one of the subtrahend to indicate a positive result; the imaginary bit of the minuend would then be a zero. In the case of subtraction, the C bit is set **if there is no carry out of the most significant bit**. The test for unsigned overflow is then simply a test of the C bit.

Consider a four-bit register, which has an unsigned range of $0 <= n < 16$, subtracting 3 from 12:

$$
\begin{aligned}
12 - 03 &= 1100 - 0011 \\
&= 1100 + (10000 - 1) - 0011 + 1 \\
&= 1100 + 1111 - 0011 + 1 \\
&= 1100 + 1101 \\
9 &= 1001
\end{aligned}
$$

As expected the carry occurred indicating a positive result.

4.8   Unsigned Number Branching Conditions

When performing unsigned arithmetic, the overflow bit, V, has no meaning, as it is related to tests on the signed numbers. The N bit has no significance when dealing with unsigned numbers. All unsigned branching tests are made, based on the state of the C and Z bits alone. The C bit is set when a carry occurs out of the most significant bit on addition and when it does not occur on subtraction.

There is a set of unsigned branch instructions that makes the following tests:

Assembler Mnemonic	Unsigned Arithmetic Branches	Condition Codes
blu	Branch on less	$C = 1$
bleu	Branch on less or equal	$C = 1$ or $Z = 1$
be	Branch on equal	$Z = 1$
bne	Branch on not equal	$Z = 0$
bgeu	Branch on greater or equal	$C = 0$
bgu	Branch on greater	$C = 0$ and $Z = 0$

4.9 Condition Code Tests

There is also a set of branches that tests the individual condition codes:

Assembler Mnemonic	Condition Code Branches		Synonym
bneg	Branch on negative	$N = 1$	
bpos	Branch on positive	$N = 0$	
bz	Branch on equal to zero	$Z = 1$	be
bnz	Branch on not equal to zero	$Z = 0$	bne
bvs	Branch on overflow set	$V = 1$	
bvc	Branch on overflow clear	$V = 0$	
bcs	Branch C set	$C = 1$	blu
bcc	Branch C clear	$C = 0$	bgeu

4.10 Multiplication

If we had to multiply 23×32 using pencil and paper, we might proceed as follows:

```
    23
    32 x
    ----
    46
  69
    ----
  736
```

In the above, we multiply the multiplicand by each digit of the multiplier, eventually adding these partial products to form the product. We might organize the calculation above somewhat. We make use of two two-digit registers to eventually hold the product. We initialize the first of these to zero and the second to the multiplier. We will examine the rightmost digit of the multiplier and then multiply the multiplicand by the digit and add it to the left-hand register. Having made use of the rightmost digit of the multiplier, we will shift the two registers right one digit before repeating the process until all digits of the multiplier have been examined. The two registers will thus hold both the partial product and the partial multiplier until after the last shift they hold the complete product.

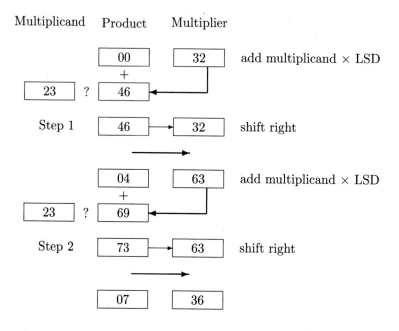

What would happen if we tried to multiply 23×-32? Let us try using 10's complement arithmetic. First we need to find the 10's complement of -32:

```
   99
   32 -
   --
   67
    1 +
   68
```

Let us now proceed to use our algorithm multiplying 23 by 68:

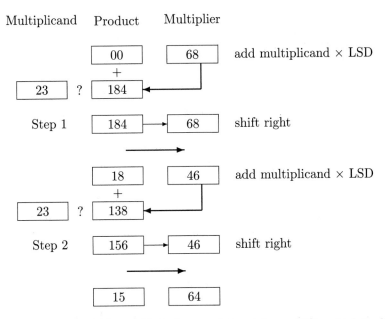

The result should be -736 or, in complement form, 9264, which it clearly is not. What went wrong? A careful examination of the algorithm will reveal that we have evaluated

$$23 \times (10^2 - 32)$$
$$23 \times 10^2 - 23 \times 32$$

The correct result is -23×32; our result is too large by 23×10^2. Do not forget that we are computing a result of twice the number of digits as the multiplier and multiplicand. When performing this computation we should be using twice as many digits when representing negative numbers. If we do not use twice as many digits when the multiplier is negative, we must subtract from the high-order part of the final result, the multiplicand, which in our case is 23×10^2:

```
23
76 9's complement
77 10's complement

1564
77    +

----
9264

0735 9's complement
0736 10's complement
```

This gives the correct result. There is no problem when the multiplicand is negative, as we are simply adding scaled versions of it to obtain the result. It is only when the multiplier is negative that we need to make the final subtraction to obtain the correct result.

Let us now turn our attention to binary arithmetic. Consider the multiplication of 3×5, or 0011×0101:

Multiplicand   Product   Multiplier

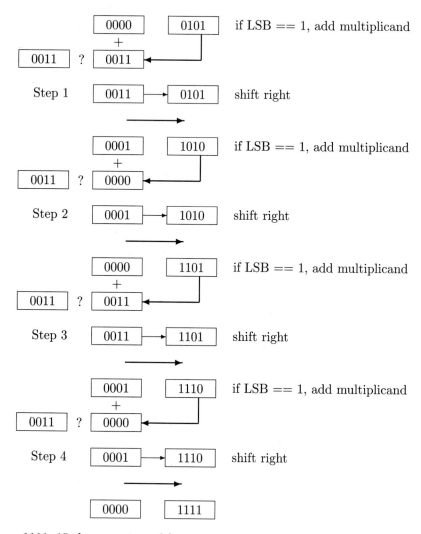

1111, 15 the correct result!

How about 3×-5? Or 0011×1011:

Multiplicand   Product   Multiplier

	0000	1011	if LSB == 1, add multiplicand
	+		
0011 ?	0011		

Step 1   0011 ⟶ 1011   shift right

⟶

	0001	1101	if LSB == 1, add multiplicand
	+		
0011 ?	0011		

Step 2   0100 ⟶ 1101   shift right

⟶

	0010	0110	if LSB == 1, add multiplicand
	+		
0011 ?	0000		

Step 3   0010 ⟶ 0110   shift right

⟶

	0001	0011	if LSB == 1, add multiplicand
	+		
0011 ?	0011		

Step 4   0100 ⟶ 0011   shift right

⟶

0010   0001

+

1101   multiplier negative → subtract multiplicand

1111   0001

As the multiplier was negative, we had to subtract the multiplicand from the high-order part of the result. The multiplier was 3, or 0011_2, and its two's complement, 1101.

Finally, let us multiply -3×-5, or 1101×1011.

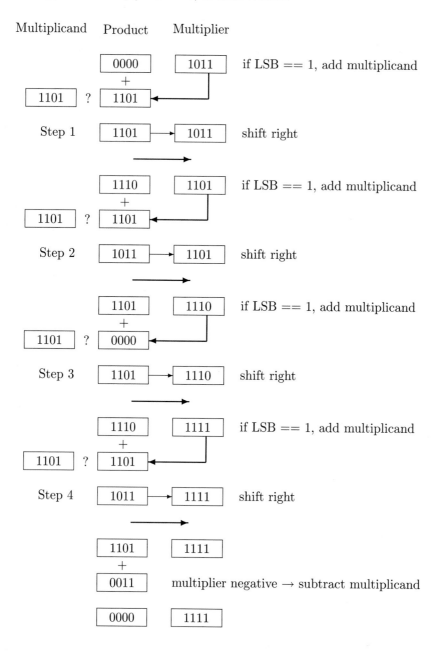

We obtain the correct result again, 15. Note the arithmetic shift right, shifting in one's when the number is negative.

4.10.1 SPARC `mulscc` Instruction

Although the SPARC architecture does not include a multiply instruction, it does have an instruction that performs one step of a multiply, the `mulscc` instruction. This instruction works in conjunction with a special machine register called the %Y register, which initially holds the multiplier and eventually holds the low-order part of the product (see Figure 4.4).

Multiplication using the `mulscc` instruction on the SPARC machine is as follows:

1. The multiplier is loaded into the %Y register and the high-order part of the product cleared to zero.

2. The multiplier is tested to set the N and V bits.

3. This is then followed by 32 `mulscc` instructions. The `mulscc` instruction shifts N ^ V into the first source register, shifting the contents of the register right one place, the bit shifted out of the right-hand end of the register is kept. The least significant bit of the Y register is tested, and if a one, the contents of the second source register or sign extended constant are added to the destination register. Finally, the kept bit, shifted out of the first source register, is shifted into the Y register, shifting the contents of the Y register right one place.

4. One additional mulscc instruction with the multiplicand zero forms a final shift to produce a two-word result with the high-order part of the product in the %rd register and the low-order part in %Y.

For example, to multiply 3×5 with the three in %o2 and five, the multiplier, in %o0, we would write

```
mov     3, %o2
mov     5, %o0

mov     %o0, %y

nop         !it takes time to get to the %y register
nop
nop
andcc   %g0, %g0, %o1   !zero the partial product
                        ! and clear N and V
mulscc  %o1, %o2, %o1   !32 mulscc instructions
mulscc  %o1, %o2, %o1
mulscc  %o1, %o2, %o1
mulscc  %o1, %o2, %o1
mulscc  %o1, %o2, %o1
mulscc  %o1, %o2, %o1
mulscc  %o1, %o2, %o1
```

```
mulscc  %o1, %o2, %o1
mulscc  %o1, %o2, %o1
mulscc  %o1, %o2, %o1
mulscc  %o1, %o2, %o1
mulscc  %o1, %o2, %o1
mulscc  %o1, %o2, %o1
mulscc  %o1, %o2, %o1
mulscc  %o1, %o2, %o1
mulscc  %o1, %o2, %o1
mulscc  %o1, %o2, %o1
mulscc  %o1, %o2, %o1
mulscc  %o1, %o2, %o1
mulscc  %o1, %o2, %o1
mulscc  %o1, %o2, %o1
mulscc  %o1, %o2, %o1
mulscc  %o1, %o2, %o1
mulscc  %o1, %o2, %o1
mulscc  %o1, %o2, %o1
mulscc  %o1, %o2, %o1
mulscc  %o1, %o2, %o1
mulscc  %o1, %o2, %o1
mulscc  %o1, %o2, %o1
mulscc  %o1, %o2, %o1
mulscc  %o1, %o2, %o1
mulscc  %o1, %o2, %o1
mulscc  %o1, %g0, %o1    !final shift
mov     %y, %o0          !high-order part back from %y
```

System routines are provided for multiplication, .mul for signed multiplication, and .umul for unsigned multiplication. The multiplicand is passed in %o0 and the multiplier in %o1. The low-order part of the result is returned in %o0 and the high-order part in %o1. In C, when two integers are multiplied together, only the low 32 bits of the product are kept. It is thus important to ensure that overflow does not occur when multiplying integers in C. Although .umul and .mul produce the same low 32 bits of the product, .umul results in fewer instructions. It is frequently used in C to multiply both signed and unsigned integers.

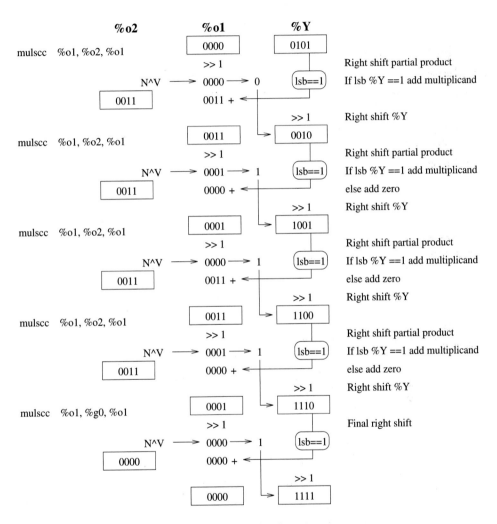

Figure 4.4: SPARC Multiplication

4.11   Division

Finally, we must consider division. For example, the division of 737 by 32:

```
        23 + 1
      ------
32  )  737
       64-
       --
        97
        96-
        --
         1
```

results in a quotient of 23 with a remainder of 1.

Binary division is much easier than decimal division. In the case of binary division, one does not have to try to estimate how many times the divisor will subtract from the dividend successfully, leaving a positive remainder which is less that the divisor. The divisor will either subtract, leaving a positive remainder, or it will not.

Consider the case of dividing 15 by 3, $00001111 \div 0011$. We may formalize the process by making use of three registers as we did in the case of multiplication. In this case the dividend occupies two registers, as did the product after multiplication. At the end of the division the registers will contain the remainder and the quotient. At each step in the division the double-length register containing the dividend is shifted left one place; the bits of the quotient may be assembled in the dividend register, from the right-hand side, bit by bit until at the end of the division the quotient occupies the register which initially contained the low part of the dividend. The remainder is left in the register which initially contained the high part of the dividend. Notice how it is only necessary to be able to add or subtract into the register containing the high part of the dividend. In the case of multiplication it was also only necessary to be able to add into the same register. Hardware multiplier/dividers use the same three hardware registers for both operations.

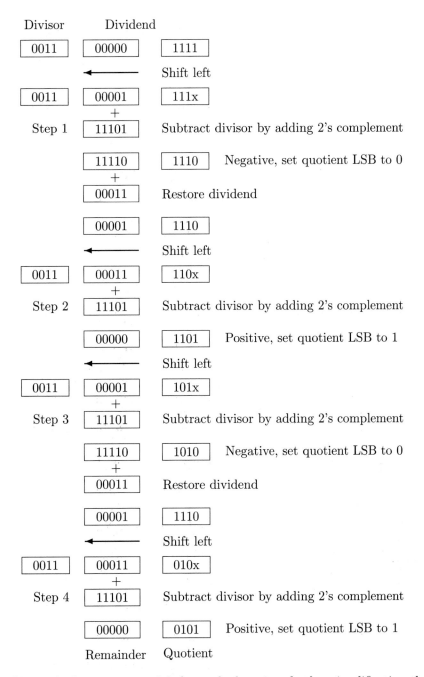

Although this is very straightforward, there is a further simplification that we should introduce: When we subtract the divisor from the dividend and the result is negative, we must add the divisor back to the dividend. We then subtract the divisor from the shifted dividend. For example, if b is the divisor and a the dividend this operation as follows:

$$((a - b) + b) - b2^{-1}$$

Regrouping terms, we obtain:

$$(a - b) + (2b - b)2^{-1}$$
$$(a - b) + b2^{-1}$$

Having subtracted and produced a negative result, we only need shift the registers and *add* in place of subtracting. This is known as *non-restoring* division [19]:

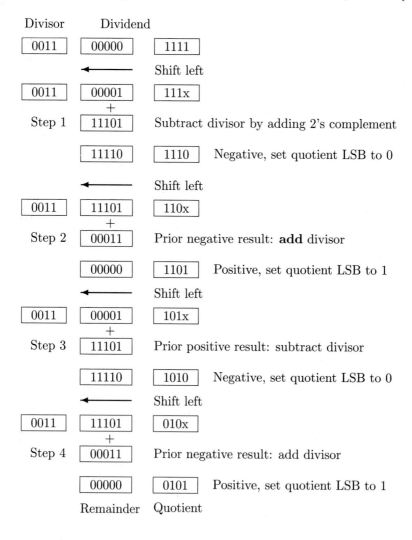

An assembly language program to perform the above division is given below. The program first creates a dividend by multiplying two numbers together; it then divides the dividend by one of the factors used to produce the dividend. The dividend is 64 bits long and is in registers %o1 and %o0. The divisor is placed into register %o2. The quotient then appears in %o0 with the remainder in %o1.

In the program, we will need to shift the contents of two registers. This is accomplished by the following code:

```
        addcc   %lo_r, %lo_r, %lo_r
        bcc     1f
        add     %hi_r, %hi_r, %hi_r
        bset    1, %hi_r
1:
```

Note the use of a numeric label, "1." The assembler allows single-digit labels to appear many times in a single source file. A branch to such a label must be distinguished by appending the single letter "b" or "f" to the digit to indicate whether it is the first occurrence of the label in the backward direction in the file or the first occurrence of the label in the forward direction in the file. The use of such numeric labels is recommended for labels that have no intrinsic significance, such as labels needed to create control structures. This relieves the programmer of the need to create names that have no significance. Numeric labels also solve a problem when writing macros that require labels, allowing the same label to appear in each incantation of the macro without leading to multiply-defined symbol errors:

```
define(lo_r, o0)              !'low part of dividend'
define(hi_r, o1)              !'high part of dividend'

define(divisor_r,o2)
define(count_r, o3)           !'number of times to iterate'

define(n_bits, 32)            !'number of bits in register'
define(quotient,0x101)        !'trial quotient'
define(dividend,0xff)         !'trial dividend'
define(remainder,0x2)         !'trial remainder'

    .global main
main:
    save    %sp, -96, %sp

    mov     quotient, %o0     !'form num as trial dividend'
    call    .umul
    mov     dividend, %o1
    add     %o0, remainder, %o0 !'add in a remainder'
```

```
        mov     dividend, %o2       !'use same number as divisor'

        mov     n_bits, %count_r    !'initialize count to n_bits'


        ba      pos                 !'start off with a shift'
        addcc   %lo_r, %lo_r, %lo_r

test:
    bge     pos
    addcc   %lo_r, %lo_r, %lo_r

neg:                                !'result negative, shift'
    bcc     1f
    add     %hi_r, %hi_r, %hi_r
    bset    1, %hi_r
1:
    ba      fin
    addcc   %hi_r, %divisor_r, %hi_r!'finished?'

pos:                                !'positive -> shift & sub'
    bcc     1f
    add     %hi_r, %hi_r, %hi_r
    bset    1, %hi_r
1:
    subcc   %hi_r, %divisor_r, %hi_r

fin:    bl      szero
    subcc   %count_r, 1, %count_r
    or      %lo_r, 1, %lo_r     !'set bit into quotient'
szero:
    bg      test
    tst     %hi_r

done:
    bge     ok                      !'restore remainder?'
    mov     1, %g1
    add     %hi_r, %divisor_r, %hi_r
ok:
    ta      0
```

Integer division occurs much less frequently in code than does multiplication, and the SPARC architecture does not provide an instruction equivalent to `mulscc` for division. Four routines are, however, provided: two for signed arithmetic `.div`, which returns the quotient, and `.rem`, which returns the remainder; two routines for unsigned arithmetic, `.udiv` and `.urem`. In all cases the dividend is in register `%o0` and the divisor in `%o1`. The result is returned in `%o0`.

4.12 Extended Precision Arithmetic

Occasionally, there is a need to perform arithmetic to greater than 32 bits of precision. Consider the case where it is desired to perform integer arithmetic with 96 bits of precision. We may store such a 96-bit number in three sequential registers with the most significant bits in the lowest of the three registers. If such a number were stored in registers `%l0`, `%l1`, and `%l2`, then the sign bit would be bit 31 of `%l0` and the least significant bit of the 96 bit number would be bit 0 of `%l2`.

4.12.1 Addition of Extended Precision Numbers

There is no machine instruction to add three register numbers; instead, we have to proceed by adding the two low registers of both numbers, bits 0–31, then adding the two registers containing bits 32–63, along with any carry that was generated when the two low registers were added. Finally, we add the two high registers containing bits 64–95 along with any carry generated when the mid registers were added. There is a machine instruction especially for this purpose that adds the contents of two registers together plus one if the C, carry, bit is set. A carry from the previous add will set the carry bit:

$$\text{addx} \quad reg_{rs1}, \ reg\_or\_imm, \ reg_{rd}$$
$$\text{addxcc} \quad reg_{rs1}, \ reg\_or\_imm, \ reg_{rd}$$

In both cases the operation result is

$$reg_{rd} = reg_{rs1} + reg\_or\_imm + \text{C}$$

with the `addxcc` instruction also setting the condition codes. Thus, if the second number were in registers `%l3`–`%l5`, with the result to go into `%o0`–`%o2`, the code for the extended precision addition would be

```
addcc   %l2, %l5, %o2   !add bits 0-31
addxcc  %l1, %l4, %o1   !add bits 32-63 + C
addx    %l0, %l3, %o0   !add bits 64-95 + C
```

4.12.2 Subtraction of Extended Precision Numbers

On subtraction we need to form the two's complement of one of the multiregister numbers. We could do this by first forming the one's complement of each register, and then add one to the low register (propagating any carry). We would then add the numbers as before:

```
not     %l5, %l5        !form complement in place
not     %l4, %l4
not     %l3, %l3
inccc   %l5             !add one to form two's comp.
addxcc  %l4, %g0, %l4   !propagate carry
addx    %l3, %g0, %l3


addcc   %l2, %l5, %o2   !add bits 0-31
addxcc  %l1, %l4, %o1   !add bits 32-63 + C
addx    %l0, %l3, %o0   !add bits 64-95 + C
```

We can reduce this to three instructions, like the multiple-precision add, by making use of the subx and subxcc instructions. These instructions subtract their second operand from their first and, in addition, subtract one more if the C bit is set:

```
subx      regrs1, reg_or_imm, regrd
subxcc    regrs1, reg_or_imm, regrd
```

In both cases the operation result is

$$reg_{rd} = reg_{rs1} - reg\_or\_imm - C$$

with the subxcc instruction also setting the condition codes.

By proceeding to use the subcc instruction directly to subtract the two low registers:

```
subcc   %l2, %l5, %o2
```

we achieve the same effect as three of the instructions above:

```
not     %l5, %l5        !form complement in place
inccc   %l5             !add one to form two's comp.
addcc   %l2, %l5, %o2   !add bits 0-31
```

If we use the subcc instruction to subtract the two midregisters:

```
subcc   %l1, %l4, %o1
```

we will perform

```
not     %l4, %l4
inc     %l4, %l4
addxcc  %l1, %l4, %o1
```

which results in a number too large by one. However, if a carry had been generated by the previous subtraction, this would be the correct result after carry propagation. If a carry were not generated by the previous subtraction, we need to subtract one. This is exactly what the subx instruction does, so that we can rewrite the entire three-word subtraction code in a form similar to the addition code:

```
subcc   %l2, %l5, %o2   !subtract bits 0-31
subxcc  %l1, %l4, %o1   !subtract bits 32-63 + C
subx    %l0, %l3, %o0   !subtract bits 64-95 + C
```

4.12.3 Multiplication of Extended Precision Numbers

By keeping track of the binary scaling of each word and remembering that each 32-bit multiplication results in a two-word, 64-bit result, we can also perform multiple-precision multiplication. Consider the case of the multiplication of two 64-bit unsigned numbers. The first number is represented by A_{32} B and the second by C_{32} D, where A, B, C, and D are the four registers containing the two numbers and the subscripts refer to the binary scaling. The product, E_{96}, F_{96}, G_{96}, H_{96}, may be written as

$$
\begin{array}{rrrrc}
 & & A_{32} & B & \\
 & & C_{32} & D & \times \\
\hline
 & & BD_{32} & BD & \\
 & BC_{64} & BC_{32} & & \\
 & AD_{64} & AD_{32} & & \\
 AC_{96} & AC_{64} & & & + \\
\hline
 E_{96} & F_{64} & G_{32} & H & \\
\end{array}
$$

This may be translated into the following code, making use of `.umul` to perform 32-bit *unsigned* multiplication. The multiply routine produces 64 bits of result, with the high-order part in `%o1` and the low-order part in `%o0`.

```
            .global main
main:

            define(A, i0)           !multiplicand
            define(B, i1)
            define(C, i2)           !multiplier
            define(D, i3)

            define(E, l0)           !product
            define(F, l1)
            define(G, l2)
            define(H, l3)

            mov     0x1, %A         !initialize A and B
            mov     0xffffffff, %B

            mov     0x1, %C
            mov     0xffffffff, %D  !initialize C and D

            mov     %B, %o0         !BD
            call    .umul
            mov     %D, %o1

            mov     %o0, %H         !H = BD
```

```
        mov     %o1, %G              !G = DB32

        mov     %B, %o0              !BC
        call    .umul
        mov     %C, %o1

        addcc   %o0, %G,   %G        !G = G + BC32
        addx    %o1, %g0,  %F        !F = BC64, no carry can occur here

        mov     %D, %o0              !AD
        call    .umul
        mov     %A, %o1

        addcc   %o0, %G,   %G        !G = G + AD32
        addxcc  %o1, %F,   %F        !F = AD64, a carry may occur here
        addx    %g0, %g0,  %E

        mov     %C, %o0              !AC
        call    .umul
        mov     %A, %o1

        addcc   %o0, %F,   %F        !F = F + AC64
        addx    %o1, %E,   %E        !E = AC96

        mov     1, %g1
        ta      0
```

Division can also be performed, in a non-restoring manner, by making use of multiple-precision addition and subtraction.

4.13   Summary

Binary arithmetic was shown to be very simple to implement using elementary logic operations, and and xor in the form of half and full adders. Modulus arithmetic was introduced to handle negative numbers. The diminished radix complement (one's complement for binary numbers) and radix complement (two's complement for binary numbers) were defined. Modulus arithmetic makes use of the top half of the representable states of an n-bit binary number to represent the negative numbers. A two's complement negative number has the most significant bit set. Subtraction may be handled in the same manner as addition, using two's complement arithmetic simplifying hardware requirements for arithmetic logic units.

Two's complement branches were described, used in conjunction with the V, N, and Z condition codes. Handling unsigned numbers was presented in terms of an imaginary high-order bit. Unsigned branches, which tested the C and Z bits, were presented. A fairly extensive discussion of multiplication was given, as the SPARC architecture does not include a multiply instruction. This section concluded with the SPARC `mulscc` instruction to provide for multiplication. The section on multiplication was followed by a section on division, introducing non-restoring division and concluding with an assembly language division routine. The chapter concluded with a section on extended precision arithmetic.

4.14   Exercises

4–1 Write addition and subtraction algorithms for two's complement numbers using the machine logical instructions:

```
and     reg_rs1, reg_or_imm, reg_rd
andn    reg_rs1, reg_or_imm, reg_rd
xor     reg_rs1, reg_or_imm, reg_rd
or      reg_rs1, reg_or_imm, reg_rd
xnor    reg_rs1, reg_or_imm, reg_rd
orn     reg_rs1, reg_or_imm, reg_rd
```

You may not use the **add** or **sub** instructions, or their cc versions. The following addition algorithm is suggested:

```
int add (int a, int b)          !addition using logical operations
  {
     int s;                      !sum
     int c;                      !carry

     c = b                       !initialize carry
     s = a ^ c;                  !sum is the xor
     while (c = (a & c) << 1)    !carry is the and of inputs
       s = (a = s) ^ c;
     return (s);
  }
```

and for subtraction:

```
int sub (int a, int b)          !subtraction using logical operations
  {
     int d;                      !difference
     int c;                      !carry

     c = ~b                      !initialize carry to one's comp of b
     d = a ^ c;                  !diff is the xor + 1
     c = (a & c) << 1 | 1;       !Note the extra one to make two's comp
```

```
   do
      d = (a = d) ^ c;
   while (c = (a & c) << 1)   !carry is the and of inputs
   return (d);
}
```

Your program should form the sum of

07707 and 00101

and the difference of

00710 and 01010

For both the addition and the subtraction you are to print out the partial sum and carry each iteration through the loop. You are also to print out the result of the addition and subtraction. Note that the input given above is in octal.

4–2 Write an addition algorithm, which also sets the condition codes, for two's complement numbers using the machine logical instructions, such as

```
   and       reg_rs1, reg_or_imm, reg_rd
   andn      reg_rs1, reg_or_imm, reg_rd
   xor       reg_rs1, reg_or_imm, reg_rd
   or        reg_rs1, reg_or_imm, reg_rd
   xnor      reg_rs1, reg_or_imm, reg_rd
   orn       reg_rs1, reg_or_imm, reg_rd
```

You may not use the **add** or **sub** instructions, or their cc versions. Your code is also to set the four condition code bits, N, V, Z, and C as outlined in the definition of addcc instruction given on page 410. The N bit is to be set if the result is negative; the V bit is to be set, indicating overflow, if the resulting number is too large to store in 32 bits; the Z bit is to be set if the result is zero; the C bit is to be set if a carry occurred on addition and if a carry did not occur on subtraction. You may use the use the logic given on page 410 to set the bits or generate the bits in the course of your algorithm. The condition codes are to be stored in the low-order four bits of a register:

```
define(Z, 8)  !'Z = 010'
define(N, 4)  !'N = 004'
define(V, 2)  !'V = 002'
define(C, 1)  !'C = 001'
```

A simplification in the boolean expression for V on page 410 is

```
V = (r[rs1]<31> & op2<31>) & ~r[rd]<31>) |
    (~(r[rs1]<31> | op2<31>)) & r[rd]<31>)
```

To compute such an expression you can perform logical operations between the registers and then test the sign bit, bit 31. The following two branches will directly test if bit 31 is set of clear:

```
bpos branch if bit 31 clear
bneg branch if bit 31 set.
```

You can run your program with different numbers in gdb by setting a breakpoint at `main` and then using the print command. For example, to set `%l0` to `0x7fffffff` and `%l1` to `-5` you could type

```
(gdb) p/x $l0 = 0x7fffffff
$1 = 0x7fffffff
(gdb) p/x $l1 = -5
$2 = 0xfffffffb
(gdb)
```

Run you program with four inputs, which demonstrate the setting of the Z, N, V, and C bits. Print out the condition codes and the sum for each pair of numbers.

4–3 Modify the algorithm on page 131 to handle signed integers as well.

4–4 Write an assembly language program to multiply two four-bit unsigned numbers together using no more than five `mulscc` instructions.

4–5 Write an assembly language program to perform the division of two unsigned integers employing the restoring division algorithm.

4–6 Write an assembly language program to perform signed 64-bit multiplication to produce 128 bits of result.

4–7 Write an assembly language program to perform unsigned 64-bit division with a 128 bit dividend.

4–8 Divide 17 by 5 using two's complement non-restoring division. Show all your work and comment the generation of each bit of the quotient.

4–9 Translate the final form of the following algorithm for multiplication into assembly language:

```
neg = multiplier >= 0 ? 0 : 1;
product = 0;
for(i = 32; --i>=0;){
  if(multiplier & 1)
    product += multiplicand;
  product/multiplier >> 1;        double register shift right
}
if(neg)                           correct product
  product -= multiplicand;
```

Which may be transformed into

```
neg = multiplier >= 0 ? 0 : 1;
product = 0;
i = 32;
while( --i>=0){
  if(multiplier & 1)
    product += multiplicand;
  product/multiplier >> 1;
}
if(neg)
  product -= multiplicand;
```

and as the loop will be executed at least once, this may be transformed into a do loop:

```
neg = multiplier >= 0 ? 0 : 1;
product = 0;
i = 32 - 1;
do {
  if(multiplier & 1)
    product += multiplicand;
  product/multiplier >> 1;
} while( --i>=0);
if(neg)
  product -= multiplicand;
```

4–10 The following algorithm adds two numbers together using only bitwise logical operations:

```
int add(int a, int b){
  int s = a ^ b;                 /* xor */
  int c;
  c = b;
  while (c = (a & c) << 1) {
    a = s;
    s = a ^ c;
  }
  return s;
}
```

It may be translated into assembly language. Here, a = a + b with a in %l0, b in %l1, and the sum, s in %o0 and carry, c in %o1:

```
        /* open subroutine to perform %l0 = %l0 + %l1
        using %o0 for carries and %o1 for the sum */

        xor     %l0, %l1, %o0    !sum = a ^ b
        ba      1f
        mov     %l1, %o1         !carry = b
2:      xor     %l0, %o1, %o0    !sum = a ^ carry
1:      and     %l0, %o1, %o1    !carry = a & carry
        sll     %o1, 1, %o1      !carry << 1
        orcc    %g0, %o1, %g0    !a = sum
        bne     2b               !while (carry)
        mov     %o0, %l0
```

Note the use of numeric labels. Labels 0–9 may be used repeatedly in a file; however, the particular branch target must be distinguished by prepending the label with a b or f depending upon whether it is the label in the backward direction in the file or the forward direction.

This code segment was generated by a macro add:

```
comment('add: a in $1, b in $2, sum in $3, carry in $4')
comment('result a + b in $1')

define(add, '
        /* open subroutine to perform $1 = $1 + $2
        using $3 for carries and $4 for the sum */

        xor     $1, $2, $3       !sum = a ^ b
```

```
          ba      1f
          mov     $2, $4   !carry = b
2:        xor     $1, $4, $3        !sum = a ^ carry
1:        and     $1, $4, $4        !carry = a & carry
          sll     $4,  1, $4        !carry << 1
          orcc    %g0, $4, %g0      !a = sum
          bne     2b                !while (carry)
          mov     $3, $1')


          add(%l0, %l1, %o0, %o1)
```

If one wished to repeat this addition a number of times, say n, the irp macro might be used:

```
define(irp, 'ifelse($1,0,,'$2irp(eval($1 - 1),'$2')')')
```

ifelse is a built-in macro; its arguments are evaluated, then if the first argument string, is the same as the second argument string the value of the macro is the third argument string, else it is the fourth argument string. Here the first argument is the repetition count n, which if zero returns nothing, else, it returns $2 irp(eval($1 - 1),'$2') printing the second argument and making a recursive call to irp with n = n - 1. Thus irp(2, '   add(%l0, %l1, %o0, %o1)') generates

```
          /* open subroutine to perform %l0 = %l0 + %l1
          using %o0 for carries and %o1 for the sum */

          xor     %l0, %l1, %o0    !sum = a ^ b
          ba      1f
          mov     %l1, %o1         !carry = b
2:        xor     %l0, %o1, %o0    !sum = a ^ carry
1:        and     %l0, %o1, %o1    !carry = a & carry
          sll     %o1,  1, %o1     !carry << 1
          orcc    %g0, %o1, %g0    !a = sum
          bne     2b               !while (carry)
          mov     %o0, %l0

          /* open subroutine to perform %l0 = %l0 + %l1
          using %o0 for carries and %o1 for the sum */

          xor     %l0, %l1, %o0    !sum = a ^ b
          ba      1f
          mov     %l1, %o1         !carry = b
2:        xor     %l0, %o1, %o0    !sum = a ^ carry
```

```
1:          and      %l0, %o1, %o1     !carry = a & carry
            sll      %o1,  1, %o1      !carry << 1
            orcc     %g0, %o1, %g0     !a = sum
            bne      2b                !while (carry)
            mov      %o0, %l0
```

You may make use of these two macros to write a macro to multiply two unsigned integer numbers together. Your macro should have five arguments: $1 the multiplicand register, $2 the product register, $3 the multiplier register, $4 a temporary register, $5 another temporary register. The algorithm should follow the algorithm in the text, page 112, where the least significant bit (LSB) of the multiplier is tested, and if one, the multiplicand is added to the product before the product and multiplier are both shifted right one place. This is done 32 times. Be careful not to lose the LSB of the product register, which should be shifted into the most sigificant bit of the multiplier register. Thus to generate code to multiply two numbers together located in %o0 and %o2, with the high part of the result to end up in the product register %o1, using %g2 and %g3 as temporaries, we might write

```
            .global main
main:       save     %sp, -96, %sp
            mov      4095, %o1
            mov      4095, %o2
            multiply(%o2, %o0, %o1, %g2, %g3)
out:        clr      %i0
            ret
            restore
out:        clr      %i0
            ret
            restore
```

The result should be

```
(gdb) p/x $o0
$1 = 0x0
(gdb) p/x $o1
$2 = 0xffe001
```

Chapter 5

THE STACK

5.1 Memory

The SPARC architecture specifies a 32-bit address providing 0x100000000 bytes of memory. Variables may be stored in memory occupying one, two, four, or eight bytes of memory. These memory data types are referred to as byte, halfword, word, and doubleword, occupying one, two, four, and eight bytes of memory, respectively [22].

While all integer instructions operate on 32-bit, four-byte quantities, variables known to have a small magnitude may be stored in one or two bytes. Instructions are provided to load a 32-bit register from a variable stored in one, two, or four bytes of memory. Instructions are also provided to store the low byte, low two bytes, or all four bytes of a register into memory. These data types correspond to the following C data types and have the following ranges:

C Type	SPARC Type	Bits	Unsigned	Signed
char	byte	8	0, 255	$-128, 127$
short	half	16	0, 65,535	$-32,768, 32,767$
int,long	word	32	$0, 4.294 \times 10^9$	$\pm 2.147 \times 10^9$

To make the implementation of the architecture efficient, all memory references must be aligned. That is to say, two-byte quantities may only be addressed in memory with addresses that are divisible by 2, even addresses. Four-byte quantities may be addressed in memory only if they are aligned on a four-byte boundary, that is, that the address is evenly divisible by 4. Similarly, an eight-byte quantity must have a memory address evenly divisible by 8.

151

5.2   The Stack

When a program is loaded into memory for execution, it is loaded into low memory; the first executable instruction is located somewhere above 0x2000 in the SPARC architecture. Subsequent instructions occupy higher memory addresses. The operating system provides additional memory for automatic variables near the top of memory. This space is called the stack and is intended to be used in a first-in last-out manner. Functions may use the stack to allocate space for automatic variables, as they observe a strict first-in last-out order. The address of the last occupied stack memory element is always kept in register %o6. This register is also know to the assembler as %sp, the stack pointer.

This stack, and the stack we discussed in Chapter 1, are entirely different. We do not push items onto this stack, nor do we pop items off the stack; nor does the machine perform arithmetic between the top two elements of the stack. The only reason that the space at the top of memory is called the stack is because it provides a first-in last-out data structure.

The stack, located at top of memory grows downward. It is also possible to grow a program upward from the bottom of memory to provide for a *heap*, space that in not handled on a first-in last-out order. This allows for the largest possible size of program in a given memory space; when the stack and heap overlap, the program can no longer execute. In this book in figures showing the stack, memory always increased down the page, as in writing programs. Thus, when we increase stack space, we subtract from the stack pointer bringing us back up the page, as if we were writing a program and assigning space at the end of the program(see Figure 5.1).

If in our program we need to obtain additional memory, we only have to subtract the number of bytes of additional storage needed from the stack pointer %sp. For example, to obtain an additional 64 bytes of memory:

```
sub     %sp, 64, %sp
```

The stack, however, is always kept doubleword aligned for reasons that will become clearer later. To ensure that the stack is doubleword aligned, the address in the stack pointer, %sp, must be evenly divisible by 8. If we want 94 bytes of stack memory space, we must ask for 96 to keep the stack aligned. Asking for two more bytes of memory than we really need is not important.

If we clear some of the low-order bits of a two's complement binary number we "chop" the number and make it evenly divisible by a power of 2. If we clear the low three bits, the number will be evenly divisible by 8. The resulting chopped two's complement number is the next largest number to the left on the axis of integer numbers evenly divisible by 8. The results is always ≤ to the number (see the table following).

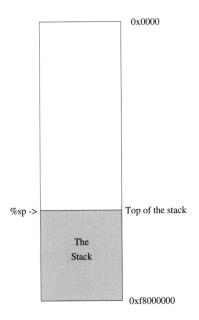

Figure 5.1: The Stack

Decimal	Binary	Chopped	Result
31	011111	011000	24
25	011001	011000	24
24	011000	011000	24
23	010111	010000	16
17	010001	010000	16
16	010000	010000	16
15	001111	001000	8
9	001001	001000	8
7	000111	000000	0
1	000001	000000	0
−1	111111	111000	−8
−2	111110	111000	−8
−7	111001	111000	−8
−8	111000	111000	−8
−9	110111	110000	−16

If instead of subtracting a positive number from the stack pointer, we were to add a chopped negative number, we would be guaranteed to obtain the additional bytes of storage we need plus the additional bytes of storage to keep the stack pointer aligned. How do we chop a number in assembly language? The assembler provides full expression evaluation just like C. We may write expressions containing constants and variables that will be evaluated by the assembler to compute a constant that may be assembled. Thus, to clear the low-order three bits, we need to form the bitwise **and** of the number with ...111111111000:

```
add      %sp, -94 & 0xfffffff8, %sp
```

The constant `0xfffffff0` is the hexadecimal representation of -8, so we might write

```
add      %sp, -94 & -8, %sp
```

This would result in 96 being subtracted from the stack pointer. In general, we always add or subtract negative numbers from the stack pointer that are evenly divisible by 8 to ensure stack double-word alignment.

The stack pointer `%sp` marks the top of the stack. Memory locations below where the stack pointer is pointing may be changed by the operating system and, indeed, frequently are. We should never refer to an address negative with respect to the stack pointer.

5.2.1   The Frame Pointer

The stack pointer is frequently changed during program execution and does not remain constant enough to reference automatic variables stored on the stack. For example, if we had a word variable stored at `%sp + 20` and subsequently changed the stack pointer to obtain more storage, the variable would no longer be located 20 bytes from the stack pointer. To solve this problem the SPARC architecture provides a second register, `%i6`, known as the frame pointer, `%fp`, into which is stored a copy of the stack pointer before it is changed to provide more storage. The frame pointer `%fp` points to what was the top of the stack before `%sp` was changed. The **save** instruction both performs an addition and saves the contents of the stack pointer in `%fp`. A **save** instruction is normally executed once at the beginning of a program to provide storage for all automatic variables. The save instruction is used to provide not only storage for automatic variables but also to provide space on the stack to save some of the registers. In Chapter 7 we describe why registers must be saved, but for now we need to provide 92 extra bytes of storage whenever executing a **save** instruction:

```
save     %sp, -92 - bytes_of_local_storage, %sp
```

Suppose, for example, that we wished to store five variables, a0–a4, on the stack instead of in the registers. We would first need to make room at the beginning of our program by

```
save     %sp, (-92 -(5 * 4)) & -8, %sp
```

which makes room for five four-byte variables together with 92 bytes in which to save registers if necessary. Note that the expression

```
(-92 -(5 * 4)) & -8
```

is evaluated by the assembler to yield a constant that is assembled in place of the expression. After executing the save instruction the stack pointer %sp points to the location on the stack in which the registers may be saved, if necessary.

The first variable, a0, will be at the memory addressed by the contents of %fp - 4, that is, four bytes above the old top of the stack. The second variable, a1, will be at %fp - 8; the third at %fp - 12, and so on (see Figure 5.2).

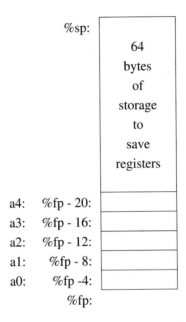

Figure 5.2: Automatic Variables on Stack

5.3 Addressing Stack Variables

How do we address stack variables and load them into and from the registers? The only instructions that reference memory are the load and store instructions, which are used to load data into registers and to store data back into memory. These instructions handle single byte, halfwords, words, and doublewords, that is, one-, two-, four-, and eight-byte quantities. Whereas bytes may be fetched and stored at any memory address, halfwords may only be loaded from, or stored into, memory addresses evenly divisible by 2. Similarly, words may only be loaded from, or stored into, memory addresses evenly divisible by 4. Finally, doubleword quantities may be only accessed from memory addresses evenly divisible by 8. In the case of double loads and stores, the register must also have an even number, as two registers are needed to store a doubleword quantity.

5.3.1   Load Instructions

The load instructions are as follows:

Mnemonic	Operation
ldsb	Load signed byte, propagate sign left in register.
ldub	Load unsigned byte, clear high 24 bits of register.
ldsh	Load signed halfword, propagate sign left in register.
lduh	Load unsigned halfword, clear high 16 bits of register.
ld	Load word.
ldd	Load double, register number even, first four bytes into register n, next four into register $n+1$.

The load instruction has two operands, with the second operand specifying the register into which the data are to be loaded. The first argument is enclosed in square brackets [ ], to indicate that the first operand is being used as a pointer, and it is the contents of the memory location addressed that is to be loaded into the register. The first argument, enclosed in square brackets, may be a register, a register plus a constant, or two registers. Where a register and a constant are specified, the memory address of the data to be loaded is the sum of the register plus the constant. Constants are stored in 13 bits in the instruction word and are first sign-extended to 32 bits before they are added to the contents of the register. Thus, the address in the register may be modified by a constant in the range $-4096 \leq$ constant ≤ 4095. Where a single register is specified, a second register, %g0, is specified by the assembler. When two registers are specified, the address is the sum of the contents of the two registers.[1] Thus, to load the first variable into %l1:

```
ld      [%fp - 4], %l1   !a0 into %l1
```

and to load the second variable, a1, into %l2:

```
ld      [%fp - 8], %l2   !a1 into %l2
```

To load the fourth variable, a3, we would write

```
ld      [%fp - 16], %l4 !a3 into %l4
```

---

[1]When a load instruction is executed, the data is not available until after the next instruction has been executed. This is due to the pipelining design of the processor (see Figure 2.2). The execution of a load instruction involves the fetching of the data from memory, and it is not until after the next cycle that the data is available. A machine interlock is, however, provided to stall the processor to prevent a program executing an instruction that would access invalid data in the next instruction cycle. A programmer should, if possible, arrange to load data into registers at least one cycle before the data are needed.

5.3.2   Store Instructions

The store instructions are as follows:

Mnemonic	Operation
stb	Store low byte of register, bits 0–7, into memory.
sth	Store low two bytes of register, bits 0–15, into memory.
st	Store register.
std	Store double, register number even, first four bytes from register n, next four from register $n+1$.

Like the load instruction, the store instruction has two operands. The first operand is the register whose contents are to be stored. The second argument is enclosed in square brackets to indicate that the second operand is being used as a pointer, and it is into the the memory location addressed that the contents, or part of the contents, of the register are to be stored. The second argument, enclosed in square brackets, may be a register, a register plus a constant, or two registers. Where a register and a constant are specified, the memory address of where the data are to be stored is the sum of the register plus the constant. Constants are stored in 13 bits in the instruction word and are first sign-extended to 32 bits before adding to the contents of the register. Thus, the address in the register may be modified by a constant in the range $-4096 \leq \text{constant} \leq 4095$. Where a single register is specified, a second register, %g0, is specified by the assembler. When two registers are specified, the address is the sum of the contents of the two registers. Notice that when storing data there is no need to distinguish between signed and unsigned data; if only part of the register is being stored, no sign extension or zeroing of high-order bits is involved. Note that the square brackets around the address part of these instructions are used to make clear that we are using the contents of the registers, plus the constant, as a pointer to address memory. Thus, to store the first variable %l1 back into a0:

```
st      %l1, [%fp - 4]   !%l1 into a0
```

and to store the second variable, %l2, into a1:

```
st      %l2, [%fp - 8]   !%l2 into a1
```

5.4   Defining Stack Variable Offsets

The constants in the operand to the ld instruction are obviously a problem, and we would prefer to define these constants symbolically, using **m4**:

```
define(a0_s, -4)
define(a1_s, -8)
define(a2_s, -12)
```

```
        define(a3_s, -16)
        define(a4_s, -20)
```

If we do this, we can write

```
    ld        [%fp + a0_s], %l1
    ld        [%fp + a1_s], %l2
    ld        [%fp + a4_s], %l4
```

which is much more readable and far less prone to error.

The macros were, however, used only to define constants representing the offset between the stack address of the variable and the frame pointer %fp. We could define macros to compute the offsets as well as to make the definitions:

```
define(local_var, 'define(last_sym, 0)')
define(var, 'define('last_sym',
  eval(last_sym - $2))$1 = last_sym ')
```

The macro local_var, used first, defines last_sym to be zero. The second macro var has two arguments, the variable name and the size of the variable in bytes. The var macro first computes the stack offset, the evaluation of last_sym - $2, and assigns this to last_sym. Note the use of the built-in macro eval to force the evaluation of its arguments as numbers. If eval were not used, an arithmetic expression would have been assigned, not its value (see Appendix C). The macro then prints the assignment

```
        $1 = last_sym
```

which will evaluated by the assembler. Pay particular attention to the single quotes in this macro.

An example of the use of these macros is

```
define(local_var, 'define(last_sym, 0)')
define(var, 'define('last_sym',
  eval(last_sym - $2))$1 = last_sym ')
        local_var
        var(a0_s, 4)
        var(a1_s, 4)
        var(a2_s, 4)
        var(a3_s, 4)


        .global main
main:
        save      %sp, (-92 + last_sym) & -8, %sp
        ld        [%fp + a0_s], %l1
        ld        [%fp + a1_s], %l2
        ld        [%fp + a3_s], %l4
```

When run through `m4` the following code results:

```
a0_s = -4
a1_s = -8
a2_s = -12
a3_s = -16
```

```
            .global main
main:
            save    %sp, (-92 + -16) & -8, %sp
            ld      [%fp + a0_s], %l1
            ld      [%fp + a1_s], %l2
            ld      [%fp + a3_s], %l4
```

To assign variables on the stack corresponding to the following C variables:

```
int a, b;
char ch;
short c;
int d;
```

using the macros we could write

```
local_var
var(a_s, 4)
var(b_s, 4)
var(ch_s, 1)
var(c_s, 2)
var(d_s, 4)
```

with the following assembler code resulting:

```
a_s = -4
b_s = -8
ch_s = -9
c_s = -11
d_s = -15
```

If, however, we then tried to access these variables by

```
ldsh    [%fp + c_s], %o0
ld      [%fp + d_s], %o1
```

we would get a nonaligned memory error and our program would stop executing; the address `%fp - 11` is not divisible by 2, which it must be for halfword access. Halfwords must be fetched from addresses divisible by 2 and words must be fetched from addresses divisible by 4. If the stack pointer and the frame pointer are doubleword aligned and thus evenly divisible by 8, `%fp - 11` is clearly not divisible by

2, nor is %fp - 15 divisible by 4. To correct this situation, we need to make sure that each variable is aligned. We do this by performing the bitwise **and** of the offset with the negative of the alignment.

```
define('var', 'define('last_sym',
eval((last_sym - $2) & -$2)) $1 = last_sym')
```

and our program now expands into

```
        a_s = -4
        b_s = -8
        ch_s = -9
        c_s = -12
        d_s = -16

        .global main
main:
        save    %sp, (-92 + -16) & -8, %sp
        ldsh    [%fp + c_s], %o0
        ld      [%fp + d_s], %o1
```

with the variables on the stack correctly aligned. Note that there is now a wasted byte after the **ch** variable to align the stack variables (see Figure 5.3).

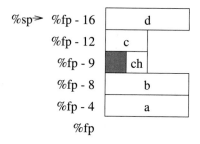

Figure 5.3: Automatic Variables Aligned on Stack

5.5 An Example

We are now in a position to write quite sophisticated programs. Consider the following C code:

```
int a, b;
char c1;
int c, d;
```

```
register int x, y, z;

x = 17;
y = -5;

for (z = 1; z < x + y; z++)
  for (a = z; a >= z * y; a -= 10)
    {
       d = a + z;
       c1 = d * b;
       c = a + y / z;
    }
```

To translate this program into assembly language, we first assign variables, to the stack and to registers making use of macros:

```
local_var
var(a_s, 4)
var(b_s, 4)
var(c1_s, 1)
var(c_s, 4)
var(d_s, 4)

define(x_r, 10)    !'x_r 10'
define(y_r, 11)    !'y_r 11'
define(z_r, 12)    !'z_r 12'
```

We might define two more macros for the program entry and exit:

```
define('begin_main','.global    main
        .align   4
main:   save    %sp, eval( -92  last_sym) & -8), %sp')

define(end_main,'mov    1, %g1
        ta        0')
```

After defining the stack offsets for automatic variables we need the program entry, macro begin_main, followed by the variable initialization statements:

```
begin_main
mov      17, %x_r         !x = 17
mov      -5, %y_r         !y = -5
```

In the case of the for loops, we branch to a test at the end of the loop, filling the delay slots with the initialization statements of the fors, before writing the loop code:

```
                local_var
                var(a_s, 4)
                var(b_s, 4)
                var(c1_s, 1)
                var(c_s, 4)
                var(d_s, 4)

                define(x_r, 10) !'x_r 10'
                define(y_r, 11) !'y_r 11'
                define(z_r, 12) !'z_r 12'

                begin_main

                mov     17, %x_r        !x = 17
                mov     -5, %y_r        !y = -5

                b       outer_test      !branch to outer loop test
                mov     1, %z_r   !use delay slot for initialization
                                        !statement

outer:                                  !code for outer loop
                b       inner_test      !similarly for inner loop
                st      %z_r, [%fp + a_s] !a = z

inner:                                  !code for inner loop
                ld      [%fp + a_s], %o0
                add     %o0, %z_r, %o0
                st      %o0, [%fp + d_s]

                ld      [%fp + d_s], %o0
                call    .mul
                ld      [%fp + b_s], %o1
                stb     %o0, [%fp + c1_s]

                mov     %y_r, %o0
                call    .div
                mov     %z_r, %o1
                ld      [%fp + a_s], %o1
                add     %o0, %o1, %o0
                st      %o0, [%fp + c_s]

inner_inc:                              !inner for increment statement
                ld      [%fp + a_s], %o0
                sub     %o0, 10, %o0
```

```
        st        %o0, [%fp + a_s]

inner_test:                               !inner for test
        mov       %z_r, %o0
        call      .mul
        mov       %y_r, %o1
        ld        [%fp + a_s], %o1
        cmp       %o1, %o0
        bge       inner
        nop

outer_inc:                                !outer for increment statement
        add       %z_r, 1, %z_r

outer_test:                               !outer for test
        add       %x_r, %y_r, %o0
        cmp       %z_r, %o0
        bl        outer
        nop

        end_main
```

We may fill the delay slots following the inner loop test by moving the first instruction of the inner loop into the delay slot and annulling the `bge` instruction. We may also fill the delay slot of the outer loop by branching directly to the inner test and filling the delay slot with the initialization test of the inner loop. We must also annul the `bl` instruction:

```
        local_var
        var(a_s, 4)
        var(b_s, 4)
        var(c1_s, 1)
        var(c_s, 4)
        var(d_s, 4)

        define(x_r, 10) !'x_r 10'
        define(y_r, 11) !'y_r 11'
        define(z_r, 12) !'z_r 12'

        begin_main

        mov       17, %x_r         !x = 17
        mov       -5, %y_r         !y = -5

        b         outer_test       !branch to outer loop test
```

```
        mov     1, %z_r !use delay slot for initialization
                        !statement

inner:                          !code for inner loop
        add     %o0, %z_r, %o0
        st      %o0, [%fp + d_s]

        ld      [%fp + d_s], %o0
        call    .mul
        ld      [%fp + b_s], %o1
        stb     %o0, [%fp + c1_s]

        mov     %y_r, %o0
        call    .div
        mov     %z_r, %o1
        ld      [%fp + a_s], %o1
        add     %o0, %o1, %o0
        st      %o0, [%fp + c_s]

inner_inc:                      !inner for increment statement
        ld      [%fp + a_s], %o0
        sub     %o0, 10, %o0
        st      %o0, [%fp + a_s]

inner_test:                     !inner for test
        mov     %z_r, %o0
        call    .mul
        mov     %y_r, %o1
        ld      [%fp + a_s], %o1
        cmp     %o1, %o0
        bge,a   inner
        ld      [%fp + a_s], %o0

outer_inc:                      !outer for increment statement
        add     %z_r, 1, %z_r

outer_test:                     !outer for test
        add     %x_r, %y_r, %o0
        cmp     %z_r, %o0
        bl,a    inner_test
        st      %z_r, [%fp + a_s] !a = z

        end_main
```

When this code is processed by **m4**, we obtain the assembly language:

```
        !local variables
        a_s = -4
        b_s = -8
        c1_s = -9
        c_s = -16
        d_s = -20

         !x_r 10
         !y_r 11
         !z_r 12

        .global main
        .align  4
main:   save    %sp, -112, %sp

        mov     17, %l0          !x = 17
        mov     -5, %l1          !y = -5

        b       outer_test       !branch to outer loop test
        mov     1, %l2           !use delay slot for initialization
                                 !statement

inner:                           !code for inner loop
        add     %o0, %l2, %o0
        st      %o0, [%fp + d_s]

        ld      [%fp + d_s], %o0
        call    .mul
        ld      [%fp + b_s], %o1
        stb     %o0, [%fp + c1_s]

        mov     %l1, %o0
        call    .div
        mov     %l2, %o1
        ld      [%fp + a_s], %o1
        add     %o0, %o1, %o0
        st      %o0, [%fp + c_s]

inner_inc:                       !inner for increment statement
        ld      [%fp + a_s], %o0
        sub     %o0, 10, %o0
        st      %o0, [%fp + a_s]
```

```
inner_test:                          !inner for test
        mov     %l2, %o0
        call    .mul
        mov     %l1, %o1
        ld      [%fp + a_s], %o1
        cmp     %o1, %o0
        bge,a   inner
        ld      [%fp + a_s], %o0

outer_inc:                           !outer for increment statement
        add     %l2, 1, %l2

outer_test:                          !outer for test
        add     %l0, %l1, %o0
        cmp     %l2, %o0
        bl,a    inner_test
        st      %l2, [%fp + a_s] !a = z

        mov     1, %g1
        ta      0
```

The program is loaded into memory by calling the C compiler. The resulting code in memory is then

```
0x106a4 <main>:           save  %sp, -112, %sp
0x106a8 <main+4>:         mov   0x11, %l0
0x106ac <main+8>:         mov   -5, %l1
0x106b0 <main+12>:        b     0x10714 <outer_test>
0x106b4 <main+16>:        mov   1, %l2
0x106b8 <inner>:          add   %o0, %l2, %o0
0x106bc <inner+4>:        st    %o0, [ %fp + -20 ]
0x106c0 <inner+8>:        ld    [ %fp + -20 ], %o0
0x106c4 <inner+12>:       call  0x208c8 <.mul>
0x106c8 <inner+16>:       ld    [ %fp + -8 ], %o1
0x106cc <inner+20>:       stb   %o0, [ %fp + -9 ]
0x106d0 <inner+24>:       mov   %l1, %o0
0x106d4 <inner+28>:       call  0x208d4 <.div>
0x106d8 <inner+32>:       mov   %l2, %o1
0x106dc <inner+36>:       ld    [ %fp + -4 ], %o1
0x106e0 <inner+40>:       add   %o0, %o1, %o0
0x106e4 <inner+44>:       st    %o0, [ %fp + -16 ]
0x106e8 <inner_inc>:      ld    [ %fp + -4 ], %o0
0x106ec <inner_inc+4>:    sub   %o0, 0xa, %o0
0x106f0 <inner_inc+8>:    st    %o0, [ %fp + -4 ]
```

```
0x106f4 <inner_test>:          mov   %l2, %o0
0x106f8 <inner_test+4>:        call  0x208c8 <.mul>
0x106fc <inner_test+8>:        mov   %l1, %o1
0x10700 <inner_test+12>:       ld    [ %fp + -4 ], %o1
0x10704 <inner_test+16>:       cmp   %o1, %o0
0x10708 <inner_test+20>:       bge,a  0x106b8 <inner>
0x1070c <inner_test+24>:       ld    [ %fp + -4 ], %o0
0x10710 <outer_inc>:           inc   %l2
0x10714 <outer_test>:          add   %l0, %l1, %o0
0x10718 <outer_test+4>:        cmp   %l2, %o0
0x1071c <outer_test+8>:        bl,a   0x106f4 <inner_test>
0x10720 <outer_test+12>:       st    %l2, [ %fp + -4 ]
0x10724 <outer_test+16>:       mov   1, %g1
0x10728 <outer_test+20>:       ta    0
```

We should make sure that we fully understand the three representations of the program: the macro version, the assembler version, and the **gdb** version. It is also important that we understand stack variables and the manner in which macros may be used to compute the offsets so that the variables will be aligned correctly. Note that **gdb** frequently prints the nop instruction as sethi %hi(0x0), g0.

5.6   One-Dimensional Arrays

A one-dimensional array, or vector, is a block of memory into which a number of variables, all of the same type, may be stored. The array address is the address of the first element of the array in memory and is a pointer to the array. The ith array element may be accessed in memory at

```
address_of_first_element + i * size_of_array_element_in_bytes
```

which is consistent with the definition of an array in C. Thus, a five-element integer array

```
int ary[5];
```

would be represented in memory as shown in Figure 5.4. It occupies 5×4 bytes of memory.

To provide space for such an array on the stack, we need to modify our stack offset macros slightly to allow us to specify a variable of a number of bytes different from its alignment. We will do this by providing an optional third argument to var, which if present specifies the total number of bytes of storage with the alignment still specified by the second argument:

```
define('var', 'define('last_sym',
eval((last_sym - ifelse($3,,$2,$3)) & -$2)) $1 = last_sym')
```

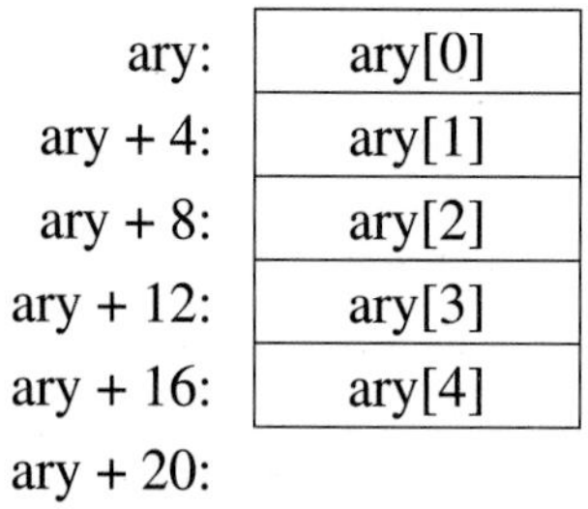

ary:	ary[0]
ary + 4:	ary[1]
ary + 8:	ary[2]
ary + 12:	ary[3]
ary + 16:	ary[4]
ary + 20:	

Figure 5.4: The Array ary[5]

This macro makes use of a new construct "ifelse." Ifelse is a built-in m4 macro that evaluates all its arguments, and then, if the first string argument is identical to the second string argument, the value of the ifelse is the third string argument. If the first two arguments are not identical, the value of the ifelse is the fourth argument. For example:

```
ifelse(a,b,c,d)
```

results in the string "d," as the string "a" is not the same as the string "b."

In the use of the ifelse in the var macro, the third argument is evaluated and compared to the null string. If the third argument is not supplied, it has the null value and so this functions as a test to see if a third argument has been supplied. Where the third argument is missing, the number subtracted from the last_sym is the second argument. Where a third argument is supplied, the third argument is subtracted. The alignment of the stack is still the second argument. For example, to declare the following automatic variables:

```
int a;
char c1;
int ary[5];
char c2;
int  d;
```

we would write

```
local_var
var(a_s, 4)
var(c1_s, 1)
var(ary_s, 4, 4 * 5)
var(c2_s, 1)
var(d_s, 4)
```

which would result in the following expansion:

```
a_s = -4
```

```
c1_s = -5
ary_s = -28
c2_s = -29
d_s = -36
```

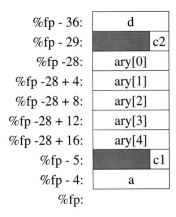

%fp - 36:	d
%fp - 29:	c2
%fp -28:	ary[0]
%fp -28 + 4:	ary[1]
%fp -28 + 8:	ary[2]
%fp -28 + 12:	ary[3]
%fp -28 + 16:	ary[4]
%fp - 5:	c1
%fp - 4:	a
%fp:	

Figure 5.5: An Array on the Stack

It will be seen in Figure 5.5 that the array begins at %fp - 28 allowing successive array elements to be accessed at higher memory locations. For example, ary[2] is located at %fp - 28 + 8. Notice that the macros generate addresses that are always aligned, assuming that the stack and frame pointers are doubleword aligned.

To load ary[i] into %o0, if i were stored in register %i_r, would be

```
sll    %i_r, 2, %o0        !'multiply i by 4'
add    %fp, %o0, %o0       !'add the frame pointer'
ld     [%o0 + ary_s], %o0
```

Consider the following program to find the maximum element in the array nums:

```
int nums[100] = {1, 45, -16, 23, 38, 45, 17};
int n = 7;              /* number of elements in array */
register int i;         /* for index */
register int max;       /* to hold the maximum element */

max = nums[0];          /* initialize max to first element */

for (i = 1; i < n; i++) /* run through rest of array */

  if (nums[i] > max)    /* storing largest number */
    max = nums[i];
```

Its translation into assembly language is as follows

```
define('local_var', '!local variables
define('last_sym', 0)')
define('align_d', 'eval($2 * ((($1 + 1) / $2) - 1))')
define('var', 'define('last_sym',
align_d(eval(last_sym - ifelse($3,,$2,$3)), $2))$1 = last_sym')
define('begin_main','.global      main
main:   save    %sp, align_d(eval(
  -92 ifdef('last_sym','+ last_sym'))), 8), %sp')
define('end_main','mov  1, %g1
        ta        0')

        local_var
        var(nums_s, 4, 100 * 4)        !'the array nums'
        var(n_s, 4)

        define(i_r, 10)           !'index in %l0'
        define(max_r, 11)         !'max in %l1'

        begin_main

/* a macro to initialize the array nums */
define(initialize, '    mov      $2, %o0
        st       %o0, [%fp + nums_s + $1]
ifelse($3,,,'initialize(
  eval($1 + 4),$3,$4,$5,$6,$7,$8,$9)')')

initialize(0, 1, 45, -16, 23, 38, 45, 17)

        mov     7, %o0    !'initialize the variable n = 7'
        st      %o0, [%fp + n_s]

        ld      [%fp + nums_s], %max_r  !'max = nums_s[0]'

        b       fortest            !'branch to the for test'
        mov     1, %i_r !'the for initialization expression'

for:    sll     %i_r, 2, %o0      !'o0 = i * 4'
        add     %fp, %o0, %o0     !'o0 = %fp + i * 4'
        ld      [%o0 + nums_s], %o0
        cmp     %o0, %max_r
        ble     keep
        nop
        mov     %o0, %max_r       !'found a larger one'
keep:
```

```
        add     %i_r, 1, %i_r   !'i++'
fortest:
        ld      [%fp + n_s], %o0         !'the test'
        cmp     %i_r, %o0
        bl      for
        nop


        end_main
```

Stack variables have to be initialized by loading the constant into a register and then storing it on the stack. We wrote a macro, `initialize`, to do this instead of writing a number of `mov` and `st` instructions. The arguments to `initialize` are the stack offset in bytes from the beginning of the array on the stack, followed by up to eight initializers. The macro generates a `mov` and `st` instruction to initialize the first array element and then uses an ifelse to check if there is an additional array element to initialize. If there is, it calls `initialize` again, with the first argument incremented by four and all the remaining arguments one place to the left (remember that missing arguments are replaced by null strings).

Note that in accessing `nums[i]` we must first multiply i by 4, which we do by left-shifting two, and then add the result to `%fp` before we can load the value using as address the register containing `%fp + i * 4` plus `nums`. We have not yet attempted to remove the `nop` instructions. The program's expansion into assembly language is as follows:

```
        !local variables
        nums_s = -400       !the array nums
        n_s = -404


                        !index in %l0
                !max in %l1


        .global main
        .align  4
main:   save    %sp, -496, %sp

/* a macro to initialize the array nums */


        mov     1, %o0
        st      %o0, [%fp + nums_s + 0]
        mov     45, %o0
        st      %o0, [%fp + nums_s + 4]
        mov     -16, %o0
        st      %o0, [%fp + nums_s + 8]
        mov     23, %o0
```

```
        st      %o0, [%fp + nums_s + 12]
        mov     38, %o0
        st      %o0, [%fp + nums_s + 16]
        mov     45, %o0
        st      %o0, [%fp + nums_s + 20]
        mov     17, %o0
        st      %o0, [%fp + nums_s + 24]


        mov     7, %o0    !initialize the variable n = 7
        st      %o0, [%fp + n_s]

        ld      [%fp + nums_s], %l1      !max = nums_s[0]

        b       fortest             !branch to the for test
        mov     1, %l0 !the for initialization expression

for:    sll     %l0, 2, %o0      !o0 = i * 4
        add     %fp, %o0, %o0    !o0 = %fp + i * 4
        ld      [%o0 + nums_s], %o0
        cmp     %o0, %l1
        ble     keep
        nop
        mov     %o0, %l1            !found a larger one
keep:
        add     %l0, 1, %l0      !i++
fortest:
        ld      [%fp + n_s], %o0          !the test
        cmp     %l0, %o0
        bl      for
        nop

        mov     1, %g1
        ta      0
```

Note the macro expansion of the initialization of the array.

We are beginning to accumulate a number of macros that we will need in all our programs. Instead of copying them into the beginning of each program, we can put them all into a file and simply include the file at the beginning of each program. This is done by the **include** macro, whose argument is the name of the file to include. The macros we have accumulated so far, and placed in a file called `macro_defs.m`, are

```
divert(-1)
define('local_var', '!local variables define('last_sym', 0)')
```

```
define('var', 'define('last_sym',
eval((last_sym - ifelse($3,,$2,$3)) & -$2)) $1 = last_sym')

define('begin_main','.global     main
        .align  4
main:   save    %sp, eval(
            ( -92 ifdef('last_sym',' last_sym')) & -8), %sp')

define('end_main','mov   1, %g1
        ta      0')
divert
```

We have surrounded the file with divert macros to avoid extra blank lines in our output.

5.7 Improvements to the Code

Observation of the macro code for the program above indicates that n should be stored in a register to avoid the need to load it repeatedly into a register:

```
include(macro_defs.m)
```

$$\vdots$$

```
        define(n_r, 12)           !'n in %12'
```

$$\vdots$$

```
        mov     7, %n_r

        ld      [%fp + nums_s], %max

        b       fortest
        mov     1, %i_r

for:    sll     %i_r, 2, %o0     !'o0 = i * 4'
        add     %fp, %o0, %o0    !'o0 = %fp + i * 4'
        ld      [%o0 + nums_s], %o0
        cmp     %o0, %max_r
        ble     keep
        nop
        mov     %o0, %max_r
keep:
```

```
        add     %i_r, 1, %i_r    !'i++'

fortest:
        cmp     %i_r, %n_r
        bl      for
        nop
```

It is possible to fill the first delay slot by moving back the increment statement, following the label keep. The increment statement is always executed, whether or not the value of max is updated. The second delay slot can be filled by moving the first instruction of the for into the slot and annulling the statement:

$$\vdots$$

```
        mov     7, %n_r

        ld      [%fp + nums_s], %max_r

        b       fortest
        mov     1, %i_r

for:    add     %fp, %o0, %o0    !'o0 = %fp + i * 4'
        ld      [%o0 + nums_s], %o0
        cmp     %o0, %max_r
        ble     keep
        add     %i_r, 1, %i_r    !'i++'

        mov     %o0, %max_r
keep:

fortest:
        cmp     %i_r, %n_r
        bl,a    for
        sll     %i_r, 2, %o0     !'o0 = i * 4'

        end_main
```

By using a pointer variable, we can replace the subscript computations that involve many instructions, with the addition of four to the pointer, to point to the next element in the array:

```
        define(ptr_r, 13)                   !'ptr_r in %13'
```

$$\vdots$$

```
        mov      7, %n_r

        add      %fp, nums_s + 4, %ptr_r      !'points to nums[1]'

        ld       [%ptr_r - 4], %max_r         !'first value'



        b        fortest
        mov      1, %i_r

for:    cmp      %o0, %max_r
        ble      keep
        add      %i_r, 1, %i_r    !'i++'

        mov      %o0, %max_r
keep:
        add      %ptr_r, 4, %ptr_r            !'ptr_r++'

fortest:
        cmp      %i_r, %n_r
        bl,a     for
        ld       [%ptr_r], %o0    !'*ptr_r'
```

Note the initialization of %ptr_r by adding %fp to nums. We have replaced the sll instruction in the delay slot by the first instruction of the for, the ld instruction. By counting down we can eliminate the cmp instruction, setting the condition codes as we decrement %i_r:

$$\vdots$$

```
        ld       [%fp + nums_s], %max_r

        orcc     %g0, 6, %i_r     !'set icc for test'

        b        fortest
        add      %fp, nums_s + 4 * 6, %ptr_r
                                  !'points to seventh element'
for:
        cmp      %o0, %max_r
        ble      keep
        subcc    %i_r, 1, %i_r    !'i--'
```

```
        mov     %o0, %max_r
keep:
        sub     %ptr_r, 4, %ptr_r
fortest:
        bg,a    for
        ld      [%ptr_r], %o0


        end_main
```

Note that we have to set the condition codes before the branch to `fortest`. If we did not use the `orcc` instruction, the condition codes would not be set for the execution of the `bg` instruction. The loop is now seven instructions long.

One final improvement is to move the pointer decrement instruction between the `ld` and the use of the loaded data in the immediately following `cmp` instruction (see footnote on page 156).

$$\vdots$$

```
        ld      [%fp + nums_s], %max_r   !'max = nums[0]'
        orcc    %g0, 6, %i_r                 !'set icc for test'
        ba      fortest
        add     %fp, nums_s + (4 * 6), %ptr_r
                                  !'points to seventh element'
for:
        sub     %ptr_r, 4, %ptr_r         !'ptr--'
        cmp     %o0, %max_r
        ble     fortest
        subcc   %i_r, 1, %i_r    !i--


        mov     %o0, %max_r
fortest:
        bg,a    for                      !testing %i
        ld      [%ptr_r], %o0
```

What would the C program to produce this code look like?

```
int nums[100] = {1, 450, -16, 23, 38, 45, 17};
register int i;        /* for index */
register int max;      /* to hold the maximum element */
register int *ptr;     /* array pointer */

for(max = nums[0], i = 6, ptr = nums + 6; i > 0; --i)
   if (*ptr-- > max)     /* storing largest number */
     max = *ptr;
```

Tests against zero are better if the test can be combined with an `addcc` or `subcc` instruction, as they generally eliminate the need for a separate `cmp` instruction. The use of pointers is generally better than an indexing, as it avoids computing an index expression, especially when stepping through an array element by element.

5.8 Summary

In this chapter we introduced the stack to store data. We also introduced the load and store instructions and described the need to align memory data. Macros were given to define stack offsets for variables to be stored on the stack. These macros handled the alignment of byte, halfword, word, and double-word data as well as defining stack offsets for arrays. A fairly extensive example was given, demonstrating the use of the stack for automatic variables and the coding of a nested for statement.

One-dimensional arrays were introduced with macros to assign space on the stack for them. A second example demonstrated the coding and optimization of a routine to find the maximum element in an array.

5.9 Exercises

5–1 Define symbolic stack offsets in an assembly language program for the following automatic variables:

```
int a, b;
char d;
int c;
short e;
```

and write the appropriate `save` instruction to provide the storage.

5–2 Define stack offsets for an assembly language program using the macros defined in `macro_defs.m`: `local_var`, `var`, and `begin_fn`, for the following automatic variables:

```
char a, b;
int d;
char c;
short e;
```

5–3 Bearing in mind alignment problems, how would it be best to declare automatic variables in C programs to minimize stack space?

5–4 Write a program to initialize an array

```
int ary[] = {3, 4, -5, 6, 2, 0}
```

and then to find the largest element by searching the array.

5–5 Write a program to initialize an array

```
int ary[] = {3, 4, -5, 6, 2, 0}
```

and then to sort the array, smallest element first.

5–6 Write a program to initialize each element of an array

```
int fact[6];
```

to the factorial of the subscript.

5–7 You are to translate the following C code into assembly language. All variables are to be allocated space on the stack using local_var and var macros. For program entry you are to use begin_main and end_main macros. In the program you are to use only registers %o0 and %o1. All variables are to be accessed from the stack such that at any time during program execution the latest values of the variables are located on the stack. You are to execute the statements in the order given. Do not try to optimize your code.

```
char ca;
short sb;
int ic;
char cd;
short se;
int ig;

ca = 17;
cd = ca + 23;
ic = -63 + ca;
ig = ic + cd;
sb = ic / ca;
se = cd * sb + ic;
```

At the end of the program the values of the variables should be ca = 17, sb = -2, ic = -46, cd = 40, se = -126, and ig = -6.

5–8 Translate the following C code to assembly language using macros suitable for processing by m4. You may include macro_defs.m, which defines local_var, var, begin_main, and end_main. Apart from the temporary registers %o0 and %o1, define all register names symbolically and allocate the space on the stack for the array.

```
int ary[10];
register int i, j, sum;

i = 0;
sum = 0;
do{
  j = 1;
  do
    sum += j++;
  while (j <= i);
  ary[i++] = sum;
}
while (i <= 10);
```

5–9 Translate the following C code to assembly language using macros suitable for processing by m4. You may include `macro_defs.m`, which defines `local_var`, `var`, `begin_main`, and `end_main`. Assign all variables to the stack, updating their values every time a new value is computed, unless they have a **register** declaration. Apart from the temporary registers %o0 and %o1, define all register names symbolically. No constants are to appear as machine instruction operands except for 2, 3, and 4. Eliminate all **nop**'s.

```
int a = 4, b = 3;
char c;
register int d, e;

c = a * b / 2;
if (a + b > c)
  d = a++;
else
  b = b / c;
c = --b;
```

5–10 Translate the following C code into assembly language using macros suitable for processing by m4. You may include `macro_defs.m`, which defines `local_var`, `var`, `begin_main`, and `end_main`. Apart from the temporary registers %o0 and %o1, define all register names symbolically. No constants are to appear as machine instruction operands except for the constant 10. Eliminate all **nop** instructions.

```
int ary[10];

register int i;
register int *ptr;
```

```
for(ptr = ary, i = 10;--i >= 0;)
   *ptr++ = i * i;
```

5–11 You are to translate the following shell sort program into assembly language
eliminating all nop instructions. Shell sort for an array of SIZE integers. The array
is initialized to the sequence SIZE - 1, ... , 1, 0 and after the sort is 0, 1, ... , SIZE
- 1.

```
#define SIZE 20
main()
{
  int v[SIZE];
  register int gap, i, j;
  register int temp;

 for (j = 0, i = SIZE; --i >= 0;) /* initialize array */
   v[i] = j++;

  for (gap = SIZE/2; gap > 0; gap /=2) /* sort it */
    for (i = gap; i < SIZE; i++)
      for (j = i - gap; j >= 0 && v[j] > v[j + gap]; j -= gap) {
        temp = v[j];
        v[j] = v[j + gap];
        v[j + gap] = temp;
      }
}
```

Chapter 6

DATA STRUCTURES

6.1 Introduction

Arrays and structures cannot be stored in registers because in both cases it is necessary to perform address arithmetic; registers do not have addresses. Multi-dimensional arrays and structures provide for more sophisticated data structuring; they add complexity at the architectural level in addressing both elements and fields. While the addressing of structures is handled at assembly time, arrays require repeated multiplication by constants and addition to compute the address of array elements. Macros to generate code for the multiplication by constants are developed in this chapter.

6.2 Array Storage and Addressing

An array is an indexable data structure whose elements are all of the same type. That is, given indices $i, j, k, ...$ the ith, jth, kth element may be accessed. We discussed one-dimensional arrays in Chapter 5, in which the ith element may be accessed by

```
address_of_first_element + i * size_of_array_element_in_bytes
```

To make space on the stack for such a one-dimensional array, for example:

```
int a[100];
```

we would use the **var** macro:

```
var(a, 4, 100 * 4)
```

which defines the offset **a** for the first element of the array and reserves 400 bytes of storage on the stack, aligned on a four-byte boundary. Accessing the i element requires a shift, an add, and a load or store instruction:

```
sll    %i_r, 2, %o0      !o0 = i * 4
add    %fp, %o0, %o0     !o0 = %fp + i * 4
ld     [%o0 + a_s], %o0  !%o0 = [%fp + a + %i_r * 4]
```

6.3   Multidimensional Arrays

Although the mapping of a multidimensional array may take many forms, two are used predominantly, row major order and column major order. The mapping, for row major order, of the ith, jth, kth element of an array ary is

```
int arr[di][dj][dk];
```

%fp + arr_s + i * dj * dk * 4 + j * dk * 4 + k * 4

or

%fp + arr_s + ((i * dj + j) * dk + k) * 4

where the 4 relates to the size of an int, four bytes.

The same array stored in column order would be addressed as

%fp + arr_s + i * 4 + j * di * 4 + k * di * dj * 4

or

%fp + arr_s + ((k * dj + j) * di + i) * 4

With the exception of Fortran, most languages, including C, use row major order for addressing arrays. Fortran uses column major order to make more efficient array addressing for a class of computations. When we are aware of the addressing arithmetic, we may find it beneficial to transpose arrays in some computations to make the addressing more efficient. We discuss here only row major order storage of multidimensional arrays.

To provide storage for a multidimensional array we may use the var macro. Consider the array

```
short ary[16][3][4][15];
```

This will require 16 * 3 * 4 * 15 * 2 bytes of storage, halfword aligned:

```
define(d1, 16)
define(d2, 3)
define(d3, 4)
define(d4, 15)
var(ary_s, 2, d1 * d2 * d3 * d4 * 2)
```

Addressing requires evaluation of

```
%fp + ary_s + (((i * d2 + j) * d3 + k) * d4 + l) * 2
```

which we might write as

```
        mov     %i_r, %o0
        call    .mul
        mov     d2, %o1         !%o0 = i * d2
        add     %j_r, %o0, %o0   !%o0 = i * d2 + j
        call    .mul
        mov     d3, %o1         !(i * d2 + j) * d3
        add     %k_r, %o0, %o0   !(i * d2 + j) * d3 + k
        call    .mul
        mov     d4, %o1         !((i * d2 + j) * d3 + k) * d4
        add     %l_r, %o0, %o0   !((i * d2 + j) * d3 + k) * d4
                                ! + %l_r
        sll     %o0, 1, %o0     !(((i * d2 + j) * d3 + k) * d4
                                ! + %l_r) * 2
        add     %fp, %o0, %o0
        ldsh    [%o0 + ary_s], %o0 !%o0 = ary[i][j][k][l]
```

In general, an n-dimensional array requires n adds and $n-1$ multiplies to compute an address.

6.3.1   Lower Bounds Different from Zero

Arrays may be declared with a lower bound differing from zero, as in Pascal [10]:

```
b: array[l1..u1, l2..u2, l3..u3] of integer;
```

Each subscript now has a dimension $u_n - l_n + 1$ and we might define the dimensions as

```
d1 = u1 - l1 + 1
d2 = u2 - l2 + 1
d3 = u3 - l3 + 1
```

The storage required is d1 * d2 * d3 * 4 bytes and thus the storage might be obtained by

```
define(d1, eval(u_1 - l_1 + 1))
define(d2, eval(u_2 - l_2 + 1))
define(d3, eval(u_3 - l_3 + 1))
var(b_s, 4, eval(d1 * d2 * d3 * 4))
```

Note that b_s is the address of b[l1, l2, l3].

The address of the ith, jth, kth element is

```
%fp + b_s + (((i - l1) * dj + (j - l2)) * dk + (k - l3)) * 4
```

or:

```
%fp + b_s + ((i * dj + j) * dk + k) * 4
        - ((l1 * dj + l2) * dk + l3) * 4
```

By defining a further constant

```
define(b0, eval(b_s - ((l1 * dj + l2) * dk + l3) * 4)
```

we may write the code to load the *i*th, *j*th, *k*th element of arr: array [-2..3, 0..9, 2..4] of integer:

```
include(../macro_defs.m)
define(l_1, -2)
define(u_1, 3)
define(l_2, 0)
define(u_2, 9)
define(l_3, 2)
define(u_3, 4)
define(d1, eval(u_1 - l_1 + 1))
define(d2, eval(u_2 - l_2 + 1))
define(d3, eval(u_3 - l_3 + 1))
define(i_r, 10)
define(j_r, 11)
define(k_r, 12)

local_var
var(arr_s, 4, d1 * d2 * d3 * 4)
b0 = arr_s - ((l_1 * d2 + l_2) * d3 + l_3) * 4

begin_main
mov     -2, %i_r
mov     0, %j_r
mov     2, %k_r

mov     %i_r, %o0
call    .mul
mov     d2, %o1          !%o0 = i * d2
add     %j_r, %o0, %o0   !%o0 = i * d2 + j
call    .mul
mov     d3, %o1          !(i * d2 + j) * d3
add     %k_r, %o0, %o0   !(i * d2 + j) * d3 + k
sll     %o0, 2, %o0      !(((i * d2 + j) * d3 + k) * 4
add     %fp, %o0, %o0
ld      [%o0 + b0], %o0 !%o0 = ary[i][j][k]
end_main
```

Thus, arrays whose lower bounds differ from zero do not require any additional instructions in the array element access.

6.3.2   Array Bound Checking

In many high-level languages, array bounds are checked before an array is accessed. For instance, in the example given above, we must check that $-2 \leq i \leq 3$ and $0 \leq j \leq 9$ and so on. To provide for this in assembly language, we must check each subscript:

lower-bound $\leq$ index $\leq$ upper-bound
$0 \leq$ index $-$ lower-bound $\leq$ upper-bound $-$ lower-bound
$0 \leq$ index $-$ lower-bound $<$ dimension

In assembly language:

```
define(l_1, -2)
define(u_1, 3)
define(l_2, 0)
define(u_2, 9)
define(l_3, 2)
define(u_3, 4)

define(d1, eval(u_1 - l_1 + 1))
define(d2, eval(u_2 - l_2 + 1))
define(d3, eval(u_3 - l_3 + 1))

define(i_r, 10)
define(j_r, 11)
define(k_r, 12)

local_var
var(arr_r, 4, d1 * d2 * d3 * 4)

begin_main

mov     -2, %i_r
mov     0, %j_r
mov     2, %k_r

subcc   %i_r, l_1, %o1  !'i - l_1'
bl      error
cmp     %o1, d1
bge     error
add     %o1, %g0, %o0    !'for consistency'
```

```
        call    .mul
        mov     d2, %o1         !'%o0 = (i - l_1) * d2'
        subcc   %j_r, l_2, %o1
        bl      error
        cmp     %o1, d2
        bge     error
        add     %o1, %o0, %o0   !'%o0 = (i - l_1) * d2 + (j - L_2)'
        call    .mul
        mov     d3, %o1         !'(i - l_1) * d2 + (j - L_2) * d3'
        subcc   %k_r, l_3, %o1
        bl      error
        cmp     %o1, d3
        bge     error
        add     %o1, %o0, %o0   !'(i - l_1) * d2 + (j - L_2) * d3'
                                !'+ (k - L_3)'
        sll     %o0, 2, %o0     !'* 4'
        add     %fp, %o0, %o0
        ld      [%o0 + arr_r], %o0 !'%o0 = ary[i][j][k]'

error:
        end_main
```

For each dimension of the array we now need three additions and one multiplication, which is quite expensive.

If the subscripts in an array access are given as constants, such as arr[-1][3][3], the offset may be computed by the assembler:

```
        define(l_1, -2)
        define(u_1, 3)
        define(l_2, 0)
        define(u_2, 9)
        define(l_3, 2)
        define(u_3, 4)

        define(d1, eval(u_1 - l_1 + 1))
        define(d2, eval(u_2 - l_2 + 1))
        define(d3, eval(u_3 - l_3 + 1))

        local_var
        var(arr_r, 4, d1 * d2 * d3 * 4)

        b0 = arr_r - ((l_1 * d2 + l_2) * d3 + l_3) * 4

        begin_main
```

```
ld   [%fp + b0 + (((-1 * d2 + 3) * d3 + 3) << 2)], %o0
                              !%o0 = ary[i][j][k]
```

```
end_main
```

and the resulting code is the same as if we had accessed a simple variable. However, not all compilers will do this and, in general, one should expect considerable arithmetic for subscript computations. Arrays should be used only when the subscripts do indeed need to be computed and are not constants. If we are using arrays with constant subscripts, structures are appropriate.

6.4 Address Arithmetic

If the array dimensions are constant, as in C, the multiplications in the array address computations involve the product of a number with a constant. If this is the case, the multiplication is better handled by shifting and adding. For example, to multiply the contents of register %o0 by five, leaving the result in %o1, we might write

```
mov     %o0, %o1        !times one
sll     %o0, 2, %o0     !times four
add     %o0, %o1, %o1   !times five
```

Given the binary representation of a number, it is a simple matter to generate such code:

```
*/ multiply %o0 by 03514 octal = 011 101 001 100 binary/*
        sll     %o0, 2, %o1     !04
        sll     %o1, 1, %o0
        add     %o0, %o1, %o1   !014
        sll     %o0, 3, %o0
        add     %o0, %o1, %o1   !0114
        sll     %o0, 2, %o0
        add     %o0, %o1, %o1   !0514
        sll     %o0, 1, %o0
        add     %o0, %o1, %o1   !01514
        sll     %o0, 1, %o0
        add     %o0, %o1, %o1   !03514
```

Scanning the multiplier from the right in binary whenever we see a one, we add the multiplicand to the product and then shift the multiplicand left one place; when we see a zero we simply shift the multiplicand left one place.

If we need to multiply by constants containing strings of ones, we may make use of the Booth recoding, which eliminates strings of ones by means of the following recoding:

$$01110 = 10000 - 10$$

Here the repeated adding and shifting are replaced by a subtraction, a shift, and an add. Bits in the multiplier are examined one by one starting from the least significant bit; the bits are compared to a state bit, which is initialized to zero. After each bit is examined, it replaces the state bit. When the comparison is made:

- If the state and the examined bit are the same, shift the multiplicand left one place.

- If the state is a one and the examined bit a zero, a one/zero transition, add the multiplicand to the product and then shift.

- If the state is a zero and the examined bit a one, a zero/one transition, subtract the multiplicand from the product and then shift.

Consider multiplying %o0 by $7 = 0111$: The initial state is zero and the first bit examined a one, thus we subtract and shift, the state becomes a one; the next bit is the same as the state, shift; the next bit is the same, shift again; finally, we encounter the high-order bit a zero, with a one/zero transition we add. In assembly language:

```
sub     %g0, %o0, %o1       !result into %o1
sll     %o0, 3, %o0         !three shifts accumulated
add     %o0, %o1, %o1       !times seven
```

Multiplication by constants occurs quite frequently and a set of macros has been developed to generate the code in line (see Appendix C).

In Appendix C a macro `cmul` is developed with arguments: the register that contains the multiplicand; the positive, constant multiplier; a temporary register into which to place the shifted multiplicand; and finally, the register into which the product is to be placed.

```
'cmul (1=multiplicand register, 2=constant multiplier, 3=temp,
      4 = product)'
```

The macro works only for positive constants and requires that the multiplicand and temp registers are different.

Making use of the `cmul` macro, we can rewrite the multiple array access code, given on page 183, as

```
cmul(   %i_r, d2, %g1, %o0)
add     %j_r, %o0, %o0  !'%o0 = i * d2 + j'
cmul(   %o0, d3, %g1, %o0)
add     %k_r, %o0, %o0  !'(i * d2 + j) * d3 + k'
cmul(   %o0, d4, %g1, %o0)
add     %l_r, %o0, %o0  !'((i * d2 + j) * d3 + k)
                        ! * d4 + %l'
sll     %o0, 1, %o0     !'(((i * d2 + j) * d3 + k)
```

```
                                 ! * d4 + %l) * 2'
        add      %fp, %o0, %o0
        ldsh     [%o0 + ary_s], %o0 !'%o0 = ary[i][j][k]'
```

which generates the following code:

```
                          !start open coded multiply for
                          !%o0 = %l0 * 3, using %g1 as temp
        sll      %l0,   2, %g1
        sub      %g1, %l0, %o0


                          ! end open coded multiply


        add      %l1, %o0, %o0 !%o0 = i * d2 + j


                          !start open coded multiply for
                          !%o0 = %o0 * 4, using %g1 as temp
        sll      %o0,   2, %o0
                          ! end open coded multiply


        add      %l2, %o0, %o0 !(i * d2 + j) * d3 + k


                          !start open coded multiply for
                          !%o0 = %o0 * 5, using %g1 as temp
        sll      %o0,   2, %g1
        add      %g1, %o0, %o0


                          ! end open coded multiply


        add      %l3, %o0, %o0 !((i * d2 + j) * d3 + k) * d4
                                ! + %l
        sll      %o0, 1, %o0    !(((i * d2 + j) * d3 + k)
                                ! * d4 + %l) * 2
        add      %fp, %o0, %o0
        ldsh     [%o0 + ary_s], %o0 !%o0 = ary[i][j][k]
```

When declaring multidimensional arrays, as in C, it is to our advantage to keep dimensions as powers of 2.

6.5   Structures

A structure is a block of contiguous memory allocated to store a number of variables.
The variables of a structure are referred to as *fields*, and a structure may contain
variables of many different types. A structure definition relates to the offsets of the
individual fields with respect to the beginning address of the structure. Individual
fields may be accessed with respect to a pointer to the beginning of the record.

Thus, the structure

```
struct example {
    int a, b;
    char d;
    short x, y;
    int u, v;
}
```

defines the following offsets:

```
example_a = 0
example_b = 4
example_d = 8
example_x = 10
example_y = 12
example_u = 16
example_v = 20
size_of_example = 24
```

The fields of the structure are shown in Figure 6.1.

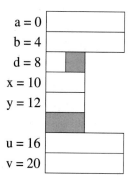

Figure 6.1: The Fields of the Structure

If a pointer to the first element in the structure is in a register, say, %l0, then
the various fields may be accessed by

```
ld      [%l0 + example_a], %o0          !%o0 = a
ld      [%l0 + example_b], %o0          !%o0 = b
ldub    [%l0 + example_d], %o0          !%o0 = d
ldsh    [%l0 + example_x], %o0          !%o0 = x
ldsh    [%l0 + example_y], %o0          !%o0 = y
ld      [%l0 + example_u], %o0          !%o0 = u
ld      [%l0 + example_v], %o0          !%o0 = v
```

We clearly need to use macros to define these offsets; however, we must be careful of memory alignment. Note that in the example above we defined the offset for `example_d` to be eight, not seven, which would have caused a memory alignment error when we tried to access the variable.

Macros to define structure field offsets are very similar to the macros used to define the local variable offsets on the stack; the difference is that structure offsets increase positively, whereas stack variable offsets increase negatively. We also need to define the size of the structure in bytes and the maximum alignment needed by the structure. We will define two symbols for these quantities, consisting of the string "size_of_" appended with the struct name and "align_of_" appended with the struct name. We will define three macros:

```
'begin defining the fields of a structure'
'$1 = struct name'
define(begin_struct, '!'define' structure $1
define('size_of_struct',0)define(
'name_of_struct',$1)define(
'align_of_struct', 0)')

'define a field of a struct'
'$1 = name of field, $2 = alignment, $3 if present no. bytes'
define(field,
  'name_of_struct'_'$1 = align_d(size_of_struct,$2)define(
  'size_of_struct', eval(align_d(size_of_struct,$2)
  + ifelse($3,,$2,$3)))define(
  'align_of_struct', ifelse(
  eval($2 > align_of_struct),1,$2,align_of_struct))')

'end definition of a struct'
'$1 = name, defines size_of_$1 to be the size in bytes aligned
to align_of_struct'
define('end_struct', 'ifelse(
$1,name_of_struct,'define(
'size_of_$1',align_d(size_of_struct, align_of_struct)) define(
'align_of_$1',align_of_struct)
        !'size_of_$1', size_of_$1 bytes','
errprint('      structure begin does not match end')')')')
```

The first macro defines two symbols, `size_of_struct` and a symbol representing the alignment of the structure, `align_of_struct`, to be zero. The second macro, `field`, has three arguments: the name of the field, its alignment, and the size in bytes if not equal to the alignment. The field name is prepended with the name of the struct. The second macro defines the field to be equal to `size_of_struct` appropriately aligned. The macro then updates the size of the structure and the alignment, keeping track of the maximum alignment so far. Note that the arithmetic relational operator ">" has the value "1" if the condition is true and "0" if false.

The `align_d` macro returns the smallest number exactly divisible by the second argument and greater or equal to the first argument:

```
'returns $1 aligned according to $2'
define('align_d', 'eval(((($1 + $2 - 1)/ $2) * $2))')
```

The final macro, `end_struct`, defines a symbol to represent the size of the structure and the alignment.

An example of the use of the macros is the representation of the C structure declaration:

```
struct ex2 {
   char  a;
   int   b;
   short c[3];
   char  d;
   int   e;
   char  f;
}
```

in assembly language as

```
begin_struct(ex2)
field(a, 1)
field(b, 4)
field(c, 2, 2 * 3)
field(d, 1)
field(e, 4)
field(f, 1)
end_struct(ex2)
```

which results in the following code being generated:

```
!define structure ex2

ex2_a = 0
ex2_b = 4
ex2_c = 8
ex2_d = 14
```

```
ex2_e = 16
ex2_f = 20

!size_of_ex2, 24 bytes
```

The fields of the structure are shown in Figure 6.2.

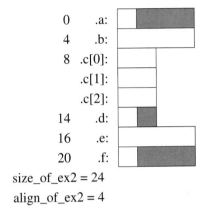

size_of_ex2 = 24

align_of_ex2 = 4

Figure 6.2: The Fields of the Structure ex2

6.6 Structures as Automatic Variables

We might declare two such structures, s1 and s2, as local variables as follows:

```
local_var
var(s1, align_of_ex2, size_of_ex2)
var(s2, align_of_ex2, size_of_ex2)
```

and then access the fields of the structure as follows:

```
begin_struct(ex2)
field(a, 1)
field(b, 4)
field(c, 2, 2 * 3)
field(d, 1)
field(e, 4)
field(f, 1)
end_struct(ex2)

local_var
var(s1, align_of_ex2, size_of_ex2)
var(s2, align_of_ex2, size_of_ex2)
```

```
begin_main

    ld      [%fp + s1 + ex2_b], %o0        !'s2.f = s1.b'
    stb     %o0, [%fp + s2 + ex2_f]


    ldsh    [%fp + s1 + ex2_c + 2 * 2], %o0 !'s2.e = s1.c[2]'
    st      %o0, [%fp + s2 + ex2_e]


end_main
```

which results in the following code being generated:

```
0x10658 <main>:         save  %sp, -144, %sp
0x1065c <main+4>:       ld    [ %fp + -20 ], %o0
0x10660 <main+8>:       stb   %o0, [ %fp + -28 ]
0x10664 <main+12>:      ldsh  [ %fp + -12 ], %o0
0x10668 <main+16>:      st    %o0, [ %fp + -32 ]
0x1066c <main+20>:      mov   1, %g1
0x10670 <main+24>:      ta    0
```

Notice that in comparison to array access, structure access is always as efficient as simple variable access. In the case of structures, it is the assembler that has to compute the offsets from the origin of the structure. This is done at assembly time, not during program execution. Structure elements, or fields, cannot be accessed by a variable index, whereas array elements can.

6.6.1   Nested Structures

Nested structures do not present any additional problem. Consider the following:

```
struct date {
  char day, month;
  short year;
}

struct person {
  char name[21];
  int ss;
  struct date birth, marriage;
  char married, sex;
}

struct date d1, d2;
```

```
    struct person p1, p2;

    d1.day = 13;
    d1.month = 5;
    d1.year = 1967;

    p1.birth = d1;
    p2.marriage.day = 3;
    p1.sex = p2.sex;
```

In assembly language:

```
begin_struct(date)
field(day,1)
field(month,1)
field(year,2)
end_struct(date)

begin_struct(person)
field(name,1,21)
field(ss,4)
field(birth,align_of_date,size_of_date)
field(marriage,align_of_date,size_of_date)
field(married,1)
field(sex,1)
end_struct(person)

local_var
var(d1,align_of_date,size_of_date)
var(d2,align_of_date,size_of_date)
var(p1,align_of_person,size_of_person)
var(p2,align_of_person,size_of_person)

begin_main

mov   13, %o0                    !'d1.day = 13';
stb   %o0, [%fp + d1 + date_day]

mov   5, %o0                     !'d1.month = 5';.
stb   %o0, [%fp + d1 + date_month]

mov   1967, %o0                  !'d1.year = 1967';
sth   %o0, [%fp + d1 + date_year]

ld    [%fp + d1], %o0            !'p1.birth = d1'
```

```
st     %o0, [%fp + p1 + person_birth]
       !'all four bytes will fit into a single register'
mov    3, %o0                    !'p2.marriage.day = 3';
stb    %o0, [%fp + p2 + person_marriage + date_day]

ldub   [%fp + p2 + person_sex], %o0    !'p1.sex = p2.sex';
stb    %o0, [%fp + p1 + person_sex]
```

After processing by m4:

```
!define structure date

date_day = 0
date_month = 1
date_year = 2

       !align_of_date, 2 bytes
       !size_of_date, 4 bytes

!define structure person

person_name = 0
person_ss = 24
person_birth = 28
person_marriage = 32
person_married = 36
person_sex = 37

       !align_of_person, 4 bytes
       !size_of_person, 40 bytes

!local variables
  d1 = -4
  d2 = -8
  p1 = -48
  p2 = -88

.global      main
      .align  4
main:    save   %sp, -184, %sp

mov    13, %o0                   !d1.day = 13;
stb    %o0, [%fp + d1 + date_day]

mov    5, %o0                    !d1.month = 5;.
```

```
        stb    %o0, [%fp + d1 + date_month]

        mov    1967, %o0                !d1.year = 1967;
        sth    %o0, [%fp + d1 + date_year]

        ld     [%fp + d1], %o0           !p1.birth = d1
        st     %o0, [%fp + p1 + person_birth]
               !all four bytes will fit into a single register
        mov    3, %o0                    !p2.marriage.day = 3;
        stb    %o0, [%fp + p2 + person_marriage + date_day]

        ldub   [%fp + p2 + person_sex], %o0    !p1.sex = p2.sex;
        stb    %o0, [%fp + p1 + person_sex]
```

Finally, the loaded version printed by gdb:

```
0x10658 <main>:        save  %sp, -176, %sp
0x1065c <main+4>:      mov   0xd, %o0
0x10660 <main+8>:      stb   %o0, [ %fp + -4 ]
0x10664 <main+12>:     mov   5, %o0
0x10668 <main+16>:     stb   %o0, [ %fp + -3 ]
0x1066c <main+20>:     mov   0x7af, %o0
0x10670 <main+24>:     sth   %o0, [ %fp + -2 ]
0x10674 <main+28>:     ld    [ %fp + -4 ], %o0
0x10678 <main+32>:     st    %o0, [ %fp + -20 ]
0x1067c <main+36>:     mov   3, %o0
0x10680 <main+40>:     stb   %o0, [ %fp + -52 ]
0x10684 <main+44>:     ldub  [ %fp + -47 ], %o0
0x10688 <main+48>:     stb   %o0, [ %fp + -11 ]
```

6.7 Summary

Data storage and access methods for multidimensional arrays and structures were presented. It was shown that there was a computational cost related to array accessing proportional to the number of subscripts involved. It was also shown that providing for arrays with subscripts differing from zero did not increase the array access code. Checking subscript ranges did, however, increase the access time. Code examples of all forms of array access were provided. In conjunction with array access, the need to multiply variables by constants was introduced together with the Booth encoding, which allowed for very efficient shift, add, and subtract code to be written to perform the multiplication, thus avoiding the need to call the multiply routine.

In the case of structures, macros were developed to define field offsets in a manner that allowed for the nesting of structures. It was shown that as in all forms of variable access, strict alignment must be maintained.

6.8   Exercises

6–1 Write a macro to generate the factorial of its argument. For example: `fact(4)` will generate the string "24".

6–2 Why is it to our advantage, in C, to declare arrays with dimensions that are powers of 2?

6–3 Why is it necessary to enclose assembly language comments in single quotes ' ' when using `m4`?

6–4 Write a macro to initialize each element of a two-dimensional automatic array, `a[i][j]`, to

```
a[i][j] = i * 10 + j;
```

6–5 Write a program to initialize an array `a[10][6]` as indicated in Exercise 6-4; then declare an array `b[6][10]` and write a program to transpose the array `a` into `b`. That is

```
b[i][j] = a[j][i];
```

6–6 Given the following C integer array definition:

```
int ary[16][3][4]
```

and its representation in assembly language as

```
define(d1, 16)
define(d2, 3)
define(d3, 4)

var(ary_s, 4, d1 * d2 * d3  * 4)
```

write code to load `ary[i][j][k]` into `%o0` if the subscripts are in registers `%i_r`, `%j_r`, and `%k_r`.

6–7 You are to translate the following C code into assembly language which generates random entries into a three-dimensional array, density, which represents some density function. 4000 random entries are generated and the appropriate elements of the array density are incremented as each number is processed. Then the array is searched for the largest entry, and the value of the entry and its subscripts are stored in `max`, `max_i`, `max_j`, and `max_k`.

```
#define D1 5
#define D2 9
#define D3 14
#define COUNT 4000

main()
{
  int density[D1][D2][D3];

  register int max = 0;        /* maximum density */
  int max_i, max_j, max_k;     /* i,j,k for maximum value */

  register int c;              /* a counter */
  register int r;              /* the random number */
  register int i, j, k;        /* array indices */
  register int *ptr;           /* pointer to clear array */

  for (ptr = **density, c = D1 * D2 * D3; --c >= 0;)
    *ptr++ = 0;                /* clear array to zero */

  for (c = COUNT; --c >= 0;) {  /* start generating entries */
    r = rand();
    i = r % D1;
    r = r / D1;
    j = r % D2;
    r = r / D2;
    k = r % D3;
    density[i][j][k]++;         /* incrementing the cell */
  }
  for(i = D1; --i >= 0;)        /* now search for the largest */
    for(j = D2; --j >= 0;)
      for(k = D3; --k >= 0;)
        if ((r = density[i][j][k]) > max) {
          max = r;              /* store the maximum */
          max_i = i;            /* and its indices */
          max_j = j;
          max_k = k;
        }
}
```

Register variables are to be stored in registers and all other variables kept on the stack. You are to use the cmul macro for the array address calculations. The rand function has no arguments and may be called like `.mul` and `.div` with

```
call       rand
nop
```

The random number will be returned in `%o0`. Use `.div` for division (/) and `.rem` for the remainder (%). Use gdb to print out the maximum value and its indices at the end of your program.

6–8 Construct a magic square of numbers.[1] The magic square consists of an array of numbers from 1 to N $\times$ N arranged in an N by N square so that the sum of each column, of each row, and of each of the main diagonals is identical.

You are to construct a square of size N $\times$ N (where N is defined to be an odd constant in your program) using the method of De La Loubere, described below:

1. Initialize a variable n to 1.

2. Store n in the center cell of the top row of the square.

3. Move to the next cell in a diagonal manner, right one place and up one place. Whenever you go off the top in this manner, go instead to the bottom row. Whenever you step off the right side, go instead to the left column. Increment n and place it in the new cell.

4. When you move to a square that has a number stored in it, move back left one cell and down two. That is, store n into the cell below the last cell you stored a number into.

5. When all cells are filled, stop.

The magic square of size 3 is

```
8    1    6
3    5    7
4    9    2
```

Print out the N x N square by calling `print_row` with arguments, a pointer to the first element of the row, and the constant N.

```c
void print_row ( int * ptr, int n) {
  while (n--)
    printf(" %3i", *ptr++);
  putchar('\n');
  return;
}
```

The C program `print_row` may be compiled to produce the machine code in a file `print_row.o` by the command

---

[1] Adapted from [7].

```
> gcc -g -c print_row.c
```

and then loaded with your assembly language program by

```
>gcc asm.s print_row.o
```

Make sure that your program is written so that it may be used to generate squares of any odd size greater than 1 simply by changing the definition of N in your program. Check in your program that N is odd, exiting otherwise. Run the program with N = 7.

6–9 Declare a **stuct powers** consisting of four fields: a byte to hold an integer, a halfword to hold the square of the integer, a word to hold the cube of the integer, and a pointer to a struct of the type powers. In C such a declaration might be

```
struct powers {
   char one;
   short two;
   int three;
   struct powers * next;
};
```

In your program declare an array of 11 such structs:

```
struct powers num[11];        /* an array of 11 structs */
```

Declare also two pointers to struct powers:

```
register struct powers * head; /* points to list of structs */
register struct powers * ptr; /* points to current struct */
```

and then initialize each **strut**, **num[i]** to

```
ptr = & num[i];            /* get pointer to struct */
ptr->one = i;              /* initialize one to i */
ptr->two = i * i;          /* two to i * i */
ptr->three = ptr->two * i; /* and three to i * i * i */
ptr->next = head;          /* add struct at head of list */
head = ptr;
```

The last two statements link the current struct into the head of a list of such structs. Initialize the structs for $0 <= i <= 10$. Then run down the list by using the pointer next. Each time you move to the next struct, print out the values of the fields one, two, and three:

```
ptr = head;
while (ptr) {
  printf ("%d square = %d, cube = %d\n",
             ptr->one, ptr->two, ptr->three);
  ptr = ptr->next;
}
```

You will need to use gdb to print the values in place of the call to printf shown above.

6–10 Write a program in assembly language to transpose a matrix. You are to declare two matrices:

```
int matrix[7][10];
int trans [10][7];
```
and initialize the first so that:
```
matrix[i][j] = i * 10 + j;
```

Then form the transpose into trans:

```
for(i = 0; i < 7; i++)
  for(j = 0; j < 10; j++)
    trans[j][i] = matrix[i][j];
```

Print out both matrices in gdb. If, for instance, the matrix were located on the stack at -280 wrt the %fp, you could print out the values, one row at a time, by

(gdb) x/10wd $fp −280

repeating the command seven times for each row, you would handle trans similarly. Use pointers whenever you are stepping through an array, element by element. Use cmul for all multiplications by constants.

Chapter 7

SUBROUTINES

7.1 Introduction

In programming there is frequently a need either to repeat a computation or to repeat the computation with different arguments. It is possible to repeat a computation by means of a subroutine. Subroutines may be either open or closed. An open subroutine is handled by the text editor or by the macro preprocessor and is the insertion of the required code whenever it is needed in the program. The `cmul` macro is an example of such an open subroutine. Its arguments are passed in three registers that are given as arguments to the subroutine. A closed subroutine is one in which the code appears only once in the program; whenever it is needed, a jump to the code is executed, and when it completes, a return is made to the instruction occurring after the jump instruction. Arguments to closed subroutines may be placed in registers or on the stack.

A subroutine also allows you to debug code once and then to be sure that all future instantiations of the code will be correct. The use of subroutines provide for the control of errors; it is also the basis for structured programming.

A subroutine represents a specialized instruction written by the programmer. As such, there is a general concept that execution of the subroutine should not change the state of the machine, except possibly for the condition codes. That means that any registers that the subroutine uses must first be saved and then restored after the subroutine completes execution. Arguments to subroutines are normally considered to be local variables of the subroutine, and the subroutine is free to change them. This is not always the case, however; `cmul`, for example, does not change the contents of the multiplicand register.

7.2   Open Subroutines

The macro we defined in Chapter 6 to handle multiplication by constants:

```
cmul(%r0, 603, %g1, %r1)
```

is called an *open subroutine*. Whenever we need to multiply by a constant we
simply expand the macro code for the multiplication. This is very efficient; in fact,
we went to great pains in writing cmul to ensure efficient code tailored to every
possible initial condition and use of registers. The cmul open subroutine to multiply
%r0 by 100 is

```
cmul(%r0, 100, %g1, %r0)
```

and expands into:

```
                    !start open coded multiply for
                    !%r0 = %r0 * 100, using %g1 as temp
        sll     %r0,   2, %r0
        sll     %r0,   3, %g1
        sub     %r0, %g1, %r0
        sll     %g1,   2, %g1
        add     %r0, %g1, %r0

                    ! end open coded multiply
```

Open subroutines are very efficient in execution, with no wasted instructions. Arguments to open subroutines are very flexible and can be as general as the programmer
wishes to make them. However, every time we need to multiply and insert the open
subroutine, we generate additional code. If the open subroutine results in a short
section of code, this is probably the correct thing to do. If the code generated were
longer, simply repeating the code every time it was needed would begin to take up
a lot of memory. It might be better to write code once, as a closed subroutine,
and to *branch* to the code when needed, and then to *return* to the next instruction
immediately after the branch.

7.3   Register Saving

Almost any computation will involve the use of registers. Historically, registers that
were needed for use by a subroutine were pushed onto the stack at the beginning
of the subroutine and were subsequently popped from the stack at the end of the
subroutine execution. This required execution of a number of instructions and involved considerable execution time overhead, especially as programmers were being
encouraged to break up their programs into many simple subroutines. Recent developments in computer architecture have related to special instructions for saving
registers. In one example this took the form of an instruction that would examine

a*register save mask* that would indicate, by bits that were set, which registers were to be saved. Such an instruction is typical of a *Complex Instruction Set Computer* (CISC), and although these instructions reduced the instruction count, they did little to reduce the time to save the registers.

The SPARC architecture provides for a register file with a mapping register that indicates the active registers. Typically, 128 registers are provided, with the programmer having access to the eight global registers, and only 24 of the mapped registers at any one time. The `save` instruction changes the register mapping so that new registers are provided. A similar instruction, `restore`, restores the register mapping on subroutine return.

The 32 registers are divided into four groups: *in*, *local*, *out*, and *general*. The eight general registers, %g0–%g7, are not mapped and are global to all subroutines. The in registers are used to pass arguments to closed subroutines, the local registers are for a subroutine's local variables, and the out registers are used to pass arguments to subroutines that are called by the current subroutine. The in, local, and out registers are mapped. When the `save` instruction is executed the out registers become the in registers, and a new set of local and out registers is provided. The mapping pointer into the register file is changed by 16 registers (see Figure 7.1).

In Figure 7.2 is shown a register set. The current register set is indicated by the current window pointer, "CWP," a machine register. The last free register set is marked by the window invalid bit, in the "WIM," another machine register. Each register set contains 16 general registers; the number of register sets is implementation dependent. After a `save` instruction is executed, the situation represented by the diagram on the right in Figure 7.2 results. Note that there are really 8×16 hardware registers and that the set selected is controlled by the `cwp`. When the `save` instruction is executed, the prior subroutine's register contents remain unchanged until a restore instruction is executed, resetting the `cwp`.

If a further five subroutine calls are made without any returns, the situation in Figure 7.3 exists. The out registers being used are from the invalid register window marked by the `wim` bit. If an additional subroutine call is made, a hardware trap occurs. The hardware trap is discussed fully in Chapter 12, but its effect is to move the 16 registers from window set seven onto the stack where the stack pointer of register window seven is pointing. The trap handler may use the local registers of the invalid window. The `cwp` and `wim` pointers are moved as shown in Figure 7.2. Note also that the pointer to the location of the saved registers on the stack is in register window set six and is accessible when it is needed to restore register window set seven. Of course, if another subroutine call is made, register set six will be written to the stack where the stack pointer, located in register set five, is pointing.

Saves and restores can be made in a range of six without window overflows or underflows occurring. Although this is efficient for general programming, it would become expensive if deeply nested recursive subroutine calls were frequently made.

Register window mapping explains the process by which the stack pointer becomes the frame pointer. The stack pointer is register %o6, which, after a `save`,

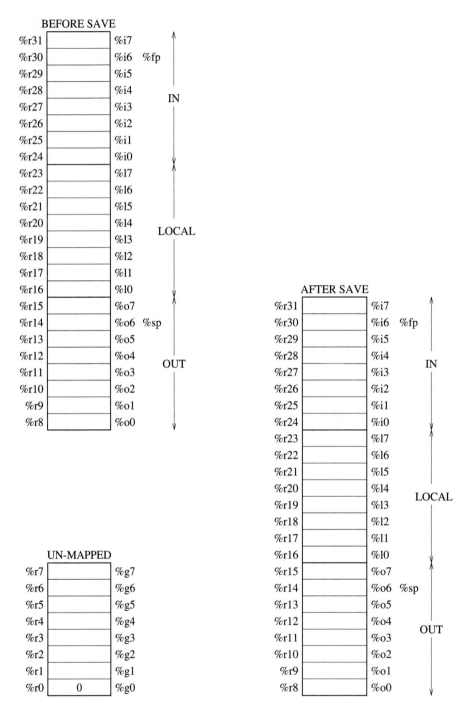

Figure 7.1: A Register Set

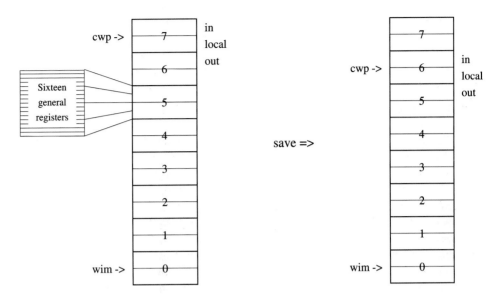

Figure 7.2: Register Sets

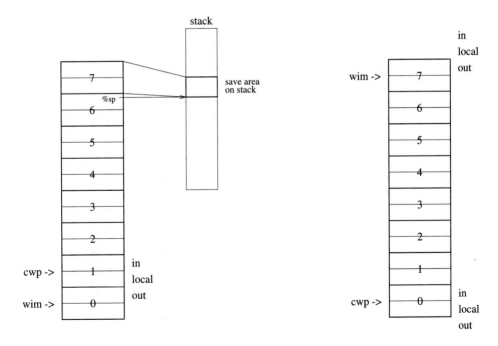

Figure 7.3: Window Overflow

becomes %i6, the frame pointer. The save and restore instructions are both also
add instructions. However, the source registers are always from the current register
set, and the destination register is always in the new register set. Thus

```
save %sp, -64, %sp
```

subtracts 64 from the current stack pointer but stores the result into the new
stack pointer, leaving the old stack pointer contents unchanged. After the save
instruction is executed, the old, unchanged stack pointer becomes the new frame
pointer.

The restore instruction, which we have not used until now, restores the register
window set. On doing this a register window can underflow if the cwp is moved to
the wim. When this happens the window trap routine restores the registers from
the stack and resets the pointers.

As we mentioned, the restore instruction is also an add instruction and is
frequently used as the final add instruction in a subroutine, as we will presently
see.

7.4   Subroutine Linkage

To branch to the first instruction of a subroutine, a ba instruction might be used;
unfortunately, if it is used there is no way of returning to the point where the subroutine was called. The SPARC architecture supports two instructions for linking
to subroutines. Both instructions may be used to store the address of the instruction that called the subroutine into register %o7. As the instruction following the
instruction that called the subroutine will also be executed, the return from a subroutine is to %o7 + 8, which is the address of the next instruction to be executed
in the main program. If a save instruction is executed at the beginning of the
subroutine, the contents of %o7 will become the contents of %i7 and the return will
have to be to %i7 + 8.

If the subroutine name is known at assembly time, the call instruction may
be used to link to a subroutine. The call instruction has as operand the label at
the entry to the subroutine and transfers control to that address. It also stores
the current value of the program counter, %pc, into %o7. Like any instruction that
changes the %pc, the call instruction is always followed by a delay slot instruction.
The call instruction delay instruction may not be annulled.

If the address of the subroutine is computed, it must be loaded into a register.
If this is done, the jmpl instruction is used to call the subroutine. Like most
other instructions, the jmpl instruction has two source arguments and a destination
register. The source may be a register and a constant or two registers. The address
of the subroutine is the sum of the register contents or the sum of the register and
the constant. It is this address to which the transfer takes place. Like all branching
instructions, jmpl is followed by a delay slot instruction. The address of the jmpl

instruction is stored in the destination register. Thus, to call a subroutine whose address is in register %o0 storing the return address into %o7, we would write:

```
jmpl    %o0, %o7
```

The assembler recognizes

```
call    %o0
```

as

```
jmpl    %o0, %o7
```

and you may use the `call` for both types of subroutine calls.

The return from a subroutine also makes use of the `jmpl` instruction. In this case we need to return to %i7 + 8 and the assembler recognizes the mnemonic `ret` for:

```
jmpl    %i7 + 8, %g0
```

Notice that in the case of the return the program counter is stored into %g0, which is discarded.

The call to a subroutine is then

```
        call    subr
        nop
```

and at the entry of the subroutine

```
subr:   save    %sp, ... %sp
```

with the return

```
        ret
        restore
```

The restore instruction is normally used to fill the delay slot of the `ret` instruction. The ret instruction, of course, is expanded by the assembler to

```
        jmpl    %i7 + 8, %g0
        restore
```

7.5 Arguments to Subroutines

Arguments to subroutines can follow in-line after the call instruction, be on the stack, or be located in registers. If the addresses and values of all arguments are known at assembly time, as in Fortran, the arguments may follow the `call` instruction. For example, a Fortran routine to add two numbers, 3 and 4, together would be called by

```
        call    add
        nop
        3
        4
```

and handled by the following subroutine code:

```
add:    save    %sp, -64, %sp
        ld      [%i7 + 8], %i0    !first argument
        ld      [%i7 + 12], %i1   !second argument
        add     %i1, %i0, %i0
        jmpl    %i7 + 16, %g0     !return address
        restore
```

Note that the return is to `%i7 + 16` jumping over the arguments. This type of argument passing is very efficient (one of the reasons why Fortran is efficient) but is limited. Recursive calls are not possible, nor is it possible to compute any of the arguments.

Placing argument onto the stack is, on the other hand, very general but time consuming. Each argument must be stored on the stack before the subroutine may be called. However, passing arguments on the stack allows us complete flexibility to compute arguments, pass any number of arguments, and support recursive calls. Placing arguments on the stack is frequently wasteful, as the arguments are generally computed in registers and are moved from there to the stack. Then, when the subroutine is called, the first thing to be done inside the subroutine is to move the arguments from the stack back into registers. The SPARC architecture recognizes this problem and allows the first six arguments simply to be placed in the out registers where the subroutine may access them directly. Unfortunately, only six out registers are available, as `%o6` is the stack pointer and `%o7` will be the return address if we call another subroutine. After execution of a `save` instruction the arguments will be in the first six in registers, `%i0`–`%i5`.

The convention established in the SPARC architecture is to pass the first six arguments in the first six out registers, `%o0`–`%o5`, with any additional arguments placed on the stack. However, space is always reserved for the first six arguments on the stack even though they are not there. In fact, the space is reserved even if there are no arguments at all. Each argument occupies one word on the stack or register, so that when passing byte arguments to subroutines, they must be moved into word quantities before passing.

The arguments are located on the stack, after the 64 bytes reserved for register window saving. However, immediately after the 64 bytes reserved for register window saving, there is a pointer to where a structure may be returned (this is discussed in Section 7.7). Thus, the structure return pointer will be at `%sp + 64` and the first argument, if it were on the stack, at `%sp + 68`.

Before arguments may be placed onto the stack, space on the stack must be provided by subtracting the number of bytes required for arguments from the stack pointer. As we will always provide for a structure pointer and six arguments we may as well create this space when we execute the **save** instruction on subroutine entry

```
.global subroutine_name
```

subroutine_name:
```
            save    %sp, -(64 + 4 + 24 + local) & -8, %sp
```

This **save** instruction will provide:

- Space for saving the register window set, if necessary

- A structure pointer

- A place to save six arguments

- Space for any local variables

keeping the stack pointer aligned on a doubleword boundary.

If we had a subroutine **vector** with local variables

```
vector ()
{
        int a, b;
        char d;
```

then the **save** instruction would be

```
        save    %sp, -(64 + 4 + 24 + 9) & -8, %sp
```

resulting in 104 bytes being subtracted from the stack pointer. The resulting stack is shown in Figure 7.4 and the stack shown again in Figure 7.5 to emphasise the difference between the current frame, referenced by %fp, and the beginning of the frame to be set up by a subroutine called by this subroutine, referenced by %sp.

Notice that the structure pointer and space to save the called routine's arguments are all accessed positively with respect to the stack pointer, whereas the local variables are accessed negatively with respect to the frame pointer. The subroutine's arguments are located positively with respect to the frame pointer.

The region of the stack addressed with respect to the frame pointer, %fp, relates to the called subroutine's local variables and incoming arguments. The region of the stack addressed with respect to the stack pointer, %sp, is the start of a call frame for any subroutine called by the current subroutine. As long as the two regions do not overlap, they are quite distinct. Of course, the two regions are both created at the same time with execution of the **save** instruction as the subroutine is entered. Note also that the register saving region for the called subroutine is addressed by the stack pointer, %sp, as if the called subroutine's registers are saved. Then the frame pointer, %fp, will be written out onto the stack in the save area and will not be available to restore the registers when an eventual window underflow occurs; the stack pointer, %sp, is saved in the next register window set and is always present when a register underflow occurs.

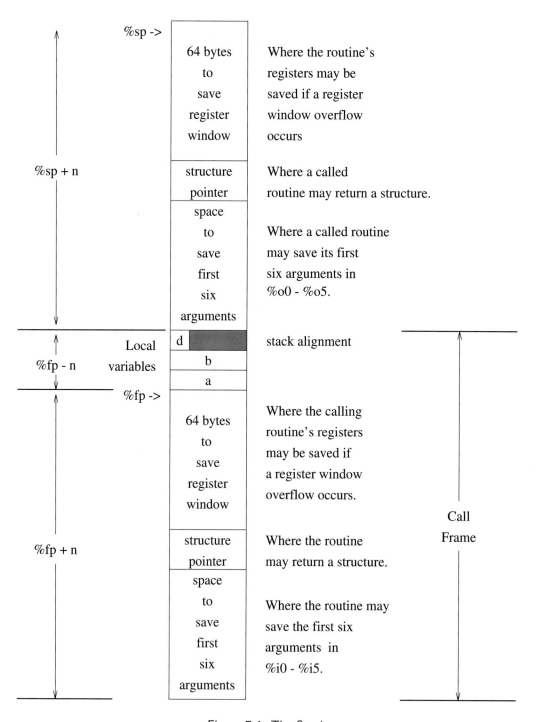

Figure 7.4: The Stack

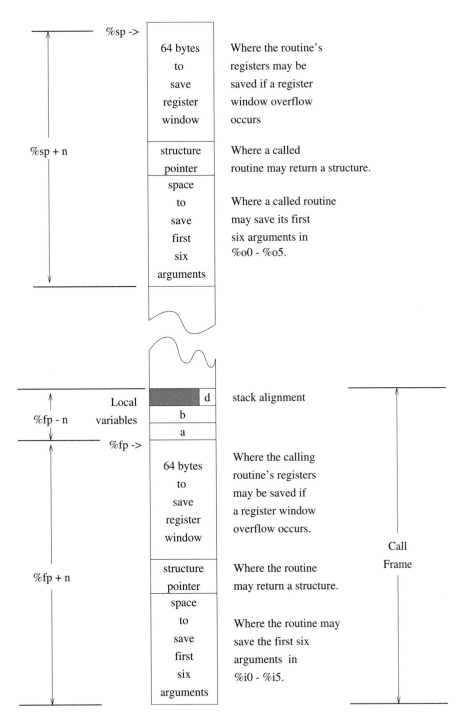

Figure 7.5: The Stack Showing Two Frames

The argument offsets are logically defined as

```
define(struct_s, 64)
define(arg1_s, 68)
define(arg2-s, 72)
define(arg3-s, 76)
define(arg4_s, 80)
define(arg5_s, 84)
define(arg6_s, 88)
```

or in terms of a macro `argd`:

```
define(struct_s, 64)
define(arg_d,'eval($1 * 4 + struct_s)')
```

and we might define a subroutine entry macro, `begin_fn`, to be called after the definition of local variables with the name of the subroutine as argument:

```
'subroutine entry, $1 = subroutine name'
define(begin_fn,'.global        $1
        .align  4
$1:     save    %sp, eval(
                    -92 ifdef('last_sym',' last_sym') & -8), %sp
undefine('last_sym')define('name_of_funct',$1)')
```

and a macro to end the subroutine with optional arguments to the `restore` instruction:

```
'subroutine end, return sequence,
 $1 = subroutine name, $2 = src1, $3 = src2 or imm, $4 = dst'
define(end_fn,'ifelse(
$1,name_of_funct,'ret      restore' 'ifelse($2,,,  '$2, $3, $4')'
        .type   name_of_funct',' #function
        .size   name_of_funct',' . - name_of_funct''undefine(
        'name_of_funct'),'errprint(
    '    subroutine begin does not match end')')')')
```

7.6 Examples

Let us look at an example. We will express the algorithm in C as follows:

```c
int example(int a, int b, char c)
{
  int x, y;
  short ary[128];

  register int i, j;

  x = a + b;
  i = c + 64;
  ary[i] = c + a;
  y = x * a;
  j = x + i;
  return x + y;
}
```

Its translation into assembly languages is

```
include(../macro_defs.m)

        define(a_r, i0)         '! a_r in %i0'
        define(b_r, i1)         '! b_r in %i1'
        define(c_r, i2)         '! c_r in %i2'

        local_var
        var(x_s, 4)
        var(y_s, 4)
        var(ary_s, 2, 128 * 2)

        define(i_r, l0)         '!i_r in %l0'
        define(j_r, l1)         '!j_r in %l1'

        begin_fn(example)

        add     %a_r, %b_r, %o0         '!x = a + b'
        st      %o0, [%fp + x_s]

        add     %c_r, 64, %i_r          '!i = c + 64'

        add     %a_r, %c_r, %o0         '!ary[i] = c + a'
        sll     %i_r, 1, %o1
        add     %fp, ary_s, %o2
```

```
    sth      %o0, [%o1 + %o2]

    ld       [%fp + x_s], %o0            '!y = x * a'
    call     .mul
    mov      %a_r, %o1
    st       %o0, [%fp + y_s]

    ld       [%fp + x_s], %o0            '!j = x + i'
    add      %i_r, %o0, %j_r

    ld       [%fp + x_s], %o0            '!return x + y'
    ld       [%fp + y_s], %o1
    ret
    restore %o0, %o1, %o0
```

This code expands into

```
                     ! a_r in %i0
                     ! b_r in %i1
                     ! c_r in %i2


    !local variables
    x_s = -4
    y_s = -8
    ary_s = -264


                     !i_r in %l0
                     !j_r in %l1


    .global example
    .align   4
example:         save     %sp, -360, %sp


    add      %i0, %i1, %o0              !x = a + b
    st       %o0, [%fp + x_s]

    add      %i2, 64, %l0              !i = c + 64

    add      %i0, %i2, %o0              !ary[i] = c + a
    sll      %l0, 1, %o1
    add      %fp, ary_s, %o2
    sth      %o0, [%o1 + %o2]

    ld       [%fp + x_s], %o0          !y = x * a
```

```
call    .mul
mov     %i0, %o1
st      %o0, [%fp + y_s]

ld      [%fp + x_s], %o0        !j = x + i
add     %l0, %o0, %l1

ld      [%fp + x_s], %o0        !return x + y
ld      [%fp + y_s], %o1
ret
restore %o0, %o1, %o0
```

with the resultant code loaded into memory:

```
0x106f8 <example>:       save  %sp, -360, %sp
0x106fc <example+4>:     add   %i0, %i1, %o0
0x10700 <example+8>:     st    %o0, [ %fp + -4 ]
0x10704 <example+12>:    add   %i2, 0x40, %l0
0x10708 <example+16>:    add   %i0, %i2, %o0
0x1070c <example+20>:    sll   %l0, 1, %o1
0x10710 <example+24>:    add   %fp, -264, %o2
0x10714 <example+28>:    sth   %o0, [ %o1 + %o2 ]
0x10718 <example+32>:    ld    [ %fp + -4 ], %o0
0x1071c <example+36>:    call  0x208f0 <.mul>
0x10720 <example+40>:    mov   %i0, %o1
0x10724 <example+44>:    st    %o0, [ %fp + -8 ]
0x10728 <example+48>:    ld    [ %fp + -4 ], %o0
0x1072c <example+52>:    add   %l0, %o0, %l1
0x10730 <example+56>:    ld    [ %fp + -4 ], %o0
0x10734 <example+60>:    ld    [ %fp + -8 ], %o1
0x10738 <example+64>:    ret
0x1073c <example+68>:    restore  %o0, %o1, %o0
```

7.7 Return Values

Subroutines that return a value are called *functions*. All subroutines in C are functions with the option that they do not have to return a value, and even if they do, it may be ignored by the caller. The value returned by a function or subroutine is always returned in register %o0, that is, %o0 of the calling program. If a save instruction has been executed, %o0 will be %i0 before the restore instruction is executed.

Functions in C may also return a structure. Consider the following:

```
struct point {
  int x, y;
};

struct point zero()
{
  struct point local;

  local.x = 0;
  local.y = 0;

  return local;
}

main()
{

  struct point x1, x2;


  x1 = zero();
  x2 = zero();
}
```

The function **zero** returns a structure. When the call is made to **zero**, a pointer to where the returned struct is to be stored is passed to the function at **%sp + 64**, the address of x1 in the example given above. The equivalent C code in assembly language would appear as

```
        include(../macro_defs.m)

        begin_struct(point)
        field(x, 4)
        field(y, 4)
        end_struct(point)

        local_var
        var(local, align_of_point, size_of_point)

        begin_fn(zero)

        ld      [%fp + struct_s], %o0    '!get pointer into %o0'
        st      %g0, [%o0 + point_x]
```

```
st        %g0, [%o0 + point_y]

end_fn(zero)

local_var
var(x1, align_of_point, size_of_point)

begin_main

add       %fp, x1, %o0
call      zero
st        %o0, [%sp + struct_s]

end_main
```

Returning structures in this manner is a little dangerous, as some called subroutine is assuming that a pointer exists to a region of memory of sufficient size to receive data. If anything were to go wrong, such a situation would be difficult to debug. To prevent such an occurrence, an additional handshaking procedure has been specified. The caller, expecting to receive data, passes a pointer to the beginning of the storage in %sp + struct_s and places the number of bytes of storage expected to be received, in-line, in the program after the delay slot of the call to the subroutine. The called function must check that the size of data it is about to return is the same as the constant stored in %i7 + 8. If not, it is not to return any data. For example:

```
local_var
var(x1, align_of_point, size_of_point)
var(x2, align_of_point, size_of_point)

begin_main

add    %fp, x1, %o0              !'pointer to x1'
call   zero
st     %o0, [%sp + struct_s]
.word size_of_point            !'size of x1'

end_main
```

The called routine first checks the size of the data to be returned and, if correct, returns the data using the pointer in %fp + struct_s. The return from the subroutine must, however, be to %i7 + 12, skipping over the data size:

```
begin_struct(point)
field(x, 4)
field(y, 4)
end_struct(point)

local_var
var(local, align_of_point, size_of_point)

begin_fn(zero)
```

```
    ld    [%i7 + 8], %o1           !'expected size in bytes'
    cmp   %o1, 8
    bne   return                   !'do nothing'
    ld    [%fp + struct_s], %o0    !'get pointer into %o0'
    st    %g0, [%o0 + point_x]
    st    %g0, [%o0 + point_y]
return:
    jmpl  %i7 + 12, %g0            !'jump over unimp'
    restore
```

If a subroutine is called that is expected to return a structure but does not do so, then the normal return will be to the size of data. Such a small constant appears to be an unimplemented instruction that will cause a system error.

7.8 Subroutines with Many Arguments

Arguments beyond the sixth are passed on the stack. In this case we must first make room for the arguments by subtracting from the stack pointer. For example, to call a subroutine with eight arguments:

```
    foo(1, 2, 3, 4, 5, 6, 7, 8)
```

which returns the sum:

```
    int foo (int a1, int a2, int a3, int a4,
             int a5, int a6, int a7, int a8)
    {
       return a1 + a2 + a3 + a4 + a5 + a6 + a7 + a8;
    }
```

We first have to make room for arguments seven and eight, which will go on the stack

```
    add    %sp, -2 * 4 & -8, %sp
```

making sure that the stack is still doubleword aligned. The seventh and eighth arguments will go onto the stack at `%sp + 92` and at `%sp + 96`, respectively. We can then pass the arguments as follows:

```
add    %sp, -2 * 4 & -8, %sp    '!make space on stack'
mov    8, %o0                   '!load args in reverse'
st     %o0, [%sp + arg_d(8)]
mov    7, %o0
st     %o0, [%sp + arg_d(7)]
mov    6, %o5
mov    5, %o4
mov    4, %o3
mov    3, %o2
mov    2, %o1
call   foo
mov    1, %o0
sub    %sp, -2 * 4 & -8, %sp    '!release space on stack'
```

The stack when `foo` has been entered is shown in Figure 7.6. Inside `foo` the arguments may be accessed by

```
define(a8_s, arg_d(8))
define(a7_s, arg_d(7))
define(a6_r, i5)
define(a5_r, i4)
define(a4_r, i3)
define(a3_r, i2)
define(a2_r, i1)
define(a1_r, i0)


begin_fn(foo)
ld     [%fp + a8_s], %o0    !'the eighth argument'
ld     [%fp + a7_s], %o1    !'the seventh argument'
add    %o0, %o1, %o0
add    %a6_r, %o0, %o0      !'the sixth argument'
add    %a5_r, %o0, %o0      !'the fifth argument'
add    %a4_r, %o0, %o0      !'the fourth argument'
add    %a3_r, %o0, %o0      !'the third argument'
add    %a2_r, %o0, %o0      !'the second argument'
end_fn(foo, %a1_r, %o0, %o0) !'the first argument'
```

7.9 Leaf Subroutines

A leaf routine is one that does not call any other routines. If one considers a program structure to be like a tree with the main function at the root and functions that are

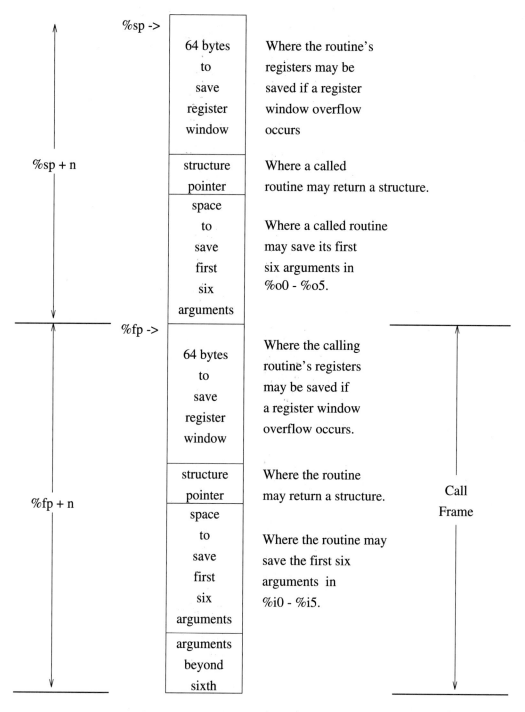

Figure 7.6: The Stack with Additional Arguments

called by the main function the first branches, the leaves of the tree are subroutines that do not call any other subroutines. These subroutines are called *leaf routines*, and a simplified calling protocol may be employed for them. For a leaf routine the register usage is restricted as follows: The leaf routine may only use the first six out registers and the global registers %g0 and %g1. A leaf routine does not execute either a save or a restore instruction but simply uses the calling subroutine's register set, observing the restrictions listed above. The elimination of register saving and restoring makes calling a leaf routine very efficient. The .mul routine is a leaf routine.

A leaf routine is called in the same manner as a regular subroutine, placing the return address into %o7. As a save instruction is not executed, the return address for a leaf routine is %o7 + 8, **not** %i7 +8. The assembler recognizes

```
retl
```

for

```
        jmpl    %o7 + 8, %g0
```

which is the correct return.

The subroutine foo should have been written as a leaf routine:

```
define(a8_s, arg_d(8))
define(a7_s, arg_d(7))
define(a6_r, o5)                        !'args in out regs'
define(a5_r, o4)
define(a4_r, o3)
define(a3_r, o2)
define(a2_r, o1)
define(a1_r, o0)
define(sum_r, o0)


    .global foo
foo:

    add     %a2_r, %a1_r, %o0 !'o0 = first + second'
    add     %a3_r, %o0, %o0   !'o0 += third argument'
    add     %a4_r, %o0, %o0   !'o0 += fourth argument'
    add     %a5_r, %o0, %o0   !'o0 += fifth argument'
    add     %a6_r, %o0, %o0   !'o0 += sixth argument'
    ld      [%sp + a7_s], %o1 !'the seventh argument'
                              !'wrt the stack pointer'
    add     %o1, %o0, %o0     !'o0 += seventh argument'
    ld      [%sp + a8_s], %o1 !'the eighth argument'
    retl
    add     %o1, %o0, %o0     !'o0 += eighth argument'
```

7.10   Pointers as Arguments to Subroutines

Let us now consider passing pointers as arguments to subroutines. Consider the classic problem of the swap function; pointers must be passed to the function in order for the values to be swapped:

```
swap(int *x, int *y)
{
    int temp;

    temp = *x;
    *x = *y;
    *y = temp;
}
```

and the assembler code:

```
include(../macro_defs.m)

local_var
var(x_s, 4)                          '!int x'
var(y_s, 4)                          '!int y'

begin_main
mov      5, %o0
st       %o0, [%fp + x_s]            '!x = 5'
mov      7, %o0
st       %o0, [%fp + y_s]            '!y = 7'
add      %fp, x_s, %o0               '!pointer to x in %o0'
call     swap
add      %fp, y_s, %o1               '!pointer to y in %o1'
end_main


         .global swap                '! a leaf routine'
swap:    ld       [%o0], %o2         '!%o2 = x'
         ld       [%o1], %o3         '!%o3 = y'
         st       %o2, [%o1]
         retl
         st       %o3, [%o0]
```

Notice how the addresses of x and y are computed and passed as function arguments for swap. Note also how swap picks up the values by means of the pointers. If we had stored x and y in registers in the main function, we would have a problem when we tried to call swap, as registers have no address. We would have to move the data onto the stack before the call and then back into the registers:

```
            include(../macro_defs.m)

            define(x_r, 10)              '!x in %10'
            define(y_r, 11)              '!y in %11'

            local_var
            var(x_s, 4)          '!where x may be stored on stack'
            var(y_s, 4)          '!where y may be stored on stack'

            begin_main
            mov     5, %x_r              '!x = 5'
            mov     7, %y_r              '!y = 7'
                                         '!now call swap'
            st      %x_r, [%fp + x_s] '!place args on stack'
            st      %y_r, [%fp + y_s]
            add     %fp, x_s, %o0        '!pass -> to args on stack'
            call    swap
            add     %fp, y_s, %o1
            ld      [%fp + x_s], %x_r '!move values to registers'
            ld      [%fp + y_s], %y_r
            end_main

            .global swap                 '! a leaf routine'
  swap:     ld      [%o0], %o2           '!%o2 = x'
            ld      [%o1], %o3           '!%o3 = y'
            st      %o2, [%o1]
            retl
            st      %o3, [%o0]
```

7.11   Summary

Subroutines simplify writing code, provide structure, and help to control programming errors. Subroutines may be expanded as open subroutines or as closed subroutines. In the case of closed subroutines the SPARC architecture provides a
register-saving mechanism to facilitate subroutine linkages. A stack frame was for-
mally introduced as storage for the registers, arguments, local variables, and the
return address. The return of both scalars and structures was discussed. Passing
arguments both in registers and on the stack was presented. The chapter concluded
with the introduction of leaf routines in which a call frame was not necessary, allowing the subroutine to access only the out registers.

7.12   Exercises

7–1 Write an open subroutine, using m4, to perform the absolute value function. The macro is to have one or two arguments, both register names. The absolute value of the first argument is to be returned in the last argument.

7–2 Write an open subroutine, using m4, to return the factorial of the first argument in the second argument. Both arguments are register names.

7–3 Write a main function to call a factorial function, which computes the factorial iteratively.

7–4 Write a main function to call a multiply function that, in turn, calls an add function, the appropriate number of times, to perform multiplication. The add function should be a leaf routine.

7–5 Write a function, max, with eight integer arguments. Max is to return the maximum of the eight arguments. Write a main function to call max with eight arguments.

7–6 Write a function, max, with up to eight integer arguments and an argument count as the first argument. This function is to return the maximum of the given arguments. Write a main function to call max with seven arguments.

7–7 Write a main function with 10 local integer variables, a1–a10, assigned on the stack. To each variable assign its square (i.e., to a3 assign 9, to a4 assign 16, etc). Then return the sum of the squares.

7–8 Translate the following functions into assembly language:

```
struct point {
   int x, y;
};

struct quad {
   struct point p1, p2, p3, p4;
};


struct quad box(int size)
{
   struct quad s;

   s.p1.x = size;
   s.p1.y = size;
   s.p2.x = -size;
   s.p2.y = size;
```

```
    s.p3.x = -size;
    s.p3.y = -size;
    s.p4.x = size;
    s.p4.y = -size;

    return s;
}

int area (struct quad *b)
{
    return (b->p1.x - b->p3.x) * (b->p1.y - b->p3.y);
}

main()
{

    struct quad s1, s2;
    int a1, a2;
    s1 = box(3);
    s2 = box(5);
    a1 = area(&s1);
    a2 = area(&s2);
}
```

7–9 Write a function that computes the factorial recursively and a main function to call the factorial function.

7–10 Translate the following C function into assembly language, making use of macros defined in `macro_defs.m`:

```
fn(int a, b, c, d, e, f, g)
{
    register int x, y, z;

    x = a + b * c;
    y = d - e / f;
    z = power(x, g);
    z = z >= 0 ? z : -z;
    return x + y + z;
}
```

7–11 Translate the following C function into assembly language, making use of macros defined in `macro_defs.m`. Translate each C statement into assembly language, filling as many delay slots as possible.

```
blah(int a, b, c, d)
{
  register int i, x, y;
  int ary[10];

  x = a + c * d;
  if (x > b)
    y = baz(a / b);
  for (i = 10; --i >= 0;)
    ary[i] = foo(--x, b);
  return x + a;
}
```

7–12 Translate the following two functions, quick and swap, into assembly language; quick will be a regular subroutine and swap will be a leaf routine. When they are written, link them with the C main function. If your assembly code is in as6.m, running m4 will produce a as6.s, which may then be assembled and linked with the C main program by

```
%gcc -g main.c as6.s -o as6
```

The functions and main program are defined as follows:

```
int ary[] = {1, -5, 27, 3, 5, 0, 89, -100, 28, 0, 25};
#define LENGTH sizeof(ary) / sizeof(int)

void swap (int * a, int f, int t)
{
  register int temp;

  temp = *(a + f);
  *(a + f) = *(a + t);
  *(a + t) = temp;
}

void quick(int * ary, int left, int right)
{
  register int i, last, pivot;

  if (left >= right)
    return;
  swap (ary, left, (left + right) >> 1);
  pivot = *(ary + (last = left));
  for (i = left + 1; i <= right; i++)
```

```
      if (*(ary + i) < pivot)
         swap (ary, ++last, i);
   swap (ary, left, last);
   quick (ary, left, last - 1);
   quick (ary, last + 1, right);
}

main()
{
   register int i, *ptr;

   for (i = 0, ptr = ary; i < LENGTH; i++)
      printf("%5d", *ptr++);
   putchar('\n');
   quick(ary, 0, LENGTH - 1);
   for (i = 0, ptr = ary; i < LENGTH; i++)
      printf("%5d", *ptr++);
   putchar('\n');
}
```

The quick function calls a function swap to exchange elements of the array being
sorted. You will at once see that quick calls itself recursively. An executable version
of the program produces the following output:

```
% a.out
      1   -5   27    3    5    0   89 -100   28    0   25
   -100   -5    0    0    1    3    5   25   27   28   89
```

7–13 A recursive definition of the binomial coefficient, nCr, is as follows:

```
int binomial(int n, int r) {
   if (r <  0 || r > n || n < 1 )
      return 0;
   if (n == 1)
      return 1;
   else
      return binomial(n - 1, r) + binomial(n - 1, r - 1 );
}
```

Translate the function above into assembly language and write a main function in
C to call it, making use of command line arguments:

```
% a.out 10 5
10C5 is 252
```

How many calls to binomial does the call binomial(10, 5) result in?

7–14 There is a monastery in Hanoi where monks are engaged in moving gold disks from one post to another; when they finish the world will come to an end. There are 64 disks and each disk is slightly smaller than the next, so that they form a sequence. There are three posts: one where the disks all start off, one to which they are going, and a spare. There is a rule that a larger disk may never be put on top of a smaller disk. The following algorithm generates the move sequence. You are to translate it into assembly language. Set breakpoints in your program to perform the output `printf` statements and run the program for a tower three high.

```c
void hanoi (int height, int from, int to, int spare)
{
  if (height == 1) {
    printf("move from %c to %c\n", from, to);
    return;
  }
  else {
    hanoi(height - 1, from, spare, to);
    printf("move from %c to %c\n", from, to);
    hanoi(height - 1, spare, to, from);
   return;
}}
main(){
  hanoi(3, 'a', 'b', 'c');
  return 0;
}
```

Chapter 8

MACHINE INSTRUCTIONS

8.1 Introduction

Instructions on the SPARC architecture occupy one word, 32 bits. Once an instruction is fetched, all the information needed to execute the instruction is encoded in the instruction word. It is important that decoding the instruction format be simple and direct if we are to execute an instruction each machine cycle. Of the 32 bits of an instruction word, 8 are reserved to specify the instruction. The need to specify three registers, each requiring 5 bits of address, leaves us with 9 bits. One of these bits is needed to specify whether there is a second source register or an immediate constant. The remaining 8 bits are then either combined, with the 5 needed to specify the second source register, to give 13 bits for a signed immediate constant or to provide an additional 8 bits to specify floating-point instructions.

8.2 Instruction Decode

Instructions are specified by two fields, op, which is two bits long, and op3, which is six bits long. The op field is decoded as follows:

op	Instruction Class
00	Branch instructions
01	call instruction
10	Format Three instructions
11	Format Three instructions

Format Three instructions are then decoded using the least significant bit of op with the remaining six bits of the op3 field.

231

8.3   Format Three Instructions

The majority of instructions executed are Format Three instructions and their
format is shown in Figure 8.1.

op	rd	op3	rs1	0		rs2
31 30 29	25 24	19 18	14 13 12		5 4	0

op	rd	op3	rs1	1	signed immediate 13 bit constant
31 30 29	25 24	19 18	14 13 12		0

Figure 8.1: Format Three Instructions

The `op` field is in bits 30 and 31, denoted by `<31:30>`. This is followed by five bits
needed to specify the destination register, bits `<29:25>`. This field is followed by
the `op3` field, which specifies the instruction, bits `<24:19>`. The first source register
is specified by bits `<18:14>`. Format Three instructions then have two options, a
constant or a second source register. The next bit, bit `<13>`, indicates whether a
constant or a second source register is to be specified. If the bit is a one, a constant
fills the remainder of the instruction word, bits `<12:0>`. If bit `<13>` is a zero, the
second source register is specified by bits `<4:0>`. A constant is specified by bits
`<12:0>`, allowing for a signed 13-bit constant. Such a constant provides for a range
from −4096 to 4095. While small constants are used in programs frequently, it is in
specifying stack offsets for variables that the constant is most needed. With 13 bits,
we may access variables with offsets up to 4096 with respect to the frame pointer.
If the field were any smaller, we would run into trouble in functions having more
bytes of local storage than allowed by the size of the constant. As the 32-bit word is
fairly standard at present, it can be seen that any change in the number of registers,
requiring more bits to specify the register, or in the number of instructions, will
cause an impact on the size of constant or the number of registers that may be
specified. This is of serious concern to computer architects.

An example of a Format Three instruction is

```
sub     %l0, 5, %o0
```

For the `sub` instruction the `op3` field is 000100, `%l0` is register 10000, and `%o0` is
register 01000:

10	01000	000100	10000	1	0000000000101
op	%rd = 8	op3	%rs1 = 16	i = 1	signed constant = 5

The instruction may be written as the hexadecimal constant 0x90242005.

The program segment

```
include(macro_defs.m)

local_var

var(ary, 4, 20)
var(res, 4)

begin_fn(main)
```

add	%fp, 2 << 2, %o0	!%l0 = ary[2]
ld	[%o0 + ary], %l0	
sub	%l0, 5, %o0	
add	%i0, %l0, %o0	!res = arg1 + ary[2]
st	%l0, [%fp + res]	

appears in the machine as

```
0x10658 <main>:        save  %sp, -120, %sp
0x1065c <main+4>:      add   %fp, 8, %o0
0x10660 <main+8>:      ld    [ %o0 + -20 ], %l0
0x10664 <main+12>:     sub   %l0, 5, %o0
0x10668 <main+16>:     add   %i0, %l0, %o0
0x1066c <main+20>:     st    %l0, [ %fp + -24 ]
```

and in hex as

```
(gdb) x/xw main
0x10658 <main>:        0x9de3bf88
(gdb)
0x1065c <main+4>:      0x9007a008
(gdb)
0x10660 <main+8>:      0xe0023fec
(gdb)
0x10664 <main+12>:     0x90242005
(gdb)
0x10668 <main+16>:     0x90060010
(gdb)
0x1066c <main+20>:     0xe027bfe8
(gdb)
```

These are all Format Three instructions and may be decoded as follows:

```
op=10,dst=01110,op3=111100,rs1=01110,i=1,1111110001000
op=10,dst=01000,op3=000000,rs1=11110,i=1,0000000001100
op=11,dst=10000,op3=000000,rs1=01000,i=1,1111111101100
op=10,dst=01000,op3=000100,rs1=10000,i=1,0000000000101
op=10,dst=01000,op3=000000,rs1=11000,i=0 ... rs2=10000
op=11,dst=10000,op3=000100,rs1=11110,i=1,1111111101000
```

Seven bits can specify $2^7 = 128$ instructions; these are listed in numeric order. Unimplemented instructions are listed as *unimp*. Many of the instructions will not be familiar, but these relate to the operating system, which are described in Chapter 13. User mode instructions are defined in Appendix D, while the reader is referred to the SPARC architecture manual [22] for the definition of instructions reserved for operating system use.

There are two tables, the first with op = 10 and the second with op = 11. The instructions with op = 10 are three-address register instructions, such as add and sub. The instructions with op = 11 are the load/store instructions, all of which refer to memory.

Examination of the table of the three address register instructions will reveal that a pattern exists to simplify decoding. The first eight instructions:

000000	add
000001	and
000010	or
000011	xor
000100	sub
000101	andn
000110	orn
000111	xnor

are decoded usng the three least significant bits. The "x" versions, addx and subx, have bit three set. The "cc" versions, addcc, subcc, etc., have bit four set. The "xcc" instructions have both bits set. This pattern changes when the most significant bit, bit five, is set, to allow for the remaining instructions to be decoded on a one-to-one basis. The floating-point instructions are all encoded within the fpop1 and fpop2 instructions, which are described in Chapter 11.

The Format Three instructions are as follows:

op = 10, Format Three Instructions			
op3	Instruction	op3	Instruction
000000	add	100000	taddcc
000001	and	100001	tsubcc
000010	or	100010	taddcctv
000011	xor	100011	tsubcctv
000100	sub	100100	mulscc
000101	andn	100101	sll
000110	orn	100110	srl
000111	xnor	100111	sra
001000	addx	101000	rdy
001001	*unimp*	101001	rdpsr
001010	*unimp*	101010	rdwim
001011	*unimp*	101011	rdtbr
001100	subx	101100	*unimp*
001101	*unimp*	101101	*unimp*
001110	*unimp*	101110	*unimp*
001111	*unimp*	101111	*unimp*
010000	addcc	110000	wry
010001	andcc	110001	wrpsr
010010	orcc	110010	wrwim
010011	xorcc	110011	wrtbr
010100	subcc	110100	fpop1
010101	andncc	110101	fpop2
010110	orncc	110110	cpop1
010111	xnorcc	110111	cpop2
011000	addxcc	111000	jmpl
011001	*unimp*	111001	rett
011010	*unimp*	111010	ticc
011011	*unimp*	111011	iflush
011100	subxcc	111100	save
011101	*unimp*	111101	restore
011110	*unimp*	111110	*unimp*
011111	*unimp*	111111	*unimp*

op = 11, Format Three Instructions			
op3	Instruction	op3	Instruction
000000	ld	100000	ldf
000001	ldub	100001	ldfsr
000010	lduh	100010	*unimp*
000011	ldd	100011	lddf
000100	st	100100	stf
000101	stb	100101	stfsr
000110	sth	100110	stdfq
000111	std	100111	stdf
001000	*unimp*	101000	*unimp*
001001	ldsb	101001	*unimp*
001010	ldsh	101010	*unimp*
001011	*unimp*	101011	*unimp*
001100	*unimp*	101100	*unimp*
001101	ldstub	101101	*unimp*
001110	*unimp*	101110	*unimp*
001111	swap	101111	*unimp*
010000	lda	110000	ldc
010001	lduba	110001	ldcsr
010010	lduha	110010	*unimp*
010011	ldda	110011	lddc
010100	sta	110100	stc
010101	stba	110101	stcsr
010110	stha	110110	stdcq
010111	stda	110111	stdc
011000	*unimp*	111000	*unimp*
011001	ldsba	111001	*unimp*
011010	ldsha	111010	*unimp*
011011	*unimp*	111011	*unimp*
011100	*unimp*	111100	*unimp*
011101	ldstuba	111101	*unimp*
011110	*unimp*	111110	*unimp*
011111	swapa	111111	*unimp*

8.4 Format One Instruction: The `call` Instruction

There is only one Format One instruction, the `call` instruction. The `call` instruction must be able to transfer control to any location in the 32-bit address space. The target of such a transfer must be an instruction and thus word aligned. A word-aligned address has the least significant two bits, both zero, so that any possible target address contains 30 bits of information. A Format One `call` instruction contains an `op` field of `<01>` followed by 30 bits of address.

Although the actual address could be stored, right-shifted two bits, in the instruction, it is the address relative to the current contents of the program counter that is stored. Why is this? Programs are frequently moved around in memory, requiring that the addresses of all labels be changed. Thus all the subroutines addressed in `call` instructions would also have to be changed. However, if the address were stored relative to the program counter, no matter where the program was moved in memory the relative address would remain the same. Program counter relative addresses do not have to be changed when a program is moved in memory and can be computed by the assembler at assembly time.

Thus, the address to which control is transferred by a `call` instruction is

```
npc = (instruction<29:0> << 2) + pc
```

and the rather tight loop:

```
        .global main
main:   call    main
        nop
```

appears in the machine as

```
0x10658 <main>:         call   0x10658 <main>
0x1065c <main+4>:       nop
```

with the machine instruction at main:

```
(gdb) x/xw main
0x10658 <main>:    0x40000000
```

8.5 Format Two Instructions

Format Two instructions are the branch instructions and an instruction we have not discussed previously, the `sethi` instruction. The `op` field for Format Two instructions is `00`.

op	a	cond	op2	displacement 22

31 30 29 28   25 24   22 21   0

Figure 8.2: Branch Instructions

8.5.1   Branch Instructions

The format of the branch instruction is shown in Figure 8.2.

In this case, the target of the branch is also stored relative to the program counter right-shifted two bits. However, in the case of a branch, only 22 bits are available for the displacement, so that the target of branches may be only $\pm 2^{21}$ instructions from the program counter. Branches to targets that are further away than $+8,388,604$, $-8,388,608$ bytes will be discussed shortly. However, such long branches are rare, almost always involve jumping out of a function and generally require special handling. The remaining fields of the Format Two instructions specify the type of branch. The op2 = 010 field specifies an integer condition code branch, the type of branch we have been using. If the branch is to be annulled, the a bit is set. Finally, the condition under which branching is to occur, the four-bit field cond, is specified as follows:

as	cond	Unconditional Branches	Condition Codes
ba	1000	Branch always, goto	1
bn	0000	Branch never	0

as	cond	Signed Arithmetic Branches	Mach. Instr.	Condition Codes
bl	0011	Branch on less than zero		N xor V
ble	0010	Branch on less or equal to zero		Z or (N xor V)
be	0001	Branch on equal to zero	bz	Z
bne	1001	Branch on not equal to zero	bnz	not Z
bge	1011	Branch on greater or equal to zero		not (N xor V)
bg	1010	Branch on greater than zero		not (Z or (N xor V))

as	cond	Unsigned Arithmetic Branches	Mach. Instr.	Condition Codes
blu	0101	Branch on less, unsigned	bcs	C
bleu	0100	Branch on less or equal, unsigned		C or Z
be	0001	Branch on zero	bz	Z
bne	1001	Branch on not zero	bnz	not Z
bgeu	1101	Branch on greater or equal, unsigned	bcc	not C
bgu	1100	Branch on greater, unsigned		not (C or Z)

as	cond	Condition Code Tests
bneg	0110	Branch on N = 1
bpos	1110	Branch on N = 0
bz	0001	Branch on Z = 1
bnz	1001	Branch on Z = 0
bcs	0101	Branch on C = 1, carry out of register
bcc	1101	Branch on C = 0
bvs	0111	Branch on V = 1, overflow
bvc	1111	Branch on V = 0

An example of a program with `call` and branch instructions is

```
include(macro_defs.m)
/* call function add to add two positive integer arguments */
include(../macro_defs.m)


        begin_main

        mov     4, %o0
        mov     3, %o1
        call    add
        nop


        end_main
/* leaf routine which adds by decrementing its second argument to
zero while incrementing its first argument */
        .global add
add:
        b       test
        nop
```

```
loop:    sub     %o1, 1, %o1
         add     %o0, 1, %o0
test:    tst     %o1
         bg      loop
         nop


         retl
         nop
```

This program may be contorted to remove `nop` instructions and to reduce the add function loop to the minimum necessary three instructions:

```
include(../macro_defs.m)
        begin_main

        mov     4, %o0
        call    add
        mov     3, %o1


        end_main


        .global add
add:
        b       test
        tst     %o1
loop:   subcc   %o1,1,%o1
test:   bg,a    loop
        add     %o0,1,%o0
        retl
        nop
```

The code loaded into memory for the second version of the program is

```
0x10670 <main>:        save  %sp, -96, %sp
0x10674 <main+4>:      mov   4, %o0
0x10678 <main+8>:      call  0x10688 <add>
0x1067c <main+12>:     mov   3, %o1
0x10680 <main+16>:     ret
0x10684 <main+20>:     restore
0x10688 <add>:         b     0x10694 <test>
0x1068c <add+4>:       tst   %o1
0x10690 <loop>:        deccc %o1
0x10694 <test>:        bg,a  0x10690 <loop>
0x10698 <test+4>:      inc   %o0
0x1069c <test+8>:      retl
```

As hex constants:

```
(gdb) x/xw &main
0x10670 <main>:          0x9de3bfa0
0x10674 <main+4>:        0x90102004
0x10678 <main+8>:        0x40000004
0x1067c <main+12>:       0x92102003
0x10680 <main+16>:       0x81c7e008
0x10684 <main+20>:       0x81e80000
0x10688 <add>:           0x10800003
0x1068c <add+4>:         0x80900009
0x10690 <loop>:          0x92a26001
0x10694 <test>:          0x34bfffff
0x10698 <test+4>:        0x90022001
0x1069c <test+8>:        0x81c3e008
0x106a0 <test+12>:       0x01000000
```

These hex constants may then be decoded as

```
0x9de3bfa0: op=10,dst=01110,op3=111100,rs1=01110,i=1,1111110100000
0x90102004: op=10,dst=01000,op3=000010,rs1=00000,i=1,0000000000100
0x40000004: op=01,disp30=000000000000000000000000000100
0x92102003: op=10,dst=01001,op3=000010,rs1=00000,i=1,0000000000011
0x81c7e008: op=10,dst=00000,op3=111000,rs1=11111,i=1,0000000001000
0x81e80000: op=10,dst=00000,op3=111101,rs1=00000,i=0 ... rs2=00000
0x10800003: op=00,rd=01000,op2=010,disp22=0000000000000000000011
0x80900009: op=10,dst=00000,op3=010010,rs1=00000,i=0 ... rs2=01001
0x92a26001: op=10,dst=01001,op3=010100,rs1=01001,i=1,0000000000001
0x34bfffff: op=00,rd=11010,op2=010,disp22=1111111111111111111111
0x90022001: op=10,dst=01000,op3=000000,rs1=01000,i=1,0000000000001
0x81c3e008: op=10,dst=00000,op3=111000,rs1=01111,i=1,0000000001000
0x01000000: op=00,rd=00000,op2=100,disp22=0000000000000000000000
```

Note the call instruction at main+8 to add:

```
0x2298 <main+8>:         0x40000004
```

The constant four indicates that the program should branch four instructions ahead. The unconditional branch instruction at add:

```
0x22a8 <add>:            0x10800003
```

decodes as a "branch always" instruction to three instructions ahead. At test is the bg,a instruction:

```
0x34bfffff op=00,rd=11010,op2=010,disp22=1111111111111111111111
```

from which we can decode the rd field as bg with the annul bit on. The target in this case is -1, or one instruction back.

8.5.2   Loading 32-Bit Constants

So far we have worked only with small constants in our programs. We were limited by the 13-bit signed-immediate field of the instruction. It would be difficult to load constants that were longer than 13 bits. If we need a larger constant, we will need to use the `sethi` instruction, which will load the high 22 bits of a register while clearing the low 10 bits. This instruction is also a Format Two instruction except that the annul bit field and the `cond` fields are combined to form a five-bit `rd` field, the register into which the constant is to be loaded. The format is shown in Figure 8.3.

op	rd	100	22 bit immediate
31 30 29 25 24 22 21			0

Figure 8.3: The `sethi` Instruction

Note that the `op2` field is 100 to distinguish this instruction from the integer branch instructions, which have `op2` of 010. The execution of this instruction results in the 22-bit immediate constant being loaded into the left-hand 22 bits of the register `rd` with the low 10 bits of the register cleared to zero. To load a 32-bit constant, two instructions are needed, a `sethi` to load the high 22 bits, followed by an `or` instruction to "or" in the low 10 bits of the constant. For example, to load register %o0 with 0x30cf0034, we would write

```
sethi   0x30cf0034 >> 10, %o0
or      %o0, 0x30cf0034 & 0x3ff, %o0
```

Notice that the 32-bit constant must be right-shifted 10 bits to become the first argument to `sethi` and that only the low 10 bits of the 32-bit constant form the second operand to the `or` instruction. The machine provides two arithmetic operators to do this, %hi and %lo. The % symbols have, in this case, nothing to do with register names but simply distinguish the symbols from other symbols the assembler has to process. These two operators, %hi and %lo, are just like other arithmetic operators, +-*/, etc. They are defined as follows:

```
%hi(x),   x >> 10
%lo(x),   x & 0x3ff
```

Thus, to load the constant 0x30cf0034 into register %o0, we could write

```
sethi   %hi(0x30cf0034), %o0
or      %o0, %lo(0x30cf0034), %o0
```

We frequently load constants in this manner in assembly language and the assembler `as` expands `set x, reg` into

```
sethi   %hi(x), reg
or      reg, %lo(x), reg
```

so that we might simply have written

```
set      0x30cf0034, %o0
```

and obtained the necessary `sethi` and `or` instructions to load the constant into the register.

8.6   Summary

The machine instruction formats were presented in this chapter with a discussion of the need for simple decoding schemes that would allow for parallel access of operands. Branch instructions and their encoding were presented. The `sethi` instruction was introduced to set the high 22 bits of a register, allowing for the loading of 32-bit constants.

The instruction formats are shown in Figure 8.4.

Format 1, call

0 1	displacement 30

31 30   0

Format 2, branch

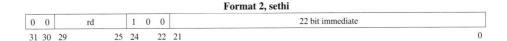

31 30 29 28   25 24   22 21   0

Format 2, sethi

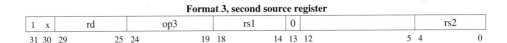

31 30 29   25 24   22 21   0

Format 3, second source register

1 x	rd	op3	rs1	0		rs2

31 30 29   25 24   19 18   14 13 12   5 4   0

Format 3, immediate constant

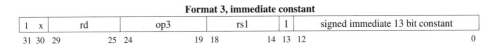

31 30 29   25 24   19 18   14 13 12   0

Figure 8.4: Instruction Formats

8.7   Exercises

8–1 Translate the following machine language into assembly language:

```
(gdb) x/x &main
0x2290 <main>:              0x9de3bfc0
(gdb)
0x2294 <main+4>:            0x90820012
(gdb)
0x2298 <main+8>:            0x1cbff75a
(gdb)
0x229c <main+12>:           0x92100012
(gdb)
0x22a0 <main+16>:           0x81c7e008
(gdb)
0x22a4 <main+20>:           0x81e80000
```

8–2 Translate the following assembly language program into machine code:

```
        .global main
main:   save    %sp, -64, %sp
        mov     4, %l1
        mov     -2, %l2
loop:   addcc   %l1, %l2, %l0
        ble,a   loop
        sub     %l1, 1, %l1

        mov     1, %g1
        ta      0
```

8–3 Write a macro to translate an eight-digit hexadecimal number into a binary Format Three instruction representation as shown on page 234.

8–4 Write a macro to translate an eight-digit hexadecimal number into a binary Format Two instruction representation.

8–5 The code that follows is a recursive factorial routine. Translate the first **three** instructions of the function (i.e., the cmp through the mov instruction) into machine language in the form of hexadecimal constants.

```
        def_reg(n, i0)
        def_reg(ret, o0)

        begin_fn(fact)
```

```
        cmp     %n_r, 1             !'if (n <= 1) return 1'
        ble     return
        mov     1, %ret_r
                                    !'return n * fact(n-1)'
        call    fact
        sub     %n_r, 1, %o0

        call    .mul
        mov     %n_r, %o1

return: end_fn(fact, %g0, %ret_r, %ret_r)
```

Chapter 9

EXTERNAL DATA AND TEXT

9.1 Introduction

So far we have made use of memory only to store our programs for execution and to store our local variables and function arguments. In this chapter we discuss external and static variables. Local variables, stored on the stack, may be addressed relative to the frame pointer; however, to make those same variables available to other functions would be very difficult. As the value of static variables in functions does not change between function calls, they may not be stored on the stack where storage is created and released between function calls. To solve this problem, external and static variables are stored in memory much like the program. Their addresses are then made available to all functions that need to access the variables.

9.2 External Variables

There are two classes of external variables, those that are to be initialized to values other than zero and those that are to be initialized to zero. When a program is loaded into memory, the program text, initialized variables, and zero-initialized variables are loaded into different regions of memory. These regions are called sections, and each generally starts on a 0x2000 byte boundary. In this way, memory protection may be applied differently to different parts of the program. Program text is normally *read-only*, meaning that if we attempt to store something into this area of memory, we will get a system trap. The other two regions are *read-write*, meaning that all accesses are valid. These three regions of memory are called the text, data, and bss sections, respectively. The text section is where the program and any read-only data are located. The text section is where the assembler puts things unless we tell it otherwise; the data section is for initialized data; and the bss

247

(block starting symbol) section is for zero-initialized data. The assembler may be told to assemble into these different sections by the pseudo-ops, section ".text", section ".data", and section ".bss". So far, of course, we have no reason to load anything but program text into memory. When the program is loaded into memory, the text and data sections are loaded first into low memory. Then space is zeroed for the bss section. These three sections are all at low memory, leaving the stack at high memory. The stack has nothing to do with program sections. In C, all the external variables that are not specifically initialized are located in the bss section. The first 0x2000 bytes of memory are reserved for the operating system and are not used by regular programs. A diagram indicating memory assignment is shown in Figure 9.1.

The assembler maintains three location counters, one for each of the text, data, and bss sections. When we issue the section changing pseudo-ops, we change the location counter that the assembler will use until the next section-changing pseudo-op. At the end of the assembly, code and data for each of the three sections are gathered together. Each of the three location counters starts at zero and increases as instructions and data are assembled.

9.3   The text Section

Code in the text section is loaded into memory starting at memory location 0x2000. Although this might seem a problem (we have always assembled the code assuming that the first instruction would be at location zero), examination of any of the programs we have written so far will reveal that they are position independent. That is, the program text may be loaded into memory starting at any location and it will execute correctly. Why is this? Obviously, all the instructions that only reference registers are position independent. The call and branch instructions' operands are all program counter relative, so that if the program is moved in memory, the program counter will be changed by the identical amount.

It is only the symbol main that is needed by the operating system in order that the program starting address may be found. This information is made available by use of the .global pseudo-op, which tells the operating system that this address is to be made available for other program sections.

9.4   The data Section

The data section is used primarily for initialized data. There are a number of assembler pseudo-ops for initializing the section. For example, .word indicates that the list of comma-separated expressions is to be evaluated and each loaded as a 32-bit constant:

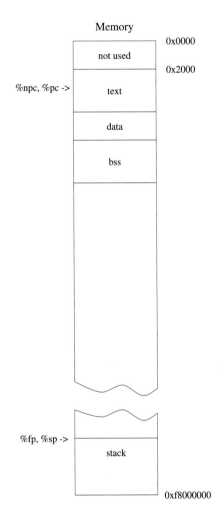

Figure 9.1: Sections in Memory

```
.section ".data"
.word    3, 3 * 3, 3 * 3 >> 3
```

would result in the following three constants in the data section:

```
3
9
1
```

Normally, such data are labeled so that they may be referred to in a program:

```
        .section ".data"
i_m:    .word    3
j_m:    .word    9
k_m:    .word    3 + 9
```

Notice that we have appended _m to all the memory addresses to distinguish these from stack offsets, (_s) and registers (_r).

To access such data, we need to load them into a register, or to store the contents of a register into addressed memory. To do this we need to load the 32-bit addresses of the data into a register before the data may be accessed. For example, to compute k = i + j, we would write:

```
        include(macro_defs.m)
        .section ".data"
        .global i_m, j_m, k_m
i_m:    .word    3
j_m:    .word    9
k_m:    .word    3 + 9

        .section ".text"
        define(i_r, 10)
        define(j_r, 11)
        define(k_r, 12)
        begin_main

        sethi    %hi(i_m), %o0
        ld       [%o0 + %lo(i_m)], %i_r
        sethi    %hi(j_m), %o0
        ld       [%o0 + %lo(j_m)], %j_r
        add      %i_r, %j_r, %o0
        set      k_m, %o1
        st       %o0, [%o1]
```

In this program we have, for the first time, labels appearing as operands to instructions as arguments of %hi and %lo. Until now, all labels have been as the target of branch and call instructions, in which case the program relative offset was stored in the instruction. The labels, addresses appearing as arguments to %hi and %lo, are to be the actual machine addresses when the program is loaded into memory. These addresses are not known until the program is loaded into memory, when a process of relocation occurs in which all the addresses are corrected so that the instructions have the correct operands. This places restrictions on the operands to %hi and %lo. The arguments may only be a label plus or minus a constant. The same restriction, of course, applies to set.

We may also initialize bytes and halfwords:

```
.half    3
.byte    7
```

If we simply need space and are not concerned with its initialization, we may use the .skip pseudo-op which only advances the location counter a specified number of bytes, thus providing space. For example:

```
ary:    .skip   4 * 100
```

will provide space for a 100-word uninitialized array, ary.

Note that external data must be aligned in memory. In the case of external data, it is the assembler that provides the correct alignment by changing the contents of the location counter. The .align pseudo-op provides for this:

```
.align   n
```

The .align pseudo-op ensures that the location counter, the address where the next data will be assigned, will be evenly divisible by n. If the value of the location counter is not evenly divisible by n (so as to produce no remainder), the .align pseudo-op will increase the value of the location counter until it is evenly divisible by n. If we are not sure that the alignment is correct, we need to use an .align 4 before any word data, an .align 2 before any halfword data, and an .align 8 before any doubleword data. Thus, if the first data word in the following example were assembled into location zero

```
a:      .word    3
b:      .byte    5
        .align   2
c:      .half    5
d:      .byte    6
        .align   4
e:      .word    17
```

the variable b will be at location four, the variable c at six, d at eight, and e at 12. Byte data are always aligned.

If we have read-only initialized data, these may be loaded into the text section. The data must, of course, be placed in the text section, where it will not be mistaken for program text and executed. Placing the data before or after any function is generally fine.

If the variables are true externals, that is, variables whose names are to be made available to other independently assembled program sections, the variables names must be declared global, using the `.global` pseudo-op:

```
        .global buf_size
buf_size:       .word   0x1000
```

If the name is to be available only to functions defined in the same file as the data definitions, external static in C, the `.global` declaration is not needed.

9.4.1 ASCII Data

We frequently make use of ASCII codes in programs. The assembler recognizes a character enclosed in double quotes "" to indicate that we want the ASCII code for that character. For example, to load the string `"hello"` into five consecutive bytes of memory, we could write it as

```
        .byte   150, 145, 154, 154, 157
```

but more clearly as

```
        .byte   "h", "e", "l", "l", "o"
```

The use of single characters is normally restricted to constants in instructions:

```
        add     %o0, "a" - "A", %o0      !convert to lowercase
```

The definition of strings is handled more directly by two other pseudo-ops, `ascii` and `asciz`. These two pseudo-ops take a string enclosed in quotes, assembling the ASCII codes for each character into successive bytes of memory. We could write the string initialization for "hello" as

```
        .ascii  "hello"
```

There are two ways of indicating the end of a string, by marking it with a zero byte, \0, or by giving the length of the string in bytes. C uses the first method, marking all strings with a byte containing a zero. Thus, our string "hello" should have an additional byte:

```
        .ascii  "hello"
        .byte   0
```

This can be achieved using the `.asciz` pseudo-op. The `.asciz` pseudo-op appends a zero byte to the end of its string argument.

```
        .asciz  "hello"
```

would generate the same zero-byte-terminated string.

Strings are frequently read-only, as in format strings. Consider the classic C program:

```
main()
{
  printf("hello, world\n");
}
```

This translates into assembly language as

```
        include(macro_defs.m)
        .global printf

fmt:    .asciz  "hello, world\n"

        .align  4
        begin_main
        sethi   %hi(fmt), %o0

        call    printf
        or      %o0, %lo(fmt), %o0

        end_main
```

Notice that the string is in the text section and is thus read-only. This program may be run from the shell producing output. The symbol `printf` is a global defined in some other code that will be loaded with our program and the addresses modified appropriately.

9.5 Pointers

When we needed pointers to variables stored on the stack we had to compute the pointer. For example, to pass a pointer to a local variable x, defined by its stack offset x_s, we would have written

```
        add     %fp, x_s, %o0
```

For external data we would use **set** instead:

```
        set     x_m, %o0
```

This synthetic instruction **set**, of course, expands into

```
        sethi   %hi(x_m), %o0
        or      %o0, %lo(x_m), %o0
```

An external array of pointers is fairly straightforward. The equivalent to the C declaration:

```
        char *month[] = {"jan", "feb", "mar", "apr", "may",
"jun", "jul", "aug", "sep", "oct", "nov", "dec"};
```

would be

```
        .align  4
        .global month
month:  .word   jan_m, feb_m, mar_m, apr_m, may_m, jun_m
        .word   jul_m, aug_m, sep_m, oct_m, nov_m, dec_m

jan_m:  .asciz  "jan"
feb_m:  .asciz  "feb"
mar_m:  .asciz  "mar"
apr_m:  .asciz  "apr"
may_m:  .asciz  "may"
jun_m:  .asciz  "jun"
jul_m:  .asciz  "jul"
aug_m:  .asciz  "aug"
sep_m:  .asciz  "sep"
oct_m:  .asciz  "oct"
nov_m:  .asciz  "nov"
dec_m:  .asciz  "dec"
```

To obtain the pointer to "jul", month[6], in register %o0, we would write

```
        set     month + (6 << 2), %o0
        ld      [%o0], %o0
```

To then obtain the second character, "u," we would write

```
        ldub    [%o0 + 1], %o1
```

9.6   The .bss Section

In the bss section we may only define labels such as

```
        .section ".bss"
        .align  4
ary:    .skip   4 * 100
i_m:    .skip   4
```

These variables will be initialized to zero immediately before the program is executed. Initialized data, other than initialized to zero, may not be in the bss section.

The `.common` pseudo-op may also used to define global labels in the `.bss` section. In the case of `.common`, a size in bytes and an alignment is also specified.

```
.common  ary, 4*100, 4
```

The same line of code may appear in many different source modules and the loader will resolve all references to the same location in memory. This allows many source modules to define a common block of data in the same manner without having to decide which module will actually assign space and which will define global references.

9.7   The switch Statement

We have deferred discussing the switch statement until this chapter, as it requires a table of pointers. Consider the following C switch statement:

```
switch (i + 3) {
case 1: i += 1;
   break;
case 2: i += 2;
   break;
case 15: i += 15;
case 3: i += 3;
   break;
case 4: i += 4;
case 6: i += 6;
   break;
case 5: i += 5;
   break;
default: i--;
   break;
}
```

The expression i + 3 is evaluated and compared to each case label. Control then transfers to the statement of the matching label. If no match occurs, the default case is executed. The labels in a switch statement must be arithmetic constants; when character labels are used, it is the ASCII code that is substituted. The comparison of the switch expression to the case labels is handled as follows:

- The smallest and largest labels are identified.

- The smallest label is subtracted from the switch expression.

- The resulting value is then checked against the range, the largest label – the smallest label.

- This value is used as an index into a pointer array where the pointers are to the switch statement code, the pointers are in switch statement order.

- Missing labels are replaced with a pointer to the next statement after the switch or to the default statement.

- If the switch expression is outside the range, either no code is executed or, if present, execution begins at the default statement.

- The code of the switch statement follows in the same order in which it was written in C to allow for statements that are not followed by **break** statements.

Following this algorithm we would translate the C above code as:

```
define(i_r, 10)            !'variable i'

define(min, 1)             !'smallest label'
define(max, 15)            !'largest label'
define(range, eval(max - min)) !'range'

    add     %i_r, 3, %o0     !'compute switch expression'
    subcc   %o0, min, %o0    !'reduce by min, and comp. to zero'
    blu     default          !'expression too small'
    cmp     %o0, range       !'compare to range'
    bgu     default          !'too large'

    .empty                   !'tell assembler that all is well'
    set     table, %o1       !'jump table'
    sll     %o0, 2, %o0      !'word offset'
    ld      [%o1 + %o0], %o0!'pointer to executable code'
    jmpl    %o0, %g0         !'transfer control'
    nop

table:
    .word L1, L2, L3, L4, L5, L6, L7, L8, L9   !in numeric order
    .word L10, L11, L12, L13, L14, L15

L1:     !'the code also in order of writing'
    ba      end
    add     %i_r, 1, %i_r    !'i++'

L2:
    ba      end
    add     %i_r, 2, %i_r    !'i += 2;'

L15:
```

```
     add      %i_r, 15, %i_r   !'i += 15; note no break;'

L3:
  ba       end
  add      %i_r, 3, %i_r    !'i += 3;'

L4:
  add      %i_r, 4, %i_r    !'i += 4; note no break;'

L6:
  ba       end
  add      %i_r, 6, %i_r    !'i += 6;'

L5:
  ba       end
  add      %i_r, 5, %i_r    !'i += 5;'


L7:                          !all defaults,  these labels could
L8:                          !also have been replaced by the
L9:                          !use of the default label in the
L10:                         !pointer table.
L11:
L12:
L13:
L14:
default:sub   %i_r, 1, %i_r    !'i--;'
end:
```

Although there is greater overhead in a switch statement, compared to a series of if else statements, it becomes increasingly efficient as the number of choices increases. The use of a switch statement becomes questionable when the number of choices is limited or when the labels have a great range. Of course, a compiler might translate such code into the if else form.

9.8 Relocation and Linking with Other Code

An important aspect of any language system designed to implement large projects is its support of separate compilation and assembly; C supports such separate compilation. A C program consists of a number of external objects, variables, and functions. These external objects may be grouped together into any number of separate source files, and each file may be compiled and assembled separately. They are combined by a program called the *loader*, ld; the loader is generally called by the compiler as a final pass. The loader's main task is to resolve the external symbols so that all references to a particular symbol refer to the same location. The scope of symbols in assembly language is the extent of the source file. If symbols are to be made available to other software modules, the .global declaration must be used.

Each assembly source file is processed by the assembler as if its text, data, and bss sections all started at memory location zero. When a program consisting of a single source module is loaded, the text, data, and bss sections will be located in memory at different addresses. This process is referred to as relocation. During assembly, all operands that refer to memory addresses, such as the operands of %hi and %lo, are marked as relocatable with respect to the section in which they are located. The value initially stored in the machine instruction is the value the symbol would have if the section started at zero. When the loader loads each section into memory, it adds the starting address of the section to the fields of the instructions, which have relocatable constants.

The .global declaration in as simply informs the assembler that a symbol is to be made available to the loader. If the global symbol is defined in the file, by appearing as a label, its address will be used to correct all references to it in other modules. If the symbol is not defined in the file (by appearing as a label), the loader will correct the reference to the address once the address is defined in some other file:

Consider the following two source files:

```
/*------------------Source file 1----------------------*/
          include(../macro_defs.m)

          .global c1, c2, a1_m, a2_m
          .global foo, baz

          .section ".data"
a1_m:     .word a2_m

          .section ".text"
          begin_fn(main)

          c1 = 17

          sethi   %hi(a2_m), %o0     !address of a2_m in %o0
          or      %o0, %lo(a2_m), %o0
          ld      [%o0], %o0         !pointer to a1_min %o0
          ld      [%o0], %o0         !what a2_m points to

          mov     c1, %o0
          call    baz
          mov     c2, %o1
```

```
            ret
            restore

foo:        sub     %o0, %o1, %o0
            retl
            nop
```

and the second source file:

```
/*-----------------Source file 2-----------------------*/
            include(../macro_defs.m)

            .global c1, c2, a1_m, a2_m
            .global foo, baz

            .section ".data"
a2_m:           .word a1_m

            c2 = 87


            .section ".text"
            .global second
second: sethi   %hi(a1_m), %o0     !address of a1_min %o0
            or      %o0, %lo(a1_m), %o0
            ld      [%o0], %o0         !pointer to a2_m in %o0
            ld      [%o0], %o0         !what a2_m points to

            mov     c1, %o0
            call    foo
            mov     c2, %o1

            ret
            restore

baz:        add     %o0, %o1, %o0
            retl
            nop
```

There are two global variables, a1_m and a2_m, one defined in each source file. Both variables are initialized to a pointer to the other variable. There are two global constants, c1 and c2, one defined in each source file. Both constants are used in both files.

When loaded into memory, we have

```
(gdb) x/25i main
0x10704 <main>:        save  %sp, -96, %sp
0x10708 <main+4>:      sethi %hi(0x20800), %o0
0x1070c <main+8>:      or  %o0, 0x10c, %o0      ! 0x2090c <a2_m>
0x10710 <main+12>:     ld  [ %o0 ], %o0
0x10714 <main+16>:     ld  [ %o0 ], %o0
0x10718 <main+20>:     mov  0x11, %o0
0x1071c <main+24>:     call  0x1075c <baz>
0x10720 <main+28>:     mov  0x57, %o1
0x10724 <main+32>:     ret
0x10728 <main+36>:     restore
0x1072c <foo>:         sub  %o0, %o1, %o0
0x10730 <foo+4>:       retl
0x10734 <foo+8>:       nop
0x10738 <second>:      sethi %hi(0x20800), %o0
0x1073c <second+4>:    or  %o0, 0x108, %o0      ! 0x20908 <a1_m>
0x10740 <second+8>:    ld  [ %o0 ], %o0
0x10744 <second+12>:   ld  [ %o0 ], %o0
0x10748 <second+16>:   mov  0x11, %o0
0x1074c <second+20>:   call  0x1072c <foo>
0x10750 <second+24>:   mov  0x57, %o1
0x10754 <second+28>:   ret
0x10758 <second+32>:   restore
0x1075c <baz>:         add  %o0, %o1, %o0
0x10760 <baz+4>:       retl
0x10764 <baz+8>:       nop
(gdb)
```

followed by

```
(gdb) x/a &a1_m
0x20908 <a1_m>: 0x2090c <a2_m>
(gdb)
0x2090c <a2_m>: 0x20908 <a1_m>
(gdb)
```

On execution:

```
1: x/i $pc  0x10708 <main+4>:    sethi  %hi(0x20800), %o0
(gdb) si
0x1070c in main ()
1: x/i $pc  0x1070c <main+8>:    or  %o0, 0x10c, %o0
(gdb) display/a $o0
2: /a $o0 = 0x20800 <_etext+65508>
(gdb) si
0x10710 in main ()
```

```
2: /a $oO = 0x2090c <a2_m>
1: x/i $pc   0x10710 <main+12>:   ld   [ %oO ], %oO
(gdb)
0x10714 in main ()
2: /a $oO = 0x20908 <a1_m>
1: x/i $pc   0x10714 <main+16>:   ld   [ %oO ], %oO
(gdb)
0x10718 in main ()
2: /a $oO = 0x2090c <a2_m>
1: x/i $pc   0x10718 <main+20>:   mov  0x11, %oO
```

etc.

9.9 Makefiles

When working with more than one source file, it is very convenient to use `make`. The following makefile combines a C main program, `main.c`, together with an assembly language program with macros, `sincos.m`, to make an executable file `as8`:

```
as8:      main.o sincos.o
          gcc -g main.o sincos.o -lm -o as8
          uptime


main.o:   main.c makefile
          gcc -g -O -c main.c


sincos.o:       sincos.m macro_defs.m makefile
          chmod -f 600 sincos.s
          m4 sincos.m > sincos.s
          chmod   400 sincos.s
          as sincos.s -o sincos.o
cleanup:
          rm -f *.o as8 *~ core
          du
```

If either `main.c` or `makefile` are changed, `main.c` is recompiled to produce machine code in `main.o`. If either of `sincos.m`, or `macro_defs.m`, or `makefile` is changed, the assembly language program is reassembled. To do this, `sincos.s` is made writable; the macro processor `m4` is run on the `.m` file to produce `sincos.s`. This is then made read-only so that it may not be inadvertently changed. Finally, the assembler is called to produce the second machine language file, `sincos.o`. The first line of the makefile checks to see if either of the two object files must be "remade;" if not, it calls `gcc` to link the two files together with debugging information and to search the math library to make the executable file, as8. The system command make will produce as8. The command make cleanup will delete all .o files along with as8 any editor backup files *~ and any core file.[1]

Suffixes may be defined in make to automate much of the detail in a makefile. The next example is a makefile which combines two source files, called global1.m and global2.m, to make an executable a.out file. Note the definition of the new suffix .m and the rules to produce a .o file from a .m source file. In this example the .s files are not produced; instead, the output of m4 is piped directly into as.

```
.m.o :
m4 $< | $(AS) - -o $@


FILES =  global1.m global2.m  macro_defs.m makefile
OBJECTS = global1.o global2.o

a.out:   $(OBJECTS)
         gcc -g $(OBJECTS)

global1.o: macro_defs.m

global2.o: macro_defs.m

print:   $(FILES)
         lpr $?
         touch print

cleanup:
         rm -f *.o a.out *~ core
         du
```

9.10   C Command Line Arguments

As we know, C main programs have arguments:

```
main(int argc, char *argv[])
```

The first is the number of strings given to the shell when the program was executed, and the second argument is a pointer to an array of pointers to the strings. There is also an additional third argument that is a pointer to an array of pointers to strings representing the environment in which the program is executing. We will not consider the environment pointer further.

Consider the following C program, which sums its command line arguments:

---

[1]If make is run in emacs by the M-x compile command, errors may be located with the C-x` command. In the case of errors in sincos.s, the lines will be found, but as the file is read-only, we will be prevented from attempting to make corrections in the .s file instead of in the .m file.

```
int summer(int *acc, char * ptr)
{
  register int n;

  n = atoi(ptr);
  *acc = *acc + n;
}

main(int argc, char *argv[])
{

  int sum = 0;

  while (--argc)
    summer(&sum, *++argv);

  printf("sum is %d\n", sum);
}
```

We could translate the summer function into assembly language and link it with a C main program with the definition of **summer** replaced with a declaration:

```
int summer(int *acc, char *ptr);

main(int argc, char *argv[])
{

  int sum = 0;

  while (--argc)
    summer(&sum, *++argv);

  printf("sum is %d\n", sum);
}
```

with the following assembly language version of **summer**:

```
          include(macro_defs.m)

          define(acc_r, i0)        !pointer to sum in %i0
          define(ptr_r, i1)        !pointer to number string in %i1

          begin_fn(summer)

          call    atoi             !call atoi to convert to number
          mov     %ptr_r, %o0
```

```
        ld      [%acc_r], %o1    !pick up sum
        add     %o0, %o1, %o0    !add new value
        st      %o0, [%acc_r]    !store the result

        end_fn(main)
```

In this case, if we had translated the `summer .m` file into a `.s` file called `summer.s`, we could then call the C compiler to compile the C program and assemble the `.s` program. If the C program were in a file called `sum1.c`:

`%gcc sum1.c summer.s`

would produce the necessary `a.out` file. The use of a makefile would, of course, be cleaner.

We could also translate the main program:

```
        include(macro_defs.m)

        define(argc_r, i0)
        define(argv_r, i1)

        local_var
        var(sum_s, 4)

fmt:    .asciz  "sum is %d\n"    !read-only string for printf

        .align  4
        begin_main

        clr     %o0                  !sum = 0
        st      %o0, [%fp + sum_s]

        b       test                 !while test
        nop

loop:   add     %fp, sum_s, %o0 !&sum
        call    summer
        ld      [%argvr], %o1    !pointer to first number string

test:   subcc   %argc_r, 1, %argc_r !decrement argc
        bg,a    loop
        add     %argv_r, 4, %argv_r !increment argv pointer

        set     fmt, %o0             !print results
        call    printf
```

```
ld      [%fp + sum_s], %o1


end_main
```

Note the handling of argc and argv. If the assembler version of the main program were in sum2.s, the C compiler could be called with

```
%gcc sum2.s summer.s
```

9.11 Summary

The ability to load a 32-bit constant into registers allows us to access external static data stored at fixed memory addresses. The access of external variables was discussed along with the three sections: text, data, and bss. Storage and accessing of strings fits into place in this chapter, in which pointers to the beginning of the string are manipulated. The C switch was introduced, in which pointers into the switch code must be handled.

The linking of individually compiled and assembled sections of code is discussed with the use of makefiles. The chapter concluded with code to handle C command line arguments and provided an example of the use of pointer arrays.

9.12 Exercises

9–1 A piecewise linear approximation has been made to some data representing an input/output relationship. These data are represented as a list of x, y pairs and are represented as follows:

```
        .align  4
diode:  .word   d1
        .half   0, 0
d2:     .word   d3
        .half   20, 5
d5:     .word   d6
        .half   40, 70
d3:     .word   d4
        .half   30, 30
d4:     .word   d5
        .half   35, 60
d1:     .word   d2
        .half   10, 1
d6:     .word   d7
        .half   45, 75
d7:     .word   0
        .half   100, 90
```

Each list element consists of a pointer to the next element on the list, a word, and then two halfwords representing the x, y pair. The list terminates with a NULL or 0. You are to write a program with two word variables, x and y. Given a value of y, you are to return the value for x based on linear interpolation from the data given above. Check that you do not run off the end of the list. Your program should start at the beginning of the list and move down the list comparing y values until you either have a match, in which case you return the element x value, or you have bracketed the y value between two list entries. In this case you should interpolate between the list x values to compute the correct value to return

9–2 This exercise is adapted from *Pascal User Manual and Report* by Jensen and Wirth [10] and relates to recursive procedures. Problems whose definition is naturally recursive lend themselves to recursive solutions. Consider the problem of translating arithmetic expressions into postfix form according to the following syntax:

```
expression ::= <term> {  + | -  <term> }

term ::= factor { * factor }

factor ::= identifier | ( expression )

identifier ::= <letter>
```

Translation is done by constructing an individual conversion function for each of the syntactic constructs, expression, term, and factor. As these syntactic constructs are defined recursively, their corresponding procedures may be activated recursively. Given the expressions

```
(a + b) * (c - d)
a + b * c - d
(a + b) * c - d
a + b * (c - d)
a * a * a * a
b + c * (d + c * a * a) * b + a.
(a period terminates the input)
```

the following program will translate the input to a postfix output:

```
ab+cd-*
abc*+d-
ab+c*d-
abcd-*+
```

```
aa*a*a*
bcdca*a*+*b*+a+

#include <stdio.h>
char ch;

main()
{
  find();
  do {
    expression();
    putchar('\n');
  } while (ch != '.');
}

find()
{
  do
    scanf("%c",&ch);
  while (ch == ' ');
  if (ch == EOF) exit();
}

term();
expression()
{
  char op;

  term();
  while (ch == '+' || ch == '-')
    {
      op = ch;
      find();
      term();
      printf("%c", op);
    }
}

factor();

term()
{
  factor();
  while (ch == '*')
```

```
    {
      find();
      factor();
      printf("*");
    }
}

factor()
{
  if (ch == '(')
    {
      find();
      expression();              /* ch == ')' */
    }
  else
    printf("%c", ch);
  find();
}
```

Translate the functions `expression`, `term`, `factor`, and `find` into assembly language to be called by the function `main` given above. Check your program against the input given above.

9–3 Given that all choices are equally probable, when is a `switch` statement more efficient than a sequence of `if else` statements?

9–4 Write an open subroutine, using `m4`, to perform the absolute value function. The macro is to have one or two arguments; arguments represent register names. The absolute value of the first argument is to be returned in the last argument.

9–5 Given the declaration for an external pointer array `months_m` initialized to point to strings representing the months of the year:

```
jan_m:   .asciz   "January"
feb_m:   .asciz   "February"
mar_m:   .asciz   "March"

  . . .

nov_m:   .asciz   "November"
dec_m:   .asciz   "December"

         .align  4
months_m: .word   jan_m, feb_m, mar_m, apr_m, may_m, jun_m
```

```
.word    jul_m, aug_m, sep_m, oct_m, nov_m, dec_m
```

write an assembly language program to accept as command line arguments three integer strings representing a date in the format mm dd yy. Your program is then to print the date with the name of the month as well as with the correct suffix, for example:

```
% a.out 9 11 90
11th. September, 1990
% a.out 9 21 90
21st. September, 1990
% a.out 9 22 90
22nd. September, 1990
% a.out 9 23 90
23rd. September, 1990
% a.out 9 24 90
24th. September, 1990
% a.out 1 1 0
1st. January, 1900
```

Be careful about the 1st, the 2nd, and the 3rd, distinguishing the 1st from the 11th from the 21st and the 31st. Don't forget the comma after the month. Your program should exit, printing an error message, if three arguments are not given:

usage mm dd yy

You will need to call **atoi** to convert strings to numbers and **printf** to produce the output.

Chapter 10

INPUT/OUTPUT

10.1   Introduction

There are two problems that must be addressed in performing input and output to and from the central processing unit. The first problem relates to matching the speed of the central processing unit to devices that are much slower. If the computer is transferring data over a modem that accepts characters at 300 per second, involving the execution of a single load byte instruction, can the computer execute other useful instructions, other than looping waiting for the next character to become available? If the computer does execute other instructions, how may it then be synchronized with the modem?

The second problem relates to mass data transfers in which bytes of data are either stored into, or written from, sequential memory locations at rates approaching the instruction rate of the computer. If the central processing unit is to execute the necessary load or store instructions, it will have little time to perform other, more useful work.

In this chapter we first discuss the interfacing of hardware devices to the computer and how the problems, outlined above, have been solved. However, we will not have the opportunity to write input/output programs, as this is not possible in a time-sharing environment where input and output are handled by the operating system. Instead, we discuss input/output within the operating system using traps.[1] The reader is referred to [15] for a full discussion of input/output at the digital logic level.

10.2   Memory Mapped I/O

Communication with input/output devices is accomplished through memory in the SPARC architecture. A section of memory, from `0xfff00000` to `0xffffe000`, might

---

[1]The implementation of traps is discussed in detail in Chapter 12.

271

be replaced by device registers. When load and store instructions have addresses in the device register section of memory, devices are activated, instead of the normal storing and retrieving of data. Each device has a unique address, or addresses, assigned to it. When the computer reads or writes to one of these reserved device memory locations, it is not addressing memory but instead communicates with the device. In this way input and output may be performed with the regular instruction set of the computer and no special input/output instructions are needed.

10.3   Character Devices

The simplest devices are those that accept or produce a single character at each input/output transaction. Many of these devices have RS232 serial connections in which the character code is sent bit by bit. These encodings may also involve the generation and checking of parity information to ensure the correctness of the data transmitted. We will not consider bit serial data transmission further here, as the subject is better treated in a digital hardware course.

To write characters to a simple character device the stb instruction is used, addressing a physical hardware device register. To read from a character device the ldub instruction is used, once again addressing a physical hardware device register. If, for example, a CRT device data register were interfaced to memory location 0xffff0000, the character "a" could be written by

```
mov     "a", %o0
set     0xffff0000, %o1
stb     %o0, [%o1]
```

Similarly, if a keyboard data register were interfaced to memory location 0xffff0008 and a key was struck on the keyboard, the ASCII code corresponding to the key struck could be obtained by loading the byte from the device register at memory location 0xffff0008. If the "h" key were struck, the following instructions would obtain 0150 in %o0:

```
set     0xffff0008, %o1
ldub    [%o1], %o0
```

10.4   Programmed I/O

In the preceding section we described device data registers, the register into which output data are stored and from which input data are loaded. There remains the problem of synchronization. How do we know when a character has been typed so that we may load it from the device data register? How do we know when a CRT is ready to accept the next character for display? This information is provided by another device register called the *status register*. For a simple device like a CRT or a keyboard, the status register would be a single byte and would be located in memory adjacent to the data register. The interfacing of a device normally results in a block of memory containing the device registers. In the status register there is normally a ready bit to indicate that the device is ready to accept data or that it has data ready to be taken from the data register. The status register may also contain an error bit to indicate that a device error has occurred. As we will see later, it also contains an interrupt for service bit.

Let us assume that the CRT status register is as follows:

ready	error	intr.	0	0	0	0	0
7	6	5	4	3	2	1	0

Before storing the ASCII character code of the byte, we wish to display into the data register, we must first check that the ready bit is set. If the ready bit is set, we may write the character to the data register. At this point the device will clear the ready bit. When the device has processed the character in its data register, it will set the ready bit to indicate that it is ready to accept another character. Code to transfer the string `"hello, world\n"` might look something like

```
crt       = 0xffff0000      !fictitious crt device

begin_struct(crt)           !crt registers
field(data, 4)              !data register
field(status, 4)            !status register
end_struct(crt)

!status register bits
crt_ready = 0x80            !ready
crt_error = 0x40            !error
crt_intr  = 0x20            !interrupt
crt_reset = 0x1             !reset device

!define registers
define(crt_r, 12)           !%12 crt base register
define(ptr_r, 13)           !%13 pointer to string
define(ptr_adr_r, 14)       !%14 address of pointer
define(data_r, 15)          !%15 data
define(status_r, 16)        !%16 status

        .global hello, ptr_m
hello:
  .asciz        "hello, world\n"
        .section ".data"
ptr_m:
  .word hello
        .section ".text"
```

```
        .align   4
begin_fn(main)

    set    ptr_m, %ptr_adr_r        !address of string pointer
    ld     [%ptr_adr_r], %ptr_r     !pointer to string
    set    crt, %crt_r              !addr. crt device struct

    mov    crt_reset, %status_r     !clear error and int status
    stb    %status_r, [%crt_r + status] !and thus set ready bit

    ldub   [%ptr_r], %data_r         !output first character
    stb    %data_r, [%crt_r + data]
next:
    inc    %ptr_r                    !increment pointer

    ldub   [%ptr_r], %data_r        !load byte of data
    tst    %data_r                  !check to see if end string
    be     done
    ldub   [%crt_r + status], %status_r !load status

wait:
    btst   crt_ready, %status_r     !device ready?
    be     wait                     !no loop
    ldub   [%crt_r + status], %status_r

    ba     next
    stb    %data_r, [%crt_r + data]!output next character

done:
    mov    crt_reset, %status_r     !and reset device
    stb    %status_r, [%crt_r + status] !clear error and int


    end_fn(main)                    !and return
```

In the code, the starting address of the CRT device registers is first defined,
"crt = 0xffff0000"; the two fields are then defined as if they were a structure,
data, and status. These registers would be addressed as ldub [%crt_r + status],
or as stb %data_r, [%crt_r + data]. The bits of the status register are then
defined: crt_ready; crt_error; crt_intr; crt_reset. Five registers are defined for use: a pointer to the CRT structure in memory; a pointer to the string
"hello, world\n"; the address of the pointer; a register to hold the byte of data;
and a register to hold the status bits. The code starts at main with the pointer
and the CRT structure base address being loaded into registers. The device is then

reset, which turns on the ready bit, at which point the first character is stored in the device data register. The next character is readied and the computer enters a wait loop at label `wait`; the status register is loaded repeatedly to check if the ready flag is set. When the flag is set, the next character is moved into the data register. When the null at the end of the string is encountered, the device is reset and the program returns. This program wastes huge amounts of time in the wait loop, `wait`. The CRT might be accepting characters once every 1000 machine cycles.

10.5   Interrupt-Driven I/O

Assuming that the computer has something useful to do while the input or output is going on, it would be efficient if the machine were able to proceed, only returning to service the input/output device when it was ready. This facility has always been provided in terms of interrupts. Input/output devices may interrupt the computer when they need service, for example, by setting the ready flag. When an interrupt occurs the state of the machine is saved and the computer then executes code related to handling the input/output device. When the device has been serviced, the computer returns to the program it was executing, first restoring the state.

The description of how interrupts are implemented on the SPARC architecture is given fully in Chapter 12; for now we assume that it is possible for the machine state to be saved and the program counters to be loaded with the device service routine address. For example, the program to print the string `"hello, world\n"` using interrupts might be as follows:

```
crt    = 0xffff0000              !fictitious crt device

begin_struct(crt)                !crt registers
field(data, 4)                         !data register
field(status, 4)                 !status register
end_struct(crt)

!status register bits
crt_ready = 0x80                 !ready
crt_error = 0x40                 !error
crt_intr  = 0x20                 !interrupt
crt_reset = 0x1                        !reset device

!define registers
define(crt_r, 12)                !%12 crt base register
define(ptr_r, 13)                !%13 pointer to string
define(ptr_adr_r, 14)            !%14 address of pointer
define(data_r, 15)               !%15 data register
define(status_r, 16)             !%16 status
```

```
  .global hello, ptr_m
hello: .asciz   "hello, world\n"
  .section ".data"
ptr_m: .word    hello
  .section ".text"
  .align        4
  begin_fn(main)


  !code to start transmission
start:
  set   ptr_m, %ptr_adr_r        !address of string pointer
  ld    [%ptr_adr_r], %ptr_r     !pointer to string
  set   crt, %crt_r              !addr. crt device struct

  mov   crt_reset, %status_r     !clear error and int status
  stb   %status_r, [%crt_r + status] !and thus set ready bit
  mov   crt_intr, %status_r      !enable interrupts
  stb   %status_r, [%crt_r + status]

  ldub  [%ptr_r], %data_r        !output first character
  stb   %data_r, [%crt_r + data]
  inc   %ptr_r                   !increment pointer
  st    %ptr_r, [%ptr_adr_r]
  end_fn(main)                   !and return


  !interrupt code
  .global next, done

next:
  set   ptr_m, %ptr_adr_r        !pointer address
  ld    [%ptr_adr_r], %ptr_r     !pointer to string
  ldub  [%ptr_r], %data_r        !load byte of data
  tst   %data_r                  !check to see if end string
  be    done
  set   crt, %crt_r              !addr. crt device struct

  stb   %data_r, [%crt_r + data]!output next character
  inc   %ptr_r                   !increment pointer
  st    %ptr_r, [%ptr_adr_r]
  !return from interrupt

done:
  clr   %ptr_r                   !just clear pointer
  st    %ptr_r, [%ptr_adr_r]
```

```
mov   crt_reset, %status_r    !and reset device
stb   %status_r, [%crt_r + status] !clear error and int
!return from interrupt
```

This program has the same definitions as the earlier program. The initialization of the registers and the device begins in the same way with the exception that after the device has been reset, the interrupt bit is set. When the interrupt bit is set the computer is interrupted whenever the ready flag is set. We have arranged that the code labeled "!interrupt code" will be executed when an interrupt occurs. At the end of this code segment, labeled by the comment "return from interrupt," the computer will continue doing whatever it was doing when the interrupt occurred.

Following initialization, when the interrupt flag is set the first character is output and the routine returns, allowing other processing to occur. The routine does not wait for the ready flag to be set.

When the ready flag is set, an interrupt occurs and the code starting at the label **next** is executed. As we will see in Chapter 12, an interrupt routine may use the local registers %12–%17; local register %10 contains the %pc and %11 the %npc at the time the interrupt occurred.

10.6   Block Devices

By using interrupts we avoid the problem of not keeping the CPU waiting for a slow device. If, however, the device transfers data at very high rates we have a different problem. The interrupt code shown above takes 10 cycles, without consideration of any overhead involved in saving the state of the machine in preparation for executing the interrupt code. Many devices, such as disks, transfer data at rates comparable to the instruction execution rate of the computer. Further, the code to transfer a block of data is very simple, involving storing or retrieving data from sequential locations in memory. Block transfer devices are capable of executing such simple transfers independently of the CPU. A block transfer device is given a starting address and an item count. The device is capable of addressing memory directly by using memory when the CPU is not. The block transfer device has a ready flag, but it sets the ready flag when it has completed the transfer of the entire block not after each data item. Thus, the computer has only to initialize a block transfer device and wait to be interrupted when the block transfer is complete.

10.7   Directory Devices

Data storage devices are either sequential, such as a CRT or a tape, or blocked, such as a disk. To write to a tape we must first position the drive at the end of the written portion of the tape and then we may resume writing. While data on tapes are written in records, with a distinguishing mark between each record, there is no information kept as to what data are located in what record. The retrieval of information from a tape involves reading the entire tape, discarding information that is not wanted. Rewriting a block on a tape involves rewriting the entire tape. Disks are unlike tapes in that they are formatted before any information is written to them. Additional information tracks are provided to locate individual records on disks. This information is only written during a formatting process. After a disk has been formatted, information may be located with respect to the formatting information. Thus, individual records on a disk may be read or rewritten in essentially a random manner.

Addressing of individual records on a disk is in terms of logical block numbers, which are translated into physical block numbers by the device. To address an individual record the logical block number must be stored in a device register. If the device is a block transfer device, the starting memory address and data item count must also be stored in device registers. Such devices have many registers and states, represented by bits of the status register. The operating system maintains a directory, relating file path names to physical locations on the device of the data.

10.8   Input/Output Processors

Handling of input/output is complicated, and some computers have additional processing units to handle input/output interfaced to the memory. These input/output processors have an instruction set relevant to data transfer with branching and arithmetic instructions. With such a system the central processor is free to perform computations, while the input/output processors handle the devices and the transfer of data to and from memory.

10.9   System I/O

Input and output are handled by the operating system [27]. It is the operating system that controls all input/output devices. The relationship between input/output and the selection of processes to run is complicated and beyond the scope of this book. However, the interface between the user and the operating system is of concern to us, as it provides our interface to the input/output devices.

To perform any input or output from a program, one must make a request to the operating system. Such a request is called a *trap*, or *system call*. We have already seen the use of a trap to *exit* at the end of a program:

```
mov     1, %g1
ta      0
```

The service requested is represented by the number in register %g1. The trap instruction `ta` is like a subroutine call in that it transfers control to a different address. Unlike a call instruction, the trap instruction has no delay slot. The address to which the trap instruction transfers control is stored in a table in the operating system (see Chapter 12). The trap instruction, as a side effect, changes the mode in which the computer is operating from user mode to supervisor mode. In supervisor mode a program may execute additional instructions and may address the input/output devices.

There are many traps, but we concern ourselves only with those related to input and output:

%g1	Service Request
3	read
4	write
5	open
6	close
8	create

All devices are represented by files in the UNIX operating system. To write to our CRT, we write to a file; to read from our keyboard, we read from a different file. These are special files; you may read from the keyboard file only when characters have been typed. When we read from a file in our directory, we are reading from a file located on a disk.

Before a file may be accessed, it must be *opened*. Opening a file relates a path name and access modes to the physical location of the data on a device. Checking also occurs at the time of opening a file in case the file is being accessed in a manner that violates the protection of the file. If the file does not exist, or if the access mode is inappropriate, the trap routine sets the carry, "C," bit. Trap routines have historically set the "C" bit to indicate an error. If the open is successful, a *file descriptor* is returned. A file descriptor is a small positive integer, usually less than 16 in magnitude. The file descriptor is used for all future accesses to the file. The arguments to a trap are stored in the out registers in exactly the same manner as in a function call. The return value from a trap instruction is located in %o0.

Our discussion of input/output parallels the discussion of low-level input/output in Kernighan and Ritchie [11]. In UNIX, the lowest-level interface to the input/output system is in terms of the following functions:

```
int n_read = read(int fd, char * buf, int n);
int n_written = write(int fd, char * buf, int n);
int fd = open(char * name, int flags, int perms);
int fd = creat(char * name, perms);
close(int fd);
```

in which fd is a file descriptor; buf is the character buffer into which characters will be read or from which characters will be written; n is the number of characters to be written or read; name is the path name of the file to be accessed; and flags and perms are described fully in the UNIX documentation. If code generated by the C compiler is examined, it will be seen that the foregoing functions simply move their arguments into the out registers and execute the appropriate trap instruction. Following the trap instruction is some error-checking code.

As an example of low-level I/O we will code the following C program, which copies a file directly into trap-handling assembly language.

```
#define PERMS 0666
#define BUFSIZ  8192

main()
{
  int ff, ft;
  int n;
  char buf[BUFSIZ];

  if ((ff = open("foo", 0, 0)) < 0)
   exit(1);

  if ((ft = creat("baz", PERMS)) < 0)
    exit(2);

  while ((n = read(ff,buf, BUFSIZ)) > 0)
    if (write(ft, buf, n) != n)
      exit(0);
}
```

The assembly language with the function calls replaced directly with traps employing the C bit as error indicator is

```
include(macro_defs.m)

define(OPEN, 5)                !'trap definitions'
define(CREAT, 8)
define(READ, 3)
define(WRITE, 4)

define(O_RDONLY, 0)            ! 'defined in <fcntl.h>'

str1:   .asciz  "foo"
str2:   .asciz  "baz"

  .align 4

define(ff_r, 10)               !'%ff_r = %10'
define(ft_r, 11)               !'%ft_r = %11'
define(n_r, 12)                   !'%n_r = %12'

define(BUFSIZ, 16)             !'buffer size'
```

```
         local_var
         var(buf, BUFSIZ, 1)              !'read/write buffer'

         begin_fn(main)

         set    str1, %o0
         clr    %o1                       !'open file to read'
         clr    %o2                       !'mode'
         mov    OPEN, %g1                 !'open file for reading'
         ta     0
         bcc    open_ok
         mov    %o0, %ff_r                !read file descriptor
         clr    %g1                       !'error, exit'
         ta     0
open_ok:
         set    str2, %o0
         mov    0666, %o1                 !file access permissions
         mov    CREAT, %g1                !'create file'
         ta     0
         bcc    creat_ok
         mov    %o0, %ft_r                !write file descriptor
         clr    %g1                       !'error, exit'
         ta     0
creat_ok:
         ba     write_ok                  !test
         mov    %ff_r, %o0                !read file descriptor
read_ok:
         add    %fp, buf, %o1             !buffer pointer
         mov    %n_r, %o2                 !number bytes to write
         mov    WRITE, %g1                !write
         ta     0
         cmp    %o0, %n_r                 !check number written
         be     write_ok
         mov    %ff_r, %o0                !read file descriptor
         clr    %g1
         ta     0                         !'error, exit'
write_ok:
         add    %fp, buf, %o1             !pointer to buffer
         mov    BUFSIZ, %o2               !max chars to read
         mov    READ, %g1                 !read
         ta     0
         addcc  %o0, 0, %n_r              !check if any chars read
         bg     read_ok
         mov    %ft_r, %o0                !read file descriptor
```

```
    be      all_done
    clr     %g1
    ta      0                           !'error, exit'
all_done:
  end_fn(main)
```

The assembly language is much more efficient than the C version, but when one takes into account the system operations involved with trap execution, the increase in efficiency becomes irrelevant.

10.10   Summary

In this chapter we discussed input/output operations in general, Unfortunately, when programming in user mode we are unable to perform input/output operations directly. Discussion started with memory mapped character devices. Programmed input/output was first discussed, then interrupt input/output motivated by its limitations. This led naturally to block devices and finally, to the input/output processor. The chapter concluded with a discussion of the trap implementation of input/output system calls under UNIX.

10.11   Exercises

10–1 Why is character input/output to a slow device handled by means of interrupts?

10–2 Write lowercase to uppercase copy.

10–3 Write word count, wc.

Chapter 11

FLOATING-POINT

11.1 Introduction

So far in our discussion of programming we have considered only integer arithmetic. We may extend our definition of the positional notation for decimal numbers (see page 99) to include fractional quantities [19]:

$$N \approx S(d_{n-1}R^{n-1} + \cdots + d_1R^1 + d_0 + d_{-1}R^{-1} + d_{-2}R^{-2} + \cdots + d_{-f}R^{-f})$$

where:

      R is the number system base, 10 for decimal numbers
      N is the the number in base R
      S is the sign, + or −
      n is the number of digits
      f is the number of digits to the right of the decimal place

A string approximating π, 3.14159, is interpreted as the number

$$3 + 1 \times 10^{-1} + 4 \times 10^{-2} + 1 \times 10^{-3} + 5 \times 10^{-4} + 9 \times 10^{-5}$$

The accuracy of representation relates to the number of decimal places, five in the example given above. The representation of a number with f decimal places is accurate to $f \pm 10^{-f}$. Many numbers do not have an exact representation with such a system. Numbers such as 1/3, result in an infinite repeating string of digits, called a *recurring binary number*. Other numbers, such as π and $\sqrt{2}$, may not be represented, only approximated. Arithmetic is performed to obtain a result accurate to a given number of decimal places.

The number 3.14159 may also be represented as a binary number with six binary places as

$$11.001001$$

where the first bit to the right of the binary point represents halves, the next bit to the right quarters, and so on, with the sixth bit to the right of the binary point representing sixty-fourths. The binary representation of π with six binary places is accurate to $\pm 2^{-6}$. The equivalent of recurring decimal numbers also occurs with binary numbers, for example, 0.1 in binary is $0.0\overline{0011}$. [1]

The simplest way to convert a decimal number to binary is first to multiply the decimal number by 2^f, where f is the number of binary places required and to then proceed to convert the integer part of the resulting number using the methods of Chapter 3.

11.2 Fixed Binary Point Numbers

Fractional quantities may be represented by shifting the binary point in an integer word. We have thus far always assumed that the binary point (the binary equivalent of the decimal point) was at the right-hand end of the word, to the right of bit zero. However, we may consider the binary point to be located anywhere in the word. Another way of looking at the problem is to consider that the integer quantity does not represent integers but might represent, for example, 1/16ths. In this case the binary point would be to the right of bit four (see Figure 11.1).

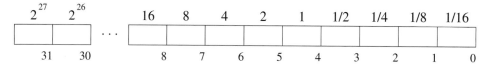

Figure 11.1: Scaled Integer Number

We may use the add and sub instructions to add and subtract such scaled numbers without any change except to note that for every additional binary place we halve the range of numbers that may be represented in a fixed-length register.

When we multiply two such numbers we generate twice as many binary places. Consider $a \times 2^{-4}$ multiplied by $b \times 2^{-4}$; the result is $a \times b \times 2^{-8}$ with eight binary places. If the multiplicand and the multiplier were both accurate to four binary places the result of the multiplication will only be accurate, at best, to four binary places, so that we should eliminate binary places beyond the fourth. This is most simply done by right-shifting four places; however, the number might also be rounded. That is, if the most significant bit of the bits to be discarded was a one, we might increment the number after shifting. We will not address rounding here, as this is properly the subject of numerical analysis, other than to mention that this is an important problem when fractional quantities are involved and approximated to a fixed number of bits of precision.

---

[1]The same problem occurs with hundredths which can cause a problem when performing accounting using Floating-Point arithmetic. It is customary to represent dollars and cents $\times 100$ to avoid this problem.

Disregarding questions of rounding, the code to multiply the two numbers would be

```
mov     %a_r, %o0        !'a * b'
call    .mul
mov     %b_r, %o1
sra     %o0, 4, %o0      !'normalize'
```

Similarly for division:

```
sll     %a_r, 4, %o0     !'pre-normalize dividend'
call    .div
mov     %b_r, %o1
```

11.3   Scientific Notation

In addition to the need to represent fractional quantities, there is the need to represent numbers of a great range, usually much greater than can be provided by conventional fixed-length registers. In general scientific calculations, a range of $\pm 10^{\pm 20}$ is quite common, with relative accuracy of 10^{-10}. This would require a register with 66 bits to represent the largest number and with an additional 100 bits to represent the smallest number to the given relative accuracy, a 166-bit register! Only the most significant 33 bits of any number would have any meaning. The remaining bits would only be needed to indicate the position of the most significant bits. Thus, we might represent such numbers in a much more practical way by storing the 30 significant bits in one word, keeping the position of the binary point in a second word. This is, of course, a binary equivalent of scientific notation in which decimal numbers are represented in the same relative precision by incorporating a multiplier of a power of 10: for example, 3.1826×10^3 to represent 3182.6, where the exponent of 10 is used to indicate the location of the decimal place. Note that the number is represented to five significant places. 3.1826×10^{-20} is also represented to five significant places but is a much smaller number.

To handle scientific notation, we might keep two words for each number; the first word would store the significand, a number between 1.0 and 2.0, the second word an exponent of base two. The number would then be interpreted as this significand, scaled by two raised to the power of the exponent. For example, the number 16 might be represented as 1.0×2^4. The significand f is normally constrained to be $1.0 \le f < 2.0$, so that the product p of two such significands will be such that $1.0 \le p < 4.0$ close to the original range. If this is done, renormalization involves at most a single arithmetic shift. The addition of two such significands also will lie between 2.0 and 4.0, once again requiring only a single shift to renormalize a sum. Of course, the significand could be much smaller or larger, but then the range of the result would no longer be so limited and renormalization would be more difficult.

For example, let us pick a representation in which the significand will represent a positive number, greater than 1.0 and less than 2.0, with the binary point located

to the right of bit 29. Bit 29 will then always be a one. This will then leave us
two bits, 30 and 31, to avoid overflow problems and to enable us to perform two's
complement arithmetic.[2] The integer contents of a register would then have to be
scaled by 2^{-29}, to be interpreted as the significand. With such a representation
multiplication would be simple, involving the product of the first pair of words and
the addition of the exponents stored in the second pair of words.

If we were to store the significands with the binary point to the right of bit 29,
we could represent unsigned numbers such as 1.5, 3 and 9 as follows:

```
one:     .word   0x30000000, 0x0      !'1 1/2 * 2^0 = 1.5'
three:   .word   0x30000000, 0x1      !'1 1/2 * 2^1 = 3'
nine:    .word   0x24000000, 0x3      !'1 1/8 * 2^3 = 9'
```

If we use umul to perform multiplication, we will obtain the product scaled
by 2^{-58} in two registers, the high-order bits in %o1 and the low bits in %o0. To
renormalize, without worrying about rounding, we would need to shift right 29
times. That involves shifting %o1 right $29 - 32 = -3$, or left 3 times.[3] The low part
in %o0 needs to be shifted right 29 times, leaving only its three most significant bits
in the register; these three bits are the low three bits of the product and must then
be ored into %o1 after it is shifted. If the product of the significands was greater
than 2 the result would need to be shifted right 30 times and the exponent of the
sum incremented. Consider the product of 3 and 9:

```
 1  /* scientific notation program to multiply two numbers */
 2            include(../macro_defs.m)
 3            .section ".data"
 4  three_m:.word    0x30000000, 0x1 !'1 1/2 * 2^1 = 3'
 5  nine_m: .word    0x24000000, 0x3 !'1 1/8 * 2^3 = 9'
 6  n27_m:  .word    0,0                  !'where to store 27'
 7            .section ".text"
 8            cdef(three_r, 10)
 9            cdef(nine_r, 11)
10            cdef(n27_r, 12)
11            cdef(mask_r, 13)
12            cdef(mask, 0x8000000) !'2 bit after mul'
13  begin_main
14     set    three_m, %three_r       !'-> three_m'
15     set    nine_m, %nine_r         !'-> nine_m'
16     set    n27_m, %n27_r           !'-> n27_m'
17     set    mask, %mask_r           !'1/2 bit after mul mask'
18     ld     [%three_r], %o0         !'multiply fractions'
19     call   .umul
20     ld     [%nine_r], %o1
```

---

[2]We address signed numbers later.

[3]The contents of the register containing the high-order part is already scaled by 2^{32}.

```
21    ld    [%three_r + 4], %o2      !'add exponents'
22    ld    [%nine_r + 4], %o3
23    !'add  %o3, %o2, %o2   move addition into delay slot'
24    andcc %o1, %mask_r, %g0       !'fraction < 2? '
25    be    shft3                    !'yes'
26    add   %o3, %o2, %o2
27    !'fraction >= 2, << 2, exp++'
28  shft2:
29    sll   %o1, 2, %o1             !'fract << 2'
30    srl   %o0, 30, %o0            !'two msb of low part'
31    ba    ok
32    inc   %o2                     !'increment exponent'
33    !'fraction < 2, << 3'
34  shft3:
35    sll   %o1, 3, %o1             !'fract << 3'
36    srl   %o0, 29, %o0            !'three msb of low part'
37  ok:
38    or    %o1, %o0, %o1           !'fract in %o1'
39    st    %o2, [%n27_r + 4]       !'store result'
40    st    %o1, [%n27_r]
41    end_main
```

The numbers are declared using two words, lines 4–6. After pointers are loaded into the registers, lines 14–18 .umul is called to perform the multiplication. The exponents are added in lines 21, 22, and 26. The high bit of the product is tested in line 24 and then either two shifts or three are made to renormalize the number, lines 28–38.

Addition and subtraction are more difficult, as we must first align the significands so that the exponents are equal. This is done by right-shifting the significand whose exponent is smaller, thus increasing its exponent for each right shift, until both exponents match. If both addends are positive, we will need at most one shift to renormalize. In the case of subtraction, assuming that we are subtracting a smaller positive number from a larger positive number, we may obtain a result with many leading zeros if the numbers are close together. In this case normalizing becomes a problem, as we have to have a loop with a test and shift for as many leading zeros as there are in the result.

Consider the subtraction of $128 - 127$:

```
1   /* Scientific notation program to subtract two numbers */
2           include(../macro_defs.m)
3           .section ".data"
4   one28_m:.word   0x20000000, 0x7 !'1 * 2^7 = 128'
5   one27_m:.word   0x3f800000, 0x6 !'1 63/64* 2^6 = 127'
6   one_m:  .word   0,0             !'where to store result'
7           .section ".text"
```

```
 8           cdef(one28_r, 10)
 9           cdef(one27_r, 11)
10           cdef(one_r, 12)
11           cdef(mask_r, 13)
12           cdef(mask, 0x20000000)          !'1/2 bit'
13  begin_main
14      set   one28_m, %one28_r  !'-> one28_m'
15      set   one27_m, %one27_r  !'-> one27_m'
16      set   one_m, %one_r      !'-> one_m'
17      set   mask, %mask_r      !'1/2 bit after mul mask'
18      ld    [%one28_r], %o0    !'fractions'
19      ld    [%one27_r], %o1
20      ld    [%one28_r + 4], %o2 !'exponents'
21      ld    [%one27_r + 4], %o3
22      sub   %o2, %o3, %o3      !'# shifts to align fract'
23      srl   %o1, %o3, %o1      !'align fractions'
24      sub   %o0, %o1, %o1      !'form difference'
25      andcc %o1, %mask_r, %g0  !'normalized?'
26      bne   ok
27      nop
28  norm:
29      sll   %o1, 1, %o1        !'fract << 1'
30  test:
31      andcc %o1, %mask_r, %g0  !'normalized?'
32      be    norm
33      sub   %o2, 1, %o2        !'exp--'
34  ok:
35      st    %o2, [%one_r + 4]  !'store result'
36      st    %o1, [%one_r]
37  end_main
```

The data are declared and pointers are loaded, lines 4–17. The exponents are then subtracted to calculate the number of shifts to align the significands, lines 22 and 23. The difference of the significands (which are now aligned) is then computed in line 24. If the high-order bit of the result in not set, line 25, a loop is entered to renormalize, lines 29–33. This body of this loop is executed once for every shift necessary to renormalize the significand.

A representation very similar to the one we have described is called *floating-point*. In floating-point format the exponent and significand are packed together in one or more words. In the SPARC architecture, floating-point numbers are normally handled by a separate processor. If a floating-point processor is not available, code very similar to that presented above must be present to perform floating-point arithmetic operations. Floating-Point numbers are normally stored in sign-magnitude format, *not* in two's complement format. In sign-magnitude format bit

31 indicates the sign of the number, a one indicates a negative number and a zero a positive number. The significand is always stored as a positive quantity. The negation of such a number simply involves complementing the sign bit.

11.4 Floating-Point

The SPARC architecture implements the ANSI/IEEE Standard 754-1985 [21] which defines three formats: floating-point single, double, and quad. The floating-point single format is shown in Figure 11.2.

Figure 11.2: Floating-Point Single Format

A floating-point single representation occupies one four-byte word. The number it represents is

$$N = (-1)^s \times 2^{e-127} \times 1.f$$

where

s is the sign bit
e is a biased exponent
f is the fractional part of the significand

The number is stored sign magnitude with only the fractional part of the magnitude of the significand present. The exponent is biased by 0x7f, so that the biased exponent is always a positive number.[4] As the significand is always to be normalized, so that the high-order bit is always a one, this bit is not stored, allowing for additional precision with the available 23 bits of significand. Before the significand can be used, 1.0 must be added to the fraction. The following table shows the representation for some simple numbers.

Number	s	e - 0x7f	e(binary)	1.f(binary)	f(binary)	Single float
1.0	0	0	0111 1111	1.000	0000	0x3f800000
-1.0	1	0	0111 1111	1.000	0000	0xbf800000
1.5	0	0	0111 1111	1.100	1000	0x3fc00000
0.5	0	-1	0111 1110	1.000	0000	0x3f000000
0.25	0	-2	0111 1101	1.000	0000	0x3e800000
2.0	0	1	1000 0000	1.000	0000	0x40000000

We could use our multiply and subtraction code with this format if we first unpack the data. The following leaf routine will do this for us, taking care of a sign as well:

---

[4]This allows an integer compare to be used to compare the magnitudes of floating-point numbers.

```
 1   /* leaf routine to unpack floating single numbers into
 2   significand, exponent, and sign in %o0, %o1, and %o2  */
 3           .global unpack
 4   unpack:
 5       orcc  %g0, %o0, %g0          !'test for negative'
 6       bpos  exp
 7       or    %g0, %g0, %o2          !'set sign positive'
 8       xnor  %g0, %g0, %o2          !'set sign'
 9   exp:
10       srl   %o0, 23, %o1           !'shift exp back into %o1'
11       andn  %o1, 0x100, %o1        !'clear sign bit'
12       sub   %o1, 127, %o1          !'unbias exponent'
13   signif:
14       sll   %o0, 9, %o0            !'place fraction into %o0'
15       srl   %o0, 3, %o0            !'normalize'
16       sethi %hi(0x20000000), %o3   !'place 1 into %o3'
17   !'or   %o0, %o3, %o0             -> delay slot'
18       retl
19       or    %o0, %o3, %o0          !'significand in %o0'
```

Here the sign is first extracted, lines 5–8, the exponent retrieved and unbiased, lines 10–12. Finally, the one is restored to the fraction and it is normalized to form the significand, lines 14–19.

The largest biased exponent we may use is 0xfe, which corresponds to 2^{127}. The largest possible biased exponent, 0xff, is restricted to represent quantities that are not numbers, such as $\sqrt{-1}$ and infinity (∞). Similarly, the smallest biased exponent, 0x0, which would correspond to 2^{-127}, is also restricted to represent subnormal numbers, which we describe in Section 11.8. The smallest biased exponent is 0x1, which corresponds to 2^{-126}.

This gives us a range of magnitudes from 1.0×2^{-126} up through $(2.0 - \epsilon) \times 2^{127}$, or from 1.17549435e-38 to 3.40282347e+38. This range of numbers would be represented in the machine as a four-byte hexadecimal quantities 0x00800000 through 0x7f7fffff. Floating single numbers are represented to approximately seven-decimal-digit accuracy. Zero is represented as a word containing 0. This is the same representation as an integer zero, which simplifies testing. Floating single numbers may be either positive or negative, and we end up with two ranges of numbers and zero, from -3.40282347e+38 to -1.17549435e-38, a gap to zero, and then another gap to the positive range from 1.17549435e-38 up to 3.40282347e+38.

11.5   The Floating-Point Processor

The SPARC architecture specified a floating-point coprocessor. This is a separate processor from the integer unit we have been discussing. The floating-point processor is capable of executing a number of floating-point instructions and has its own set of registers. The floating-point processor cannot, however, address memory or fetch instructions. This is done by the integer unit. The integer unit has additional instructions to load and store the floating-point registers. When the integer unit fetches a floating-point instruction it simply passes it to the floating-point unit for execution. As soon as it has done this, it may fetch the next instruction and start the execution of that instruction in parallel. The execution of floating-point instructions is handled within the floating-point processor by a number of specialized floating-point arithmetic units. These may include one or more adder/subtractor, multiplier/divider units. The processor keeps track of which units are working on what instructions, which floating-point registers they need for their input, and which registers they will change when they have completed their computation. The floating-point processor makes sure that no invalid computations take place by stalling individual processors until the valid data have been computed. All this is transparent to the user; however, understanding the nature of the floating-point processor is helpful in writing code for efficient execution. For example, if a number of multiplications and additions of unrelated data must take place, the interleaving of additions with multiplications will allow the processor to perform at twice its rate rather than performing all the additions first and the multiplications later. The floating-point processor can also compare floating-point numbers. Subsequent branching would, of course, have to be done by the integer unit, which is fetching instructions. This is provided for by the addition of a number of floating-point branch instructions, which test the floating-point condition codes.

The floating-point processor has 32 registers, referred to as %f0 through %f31, which may hold integer data or floating-point data. Unlike the integer unit there is no register file and all registers that contain data must be saved when calling a function.

The floating-point registers may be loaded and stored into memory by the integer unit by executing the following instructions:

Mnemonic	Operation
ldf	Load word into floating-point register.
stf	Store floating-point register into memory.

The assembler does not actually recognize the mnemonic ldf or stf but will assemble these instructions when the instructions ld and st refer to a floating-point register. The operands to these two instructions are identical to the integer load and store instructions; namely, the address is the sum of the contents of two registers, or a register and a constant, with the exception that the source or destination is a floating-point register. The address registers are specified by rs1 and rs2, while the floating-point register is specified by the rd. The address is, as usual, enclosed in square brackets.

The single floating instructions that are executed by the floating processor are as follows:

Mnemonic	Operands	Description
fadds	$freg_{rs1}$, $freg_{rs2}$ $freg_{rd}$	Add.
fsubs	$freg_{rs1}$, $freg_{rs2}$ $freg_{rd}$	Subtract.
fmuls	$freg_{rs1}$, $freg_{rs2}$ $freg_{rd}$	Multiply.
fdivs	$freg_{rs1}$, $freg_{rs2}$ $freg_{rd}$	Divide.
fsqrts	$freg_{rs2}$ $freg_{rd}$	Square root.
fmovs	$freg_{rs2}$ $freg_{rd}$	Move data between floating registers.
fnegs	$freg_{rs2}$ $freg_{rd}$	Negate.
fabss	$freg_{rs2}$ $freg_{rd}$	Absolute value.

Add, subtract, multiply, and divide operate to combine the contents of two floating registers to produce a result for a third register. The square root instruction, while appearing somewhat sophisticated, turns out to be very simple to implement in floating-point. This instruction, and those that follow, takes a single source register to compute a result. The last three instructions are very simple, involving no more than copying the data and modifying the sign bit.

Converting between integer format and floating-point is quite complicated and occurs frequently, so that conversion instructions are also provided. In this case an integer is loaded into a floating register or stored from one.

Mnemonic	Operands	Description
fitos	$freg_{rs2}$ $freg_{rd}$	Convert integer to single float.
fstoi	$freg_{rs2}$ $freg_{rd}$	Convert single float to integer.

Finally, there is a compare instruction:

Mnemonic	Operands	Description
fcmps	$freg_{rs1}$ $freg_{rs2}$	Compare.

The compare sets a condition code in a manner similar to the integer unit compare instruction. However, the condition code represents different information. The condition codes are:

fcc	Mnemonic	Relation
0	E	fs1 = fs2
1	L	fs1 < fs2
2	G	fs1 > fs2
3	U	fs1 ? fs2, unordered

The last condition code, U, indicates that one or both numbers were not floating-point numbers, so that an ordering relationship could not be established. These floating condition codes may be tested by the integer processor in much the same manner as the integer conditional branch instructions operate. The testing instructions are:

as Mnemonic	cond op2 = 110	Floating Unconditional Branches	Condition Codes
fba	1000	Branch on always	1
fbn	0000	Branch never	0

as Mnemonic	cond op2 = 110	Floating Conditional Branches	Condition Codes
fbo	1111	Branch on ordered	E or L or G
fbu	0111	Branch on unordered	U
fbul	0011	Branch on unordered or less	L or U
fbl	0100	Branch on less	L
fbule	1110	Branch on unordered or less or equal	E or L or U
fble	1101	Branch on less or equal	E or L
fbue	1010	Branch on unordered or equal	E or U
fbe	1001	Branch on equal	E
fbne	0001	Branch on not equal	L or G or U
fblg	0010	Branch on less or greater	L or G
fbuge	1100	Branch on unordered or greater or equal	E or G or U
fbge	1011	Branch on greater or equal	E or G
fbug	0101	Branch on unordered or greater	G or U
fbg	0110	Branch on greater	G

A word of caution: A floating branch instruction may not follow immediately after a floating compare instruction.

11.6 A Floating-Point Program

Given these instructions, let us look at a sample program. The following program computes the inner product of two six-vectors represented by single floating-point numbers:

```
1   /* Compute the magnitude of the dot product of two six
2   element vectors, a and b stored as float singles */
3           include(../macro_defs.m)
4           .section ".data"    !'floats must be initialized in memory'
5   a_m:    .single 0r1.0, 0r1.5, 0r-1.5
6           .single 0r10E2, 0r-1.0, 0r16.0
7   b_m:    .single 0r2.0, 0r4.0, 0r0.125
8           .single 0r0.0625, 0r3.0, 0r5.0
9   zero_m: .single 0r0.0

10          .section ".text"
11          cdef(ap_r, 10, 'pointer to vector a')
12          cdef(bp_r, 11, 'pointer to vector b')
13          cdef(i_r, 12, 'loop counter')
14          cdef(mag_r, f0, 'magnitude')
15          cdef(sum_r, f1, 'sum of products')
16          cdef(a_r, f2, 'component of a')
17          cdef(b_r, f3, 'component of b')
18          cdef(prod_r, f4, 'product')
19  begin_main
20     set     a_m, %ap_r              !'set up pointers'
21     set     b_m, %bp_r
22     mov     6, %i_r                 !'loop counter'
23     set     zero_m, %o0             !'sum = 0'
24     ld      [%o0], %sum_r

25  loop:
26     ld      [%ap_r], %a_r           !'first components'
27     ld      [%bp_r], %b_r
28      fmuls %a_r, %b_r, %prod_r
29     add     %ap_r, 4, %ap_r         !'increment pointers'
30     add     %bp_r, 4, %bp_r
31     subcc %i_r, 1, %i_r             !'decrement counter'
32     bg      loop
33      fadds %sum_r, %prod_r, %sum_r

34      fsqrts %sum_r, %mag_r          !'obtain sqrt'
35          end_main
```

Notice the `.single` pseudo-op in lines 5–9 It assembles the floating-point representation for each of its floating-point operands. It accepts anything that C would recognize as a floating-point number; however, each number must be preceded by 0r to let the assembler know that the number that it is reading is to be read as floating-point. As there is no literal mode for floating-point, all numbers must be initialized in memory, including zero. There is no instruction to zero a floating-point register.[5] In the program we declare registers to hold pointers to the two arrays, lines 11 and 12. We will use a do loop with index variable i declared in line 13. Floating-Point registers are declared to hold the magnitude, the sum, a pair of components, and the product, lines 14–18.

The program first initializes the pointers, the index variable i, and zeros out the sum, lines 20–24. Computation is then in a loop executed six times. Two components are loaded into %a_r, and %b_r, their product computed, both pointers incremented, and the loop index decremented. The addition of the product to the sum is placed in the delay slot. When the loop exits, the magnitude is computed in line 34 before the program exits.

Note that we have indented the floating-point instructions to indicate that they are being computed in parallel with the instructions that follow. The fmuls instruction, line 28, will start computing a product while the integer processor goes on to increment the pointers. If the computation of the product has been completed by the time the processor reaches line 33, the fadds instruction will start while the integer processor moves ahead to load the next two components into the floating-point registers, line 26. If the fmuls instruction was still executing, the floating-point processor would stall at line 33 until the multiply instruction completes.

11.6.1   Debugging Single Presision Floating-Point Code

The contents of the floating-point registers may be addressed in gdb by $fn, where $0 \le n \le 32$. The contents of a floating-point register are always interpreted by gdb as a single floating-point number so that if a floation-point 5 had been loaded into %f0, the following printout would occur within gdb:

```
(gdb) p/f $f0
$1 = 5
(gdb) p/d $f0
$2 = 5
```

In the second case, gdb converts the single floating-point number to an integer before printing it out. Even using p/x $f0 would fare no better, as now the integer is printed as a hexadecimal number. It is not possible to see the bit representation of numbers stored in floating-point registers.

```
(gdb) p/x $f0
$3 = 0x5
```

---

[5]If any floating-point register contains a valid floation-point number, a floating subtract instruction may be used to subtract the contents of the register from itself, storing the resulting zero in the desired register.

When examining memory we may specify how many bytes are to be examined and in what format the bytes examined are to be printed, so that if the floating single constant 5.0 were located in memory at 0x2088c, the following printout would occur:

```
(gdb) x/wf 0x2088c
0x2088c <b_m+20>:            5
(gdb) x/wx 0x2088c
0x2088c <b_m+20>:            0x40a00000
(gdb) x/wd 0x2088c
0x2088c <b_m+20>:            1084227584
```

11.6.2 An Improved Version of the Code

An improved version of the program follows, obtained by unrolling the loop once. We will compute two products in the loop, executing the loop only half as many times. This has the obvious advantage of halving the number of times we have to increment pointers and make the test on the loop variable. However, with a floating-point coprocessor with a number of multipliers and adders, we may make use of more than one of these units, possibly avoiding any processor stall to wait for a floating-point computation to complete. To do this we need to make sure that the multiplier and adder units access their own registers.

```
 1   /* Compute the magnitude of the dot product of two six
 2   element vectors, a and b stored as float singles */
 3           include(../macro_defs.m)
 4           .section ".data"   !'floats must be initialized in memory'
 5   globals:
 6   a_m:     .single 0r1.0, 0r1.5, 0r-1.5
 7           .single 0r10E2, 0r-1.0, 0r16.0
 8   b_m:     .single 0r2.0, 0r4.0, 0r0.125
 9           .single 0r0.0625, 0r3.0, 0r5.0
10   zero_m: .single 0r0.0
11           .section ".text"
12           cdef(ap_r, 10, 'pointer to vector a')
13           cdef(bp_r, 11, 'pointer to vector b')
14           cdef(i_r, 12, 'loop counter')
15           cdef(base_r, 13, 'base pointer to globals')
16           cdef(mag_r, f0, 'magnitude')
17           cdef(sum_r, f1, 'sum of products')
18           cdef(a1_r, f2, 'component of a')
19           cdef(b1_r, f3, 'component of b')
20           cdef(a2_r, f4, 'component of a')
21           cdef(b2_r, f5, 'component of b')
22           cdef(prod1_r, f6, 'product')
```

```
23              cdef(prod2_r, f7, 'product')
24  begin_main
25    sethi  %hi(globals), %base_r
26    or     %base_r, %lo(a_m), %ap_r   !'set up pointers'
27    or     %base_r, %lo(b_m), %bp_r   !'set up pointers'
28
29    ld     [%base_r + %lo(zero_m)], %prod1_r !'zero prod1'
30    mov    6, %i_r                     !'loop counter'
31    fmovs  %prod1_r, %prod2_r          !'zero prod2 and sum'
32    fmovs  %prod1_r, %sum_r

33  loop:
34    ld     [%ap_r], %a1_r             !'first components'
35    ld     [%bp_r], %b1_r
36    fadds  %sum_r, %prod1_r, %sum_r
37    add    %ap_r, 8, %ap_r
38    fmuls  %a1_r, %b1_r, %prod1_r
39    ld     [%ap_r - 4], %a2_r         !'second components'
40    ld     [%bp_r + 4], %b2_r
41    fadds  %sum_r, %prod2_r, %sum_r
42    subcc  %i_r, 2, %i_r  !'decrement counter'
43    fmuls  %a2_r, %b2_r, %prod2_r
44    bg     loop
45    add    %bp_r, 8, %bp_r

46    fadds  %sum_r, %prod1_r, %sum_r !'final additions'
47    fadds  %sum_r, %prod2_r, %sum_r
48    fsqrts %sum_r, %mag_r           !'obtain sqrt'
49  end_main
```

This time we have tried to optimize the loading of pointers by first loading the high-order 22 bits of the address of the first of the globals into a register %base, line 25. We are then able to load the pointers using only a single **or** instruction for each one, lines 26–27. To zero out the registers we first load zero into the first of the registers that we wish to zero, line 29, and then **fmove** it to zero out the other needed registers, lines 31–32.

In the loop we will need twice as many floating-point registers to be able to compute two products. These are declared in lines 16–23. The unrolled loop starts by loading two components into %a1 and %b1. The product, previously computed into %prod1, is then added to %sum before the contents of %a1 and %b1 are multiplied into %prod1, lines 33–38. Note that one of the pointer incrementing instructions is moved between the two floating-point instructions to keep the integer unit computing while instructions are passed to the floating-point unit, line 37. The next two vector components are then loaded into %a2 and %b2 before the product computed

into %prod2 is added into %sum, freeing up %prod2 to receive the second product,
lines 39–43. Here the decrement of the loop variable i is inserted between the two
floating-point instructions. The second pointer is incremented in the delay slot at
the end of the loop. When the loop exits, the final two additions are made and
the square root obtained, probably involving some processor stalls, but as the code
is not in a loop, the extra time involved is not too significant. Note that in this
program two multiplier units are used and that each unit has the time it takes to
execute seven integer unit instructions to compute the product. In the previous
version of the program time for only four instructions existed. Notice also that
instructions intervene between loading a register and using its contents for a computation: a1 and b1 are loaded in 34 and 35 followed by an add instruction in 37
before the fmuls using them in 38. In some processors a wait might happen if the
result of a load instruction is used immediately in the following instruction.

If we were writing in C we would need to write the program in the following
style to obtain the same efficiencies:

```
1   #include<math.h>
2   static float a[] = { 1.0, 1.5, -1.5, 10E2, -1.0, 16.0};
3   static float b[] = { 2.0, 4.0, 0.125, 0.0625, 3.0, 5.0};
4   main()
5   {
6     register int i = 6;
7     register float *ap = a, *bp = b;
8     register float magnitude, sum = 0.0;
9     register float a1, b1, a2, b2, prod1 = 0.0, prod2 = 0.0;

10    do{
11      a1 = *ap;
12      b1 = *bp;
13      sum += prod1;
14      ap += 2;
15      prod1 = a1 * b1;
16      a2 = *(ap - 1);
17      b2 = *(bp + 1);
18      sum += prod2;
19      bp += 2;
20      prod2 = a2 * b2;} while ((i -= 2) > 0);
21    sum += prod1;
22    sum += prod2;
23    magnitude = sqrt(sum);
24  }
```

Notice that the C code follows the same structure as the assembly language
given above.

11.7 Floating NaNs

Floating single numbers with a biased exponent of `0xff` do not represent conventional numbers but are instead reserved to represent quantities that may not be represented as numbers, like $\sqrt{-1}$ and infinity ∞. Plus ∞ is represented by `0x3f800000`, that is, a biased exponent of `0xff` and a zero fraction. Minus ∞ is the same as (∞) but with the sign bit set, `0xff800000`. Infinity will be the result of a floating divide of 1.0 by 0.0. Infinity compared to infinity is considered equal, whereas infinity compared to any other number is considered larger. The representation of ∞ is useful in such cases as `atan`(∞), which can be programmed to return the correct result of $+\pi/2$.

All other numbers with a biased exponent of `0xff` are considered to represent quantities that cannot be represented as numbers. It is customary to initialize all uninitialized single floating variables to integer -1, which is, of course, `0xffffffff`, a NaN. The hardware can detect such an inappropriate floating operand and cause a floating exception, which, in turn, may cause a trap.

11.8 Subnormal Numbers

Single floating numbers with a biased exponent of `0x00` are not interpreted as normal floating-point numbers but instead represent "subnormal" floating-point numbers. When the smallest number that can be represented, `1.17549435e-38`, is reached, there is a gap until zero is reached and then another gap until we reach `-1.17549435e-38`. To soften the encounter with this gap, subnormal numbers were defined. They are represented with a biased exponent of `0x00` and are interpreted as

$$N = (-1)^s \times 2^{-126} \times 0.f$$

where

  s is the sign bit
  f is the significand now a fraction

Note that the implicit one of the significand is no longer present and that the fraction is indeed just that, a fraction. We can now move down from the smallest single float `1.17549435e-38`, represented as `0x00800000`, to `1.17549421e-38` represented as `0x007fffff`, and continue down till we reach `1.40129846e-45`, represented as `0x00000001`. The numbers are now being represented with constant absolute accuracy, no longer with constant relative accuracy. The smallest subnormal, `1.40129846e-45`, is represented to $\pm 1.4 \times 10^{-45}$ with a relative accuracy of $\pm 50\%$. While subnormal numbers increase the range of floating-point numbers, they do not dramatically increase that range and they are a problem to implement in hardware; subnormal numbers are frequently handled in software by arranging that the floating-point processor traps when such a number is encountered.

11.9   Extended Precision Floating-Point

While single floating numbers and the associated floating-point processor apparently solve the problem of representing real numbers of considerable range, the
range $\pm 1.0 \times 10^{\pm 38}$ is quite limited and the relative accuracy of seven digits is also
limited. Numerical analysis frequently requires a much larger range of numbers
represented to greater relative significance. To this end, two additional floating-
point formats are specified, floating-point doubleword, and floating-point quad-
word. Hardware normally exists to perform floating double computations, while
floating-point quad is normally handled (very slowly) in software. The C programming language performs most calculations involving real numbers in floation-point
double.

The floating-point double representation takes eight bytes (see Figure 11.3) and
is interpreted as follows:

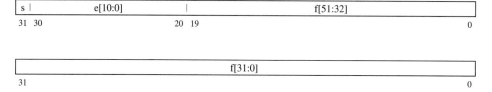

Figure 11.3: Floating-Point Double Format

$$N = (-1)^s \times 2^{e-1023} \times 1.f$$

where

> s is the sign bit
> e is a biased exponent
> f is the fractional part of the significand

Floating double numbers have a range starting from the very small number
2.2250738585072014e-308 up to 1.7976931348623157e+308 and are represented
with approximately 17 decimal digit relative accuracy. As with floating single
numbers, the largest biased exponent is reserved to represent ∞ and NaNs. Plus
infinity is represented as

.word 0x7ff00000, 0

Minus infinity is represented as

.word 0xfff00000, 0

and NaNs as anything with the biased exponent 0x7ff and the fraction nonzero.
Initializing double floating variables to integer -1 will enable the detection of uninitialized variables during computation.

Instructions exist for loading and storing double floating operands. In the case of double floating operands, each occupies two floating-point registers and the first register of a pair must be even. Thus, we can load a floating double into %f0 and into %f2 but not into %f1. Instructions lddf and stdf exist for this purpose but the assembler recognizes ldd and std in their place when the register is a floating register. Of course, floating doubles must be stored in doubleword aligned memory locations.

Mnemonic	Operation
ldd	Load doubleword into two floating-point registers.
std	Store two floating-point registers into memory.

All the single floating instructions also exist in floating double form, including a multiply instruction, fsmuld, whose source operands are single and the result double:

Mnemonic	Operands	Description
faddd	$freg_{rs1}$, $freg_{rs2}$ $freg_{rd}$	Add.
fsubd	$freg_{rs1}$, $freg_{rs2}$ $freg_{rd}$	Subtract.
fmuld	$freg_{rs1}$, $freg_{rs2}$ $freg_{rd}$	Multiply.
fsmuld	$freg_{rs1}$, $freg_{rs2}$ $freg_{rd}$	Multiply single to double.
fdivd	$freg_{rs1}$, $freg_{rs2}$ $freg_{rd}$	Divide.
fsqrtd	$freg_{rs2}$ $freg_{rd}$	Square root.

Once again the registers refer to the first register of the pair containing the operands.

The three single floating move instructions fmovs, fnegs, and fabss do not exist for floating doubles, as a double may be handled by using fmovs, fnegs, or fabss to move the high part and a second fmovs to handle the remainder of the fraction:

```
\* f0 = | f2 | *\

fabss %f2, %f0
fmovs %f3, %f1
```

Conversion routines exist between double and integer data as well as between single and double floating-point:

Mnemonic	Operands	Description
fitod	$freg_{rs2}$ $freg_{rd}$	Convert integer to double float.
fdtoi	$freg_{rs2}$ $freg_{rd}$	Convert double float to integer.
fdtos	$freg_{rs2}$ $freg_{rd}$	Convert double float to single float.
fstod	$freg_{rs2}$ $freg_{rd}$	Convert single float to double float.

Finally, there is a compare instruction that sets the four status bits G, L, E, and U:

Mnemonic	Operands	Description
fcmpd	$freg_{rs1}$ $freg_{rs2}$	Compare.

The integer unit branch instructions are the same for all floating compares.

Let us look at an example of double precision floating-point, the computation of a vector cross product:

```
 1   /* vector cross product:
 2           c_x = a_y * b_z - a_z * b_y
 3           c_y = a_z * b_x - a_x * b_z
 4           c_z = a_x * b_y - a_y * b_x
 5   */
 6           include(../macro_defs.m)
 7           .section ".data"
 8           .align  8
 9   globals:
10   a_m:    .double 0r1.0, 0r0.0, 0r0.0 !'vect a'
11   b_m:    .double 0r0.0, 0r1.0, 0r0.0 !'vect b'
12   c_m:    .skip 8 * 4                 !'vect c'
13           .section ".text"
14           cdef(ap_r, 10, 'points to a')
15           cdef(bp_r, 11, 'points to b')
16           cdef(cp_r, 12, 'points to c the result')
17           cdef(base_r, 13)
18           cdef(cx_r, f0, 'vector components')
19           cdef(cy_r, f2)
20           cdef(cz_r, f4)
21           cdef(ax_r, f6)
22           cdef(ay_r, f8)
23           cdef(az_r, f10)
24           cdef(bx_r, f12)
25           cdef(by_r, f14)
```

```
26              cdef(bz_r, f16)
27              cdef(cx1_r, f18, 'product terms')
28              cdef(cx2_r, f20)
29              cdef(cy1_r, f22)
30              cdef(cy2_r, f24)
31              cdef(cz1_r, f26)
32              cdef(cz2_r, f28)
33              cdef(subx, '+ %g0') !'subscript offsets'
34              cdef(suby, '+ 8')
35              cdef(subz, '+ 16')
36   begin_main
37     sethi  %hi(globals), %base_r !'load base address'
38     or     %base_r, %lo(a_m), %ap_r !'vector pointers'
39     ldd    [%ap_r suby], %ay_r    !'load a_y'
40     or     %base_r, %lo(b_m), %bp_r
41     ldd    [%bp_r subz], %bz_r    !'load b_z'
42     fmuld  %ay_r, %bz_r, %cx1_r   !'first comp. of c_x'
43     ldd    [%ap_r subz], %az_r
44     ldd    [%bp_r suby], %by_r
45     fmuld  %az_r, %by_r, %cx2_r   !'sec. comp. of c_x'
46     ldd    [%bp_r subx], %bx_r
47     ldd    [%ap_r subx], %ax_r
48     fsubd  %cx1_r, %cx2_r, %cx_r  !'c_x'
49     fmuld  %az_r, %bx_r, %cy1_r   !'first comp. of c_y'
50     or     %base_r, %lo(c_m), %cp_r
51     fmuld  %ax_r, %bz_r, %cy2_r   !'sec. comp. of c_y'
52     std    %cx_r, [%cp_r subx]
53     fsubd  %cy1_r, %cy2_r, %cy_r  !'c_y'
54     std    %cy_r, [%cp_r suby]
55     fmuld  %ax_r, %by_r, %cz1_r   !'first comp. of c_z'
56     fmuld  %ay_r, %bx_r, %cz2_r   !'sec. comp. of c_z'
57     fsubd  %cz1_r, %cz2_r, %cz_r  !'c_z'
58     std    %cz_r, [%cp_r subz]
59   end_main
```

Note the use of the `.double` pseudo-op to assemble double precision numbers in lines 10–12. In the program we have attempted to interlace integer unit instructions with floating-point instructions. We have also tried to optimize for the availability of two floating multiplier units; however, the code is equally efficient when there is only one. Note that the optimization tends to fall off at the end of the program, as we have to wait for all our results to be available.

11.10   Debugging Floating Double Programs

It is hard to debug programs containing floating double, as `gdb` is unable to print the contents of two floating-point registers interpreted as a floating double directly. Double floats stored in memory can be examined by using the giant format to specify eight bytes:

```
(gdb) x/gf 0x4098
0x4098 <f1>:    3.5
```

If we wish to be able to print out the values of floating doubles stored in registers, we can follow the approach of C with the debugging option `-g`. Here symbol table entries are made to inform the debugger of the location and contents of all variables, including floating doubles in registers. The macro file `reg_defs.m` (see Appendix B), defines a macro `def_reg` with the following arguments:

1. A symbolic register name

2. A SPARC register such as o0, l3, f0, f8

3. A data type which describes the data that the register contains

   - word - The register contains a signed 32-bit integer.
   - byte - The register contains a character.
   - half - The register contains a signed short integer.
   - single - The register contains a single float.
   - double - The register contains a double float.

4. An optional comment, best enclosed in ' and '

The macro file `reg_defs.m` needs to be included at the beginning of the file, as it defines the register types. For example, we may define registers in the following program:

```
        include(../macro_defs.m)
        include(../reg_defs.m)
/* computes
main() {
        register int i;
        register char c;
        register float f;
        register double d;

        f = -1.5;
        d = 33.0 * f;
        c = 'a';
```

```
          i = c + 10E5 * f;
}
*/
          .section        ".data"
          .align  4
c10e5:    .single 0r10E5
c15:      .single 0r-1.5
          .align  8
c33:      .double 0r33.0

          .section        ".text"
          def_reg(f_f, f0, single, 'the value of f')
          def_reg(t_fs, f2, single, 'single temp')
          def_reg(t_fd, f2, double, 'double temp')
          def_reg(t_fi, f2, word,   'int temp')
          def_reg(c_r, 10, byte)
          def_reg(i_r, 11, word)
          def_reg(d_f, f4, double)

          local_var
          var(ftoi, 4)

          begin_fn(main)
          set     c15, %o0         ! 'f = -1.5'
          ld      [%o0], %f_f
          set     c33, %o0         ! 'd = 33.0 * f'
          ldd     [%o0], %d_f
          fstod   %f_f, %t_fd
          fmuld   %d_f, %t_fd, %d_f
          mov     'a', %c_r        ! 'c = 'a''
          set     c10e5, %o0       ! 'i = c + 10E5 * f;'
          ld      [%o0], %t_fs
          fmuls   %f_f, %t_fs, %f_f
          st      %c_r, [%fp + ftoi]
          ld      [%fp + ftoi], %t_fi
          fitos   %t_fi, %t_fs
          fadds   %f_f, %t_fs, %f_f
          fstoi   %f_f, %t_fi
          st      %t_fi, [%fp + ftoi]
          ld      [%fp + ftoi], %i_r
          end_fn(main, %g0, %g0, %o0)
```

You will see in the program above that floating register %f2 is defined three times to contain a single, a double, and an int.

The assembly language contains the register definitions followed by a number of symbol table entries, .stabs, followed by the program

```
            .stabs "null",100,0,0,.LLtext0
.LLtext0:
.stabs "word:t1=r1;-2147483648;2147483647;",128,0,0,0
.stabs "byte:t2=r2;0;127;",128,0,0,0
.stabs "half:t8=r1;-32768;32767;",128,0,0,0
.stabs "single:t12=r1;4;0;",128,0,0,0
.stabs "double:t13=r1;8;0;",128,0,0,0
.stabs "void:t19=19",128,0,0,0


/* computes
main() {
        register int i;
        register char c;
        register float f;
        register double d;

        f = -1.5;
        d = 33.0 * f;
        c = 'a';
        i = c + 10E5 * f;
}
*/
            .section        ".data"
            .align  4
c10e5:      .single 0r10E5
c15:        .single 0r-1.5
            .align  8
c33:        .double 0r33.0


            .section        ".text"

            .stabs "f_f:r12",64,0,0,32 !f_f = %f0 the value of f

            .stabs "t_fs:r12",64,0,0,34 !t_fs = %f2 single temp

            .stabs "t_fd:r13",64,0,0,34 !t_fd = %f2 double temp

            .stabs "t_fi:r1",64,0,0,34 !t_fi = %f2 int temp
```

```
        .stabs "c_r:r2",64,0,0,16 !c_r = %l0

        .stabs "i_r:r1",64,0,0,17 !i_r = %l1

        .stabs "d_f:r13",64,0,0,36 !d_f = %f4

        !local variables
        ftoi = -4

        .global        main
        .align  4
main:       save    %sp, -96, %sp

        set     c15, %o0         ! f = -1.5
        ld      [%o0], %f0
        set     c33, %o0         ! d = 33.0 * f
        ldd     [%o0], %f4
        fstod   %f0, %f2
        fmuld   %f4, %f2, %f4
        mov     'a', %l0         ! c = a''
        set     c10e5, %o0       ! i = c + 10E5 * f;
        ld      [%o0], %f2
        fmuls   %f0, %f2, %f0
        st      %l0, [%fp + ftoi]
        ld      [%fp + ftoi], %f2
        fitos   %f2, %f2
        fadds   %f0, %f2, %f0
        fstoi   %f0, %f2
        st      %f2, [%fp + ftoi]
        ld      [%fp + ftoi], %l1
        ret
        restore %g0, %g0, %o0
        .type   main, #function
        .size   main, . - main
```

On executing the program in gdb we may print out the register contents by referring to them by name, not as $f0, etc.

```
...
1: x/i $pc  0x1068c <main+12>:  ld   [ %o0 ], %f0
(gdb) p f_f
$1 = -1.5
(gdb) si
...
1: x/i $pc  0x10698 <main+24>:  ldd   [ %o0 ], %f4
```

```
(gdb)
0x1069c in main ()
1: x/i $pc  0x1069c <main+28>:  fstod  %f0, %f2
(gdb) p d_f
$2 = 33
(gdb) si
0x106a0 in main ()
1: x/i $pc  0x106a0 <main+32>:  fmuld  %f4, %f2, %f4
(gdb) p t_fd
$3 = -1.5
(gdb) si
0x106a4 in main ()
1: x/i $pc  0x106a4 <main+36>:  mov  0x61, %l0
(gdb) p d_f
$4 = -49.5
(gdb) p c_r
$5 = 97 'a'
(gdb) si
...
1: x/i $pc  0x106b4 <main+52>:  fmuls  %f0, %f2, %f0
(gdb) p t_fs
$6 = 1000000
(gdb) si
0x106b8 in main ()
1: x/i $pc  0x106b8 <main+56>:  st  %l0, [ %fp + -4 ]
(gdb)
0x106bc in main ()
1: x/i $pc  0x106bc <main+60>:  ld  [ %fp + -4 ], %f2
(gdb) si
0x106c0 in main ()
1: x/i $pc  0x106c0 <main+64>:  fitos  %f2, %f2
(gdb) p t_fi
$8 = 97
(gdb) si
0x106c4 in main ()
1: x/i $pc  0x106c4 <main+68>:  fadds  %f0, %f2, %f0
(gdb) p t_fs
$9 = 97
(gdb) si
0x106c8 in main ()
1: x/i $pc  0x106c8 <main+72>:  fstoi  %f0, %f2
(gdb) p f_f
$10 = -1499903
(gdb) si
```

```
0x106cc in main ()
1: x/i $pc  0x106cc <main+76>:  st   %f2, [ %fp + -4 ]
(gdb) p t_fi
$11 = -1499903
(gdb) si
0x106d0 in main ()
1: x/i $pc  0x106d0 <main+80>:  ld   [ %fp + -4 ], %l1
(gdb)
0x106d4 in main ()
1: x/i $pc  0x106d4 <main+84>:  ret
(gdb) p i_r
$12 = -1499903
(gdb)
```

11.11 Floating Quad Format

Finally, we need to mention quad floating-point. Floating quad numbers occupy 16 bytes of memory and four floating-point registers (see Figure 11.4). Quad floats may only be stored in registers %fn, where n is divisible by 4 with no remainder.

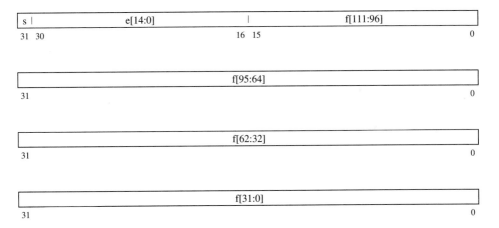

Figure 11.4: Floating-Point Quad Format

The range of such numbers with 15 bits for the biased exponent and 112 bits of precision should satisfy even the most demanding numerical analysts. A full set of instructions is provided for handling quad numbers. Instruction execution is, however, frequently emulated in software and not implemented in hardware. We will not discuss quad floating numbers further here.

11.12 Function Calls

When a function call is made, the first six arguments are placed in registers %o0 through %o5, with any additional arguments placed on the stack. In C, floating-point value arguments are also passed in %o0 through %o5 with any additional arguments placed on the stack. As a floating-point double argument will occupy two integer registers, this means that at most, three double-float arguments may be passed by value in registers %o0 through %o5. A pointer to a floating-point argument, of course, occupies only one register. If a function is called with an integer argument followed by three double-floats, the integer argument will be in %o0 and the next two double-floats in %o1–%o4. Notice that the double-float value arguments are not in even registers so that they may *not* be loaded there by a ldd instruction; instead, each part of the value argument must be loaded by a ld instruction. Furthermore, while the high-order part of the last float argument will be in %o5, its low-order part will be on the stack at %sp + 92. This can make passing double-float arguments by value difficult.

Furthermore, when the function is entered, the floating arguments will be needed in the floating registers, not in the out registers. There is no instruction to move the contents of an integer register to a floating register. To move data between the floating-point processor registers and the integer unit registers, the data must be first stored in memory, from one processor and then loaded, from memory, into the other processor's registers. Space in the stack frame is normally allocated for this purpose.

For example, to call the following function:

```
double fsum(int i, double a1, double a2, double a3, double a4)
{
  double sum = a1;
  if (--i) sum += a2; else return sum;
  if (--i) sum += a3; else return sum;
  if (--i) sum += a4; else return sum;
  if (--i) exit(); else return sum;
}
```

assuming that the arguments to be passed were in floating-point registers: %f0, %f2, %f4, and %f6. and that we had provided a temp space on the stack to move double-floats between processors:

```
        var(ftemp, 8)
```

We would proceed as follows:

```
1    add    %sp, -(3 * 4) & -8, %sp  !'make room for args'
2    mov    4, %o0                   !'first int arg'
3    std    %f0, [%fp + ftemp]       !'store second arg'
4    ld     [%fp + ftemp], %o1       !'high-order part'
```

```
5    ld    [%fp + ftemp + 4], %o2    !'low-order part'
6    std   %f2, [%fp + ftemp]        !'third arg'
7    ld    [%fp + ftemp], %o3
8    ld    [%fp + ftemp + 4], %o4
9    std   %f4, [%sp + arg_d(6)]     !'fourth arg into
10                                   ! %fp + arg6_s
11                                   ! and %fp + arg7_s'
12   ld    [%sp + arg_d(6)], %o5      !'high-order part
13                                   ! back into %o5'
14   call  fsum
15   std   %f6, [%sp + arg_d(8)]       !'fifth arg to stack'
16   sub   %sp, -(3 * 4) & -8, %sp !'release space for args'
```

Note that while the first two float arguments may be stded to the stack, they must be lded back into the out registers, lines 3–8. Note also that because space is left on the stack for the **struct** pointer, the argument location, `%sp + arg6_s`, is doubleword aligned, as is `%sp + arg8_s`, we may use the **std** instructions to store the arguments onto the stack, lines 9 and 15. The high-order part of the third floating argument has to be put back into `%o5` so that the first six words of arguments are in the registers.

Once in the function, the reverse operation has to occur to move the arguments back into registers:

```
1    st    %i1, [%fp + ftemp]        !'high-order part'
2    st    %i2, [%fp + ftemp + 4]    !'low-order part'
3    ldd   [%fp + ftemp], %f0        !'first float'
4    st    %i3, [%fp + ftemp]
5    st    %i4, [%fp + ftemp + 4]
6    ldd   [%fp + ftemp], %f2        !'second float'
7    st    %i5, [%fp + arg_d(6)]      !'high-order part
8                                    ! back onto stack'
9    ldd   [%fp + arg_d(6)], %f4      !'third float
10   ldd   [%fp + arg_d(8)], %f6      !'fourth float'
```

The function is of type double and will thus return a double-float. Single floating values are returned in `%f0`, doubles are returned in `%f0` and `%f1`, and quad floats are returned in `%f0` through `%f3`.

If we had passed pointers to the double arguments in the function

```
double
fsum(int i, double &a1, double &a2, double &a3, double &a4)
```

then the call would be vastly simplified:

```
1    mov 4, %o0 !'first int arg'
2    set a1_m, %o1 !'&second arg'
```

```
3     set a2_m, %o2 !'&third arg'
4     set a3_m, %o3 !'&fourth arg'
5     sethi %hi(a4_m), %o4 !'high part'
6     call fsum
7     or %o4, %lo(a4_m), %o4 !'low part of adr'
```

and the movement of the double arguments into the floating-point registers also vastly simplified:

```
1     ldd [%i1], %a1_r !'store second arg'
2     ldd [%i2], %a2_r  !'third arg'
3     ldd [%i3], %a3_r  !'fourth arg'
4     ldd [%i4], %a4_r !'fifth arg'
```

In general, it is much more efficient to pass a pointer to any data element larger than the register length of a machine.

We mentioned earlier that there was no register file of floating-point registers, only the 32 registers that are unaffected by **save** and **call** instructions. Some protocol has to be established for a function call, either the calling function must save all its active floating-point registers or the called function must save any registers that it uses. There are, of course, more complicated arrangements, such as saving some of the registers, etc. In the SPARC architecture the protocol is that the calling function must save all its active floating-point registers, that is, all the registers that contain valid data. This then allows a called function to use any of the floating-point registers without having first to save them.

This convention has implications. Consider the program on page 298 that places most of its local variables into registers. If it were to call another function, all its floating-point registers would have to be moved onto the stack before the call could be made, thus invalidating the storage of the variables in the floating-point registers in the first place. If the function called performed only a trivial computation, it would be better replaced by a macro to be expanded, in-line, by **cpp** whenever needed, thus avoiding the need to move all the registers to and from the stack. It really only makes sense, in this architecture, to assign floation-point variables to registers in functions that do not call any other functions, leaving floating-point variables in other functions on the stack to be loaded and stored into the floating registers as needed. The loading and storing of floating-point variables to and from the stack do not, however, have to slow down the machine if the loads and stores are interleaved with floating-point computations.

11.13 Tagged Arithmetic

In some computer languages, such as Prolog, Smalltalk, and Lisp, it is difficult to determine the type of variables until the program is executed. So far we have assumed that we knew the type of all variables when we wrote a program. We loaded

an integer variable into a register and then added it to another integer, or we loaded
the pointer to an array into a register and then accessed a particular element in the
array. In the case of multidimensional arrays, this was quite complicated, requiring
knowledge of the dimensions of each of the subscripts. If we did not know the
type of variables at execution time, we would have to access all variables through a
data structure that would specify the type, and access information. For example,
the first element of the list could be a type field: int, float, double, int vector,
int multidimensional array, and so on. Additional elements might then specify
the subscript bounds for arrays, types of structure fields, and so on. Finally, there
would be a value field where the actual value, or values, would be stored. Arithmetic
operators, such as **add** and **sub**, would then be given pointers to these lists, through
which the data could be accessed and the appropriate operation performed. For
example, if both data types were ints and the operation was an add, the **add**
instruction would be executed when the values had been loaded into registers. If
the data types were integer vectors of the same dimension, a loop would be executed,
adding pairs of values together a much more complicated procedure.

11.13.1   Lisp

Lisp is a language in which types are very general and are determined at execution
time. The Lisp language is based on a binary tree representation in which lists
may also be represented. The Lisp language was based on a paper written by
John McCarthy in 1960 [16] and implemented by Stephen Russell and Daniel J.
Edwards in the same year [17]. The language defined atomic symbols which might
have properties and values which could be of any type. Atomic symbols could be
combined together to make *S-expressions*. The most basic operation is to take two
atomic symbols and combine them to make an S-expression. If A and B are atomic
symbols (A . B) is an S-expression. The function cons[A,B] = (A.B) creates
such a *dotted pair* represented by two adjacent pointers, one addressing A and the
other B. The result of the **cons** function execution is a pointer to one element of
the pair (see Figure 11.5). Pairs of pointer cells to form dotted pairs are usually
taken from a free list. Such cells are returned by a *garbage collector* to the free list
when they are no longer needed.

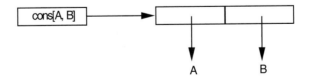

Figure 11.5: An S-Expression

A list of atomic symbols is obtained by *consing* them together with a special
atom NIL used to represent the end of lists (see Figure 11.6).

```
(A, B, C) = (A. (B . (C . NIL)))
```

obtained by

```
cons[A, cons[B, cons[C, NIL]]]
```

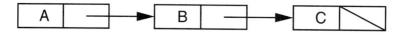

Figure 11.6: A List

A function `car` is provided to obtain the first element of a list, and a function `cdr` is provided which returns the remainder of the list:

```
car[(A, B, C)] = A
cdr[(A, B, C)] = (B, C)
```

Atoms are represented by a list whose `car` is a flag -1 followed by a list of properties. Each property is preceded by a flag indicating the type of property, followed by a pointer to the data structure representing the property. Properties range from an integer value to complex data and list structures. All atoms have a property PNAME, indicating their print names used on input and output. Numbers are treated separately with a flag to indicate the type, followed by a pointer to the data representing the number.

How to distinguish flags from pointers? The two low-order bits of a word may be reserved as a tag, as pointers are word addresses and, as a result, have both their low-order bits zero. However, they point to a pair of words, the `car` and the `cdr`, so that while the first may be addressed by the pointer directly, the second must be addressed by the pointer ± 4. If we were always to *set* both the two low-order bits in a pointer, the tag, the `car` and `cdr` of the dotted pair, might be addressed as

```
        ld      [%o0 - 3], %car
        ld      [%o0 + 1], %cdr
```

assuming that, in this example, the pointer was in %o0.

If the tag is a three, the list cell, which contains two pointers and occupies two words, is accessed as word data. The first cell is addressed as the pointer -3. The second cell is addressed as the pointer $+1$. If the tag is not three, a memory alignment trap will occur, indicating invalid data.

If we follow this rather convoluted procedure, we may, however, represent integers directly by scaling them by 4 so that they appear to be flags; this procedure will limit the range of integers to between -2^{-29} and $2^{29} - 1$. For example, a function to add its two untyped operands together might first check to see if its two arguments are both flags, meaning that they were both integers, and if so, add them directly. If either is a pointer, more complicated processing will be required first to ascertain the types, then to retrieve the data, and finally, to apply the appropriate addition function to the data. Consider, as a simple example, handling just two types, int and double. We will represent ints as flags and represent double precision numbers with a tag −2 with a pointer to the double word representing the data. See Figure 11.7 for the data structure to represent 3.5.

Figure 11.7: A Double Precision Number

The add function might then be

```
include(../macro_defs.m)
include(../reg_defs.m)

begin_struct(list)        ! 'define list structure'
field(car, 4)
field(cdr, 4)
end_struct(list)

DOUBLE_FLAG = -2

begin_fn(cons)            ! 'the cons function'
call    malloc
mov     size_of_list, %o0
st      %i0, [%o0 + list_car]
st      %i1, [%o0 + list_cdr]
end_fn(cons, %o0, 3, %o0) ! 'make it a pointer'

local_var
var(int2f, 8)
begin_fn(add)            ! 'the add function'
def_reg(l, i0, word)
def_reg(r, i1, word)
def_reg(ptr1, i2, word)
def_reg(ptr2, i3, word)
def_reg(sum, i4, word)
andcc   %l, 3, %g0       ! 'int int?'
bne     1f
andcc   %r, 3, %g0
bne     1f
add     %l, %r, %o0      ! 'yes just add them and return'
ret
restore %o0, %g0, %o0
```

```
1:        sub      %l, 3, %ptr1       ! 'get the possible argument pointers'
          sub      %r, 3, %ptr2
          call     malloc             ! 'create space for the result'
          mov      8, %o0
          mov      %o0, %sum

          andcc    %l, 3, %g0         ! 'int double?'
          bne      1f
          nop
          ld       [%ptr2 + list_car], %o1 ! 'check second flag'
          cmp      %o1, DOUBLE_FLAG
          bne      1f
          sra      %l, 2, %o1         ! 'convert first arg to int'
          st       %o1, [%fp + int2f]
          ld       [%fp + int2f], %f2
          fitod    %f2, %f2           ! 'convert first arg to double'
          ld       [%ptr2 + list_cdr], %o1
          ldd      [%o1 - 3], %f4
          faddd    %f2, %f4, %f2      ! 'add them and store result'
          ba       done
          std      %f2, [%sum]

1:        andcc    %r, 3, %g0         ! 'double int?'
          bne      1f
          nop
          ld       [%ptr1 + list_car], %o1 ! 'check first flag'
          cmp      %o1, DOUBLE_FLAG
          bne      1f
          sra      %r, 2, %o1         ! 'convert second arg to int'
          st       %o1, [%fp + int2f]
          ld       [%fp + int2f], %f2
          fitod    %f2, %f2           ! 'convert second arg to double'
          ld       [%ptr1 + list_cdr], %o1
          ldd      [%o1 - 3], %f4
          faddd    %f2, %f4, %f2      ! 'add them and store result'
          ba       done
          std      %f2, [%sum]

1:        ld       [%ptr1 + list_car], %o0! 'double dobule?'
          cmp      %o0, DOUBLE_FLAG
          bne      done
          nop
          ld       [%ptr2 + list_car], %o1
```

```
        cmp     %o1, DOUBLE_FLAG
        bne     done
        nop
        ld      [%ptr1 + list_cdr], %o1 ! 'get both args'
        ldd     [%o1 - 3], %f2
        ld      [%ptr2 + list_cdr], %o1
        ldd     [%o1 - 3], %f4
        faddd   %f2, %f4, %f2     ! 'and add them'
        std     %f2, [%sum]

done:   mov     DOUBLE_FLAG, %o0 ! 'set flag and cons it to data'
        call    cons
        add     %sum, 3, %o1

done:   end_fn(add, %o0, %g0, %o0)
```

The following main function creates two ints and two doubles and calls add to perform their addition:

```
        .align  8
double_seven:     .double 0r7.0
double_three_five:        .double 0r3.5
        .align  4
        begin_fn(main)
        def_reg(n1, 10, word)
        def_reg(n2, 11, word)
        def_reg(n3, 12, word)
        def_reg(n4, 13, word)
        def_reg(r1, 14, word)
        def_reg(r2, 15, word)
        def_reg(r3, 16, word)
        def_reg(r4, 17, word)

        mov     2 << 2, %n1             ! '2'
        mov     -5 << 2, %n2            ! '-5'
        set     double_seven + 3, %o1  ! '7.0'
        call    cons
        mov     DOUBLE_FLAG, %o0
        mov     %o0, %n3

        set     double_three_five + 3, %o1 ! '3.5'
        call    cons
        mov     DOUBLE_FLAG, %o0
        mov     %o0, %n4
```

```
        mov       %n1, %o0
        call      add
        mov       %n2, %o1
        mov       %o0, %r1

        mov       %n3, %o0
        call      add
        mov       %n4, %o1
        mov       %o0, %r2

        mov       %n1, %o0
        call      add
        mov       %n4, %o1
        mov       %o0, %r3

        mov       %n3, %o0
        call      add
        mov       %n2, %o1
        mov       %o0, %r4
        end_fn(main)
```

Note that the sum of two doubles requires two calls to `malloc`, which we are using to simulate the free list in this example, with a number of additional loads and stores, whereas the sum of two ints requires only two tests and an addition. If integer arithmetic occurs frequently, this scheme will reduce the overhead of supporting dynamic typing.

11.13.2 Tagged Arithmetic Instructions

The SPARC architecture provides tagged arithmetic instructions to simplify this process even further. Tagged add and sub instructions exist that will set the overflow V bit if the tags are not both zero (or if an overflow occurs): `taddcc` and `tsubcc`.

In this case the tagged instructions may be used in-line in the main program followed by a test of the V bit to jump over code to call the add function. The add function now handles all cases *but* that of the addition of two integers.

```
        .align  8
double_seven:       .double 0r7.0
double_three_five:        .double 0r3.5
        .align  4
        begin_fn(main)
        def_reg(n1, 10, word)
```

```
        . . .

        taddcc  %n1, %n2, %r1   ! assume they are its and add them
        bvc     1f              ! check our assumption
        mov     %n1, %o0        ! not both ints, better call add
        call    add
        mov     %n2, %o1
        mov     %o0, %r1

1:      taddcc  %n3, %n4, %r2   ! assume they are its and add them
        bvc     1f              ! check our assumption
        mov     %n3, %o0        ! not both ints, better call add
        call    add
        mov     %n4, %o1
        mov     %o0, %r2

1:      taddcc  %n1, %n4, %r3
        bvc     1f

        . . .


        end_fn(main)
```

The function add now only performs the addition of: int — double, double — int,
double — double.

```
        local_var
        var(int2f, 8)
        begin_fn(add)
        def_reg(l, i0, word)
        def_reg(r, i1, word)
        def_reg(ptr1, i2, word)
        def_reg(ptr2, i3, word)
        def_reg(sum, i4, word)

        sub     %l, 3, %ptr1
        sub     %r, 3, %ptr2
        call    malloc
        mov     8, %o0
        mov     %o0, %sum

        andcc   %l, 3, %g0      ! 'int double?'
        bne     1f
```

```
        .  .  .

done:   mov     DOUBLE_FLAG, %o0
        call    cons
        add     %sum, 3, %o1

done:   end_fn(add, %o0, %g0, %o0)
```

The use of the taddcc instruction reduces the number of instruction cycles from seven to two in the case of the addition of two ints.

Two additional instructions, taddcctv and tsubcctv, exist which will cause a trap if the V bit is set as a result of overflow or if the tags are not both zero. In these cases the tagged add or subtract instruction can be coded in-line with a trap occurring if either operand is noninteger. This requires a trap handler to obtain the operands, perform the extended arithmetic operation, and return the result in the correct register. The use of the trap instructions reduces the number of instructions from two to one. By using tagged arithmetic we can support dynamic typing without paying a heavy computational penalty for the most frequent case of the addition or subtraction of two integers.

11.14   Summary

The floating-point format was first introduced to allow for the representation of real numbers. Examples of integer processor code to add and to multiply such number formats were then given. The floating-point processor was then introduced to handle these floating-point format numbers directly. The floating-point unit has its own register set, capable of holding 32 single precision floating-point numbers and executes floating-point instructions fetched by the integer processor.

The single precision floating-point format was first introduced together with the single precision floating-point instructions. Conversion instructions between floating-point and integer format were presented with the floating-point compare instruction. The floating-point compare instruction sets floating condition codes that may be tested by the integer processor by means of a complete set of floating-point branch instructions; it is the integer unit that fetches instructions and controls the instruction flow. Debugging floating-point programs with gdb was discussed in terms of an example that reveals some of the intricacies of the multiple arithmetic units within the floation-point processor.

Floating-Point Not a Numbers (NaNs) were discussed with subnormal numbers. Double precision floating and extended precision floating-point numbers were described along with methods of handling doubles in registers by gdb. The section on floation-point concluded with a discussion of function calls involving floating-point arguments and return values. The chapter ended with a description of tagged arithmetic.

11.15 Exercises

11–1 Write functions to add, subtract, multiply, and divide integer quantities representing dollars and cents in terms of cents.

11–2 The following program prints the Cartesian coordinates of a vector in a coordinate system that is rotated -90 degrees about the z axis and translated by x = 10, y = 20, z = 1. Input of 0, 0, 0 produces output of: 10.00 20.00 1.00. Input of 10, 0, 0 produces output of: 10.00 10.00 1.00. Translate the main function and the function matmul into assembly language.

```
double atof (char *);

matmul(float r[4], float a[4][4], float b[4])
{
  register int i, j;          /* indices */
  double sum;                 /* dot product */

  for (i = 0; i < 4; i++)     /* for each row */
    {                         /* compute dot product */
      sum = 0.0;
      for (j = 0; j < 4; j++)
        sum += a[i][j] * b[j];
      r[i] = sum;             /* store result */
    }
}

float a[4][4] = {             /* rotated -90 deg */
  { 0, 1,  0, 10},            /* about z axis */
  {-1, 0,  0, 20},            /* located at 10, 20, 1 */
  {0, 0,  1,  1},
  {0, 0,  0,  1}};

main(int argc, char * * argv)
{
  register int i;             /* index */
  float c[4];                 /* result vector */
  float b[4];                 /* input vector */

  if (argc != 4)              /* check number of args */
    {
      printf("usage, ax, bx, cx\n");
      exit(1);
    }
  for (i = 0; i < 3; i++)     /* convert args into floats */
```

```
      b[i] = atof(*++argv);
    b[3] = 1.0;

    matmul (c, a, b);                    /* transform the vector */

    for (i = 0; i < 3; i++)              /* print the result */
      printf ("%8.2f", c[i]);
    printf("\n");
}
```

11–3 Write a 4 by 4 floating-point matrix multiply routine. Such matrices are used in computer graphics and in robotics to represent translation and rotation between objects in space. Determination of the absolute or relative position of objects involves the multiplication of such matrices. Hardware is normally provided in graphics workstations, but in this assignment we investigate the writing of an efficient matrix multiply routine.

```
The matrix product is simply written as
*/
matmul(float r[][4], float a[][4], float b[][4])
{

    register int i, j, k;

    double sum;

    for (i = 0; i < 4; i++)
      for (j = 0; j < 4; j++)
        {
          sum = 0.0;
          for (k = 0; k < 4; k++)
            sum += a[i][k] * b[k][j];
          r[i][j] = sum;
        }
}

/* given the data */
float a[4][4] = {                    /* object rotated 90 deg */
  { 0, 1,  0, 10},                   /* about z axis */
  {-1, 0,  0, 20}, /* located at 10, 20, 1 */
  {0,  0,  1,  1},
  {0,  0,  0,  1}};

float b[4][4] = {                    /* rotate 90 deg about x*/
```

```
     {1,   0,   0,   0},              /* and translate z=10 */
     {0,   0,  -1,   0},
     {0,   1,   0,  10},
     {0,   0,   0,   1}};

float c[4][4];                        /* the result of a * b */

main()
{

   register int i, j;

   matmul (c, a, b);

   for (i = 0; i < 4; i++)
     {
       for (j = 0; j < 4; j++)
         printf ("%8.2f", c[i][j]);
       putchar('\n');
     }
   putchar('\n');
}

/* produces the following output:
    0.00     0.00    -1.00    10.00
   -1.00     0.00     0.00    20.00
    0.00     1.00     0.00    11.00
    0.00     0.00     0.00     1.00
```

The matrix multiply, as written, is not very efficient. As the elements of the matrices being multiplied, a and b, are accessed four times each, they should be moved into floating-point registers once. Unfortunately, there are not sufficient registers. All the elements of the matrix a may, however, be moved directly into the floating-point registers, leaving 16 registers free. A single column of the matrix b may then be moved into four more registers to be used to generate the first column of the result. Then the next column may be moved into the same floating-point registers and the second column produced. All this will involve some pointer arithmetic. Note that while the multiplies may be done in single precision, the addition must be done in double precision. You are to write the improved matmul routine, described above, with the three matrices as arguments, in assembly language to be called by the main program, given above, using the global data, also given above.

11–4 Write a C main program that will call vector functions written in assembly language to verify the following vectorial equality:

$$a \ x \ (b \ x \ c) = b \ (\ a \ . \ c \ ) - c \ (\ a \ . \ b \ )$$

where a, b, and c are three-dimensional vectors (i.e., 3-tuples of the form `<x,y,z>`), and the symbols "." and "x" denote dot product and cross product, respectively. Your C program should start with the following external data definitions:

```
double a[] = {1.0, 2.0, 3.0};
double b[] = {4.0, 2.0, 0.0};
double c[] = {4.0, 2.0, 5.0};
double res1[3];
double res2[3];
double tmp[3];
double tmp2[3];
```

This initializes a, b, and c to be three-element double arrays and declares some other arrays that you will need to store temporary and the final result. Your C program should have a main program, which will set up arguments and call auxiliary functions, which you are to write in assembly language, to perform cross product, dot product, scale operation, and vector subtraction. These function names must be prepended by an _ and declared as external symbols by using the .global pseudo-op.

Your program should compute the left-hand side of the equation and store the resulting vector triple in the array **res1**. It should then independently compute the right-hand side of the equation and store the result in **res2**. The two triples should be equal and, in fact, should be `<60.0, 30.0,-40.0>`. A C main program to do this is as follows:

```
main()
{
  cross(res1, a, cross(tmp, b, c));
  subv(res2, scale(tmp, b, dot(a, c)) ,scale(tmp2, c, dot(a, b)));
  printf(" a x ( b x c )  = %8.2f%8.2f%8.2f\n",
         res1[0], res1[1], res1[2]);
  printf("b(a.c) - c(a.b) = %8.2f%8.2f%8.2f\n",
         res2[0], res2[1], res2[2]);
}
```

Note that the functions that compute vector results all return a pointer to the result vector, which enables you to write the infix style of C shown above. Do not forget to declare your external functions in the C program:

```
double *cross( double *result, double *a, double *b);
double dot(double *a, double *b);
double *subv(double *result, double *a, double *b);
double *scale(double *result, double *a, double f);
```

```
*/
double a[] = {1.0, 2.0, 3.0};
double b[] = {4.0, 2.0, 0.0};
double c[] = {4.0, 2.0, 5.0};
double res1[3];
double res2[3];
double tmp[3];
double tmp2[3];

double *cross( double *result, double *a, double *b);
        /* result = a x b */
double dot(double *a, double *b);
        /* returns a . b */
double *subv(double *result, double *a, double *b);
        /* result = a - b */
double *scale(double *result, double *a, double f);
        /* result = a scaled by f */

main()
{
  cross(res1, a, cross(tmp, b, c));
  subv(res2, scale(tmp, b, dot(a, c)),
        scale(tmp2, c, dot(a, b)));
  printf(" a x ( b x c )  = %8.2f%8.2f%8.2f\n",
        res1[0], res1[1], res1[2]);
  printf("b(a.c) - c(a.b) = %8.2f%8.2f%8.2f\n",
        res2[0], res2[1], res2[2]);
}
```

11–5 You are to write an assembly language program to compute the cube root of positive real numbers, in double precision, using Newton's method. You are to use command line arguments to input the number whose cube root is desired, val. Assume the initial guess for the cube root to be the $x = val / 3.0$. Compute y, the cube of your current guess x:

```
y = x * x * x;
```

and the difference between y and the desired val:

```
dy = y - val;
```

Compute the derivative $dy/dx = 3.0 * x * x$ and the new trial value for x as

```
x = x - dy / dy/dx;
```

and try again until the error | dy | < val * 1.0e-10;

Finally, print out the results in a %g format by calling the function printf:

```
% as8 1e-9
cube root of 1e-09 is 0.001
% as8 1.0e27
cube root of 1e+27 is 1e+09
```

11–6 The following program is based on the Newton-Raphson method for finding roots of a polynomial. The program first computes the value of the polynomial y and then computes the first derivative yp. A better value for the root x is then x - y / yp. The program iterates until abs(dx/x) < 1.0e-15 or until N iterations have occurred without convergence. Once this method starts to converge, convergence is extremely rapid. Input to the program is an initial guess for the root passed as a command line argument. You are to test that your program exits appropriately when no argument is given. You are then to look for roots near x = {-500.0, -8.0, 1.0, 4.0, and 2000.0}. You are also to test your program with x = 20000.0 when the program fails to converge. You are to reimplement the program in assembly language, taking command line arguments and printing error messages identical to the C program. The C program is executable and your output must be identical to the C program output.

```c
#include<stdio.h>
#include<stdlib.h>
#define A5   1.0
#define A4  -696.483
#define A3  -302610.3939
#define A2  -915510.7286
#define A1   8953489.814
#define A0  -8983379.828
#define B4 5.0 * A5
#define B3 4.0 * A4
#define B2 3.0 * A3
#define B1 2.0 * A2
#define B0 A1
#define EPS 1.0e-15
#define N 20
main(int argc, char ** argv)
{
  double x, y, yp, dx;
  int i = N;
  if (argc != 2)
    printf("missing starting value for x\n"), exit(1);
```

```
    x = atof(argv[1]);
    do {
       y = (((((A5 * x + A4) * x + A3) * x + A2) * x + A1) * x + A0;
       yp = ((((B4 * x + B3) * x + B2) * x + B1) * x + B0;
       x -= dx = y / yp;
       printf("For x = %22.15e, y = %10.3e and y' = %9.2e\n", x, y, yp);
    }while ((dx/x > 0.0 && dx/x > EPS ||  -dx/x > EPS) && --i);
    if (! i)
       printf("Failed to converge after %d iterations\n", N);
 return 0;
 }
```

11–7 One of the earliest calculations of π (3.14159...) was done by Archimedes, who compared the (unknown) circumference of a circle with the (known) circumference of a regular polygon inscribed within the circle. If the circle has unit radius and a square is inscribed within the circle, the circumference is 4 * sqrt(2). This is the first approximation to the circumference, which we will call p1. The kth approximation is:

```
    pk = 2 ** k sin (theta_k)
```

where ** represents exponentation and `theta_k` is `pi / 2 ** k`. Given pk we may find pk+1:

```
    pk+1 = sqrt(2) * 2 ** n sqrt{ 1 - sqrt[ 1 - (pk / 2 ** k) ** 2]}
```

Archimedes, looking for computational efficiency, decided to code the above in C, rejecting ML and C++. His code follows:

```
#include <math.h>
main()
{
  double pk, rt;
  register int k = 2, n = 4;

  rt = sqrt(2.0);
  pk = 2.0 * rt;

  printf("    k           n            pk\n");
  do {
    printf( "%5d, %11d, %16.10f\n", k, n, pk);
    pk = rt * n * sqrt( 1.0 - sqrt( 1.0 - (pk / n) * (pk / n)));
    n += n;
  } while (++k < 31);
}
```

He didn't get quite the result he was expecting but decided that it was due to the round-off when using grains of sand to represent numbers. He was probably right. Code up the algorithm above in assembly language using the variable types given above. Describe what goes wrong as k becomes large.

11–8 In this assignment you are to write a floation-point routine that computes both the sine and cosine of an angle given in degrees. Your routine is called by a main program written in C

```
#include <stdlib.h>
struct rectangular {
  double theta, sin, cos;
}

main(int argc, char ** argv)
{

  struct rectangular r1;

  if (argc != 2)
    printf("usage: theta\n"), exit(1);

  r1.theta = atof(*++argv);

  sincos(&r1);

  printf("theta = %f, sin = %f, cos = %f\n", r1.theta, r1.sin,
 r1.cos);
}
```

This main program first declares a struct to hold the angle in degrees along with the sine and cosine. The routine you are to write expects one argument, a pointer to a struct rectangular. You are to compute the sin and cos according to the following series expansions:

```
sin(x) = x - x^3 / 3! + x^5 / 5! - ...

cos(x) = 1 - x^2 / 2! + x^4 / 4! - ...
```

You are to continue to accumulate terms until the absolute value of the term is less than 1.0e-10. All real variables should be kept in double precision. You might need the constant $\pi/2 = 1.57079632679489661923$.

Chapter 12

TRAPS AND EXCEPTIONS

12.1 Introduction

To execute our program the operating system first loads the program into memory along with any library programs we will need, such as `printf`. After loading our program into memory, the `shell` collects the program arguments (typed after the program file name) and places them into a pointer array of strings. The operation system then executes a `call` to the `_main` function with two arguments, the number of arguments typed to the `shell`, and array of strings. When the program completes execution, it returns to the operating system by executing a `ret` instruction.

When the program executes there are two additional types of functions executed that we probably did not write: those that do not involve any shared resources, such as `sin` and `sscanf`, and those that do involve shared resources, such as `read` and `write`. During execution we may examine the first type of routine with `gdb` and may single-step through its execution if we wish. The second type of routine, which accesses a shared resource, is executed by the operating system and we may neither examine the code nor single-step through it. Why is this? A shared resource must be handled in such a manner that a programming error on your part does not invalidate the use of the resource for us or for others. Consider the file system: If we accidentally wrote over a directory block we could destroy data, our own and possibly others. Shared resources are handled by the operating system, and their access to users is protected.

The mechanism for preventing access to shared resources and the operating system itself is by means of two mechanisms, a different mode of execution and the `trap` mechanism. Programs may execute in two modes in the SPARC architecture, supervisor and user. Certain instructions may only be executed in supervisor mode, such as those that access state registers and input/output devices. We cannot access the processor state register when executing a program in user mode, but the operating system may read and write the register. The current state of the processor, supervisor or user, is kept in the processor status word. A number of load and store instructions exist to access other segments of memory that contain the devices and memory management. These load and store alternative instructions may only be executed in supervisor mode and are know as *privileged instructions*.

Access to memory is also limited by current execution mode. In user mode we have only limited access to memory, whereas in supervisor mode all of memory may be accessed. The operating system code along with all system tables is located in memory, which may only be accessed in supervisor mode. To call the operating system to perform a function, a trap instruction is executed. This instruction causes the machine to change to supervisor mode and to branch to system code to determine what service the user needs. As both system and user are loaded together in memory, it is very simple for the operating system to locate variables and data buffers in the user memory. Once the system has performed the service, it returns execution to the user program by executing a return from trap, `rett`, instruction, which among other things restores the state of the machine to its previous mode. The `rett` instruction is privileged so that a user may not inadvertently move into supervisor mode. It is very simple and efficient to move from user mode to supervisor mode, involving at most only a few instructions. The trap instruction is a nondelayed branch and does not involve the execution of a delay slot instruction.

Traps also occur when the user tries to execute a privileged or unimplemented instruction, or tries to access memory that has not been assigned to the program. Additional events can be programmed to cause a trap; divide by zero causes an exception flag to be set in a state register, and if the trap enable bit is also set, a trap will occur.

Traps are also used to handle input/output devices. When an input/output device requires service, it generates an interrupt, which may then cause a trap.

To understand trap handling, we need first to look at the various processor state registers. There are a small number of these and we will describe them in the following section. The reader is referred to the SPARC architecture handbook for a complete discussion of processor state registers and trap handling [22].

12.2   Processor State Registers

The integer processor has the following state registers: the multiply/divide register, Y; the program counters, PC and nPC; the processor state register, PSR; the window invalid mask, WIM; the trap base register, TBR.

The multiply/divide register, Y, discussed in Section 4.10.1, is used in conjunction with integer multiplication and division; it is readable and writable by the `rdy` and `wry` instructions in user mode. The program counters, PC and nPC, are not readable or writable directly but only indirectly by instructions such as `jmpl`. The other registers relate to the state of the processor, which we will describe now in some detail.

12.2.1 Processor State Register

The processor state register, PSR, is shown in Figure 12.1.

Figure 12.1: The Processor State Register

The various fields are as follows:

Bits	Field	Description
23:20	icc	The integer condition codes, N Z V and C.
12	EF	The floating-point processor enabled.
11:8	PIL	The interrupt level at which the processor will accept external device interrupts.
7	S	Supervisor mode.
6	PS	Processor execution mode at the time of the most recent trap.
5	ET	Traps enabled.
4:0	CWP	The current window pointer. The hardware decrements CWP on a `save` instruction and increments it on a `restore` instruction execution.

The integer condition codes are stored in the PSR whenever an instruction that sets the condition codes is executed; they are tested by the integer branch instructions. The EF bit refers to the presence of the floating-point processor. The PIL field stores the interrupt level at which the processor will accept interrupts, which we discuss in Section 12.3. Bit 7 is the supervisor mode bit; when set, the machine is in supervisor mode; when zero, the processor is in user mode. Whenever a trap occurs the current mode is saved by copying the S bit into the PS bit. The ET bit is set when traps are enabled. When a trap occurs, this bit is cleared; it is set again, by the `rett` instruction. The machine may handle only one trap at a time, if a trap occurs, when the ET bit is cleared, the machine resets and current execution halts. Finally, the current window pointer is stored in the CWP field of the PSR. Two privileged instructions, `rdpsr` and `wrpsr`, allow the operating system to read and write the psr.

12.2.2 Window Invalid Mask Register

The second of the integer unit state registers is the window invalid mask register, WIM. This register, 32 bits long, has active bits for each register set present and has one of the bits set for the register window set which is invalid, WIM[CWP] = 1; all other bits are zero. After registers are saved to the stack the invalid bit is rotated right once, and when a register set is restored from the stack the bit is rotated left. The operating system can read and write the `wim` with the privileged instructions `rewim` and `wrwim`. A `wrwim` with all 32 bits set followed by a `rewim` returns a word with bits set for each register set present; from 2 to 32 sets are possible.

12.2.3   Trap Base Register

The trap base register, TBR, holds the memory address of the first of four instructions of the code to handle the trap. As the code to handle all but the most trivial traps will typically be many instructions long, a branch instruction, along with its delay slot instruction, will typically be located among the first four instructions in the table. There are 256 possible trap types specified, half software traps and half hardware. When a trap occurs it is uniquely identified by its trap type `tt` number. When a trap occurs, the trap number field, eight bits long, is written into TBR[11:4]. The low four bits of the TBR, TBR[3:0], are always zero, as the TBR addresses memory in four-word increments, providing room for the first four instructions of each trap handler. The high-order 20 bits of the TBR, the trap base address, TBA, are written by `wrtbr` and read by `rdtbr`. These privileged instructions are used by the operating system to set the address of the table of trap handler code entries. The TBR is shown in Figure 12.2.

Figure 12.2: The Trap Base Register

12.2.4   Floating-Point Processor State Register

Like the PSR for the integer unit, the FSR keeps track of the state of the floating-point processor. It is shown in Figure 12.3. Due to the nature of the floating-point processor, with multiple floating-point arithmetic units, floating-point exceptions may occur in one of a number of floating-point instructions currently under execution. A floating-point instruction queue is kept by the floating-point processor and by this means the integer unit can determine which instruction caused an exception. This is fairly complicated and outside the scope of this book; we only describe those fields of the FSR that relate to rounding and condition codes. The various fields of the FSR are as follows:

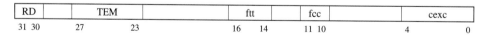

Figure 12.3: The Floating-Point Processor State Register

The RD field controls how rounding is to be handled:

RD	Round Toward
0	Nearest number (even, if equally close)
1	0
2	$+\infty$
3	$-\infty$

The `fcc` field is set by the floating-point compare instructions and has the following interpretation:

fcc	Relation
0	fs1 = fs2
1	fs1 < fs2
2	fs1 > fs2
3	fs1 ? fs2, unordered

The floating-point exception field, `cexe`, is set when each floating-point instruction completes execution. Its bits represent:

cexe	Condition
0x10	Invalid operation such as $\infty - \infty$ or $0 \div 0$
0x08	Floating overflow
0x04	Floating underflow, number not zero and too small to represent as a normalized floating-point number
0x02	Division by zero
0x01	Result inexact

The TEM field is the trap enable mask. After each instruction completes, the `cexe` field is ored with the TEM field, and if the result is nonzero, a trap is generated. The `ftt` field indicates the type of floating-point trap:

ftt	Trap Type
0	None
1	Floating-Point exception, coded in `cexe`
2	Unfinished floating-point operation
3	Unimplemented floating-point instruction
6	Invalid floating-point register

In the case of `fcc` 2 or 3, software would be expected to execute or complete the instruction execution.

12.3 Traps

For each exception that may cause a trap and for each external interrupt request a priority and trap type `tt` are defined (see Table 12.1). The traps are grouped together in the table: machine and memory failure, page faults, window overflow and underflow, privileged and illegal instructions, floating-point, arithmetic, trap instructions, interrupts. Memory access errors relate to direct failures, whereas exceptions relate to reading and writing protected memory. The MMU_miss traps relate to virtual memory accesses to sections of program or data that are not in physical memory, discussed in Section 13.2. When a trap instruction is executed, the least significant seven bits of its effective address, plus 128, are written into the tt field; hence, tt fields 0x80–0xff are reserved for trap instructions. Interrupts follow traps in priority level, with interrupt_level_15 having the highest priority of 17. Interrupt_level_1 has the lowest level of 31.

While ET is set, the integer processor, between instruction executions, prioritizes exceptions and external interrupt requests according to Table 12.1. Only interrupts whose level is greater than the processor interrupt level, or an interrupt at level 15, can cause a trap. It is assumed that interrupts at lower levels will persist until they are eventually acknowledged. The processor interrupt level is stored in the PIL field in the processor state register, PSR. When a trap occurs the following events take place:

1. The ET bit is cleared. If ET is already clear, the machine executes a reset trap. A reset trap loads the pc with 0 and the npc with 4 and the machine enters an error state. A reset trap may also be caused externally by a signal on the processor bus. When ET is set to zero, all further interrupt requests are ignored, including those at level 15.

2. The current processor execution state, stored in the S bit of the PSR, is stored into the previous state bit PS and the S bit set. This places the processor into supervisor mode.

3. The current window pointer, CWP, is decremented without testing for window overflow. This will allow the trap handling code to use the local registers in the new window. Even if decrementing the CWP would have caused a window overflow, the local registers are always free; it is the out registers in the overflowed window that must be saved.

4. The pc, npc, and psr are stored in the first three local registers, leaving the remaining five local registers for the trap handling code.

5. The tt field of the trap base register, TBR, is then written from the trap table, and pc = TBR, npc = TBR + 4.

The trap handler code is then executed with the processor in supervisor mode able to access all memory and input/output devices. The pc stored in %l0 gives the location in the user code of the source of the trap. If a register window will be needed, the trap handler must check if the current register window must be saved, and if so, save it to the stack. The global registers must also then be saved, and if the trap was caused by an interrupt, the processor interrupt level must be

Exception or Interrupt Request	Priority	tt
reset	1	–
instruction_access_error	3	0x21
data_access_error	12	0x29
register_access_error	4	0x20
instruction_access_exception	5	0x01
data_access_exception	13	0x09
mem_address_not_aligned	10	0x07
instruction_access_MMU_miss	2	0x3c
data_access_MMU_miss	12	0x2c
window_overflow	9	0x05
window_underflow	9	0x06
privileged_instruction	6	0x03
illegal_instruction	7	0x02
fp_disabled	8	0x04
fp_exception	11	0x08
division_by_zero	15	0x2a
tag_overflow	14	0x0a
trap_instruction	16	0x80–0xff
interrupt_level_15	17	0x1f
interrupt_level_14	18	0x1e
interrupt_level_13	19	0x1d
interrupt_level_12	20	0x1c
interrupt_level_11	21	0x1b
interrupt_level_10	22	0x1a
interrupt_level_9	23	0x19
interrupt_level_8	24	0x18
interrupt_level_7	25	0x17
interrupt_level_6	26	0x16
interrupt_level_5	27	0x15
interrupt_level_4	28	0x14
interrupt_level_3	29	0x13
interrupt_level_2	30	0x12
interrupt_level_1	31	0x11

Table 12.1: Traps

changed appropriately. Traps are then reenabled by resetting the ET bit and the trap handled by higher-level code.

To return from a trap, the `rett` instruction is used. First, if register windows were used, a window may have to be restored along with the global registers; the processor interrupt level might also need to be reset. With the ET bit then clear, the `rett` instruction performs the following actions:

1. The CWP is incremented.

2. A delayed transfer to the effective address of the `rett` instruction is initiated by loading `npc`.

3. Restore the S bit from the PS bit.

4. Set ET to 1.

The instruction executed immediately before the `rett` instruction **must** be a `jmpl` instruction; otherwise, the instruction following the `rett` will be fetched from supervisor memory when the processor in in user mode. A `jmpl` instruction can first be used to load the `pc` and the following `rett` loads the `npc`.

If the return is to reexecute the instruction that caused the trap (a **save** instruction, for example, which caused a window overflow trap), the following sequence will have the desired effect:

```
jmpl    %l0, %g0        !load npc with saved pc
rett    %l1             !load npc with save npc
```

When the `jmpl` instruction is about to be executed:

```
pc -> jmpl and
npc -> rett
```

When the `rett` instruction is about to be executed:

```
pc -> rett and
npc -> saved pc
```

After the `rett` instruction has been executed:

```
pc -> saved pc and
npc -> saved npc
```

This two-instruction sequence is required, as the trap instructions do not have delay slot instructions and thus the contents of the `npc` would be lost if not restored in the manner described above.

To return to the instruction after that which caused the trap, such as a system call (`ta 0`), we would use the following sequence:

```
        jmpl    %11, %g0         !load npc with saved npc
        rett    %11 + 4          !load npc with saved npc + 4
```

In this case, when the `jmpl` instruction is about to be executed:

    pc -> jmpl and
    npc -> rett

When the `rett` instruction is about to be executed:

    pc -> rett and
    npc -> instruction following trap

After the `rett` instruction has been executed:

    pc -> instruction following trap and
    npc -> instruction following, instruction following trap

which follows the instruction that followed the trap. Note that even if the instruction that followed the trap were a branch instruction, the instruction that followed it would be the delay slot instruction.

The `rett` instruction is a privileged instruction that will cause a trap if executed in user mode. The supervisor normally also clears the stack and any register windows it has used before returning from a trap.

12.4 Window Traps

To describe window overflow trap handling we will give a detailed account of a machine that has only four register sets. The initial situation is shown in Figure 12.4. The user is in the first register set, set 3. Sets 3, 2, and 1 are marked valid by corresponding zero bits in the window invalid mask register (WIM); register set 0 is marked invalid by a 1 WIM bit. The current window pointer (CWP) field of the processor status register indicates the currently active registers. The stack pointer `%sp` points to an area of the stack where the in and local registers may be saved if necessary.

If a new set of registers is needed, the SAVE instruction is executed. If the WIM bit of the next register set is zero, indicating that the register set is valid, the CWP is decremented and the next set of registers becomes the current set (see Figure 12.5). The out registers of the calling function become the in registers of the called function. The called function is provided with eight new local registers and eight new out registers. The local registers are used for temporary results and variables of the called function. The out registers are used to pass arguments to a called function.

If the current function calls yet another function, the situation is shown in Figure 12.6, as might be expected.

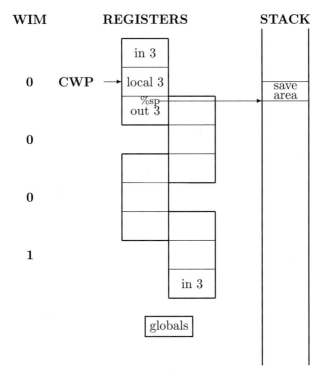

Figure 12.4: The Initial State of the Registers with the User in Set 3

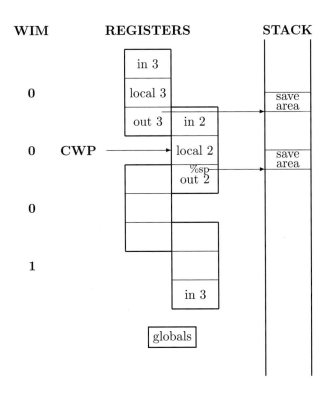

Figure 12.5: The Second Function Call with the User in Set 2

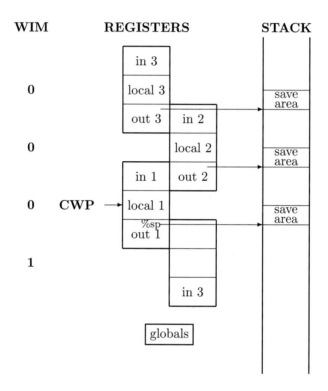

Figure 12.6: The Third Function Call with the User Now in Set 1

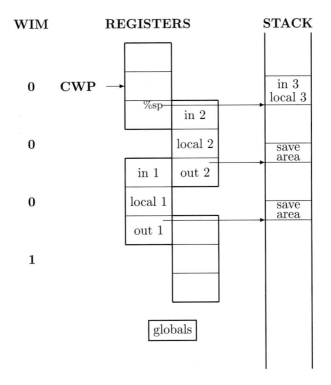

Figure 12.7: Registers Saved on Stack from within Window Overflow Trap

If another function call is made when the SAVE instruction executed, the CWP will point to the window, which has its WIM bit a one, marking it invalid. It is invalid, as its out registers are being used as the in registers of register set 3, the first register set used. Remember that the registers form a ring.

As the window is marked invalid, the attempt to execute the SAVE instruction results in a window overflow trap. When this happens the CWP is decremented to point to the invalid window and the two PCs stored in two of the local registers. Note that the local registers are never used by either the calling function's register set or by the first register set in the ring.

The trap routine first decrements the CWP again so that it points to register set 3, the first set used. The local and in registers are then saved on the stack where the %sp register is pointing. Remember that the CWP points to the current register set (see Figure 12.7).

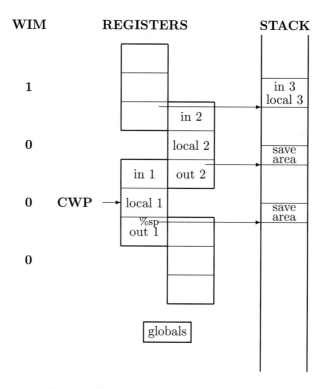

Figure 12.8: Register Set Invalid Mask Rotated and CWP Restored

Note that after the registers have been saved on the stack the pointer to their saved location is still in a valid register, %i6 of register set 2. After the registers have been saved, the CWP is incremented twice and the WIM is rotated one bit to mark the first register set as invalid, leaving register set 0 available for the function call (see Figure 12.8).

When the window overflow trap returns the SAVE instruction is reexecuted and now completes successfully (see Figure 12.9). If another function were called, the in and local registers of register set 2 would be saved on the stack and the WIM rotated again (see Figure 12.10). Note that the pointer to the in and local registers of set 3 is now also saved on the stack with the in registers of set 2. This is not a problem, however, as register set 2 would have to be restored before register set 3 could be restored, and the necessary pointer would be in a register before it was needed.

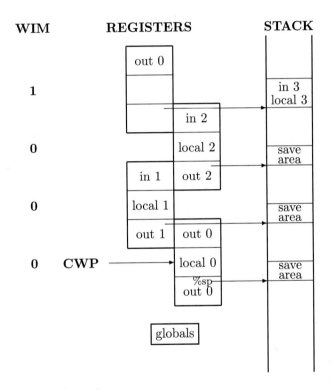

Figure 12.9: The Fourth Function Call with the User in Set 0

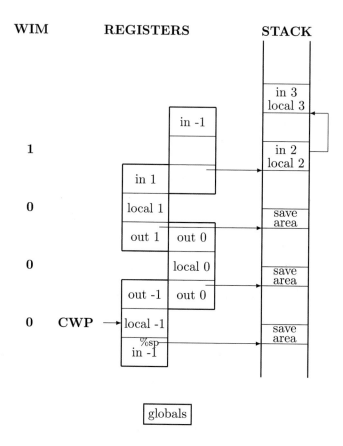

Figure 12.10: Registers after the Fifth Function Call

12.5 Summary

Traps provide the communication facility between a user program and the operating system. A processor state is maintained in a small number of registers: the processor state register, the window invalid mask register, and the floating-point status register. These registers facilitate the handling of traps and maintenance of the integrity of a multiuser computing environment.

Chapter 13

MEMORY MANAGEMENT

13.1 Introduction

If a computer is to be utilized efficiently it must continually execute useful instructions. This is difficult to achieve in the case of a workstation designed for a single user, where the processor may remain idle for long periods of time waiting for user input. The lack of economy of utilization of workstations and personal computers is balanced by the convenience of use. As the performance of a computer goes up, so does the cost, and the economics of a single-user machine grows steadily worse, so that more powerful machines are generally designed to support a number of users at the same time. This is called *time-sharing*, handled by switching the processor between users for some fraction of a second each, so that all users appear to have a less powerful machine entirely to themselves. When one user's program is not executing, the processor is free to concentrate on executing other programs that are runable. The machine switches between users after executing some quantum of time, typically 1/60 of a second, and whenever a process performs some input/output or other operation that would idle a user's program or process. When a process stops for user input, the processor will immediately be switched to another user who has a runable process. The machine will not be switched back to the process waiting for user input until the input is provided, when an interrupt occurs. Switching between users occurs with interrupts. The time quanta are governed by a clock, which also interrupts the processor at some fixed interval of time. Switching between users, called a *context switch* is handled by the operation system. The efficiency of handling a context switch is an important attribute of a computer. Switching between users is relatively simple in the SPARC architecture in supervisor mode; the register file is saved along with the program counters and some other minimal state information. A `rett` instruction is then used to continue another user, at his or her saved process state, returning the processor to user mode. We will be describing a context switch in Section 13.5. If we are to be able to switch between users it is, however, *imperative* that both users' processes are resident in memory. It would obviously be inefficient if, at the time of a context switch, the processor had to write to a disk the entire contents of memory and then to reload the entire memory with another user's process.

Memory is handled in the SPARC architecture by a unit called the *memory management unit*, MMU [22], which is presented with virtual addresses by the processor and translates these addresses into addresses of the physical memory attached to the memory management unit (see Figure 13.1).

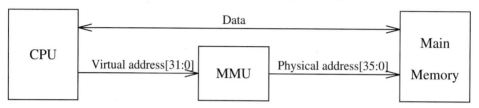

Figure 13.1: The Memory Management Unit

The MMU can map virtual addresses into different physical addresses to allow more than one user to occupy physical memory at the same time. This is especially important, as each process that is to be executed has the same starting virtual address, 0x2000, expects to find the stack at 0xf8000000, and so on. The mapping of virtual addresses into physical addresses takes into account a context register. Each user process is assigned a unique context number. This MMU register is loaded by the operating system with the context number of the user whose memory is to be mapped. The context is included with the virtual address to produce a unique physical memory address for similar virtual addresses, but with different context numbers.

13.2   Virtual Memory and Paging

The SPARC architecture specifies a 32-bit virtual address and a 36-bit physical memory address. Memory is byte addressable. The 36-bit physical address is obtained most simply from a virtual address and a context by means of a page table entry in a context table that is itself located in physical memory. The page table entry describes the location and access permission of a page of memory. A page of memory may be as large as four gigabytes, or as small as four kilobytes; the mapping we discuss first here is for four gigabyte pages, that is, an entire 32-bit process virtual address space. Such a page is called a *context* and 16 such contexts would occupy the entire 36-bit physical memory. We discuss smaller pages shortly.

The context table is located in physical memory by an MMU register, the context table pointer register, and is indexed with the contents of the MMU context register. The high 30 bits of the context table pointer register, left-shifted four bits, are **ored** with the contents of the context register, left-shifted two bits, to form the 36-bit physical address of the page table entry in physical memory (see Figure 13.2).

The process of **oring** registers together is extremely fast compared to the operation of addition, which might have seemed more logical in handling pointers. The low two bits of the context table pointer register must be zero to allow for 16 contexts to be addressed by **oring** the context table pointer register with the context register (see Figure 13.2).

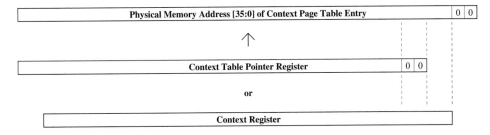

Figure 13.2: Forming the Address of the Page Table Entry

Either page table entries or page table descriptors are stored in the context table. We will discuss page table descriptors shortly.

A page table entry is a 32-bit word, shown in Figure 13.3, with the following fields:

PPN [31:8]	C	M	R	ACC	1	0

Figure 13.3: The Page Table Entry

- PPN, physical page number, the high-order 24 bits of the 36-bit physical address

- C, cacheable (see Section 13.4)

- M, modified, memory page has been written

- R, referenced, memory page has been read or written

- ACC, access permission

ACC	User Access	Supervisor Access
0	Read only	Read only
1	Read/write	Read/write

The first time a process accesses memory, the R bit is set; when it first writes to memory, the M bit is set. If it becomes necessary to replace a page of memory the M bit is tested and, if set, the page of memory has to be written to an external device, such as a disk, before a new page is read in. If the M bit is clear, the page does not have to be written but may simply be replaced with another page. If the R bit has not been set, a page is an obvious choice for replacement. Access permission is used in conjunction with the supervisor mode bit of the processor status word, PSR. By this means a user is prevented from accessing operating system pages of memory.

The translation of a virtual address to a physical address in its most simple form uses the context to index into the context table to retrieve the page table entry, PTE. If the access permission is correct, the physical memory address is formed by the **or** of the high 24 bits of the PTE and the virtual address. If we are using an **or** to form the address, all but the high 4 bits of the 24-bit PPN of the PTE must be zero. Physical pages in memory must be aligned on page boundaries; for example, if the page size is four gigabytes, 32-bits, pages must be aligned on 32-bit boundaries. If this alignment exists, the PPN entry for four-gigabyte pages will indeed have all but the four high-order bits zero. This mapping is shown in Figure 13.4.

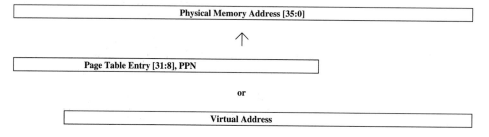

Figure 13.4: Mapping Four-Gigabyte Pages

Mapping four-gigabyte pages, *contexts*, of memory is rather unwieldy, and very few installations have 64,000 megabytes of physical memory. A further problem is that with only one page table entry, PTE, for each context the entire context must be executed entirely in supervisor mode or in user mode; furthermore, the entire virtual address space of the context must be either all read-only or all read/write.

Smaller sections of memory may be mapped; the first division below a context is called a *region*. A region of memory is 16 Mbytes long, and 256 regions will make up a four-gigabyte context (see Appendix G).

How are regions mapped? A page table entry, PTE, is characterized by having its two low-order bits <1:0> = 10. A page table entry may be replaced in the context table by a *page table descriptor*, PTD, distinguished by having its two order bits <1:0> = 01 (see Figure 13.5).

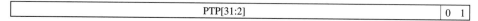

Figure 13.5: A Page Table Descriptor

When a PTD is encountered in the context table, the high-order eight bits of the virtual address are used to index into a second-level mapping table. This table is addressed by the page table descriptor. The high 30 bits of the page table descriptor are called the *page table pointer*, PTP (see Figure 13.6).

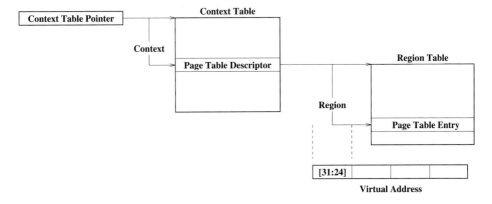

Figure 13.6: Mapping Regions

The PTP is left-shifted four places and ored with the high eight bits of the virtual address to form a pointer to the page table entry. The page table entry will now address individual 16-Mbyte regions, each of which may carry its own protection and access information (see Figure 13.7).

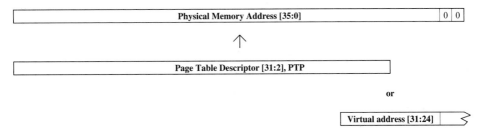

Figure 13.7: Forming the Address of the Region Page Table Entry

The low four bits of the page table pointer, PTP, must be zero to allow the or operation to access a table of 1024 word entries. If the accessed entry in the region table is a page table entry, characterized by having its two low bits 10, the memory address is formed by oring the high-order 24 bits of the PTE, the PPN, with the remaining 24 low-order bits of the virtual address. The high-order eight bits have already been used to fetch the region page table entry (see Figure 13.8). All but the 12 high-order bits of the PPN must be zero when we are addressing regions.

The UNIX operating system occupies the four top regions in memory, and the mapping tables for all contexts have identical mappings to the same region table for the top four regions. The next region will be mapped to physical memory for the stack for each user process; these will all be unique mappings to physical memory.

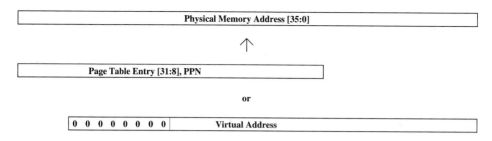

Figure 13.8: Mapping 16-Megabyte Pages

There can then be a hole with many zero entries in the region table indicating that these virtual addresses are not currently mapped. In fact, for all but user processes larger than 16 Mbytes, all but the first region will be zero. Note that the protection and access permission for the kernel will be different from the protection and access permission for the user regions. With the use of regions, a context switch can now change between users, keeping the same operating system kernel common to both.

Regions are still rather large units of memory, and regions may be further divided into 64 segments each of 256 kilobytes. This is done by replacing the page table entry in the region table with another page table descriptor. If a page table descriptor is found in the region table, the next six high-order bits of the virtual address are used to locate an entry in a segment table (see Figure 13.9).

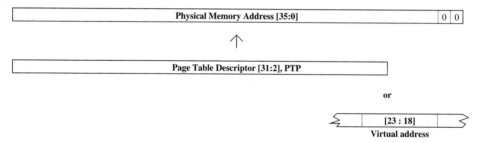

Figure 13.9: Forming the Address of the Segment Page Table Entry

If the entry in the segment table is a page table entry, the physical address is then formed by oring the low 18 bits of the virtual address with the PPN. Here, all but the high 18 bits of the PPN must be zero (see Figure 13.10).

One further division may be made to map individual four-kilobyte pages, known simply as *pages*, by locating yet another page table descriptor in the segment page table. To do this another six bits are selected from the virtual address to form an index into a page table containing, in this case, only page table entries. The final address is formed with PPN and the low 12 bits of the virtual address, commonly known as the *offset*, (see Figure 13.11). Here the entire 24 bits of the PPN are combined with the 12-bit offset to form the memory address.

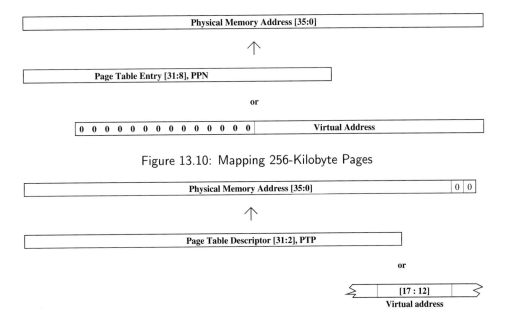

Figure 13.10: Mapping 256-Kilobyte Pages

Figure 13.11: Forming the Address of the Page, PTE

The complete hierarchical mapping scheme to map individual pages is shown in Figure 13.12.

With paging, an entire program does not have to be resident in memory for the program to be executed. Only a few pages are necessary to start the program, an initial text page, data page, bss segment page, and a page of stack. Such a set of pages is called a *working set*. When a process starts, a context number is assigned by the operating system and a region table created occupying 1024 bytes of memory. The top four entries in the region table are filled in to point to the kernel address space. The fifth entry from the top is filled in with a pointer to a newly created segment table for the stack. The remainder of the region table is zeroed except for a pointer in the first entry, which is initialized to point to another newly created segment table for the program. These two segment tables will each occupy 256 bytes of physical memory. The stack segment table will be zero except for the top entry, which will contain a pointer to a newly created page table. Similarly, the program segment table will be zero except for the first entry. This entry will point to another newly created page table. The stack and program page tables will use only another 256 bytes each of memory. The top entry of the stack page table will be set to point to an initial page of the stack. Finally, the first three entries in the program page table will be set to point to memory for program text, data, and bss segments.

When a page that is not in main memory is accessed and the zero page table entry encountered, a *page fault trap* occurs. The operating system then arranges to

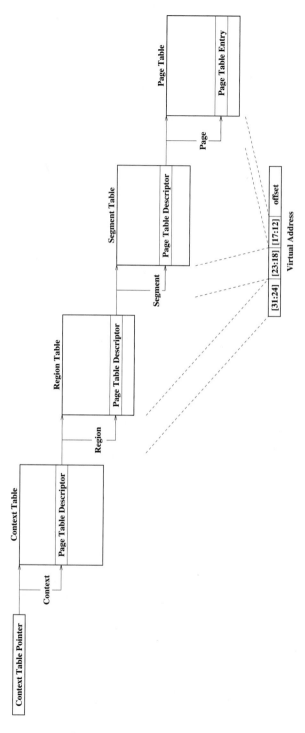

Figure 13.12: Mapping Pages

have the missing page placed somewhere into memory and the page table updated. During this time, called *paging*, some other process is run. When the page has been loaded into memory and the page table updated, the system executes a `rett` instruction to reexecute the instruction that caused the page fault. By this means the operating system can keep many more than 16 contexts in memory and ready to execute. The replacement of pages, when memory becomes full, is based on a count kept for each page relating to its access; the least recently used page is replaced. This is called an *LRU replacement policy*.

13.3 Page Descriptor Cache: The Translation Lookaside Buffer

In the mapping scheme we have described, accessing memory for each instruction fetch or data load/store would take four physical memory fetches if we had mapped memory in pages. This is far too slow. To speed up the process, the memory management unit maintains a cache of descriptor translations. This cache is an associative memory entered with the virtual address, less any offset, and the context, together called a *tag*. If this tag is found in the cache the corresponding page table entry is returned immediately. If a *miss* occurs, that is, for a virtual address and context presented by the processor, no page table entry is located, the process we described in the preceding section takes place; this process, called *table walking* is handled by hardware, necessitating up to four memory fetches. When a page table entry is retrieved by this process, it is first used to access memory for the processor, and then the page table entry is placed into the page descriptor cache along its associated tag (see Figure 13.13). Memory fetches take only one cycle, as for an unmapped memory, with the page descriptor cache once the cache has been loaded with page table entries.

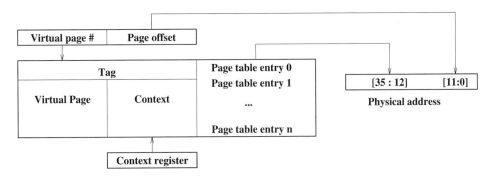

Figure 13.13: Page Descriptor Cache

13.4 Cache Memory

Even with a page descriptor cache, accessing memory is too slow for the processor, which has a cycle time considerably faster than that of the fetch or store time of conventional memory. To provide data and instructions from memory at speeds approaching that of the processor, a cache memory is provided. The cache memory is an expensive, small, high-speed memory that can match the processor's speed of operation. Whenever a fetch is made to main memory, a *line* of data or instructions is fetched and placed in the cache memory. This line is up to 128 bytes of instruction or data. If any of this line of data is subsequently required, it can be fetched from the cache memory. It has been shown that programs exhibit considerable locality of reference to memory. For example, instructions are typically fetched from sequential locations in memory. When a write to memory occurs, the processor simply writes to the cache, and then the cache writes to main memory without delaying the processor.

The cache memory is in parallel with the memory management unit and both attempt to provide data to the processor (see Figure 13.14). If the data are in the cache the cache wins out and the MMU stops its fetch. If the data are missing from the cache, the MMU provides the data to both the processor and the cache. This might simply involve using the page table descriptor cache, or it might involve accessing page tables to retrieve both the data and the page table entry.

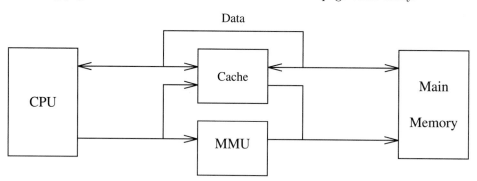

Figure 13.14: Cache Memory

In addressing the cache memory, a virtual address is broken up into three fields, the tag, line, and byte. The *byte* is the address of a particular byte in the line, up to 128 bytes. The line then addresses lines in the cache memory, and the number of bits dedicated to the line depends on the size of the cache. A 64-Kbyte cache with 32-byte lines would need 5 bits to address the byte in a line and 10 more bits to address the line in the cache. This would leave the 17 bits for the tag (see Figure 13.15).

The cache tag combines the context number with the tag part of the virtual address. Associated with the tag are the access information and protection bits.

Tag [31:15]	Line [14:5]	Byte [4:0]

Virtual Address

Figure 13.15: Cache Memory

When an address is presented to the cache, the tag is accessed by the line number; if the tag matches the rest of the address, and the protection and access permission are correct, the data are provided to the processor. If a miss occurs, the line in the cache is replaced automatically from main memory and the tag updated.

13.5   Context Switching

When it becomes necessary for the operation system to switch between users, the following actions take place to save the state of the current user's process and to restore the state of the process of the next user to run:

- Save the stack pointer, %sp.

- Save the program counter, pc, the return address.

- Save the global registers.

- Save the floating-point registers.

- Execute NWINDOWS - 2 save instructions to flush all the active active register windows of the process to the stack. One window is always invalid and the operating system will be in the other window.

- Execute NWINDOWS - 2 restore instructions to move the CWP back to the original window so that the next restore instruction, at the end of the context switch, will cause a window underflow, restoring the first new window from the new stack.

- Change context in the MMU.

- Restore floating-point registers.

- Restore global registers.

- Load new pc.

- Load new %sp.

- restore.

- Return.

The program counters and stack pointers are first saved, then the active registers are written out to the stack by performing `NWINDOWS - 2 save` instructions. Note that execution of the `save` instructions does nothing but decrement the `cwp` unless there are active registers, in which case the registers are written to the stack. The MMU context is then changed and the next user's registers restored along with the program counters and stack pointers.

13.6   Summary

Sharing the processor with a number of users is important for efficient utilization of the machine. To share the processor, more than one process must be resident in main memory at the same time. An elaborate memory mapping scheme was defined for the SPARC architecture, which was described in detail defining contexts, regions, segments, and pages. The mapping is accomplished by the memory mapping unit, the MMU. Supporting memory mapping, to make it efficient, is the use of a translation lookaside buffer and a cache memory.

Chapter 14

OTHER ARCHITECTURES

14.1 Introduction

The SPARC architecture is a Reduced Instruction Set Computer, RISC. It is in many respects similar to the earliest computers, which certainly had very limited instruction sets, as they were made out of discrete components all of which had to be assembled into printed circuit boards to process each and every instruction. The development of computers followed developments in technology, and we will trace that development in this chapter. The first computer we describe is the PDP-11, whose development coincided with creation of the C programming language [11]. The second machine we discuss is the VAX-11, which was an extension of the PDP-11 to provide for virtual memory. The VAX-11 is now known as a Complex Instruction Set Computer, CISC, and the SPARC, Reduced Instruction Set Computer, RISC, represented a radical change of technological development [19]. The last machine we discuss is the MIPS, another RISC machine developed at the same time as the SPARC architecture.

The PDP-11 was one of the first minicomputers powerful enough to perform useful computations, but smaller than the large machines prevalent at the time of their introduction. Until the 1970s, computers were large and were located in central computer rooms where programs were brought to be executed. Programs were stored on punched cards and were executed in batch mode, in which program after program was be loaded into the machine's memory and executed until it completed and was replaced by the next program to be executed. Minicomputers were designed to be used in either dedicated control applications or in small computing environments where the machine cost was not so great as to necessitate the maximization of the computer's use. These machines typically had small address spaces of 16 bits, and a modest number of registers. They were not suitable for executing large programs and were equivalent in power to today's personal computer. The concept of a personal computer in which a computer would be dedicated to a single user and his or her file system had not yet evolved.

While computer hardware was becoming cheaper due to the rapid development of integrated circuits, computer memory was neither cheap nor fast. To maximize the speed of a machine, instructions were made more powerful to minimize the number of instruction to be stored and then fetched from memory, and a register set was provided to hold temporary results, eliminating the need to store temporary results back into memory. The PDP-11 was such a machine. It provided a multiply and divide instruction, a mark of a sophisticated machine at that time, and provided eight general-purpose registers. It provided for no virtual memory management, and its 16-bit address space supported only 64 Kbytes of memory, small even at the time it was introduced.

The VAX-11 computer was a virtual memory version of the PDP-11. Its virtual address space was, like the SPARC machine's, 32 bits, allowing four gigabytes of virtual memory to be addressed. Physical memory was still, however, very limited and the 32-bit virtual address was only translated into a 24-bit physical address. Contrast this to the SPARC architecture, in which the 32-bit virtual address is translated into a 36-bit physical address! With the development of the VAX-11 came microprogramming, in which instructions were decoded into a stream of microinstructions located in extremely fast memory [26]. This allowed the machine to implement very sophisticated instructions. These machines are now known as Complex Instruction Set Computers, (CISC).

Although it was thought that the more complex instructions would make a computer more efficient, programmers were no longer writing in assembly language and the compilers rarely made use of the more esoteric instructions. Compiler writing technology was also advancing dramatically during this time period with more sophisticated translation of high-level languages into very efficient assembly language. Together with CISC computers came breakthroughs in memory technology, reducing the need to provide for powerful instructions to reduce storage requirements. The response to these changes in compiler and memory technology was the Reduced Instruction Set Computer, RISC, of which the SPARC machine was one of the first.

14.2   The PDP-11

The PDP-11 provided eight general registers and a 16-bit unmapped address space supporting 64 Kbytes of memory. Memory was byte addressable and the machine provided instructions that operated on single and two-byte quantities, referred to as *words* [5]. Sixteen-bit-word quantities had to be aligned on even-byte addresses as in the SPARC architecture. The address of a word quantity in the PDP-11 was of the low byte with the more significant byte at the next-higher odd address. This is referred to as *little endian addressing* . In the SPARC architecture, the address of multibyte data types halfword, word, single, double, and quad, is of the most significant byte, with less significant data lying at higher-byte memory addresses;

the SPARC memory addressing is called *big endian*.[1] These differences in data storage and access of multibyte data do not cause problems unless binary data is to be exchanged between machines of different endian.

Two of the eight general registers of the PDP-11 were reserved for use as a stack pointer and as the program counter. In the PDP-11 architecture the program counter was one of the general-purpose registers. The PDP-11 was not a load/store machine but allowed for operands to be located in memory or in registers. There were not sufficient registers into which all relevant variables could be loaded in the PDP-11 as there are in the SPARC architecture; nor were there sufficient bits to specify more registers in the 16-bit instruction word. To allow for the flexibility in addressing, two levels of instruction decoding were employed. In the SPARC architecture, the bit fields specifying register arguments may be decoded and fetched directly, while in the PDP-11 additional stages of decoding were necessary, leading to a much slower machine in instruction execution.

Instruction operands of the PDP-11 were specified by a six-bit field. Three bits were used to specify the addressing mode and three to specify a register. The direct addressing modes were as follows:

Mode	Assembler	Description
0	Rn	Register direct mode, the register specified contains the operand.
2	(Rn)+	Auto increment mode, register is used to a pointer to data and then incremented after use (by one for a byte operation and by two for a word operation).
4	-(Rn)	Auto decrement mode, register is decremented before use (by one for a byte operation and by two for a word operation) and then used to a pointer to data.
6	X(Rn)	Displacement mode, value X is added to the contents of Rn to produce a pointer to the operand. Neither X nor (Rn) are modified.

If the addressing mode was odd, a deferred addressing mode was specified:

---

[1]The terms *big endian* and *little endian* are due to Jonathan Swift, whose *Gulliver's Travels* referred to politicians who made war over which end of an egg should be opened, the big end or the little end. The term was introduced into computer science by Cohen in 1981.

Mode	Assembler	Description
1	*Rn	Register deferred mode; the register specified contains a pointer to the operand.
3	*(Rn)+	Auto increment mode deferred; register is used to a pointer to a pointer to the data. Register is then incremented after use by two (a pointer is always a word quantity).
5	*-(Rn)	Auto decrement mode deferred; register is decremented before use by two and then used to a pointer to a pointer to the data.
7	*X(Rn)	Displacement mode deferred; value X is added to the contents of Rn to produce a pointer to a pointer to the operand. Neither X nor (Rn) is modified.

When an instruction was decoded, except in the case of register direct mode, another register would have to be fetched and used to form the address of the operand. It might take another memory access to obtain a constant, and if a deferred addressing mode was specified, yet another memory access was required to obtain an operand. This process resembled the table walking algorithm employed by the memory management unit of the SPARC when a cache miss occurs and the page table entry is not in the translation lookaside buffer. In the case of the SPARC architecture this occurs only once for every 4 Kbytes of mapped memory and not for every operand fetched. Constants could be loaded into general registers of the PDP-11 by specifying the program counter as the register of the addressing mode. Consider the following mov instruction, which moves data from their first, source, operand to their second, destination, operand:

```
mov     (pc)+, r0
.word   3756
```

The program counter is always incremented by two in the PDP-11, so that after the mov instruction has been fetched the program counter has the address of the .word 3756. When the mode-register pair is decoded, the program counter is used as a pointer to the data, 3756, which is then accessed. As soon as the constant has been accessed, the program counter is again incremented to point to the next instruction in memory. The second mode register pair is decoded to determine that the source operand, 3756, is to be loaded into register r0. In the PDP-11, r0 was like the other general-purpose registers and did not discard data or return zero as it does in the SPARC architecture.

If we wished to copy the contents of location 3756 into location 4024:

```
mov     *(pc)+, *(pc)+
.word   3756
.word   4024
```

Here the program counter, pointing to the .word 3756, is used to retrieve the 3756, which it will then use as a pointer to the data. It then increments the program counter to point to the `.word 4024`. When the second operand mode register pair is decoded, the program counter is once again used to retrieve the 4024 used to determine where the data obtained from 3756 are to be stored. The program counter is again incremented to point to the following instruction.

If, as is normally done, we wished to use program counter relative addressing, assuming that the `mov` instruction was located at 100 in memory, we would have written

```
100:    mov     (3756 - 104)(pc), (4024 - 106)(pc)
```

Here the constants $(3756 - 104)$ and $(4024 - 106)$ are evaluated by the assembler to yield

```
100:    mov     3652(pc), 3918(pc)
```

The displacement is stored in line after the instruction, the following two words in the example above, and although it is not indicated in the addressing mode, the program counter is incremented by two each time it is used to fetch the displacement constants. Before the addition of the constant to the specified register, the program counter is incremented.

These addressing modes are used extensively and the programmer is not required to compute the constants, especially the program counter relative constants; instead, the following assembler syntax specifies the modes above:

Mode	Assembler	Description
2	`#n`	Operand follows instruction.
3	`*#A`	Absolute address follows operand.
6	`A`	Relative address follows operand (assembler will compute program counter relative address).
7	`*A`	Displacement value is the relative address of a pointer to the operand.

So we might have written the three instructions above as:

```
mov     #3756, r0
mov     *#3756, *#4024
mov     3756, 4024
```

One would, of course, normally use assembler labels as operands. The use of the program counter was novel in this context, as was the use of `%g0` novel in the SPARC architecture to increase the apparent number of instructions.

The similarity of the `PDP-11` instruction set and the C programming language is striking. Consider the code to copy a string:

```
*t++ = *f++;
```

and assuming that pointers to `t` and `f` were in registers `r2` and `r3`:

```
movb    *(r3)+, *(r2)+
```

The PDP-11 introduced the concept of condition codes, the N,Z,V, and C bits of the SPARC architecture. However, in the case of the PDP-11, which was not a pipelined machine, all instructions set the condition codes if appropriate. Branching instructions tested the condition codes as in the SPARC architecture.

Byte and word instructions were normally distinguished in the PDP-11 by the most significant bit of the instruction. If set, the instruction used byte operands; if clear, the instruction used word operands. The instruction set consisted of several two-operand instructions:

Mnemonic	Op Code	Operation
mov(b)	x1SSDD	Move, d <- s
cmp(b)	x2SSDD	Compare, s - d
add	06SSDD	Add, d <- s + d
sub	16SSDD	Sub, d <- d - s
bit(b)	x3SSDD	Bit test, s & d
bic(b)	x4SSDD	Bit clear, d <- (!s) & d
bis(b)	x5SSDD	Bit set, d <- s | d

The opcode referred to in the table above is in octal digits. Each SS and DD refers to a source and destination mode register pair. The leading x is a one if it is a byte instruction and zero if a word instruction.

There are a few more instructions involving one general operand, specified by a mode register pair, and the other operand located only in a register and needing only three bits to specify the register:

Mnemonic	Op Code	Operation
mul	070RSS	Multiply, r < r * s
div	071RSS	Divide, r <- r / s
ash	072RSS	Shift arithmetically
ashc	073RSS	Shift arithmetically combined
xor	074RDD	Exclusive or

These instructions use the bits <14:12> to decode the instruction. Notice that the PDP-11 provided a multiply and divide instruction. The low speed of instruction execution precluded the mulscc approach of the SPARC architecture. Also, at the time of introduction of the PDP-11, the presence of a multiply and divide instruction was an important selling point, setting the machine apart from the microprocessors of the day, which provided only very primitive instructions. However, the timing of these multiply and divide instruction was orders of magnitude greater than a mov or add instruction.

The remaining instructions are either single-address instructions or branch instructions. These instructions all have <14:12> = 0 and use <11:6> to decode the instruction. The single-address instructions are as follows:

Mnemonic	Op Code	Operation
clr	x050DD	Clear, d <- 0
com	x051DD	Complement (1's), d <- !d
inc	x052DD	Increment, d <- d + 1
dec	x053DD	Decrement, d <- d - 1
neg	x054DD	Negate (2's comp.), d <- -d
tst	x057DD	Test, setting condition codes
ror	x060DD	Rotate right one bit, ->C,d
rol	x061DD	Rotate left one bit, C,d<-
asr	x062DD	Arithmetic shift right one bit, d/2
asl	x063DD	Arithmetic shift left one bit, 2d
swab	0003DD	Swap bytes in word
adc	x055DD	Add carry, d <- d + C
sbc	x056DD	Subtract carry, d <- d - C
sxt	0067DD	Sign extend

Notice that the PDP-11 lacked a register that always returned zero. Instead of providing the minimal set of logic instructions, as in the case of the SPARC architecture, which could be combined with %r0 to provide operations such as mov and clr, these instructions were provided explicitly in the PDP-11 at the expense of the more general logic instructions.

Notice also that the shift instructions only shifted one place. In this case the instruction reflected the implementation in which shifting was an expensive operation proportional in time to the number of shifts. In the case of the implementation of the shift instruction in the SPARC architecture, the instructions are implemented in a manner in which the number of shifts does not affect the timing of the instruction.

The branch instructions of the PDP-11 are identical to the branch instructions on the SPARC architecture and occupy opcodes 0004000 through 0034000 and from 1000000 through 1034000. The branch address was word relative with respect to the program counter, and the offset occupied the low-byte of the branch instructions. Branching was possible only to instructions $-128 \leq$ pc < 128.

To jump to any address in memory, a jmp instruction was provided in which its effective operand replaced the contents of the program counter. Of course, on the PDP-11, with the program counter an accessible general register, a jump could be effected by a mov instruction:

```
mov     _main, pc
```

Subroutine linkage was provided for by a jsr, rts instruction pair. The jsr instruction transferred control to its effective address storing the current pc in the specified register.

Mnemonic	Op Code	Operation
jmp	0001DD	pc <- dst
jsr	004RDD	pc <- dst, R <- pc
rts	00020R	pc <- R

The `rts` instruction moved the address from a register back into the `pc`. The stack was normally used to store the return address as well as subroutine arguments. No separate frame pointer was provided, although it could be provided by a programmer, but rarely was, due to the limited number of registers available.

The `PDP-11` provided for user and supervisor mode with trap instruction and a return from trap instruction in a manner similar to the SPARC. The top 4 Kbytes of memory were reserved for device registers, limiting even further the memory available to a program. The `PDP-11` provided floating-point hardware only in certain of its implementations. The rapidly decreasing cost and increasing speed of memory made the `PDP-11` obsolete as programmers moved to writing in high-level languages, making use of much larger memories.

14.3   The VAX-11

The `VAX-11` was introduced in the 1980s [6] [14] . The premier feature of the `VAX-11` was the provision of a 32-bit virtual memory. One of the principal limitations of the `PDP-11` had been its severely limited address space. The `VAX-11` was a microprogrammed machine in which the machine instructions, referred to as *macro instructions*, were decoded to a number of *micro instructions*. The micro instructions were located in a very high speed memory, called a *micro store*. Microprogramming allowed the development of many specialized instructions. This was used in two ways, to design a machine with instruction sets appropriate to many different application fields, and to reduce the instruction fetch bandwidth. It was thought that the provision of machine instructions to perform code sequences, such as at the end of loops or in subroutine calls, would simplify a programmer's task and speed up the execution of programs. Unfortunately, very few programmers were writing in assembly language at the time of introduction of the `VAX-11` and the complicated instructions found little favor with compiler writers, who would have to "special case" their compilers for every such machine. Many of the most complicated instructions were never used in high-level languages. A second problem with microcoded machines was that the overhead of micro decoding instructions added a time overhead to all instructions, even the simplest. The `VAX-11` was a classic example of a complicated instruction set computer, CISC. The `VAX-11` had over 240 instructions with over 20 addressing formats. The `VAX-11` even had a *compatibility mode*, which, making use of micro programming, allowed it to execute all `PDP-11` instructions.

Such an architecture has to be considered in terms of technology, at the time of introduction of the `VAX-11`, microcoding was the technologically correct approach. However, as memory continued to drop in cost and to increase in speed, reducing instruction bandwidth became less important; what was necessary was to increase the execution speed of instructions fetched, and this trend, of course, led to the RISC machines. Another technological factor favoring RISC machines was development in compiler writing, allowing for highly optimized code to be generated for simple instruction sets. Finally, writing microcode was difficult, and like the assembly language programs of the past, machine specific; this increased the cost of reimplementing an architecture in a different technology. There were some hundreds of thousands of bytes of microcode to implement the VAX-11 instruction set.

The VAX-11 supported one-, two-, and four-byte integer quantities along with single and double floating-point data. The machine had sixteen, 32-bit general registers which could hold any of the foregoing data types. Byte and halfword data, however, only occupied the low-order bits in the register and did not change the high order contents of the register. Double precision data occupied two registers.

Instructions were provided to manipulate all data types; for example, there were the following add instructions:

Mnemonic	Op Code	Operation
addb2	80	add byte, dst <- src + dst
addb3	81	add byte, dst <- src1 + src2
addw2	A0	add halfword, dst <- src + dst
addw3	A1	add halfword, dst <- src1 + src2
addl2	C0	add word, dst <- src + dst
addl3	C1	add word, dst <- src1 + src2
addf2	40	add single float, dst <- src + dst
addf3	41	add single float, dst <- src1 + src2
addd2	60	add double float, dst <- src + dst
addd3	61	add double float, dst <- src1 + src2

The opcode occupied a single byte. As in the PDP-11, operands were specified by register-mode pairs. In the case of the VAX-11 with 16 registers, four bits were needed to specify the register. The addressing modes were expanded from the 8 of the PDP-11 to 16 for the VAX-11. The addressing modes were as follows:

Mode	Assembler	Description
0-3	#literal	Register/mode byte represents literal < 64.
4	[Rx]	Index mode, after computing address use register as an index.
5	Rn	Register direct mode; the register specified contains the operand.
6	*Rn	Register deferred mode; the register specified contains a pointer to the operand.
7	-(Rn)	Auto decrement mode; register is decremented before use and then used to a pointer to data.
8	(Rn)+	Auto increment mode; register is used to a pointer to data and then incremented after use.
9	*(Rn)+	Auto increment mode deferred; register is used to a pointer to a pointer to the data. Register is then incremented after use by four (a pointer is always a word quantity).
A	X(Rn)	Byte displacement mode; byte X is added to the contents of Rn to produce a pointer to the operand. Neither X nor (Rn) is modified.
B	*X(Rn)	Byte displacement mode deferred; byte X is added to the contents of Rn to produce a pointer to a pointer to the operand. Neither X nor (Rn) is modified.
C	X(Rn)	Halfword displacement mode; halfword X is added to the contents of Rn to produce a pointer to the operand. Neither X nor (Rn) is modified.
D	*X(Rn)	Halfword displacement mode deferred; halfword X is added to the contents of Rn to produce a pointer to a pointer to the operand. Neither X nor (Rn) is modified.
E	X(Rn)	Word displacement mode; word X is added to the contents of Rn to produce a pointer to the operand. Neither X nor (Rn) is modified.
F	*X(Rn)	Word displacement mode deferred; word X is added to the contents of Rn to produce a pointer to a pointer to the operand. Neither X nor (Rn) is modified.

As many small constants appear in programs, literal mode allowed for constants, of magnitude less than 63, to replace the register/mode byte directly. The displacement modes of the PDP-11 were extended in the VAX-11 to handle byte, halfword, and word offsets. Index mode was used in array addressing, in which the base address of the array could be formed with any of the addressing modes and then indexed by the contents of another register containing the index into the array. Depending on the data type of the instruction (byte, halfword, word, single, or double) the contents of the index register would be multiplied by 1, 2, 4, or 8 before being added to the address of the base of the array. This allowed for index variables to be used in loops, without prior shifting, before being used in address computations.

As with the PDP-11, the program counter was a general register, register 0xF, and could be used to extend the addressing modes:

Mode	Assembler	Description
8	#n	Operand follows instruction.
9	*#A	Absolute address follows operand.
A	A	Byte relative address follows operand (assembler will compute program counter relative address).
B	*A	Byte relative value is the program counter relative address of a pointer to the operand.
C	A	Halfword relative address follows operand (assembler will compute program counter relative address).
D	*A	Halfword relative value is the program counter relative address of a pointer to the operand.
E	A	Word relative address follows operand (assembler will compute program counter relative address).
F	*A	Word relative value is the program counter relative address of a pointer to the operand.

Depending on the distance of the operand from the instruction to which the program counter was pointing, the assembler could decide to use byte, halfword, or word relative addressing. This choice was very difficult to make and assemblers frequently ignored this feature, always using word relative addressing.

The instruction format of the VAX-11 was a one-byte opcode followed by a number of operand register/mode bytes with constants in the instruction stream. The length of instructions varied from one, such as halt, to approximately 64. Instruction decode was slow, as each operand had to be processed sequentially.

Some of the 16 general registers some were reserved for special purposes:

Register	Use
R0	General use, also for the result of certain instructions
R1	General use, also for result of certain double precision instructions
R2 - R5	General use, used to store temporary results of string operations if interrupted
R6 - R11	Local registers
R12	Argument pointer
R13	Frame pointer
R14	Stack pointer
R15	Program counter

The first six registers, R0–R5, were for temporary results, much like the six %o0–%o5 registers on the SPARC. The next six registers, R6–R11, were similar to the local registers on the SPARC. The VAX-11 did not use registers for passing arguments to subroutines.

The integer and floating-point instructions on the VAX-11 were almost identical to the PDP-11 with additional features. Instructions were provided for all data types, byte, halfword, word, single, and double precision; three and two-operand forms of many instructions existed, such as addw2 and addw3; instructions existed to convert between all possible data formats similar to the convert instructions on the SPARC. Instructions also existed to evaluate a polynomial in either single or double precision, POLYS and POLYD; these instructions had as one operand a pointer to a list of coefficients. The poly instructions were used by library routines to evaluate such functions as sin and cos.

The VAX-11 also provided specialized instructions that did not exist in the PDP-11. An index instruction provided for array indexing and array bound checking; queue instructions provided for inserting and removing items from doubly linked lists representing queues; other instructions made it possible to work with arbitrarily specified sub-bitfields in words. For example, the index instruction had six operands, any of which might be any one of the possible 16 addressing modes:

```
opcode subscript, low, high, size, indexin, indexout
```

The operation of this instruction was as follows:

```
indexout = (indexin + subscript) * size;
if (subscript < low || subscript > high)
    trap(subscript range);
```

This would enable us to translate the code for multidimensional array access given on 185 as

```
                  define(l_1, -2)
                  define(u_1, 3)
                  define(l_2, 0)
                  define(u_2, 9)
                  define(l_3, 2)
                  define(u_3, 4)

                  d1 = eval(u_1 - l_1 + 1)
                  d2 = eval(u_2 - l_2 + 1)
                  d3 = eval(u_3 - l_3 + 1)

                  define(i_r, 10)
                  define(j_r, 11)
                  define(k_r, 12)

                  local_var
                  var(arr_r, 4, d1 * d2 * d3 * 4)

                  begin_main

                  mov       -2, %i_r
                  mov       0, %j_r
                  mov       2, %k_r

          index %i_r, l_1, u_1, d2, %g0, %o0
          index %j_r, l_2, u_2, d3, %o0, %o0
          index %k_r, l_3, u_3, 4,  %o0, %o0
                  add       %fp, %o0, %o0
                  ld        [%o0 + arr_r], %o0 !'%o0 = ary[i][j][k][l]'
```

Although this appears to be very attractive, the time to execute each **index** instruction was much greater than that for simple instructions, such as **add**, and required fairly extensive modifications to a compiler that was already capable of generating the code shown on page 185.

Branching instructions, making use of the condition codes existed on the **VAX-11**; however, the branch target had to lie within -127 and $+128$ bytes of the branch instruction. If the target of the branch was further, a jump instruction had to be added to the code (the sense of the branch must be complemented and targeted to skip over the next instruction, a jump to the target of the branch). There were additional loop control statements, such as add, compare, and branch, which would increment an index variable, make a comparison to a loop-terminating condition, and branch back to the beginning of the loop if appropriate. There was also a **case** statement that replaced the dispatch table (see page 256).

The **VAX-11** provided special instructions to handle function calls. Subroutine calls were difficult to implement on the PDP-11: The arguments had first to be placed on the stack; the call made; registers saved to the stack; arguments placed into registers; the subroutine code executed; registers restored from the stack; the return made. All the above required explicit instructions. There was no register file as in the SPARC architecture and, of course, no `save` and `restore` instructions on either the PDP-11 or on the VAX-11. At about the time of the introduction of the VAX-11 structured programming was becoming popular, and programs were broken up into many small subroutines, making the need for efficient subroutine handling important. The VAX-11 `calls` instruction was provided for arguments passed on the stack. Having moved the arguments onto the stack, a `calls` instruction was executed with two arguments, the number of arguments placed onto the stack and the address of the subroutine entry. At the address of the subroutine entry was a register save mask with bits indicating which registers would be used in the subroutine and needed to be saved on the stack.

When the `calls` instruction is executed the following actions take place:

1. The number of arguments; the first argument to `calls` is pushed onto the stack.

2. The register save mask is scanned from bit 11 through bit 0 and a register whose number corresponds to a set bit is pushed onto the stack.

3. The program counter, the return address, is pushed onto the stack.

4. The frame pointer is pushed onto the stack.

5. The argument pointer is pushed onto the stack.

6. The condition codes are cleared.

7. The processor status word and the register save mask are pushed onto the stack.

8. A zero is pushed onto the stack, which might be replaced with a trap handler if necessary from within the subroutine.

9. The frame pointer is replaced by the stack pointer.

10. The argument pointer is set to point to the word on the stack containing the number of arguments passed to the subroutine. This work is immediately above the first of the arguments.

11. The program counter is replaced by the subroutine address +2 to point to the first executable instruction in the subroutine.

The VAX-11 `calls` instruction does a lot and, unfortunately, takes a lot of time to execute. The SPARC architecture replaces many of the functions by making use of a hardware solution, the register file, and by passing arguments in registers.

To return from a subroutine, the `VAX-11` `ret` instruction is used:

1. The stack pointer is replaced by the frame pointer +4.

2. The saved processor status word and the register save mask are popped from the stack.

3. The program counter is popped from the stack.

4. The frame pointer is popped from the stack.

5. The argument pointer is popped from the stack.

6. Registers are restored by scanning the register save mask from bit 0 through bit 11.

7. A word containing the number of arguments is popped from the stack.

8. Four times the number of arguments, just popped from the stack, are added to the stack pointer, thus removing the arguments from the stack.

Such a subroutine linkage is very general, but wasteful if its only purpose is to structure programs.

Although we have only discussed the integer and floating-point instructions of the `VAX-11` the `VAX-11` also had instructions for handling strings of characters very efficiently, and for editing text strings, making the machine appropriate for the execution of COBOL programs.

The `VAX-11` virtual memory was handled by a single level of mapping tables resident in memory. This was combined with a scheme of memory segmentation in which the kernel occupied the top half of virtual memory and the user the lower half. Further, these segments were broken into regions that could grow up from the bottom and down from the top, making single-level mapping possible. The `VAX-11` also needed cache memory and a translation lookaside buffer to make the handling of virtual memory efficient.

14.4 The MIPS Architecture

The final architecture we discuss is the MIPS architecture, a contemporary of the SPARC and, as we will see, very similar. Both machines were developed at the same time: SPARC at Berkeley and MIPS at Stanford. They are both 32-bit RISC load/store machines and have very similar instruction sets [8].

The instruction formats are shown in Figure 14.1. All instructions are decoded first on their opcode and then, in the case of opcodes 0 and 1, further decoded based on the op2 field. In the case of MIPS, the immediate form of instructions have different opcodes from their register equivalents. For example, `add %r1, %r2, %r3` has the following machine code, 0,1,2,3,0,040, where each of the fields

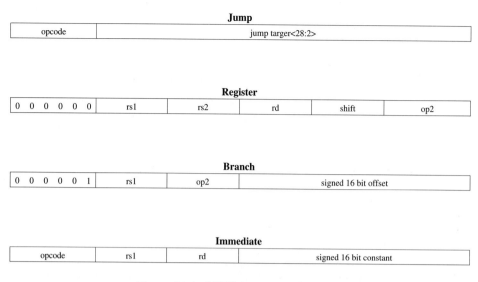

Figure 14.1: MIPS Instruction Formats

is given in octal; when the op field is zero, this indicates that decoding is to take place based on the op2 field, which in the case of the add instruction is, 040. On the other hand, the addi %r1, 17, %r3 instruction has the following machine code: 010,1,3,17. In this case, the opcode is 010 and the low 16 bits of the instruction are treated as a signed 16 bit constant, to be sign extended to 32 bits before use. The MIPS architecture allows for 16 bit constants in contrast to the 13-bit constants of the SPARC, thus allowing for much larger blocks of memory to be accessed with respect to a single base register.

The MIPS processor is also pipelined so that delay slot instructions are necessary after all instructions that change the contents of the program counter. In the case of MIPS, however, the load instruction is not interlocked to prevent the destination register of a load instruction being used in the following instruction.[2] In the MIPS architecture an instruction must be inserted between the load instruction and a following instruction that uses the loaded data.

There are no condition codes in the MIPS architecture, but branch instructions are provided to compare a register to zero and branch if the appropriate conditions are met. The SPARC cmp instruction is equivalent to the *set less than*, slt, instruction in MIPS; this instruction will set the destination register true if its first operand is less than its second. For example, the C code

```
    if (a > b)
        a++;
```

would be translated in SPARC as

---

[2]Hence the acronym for MIPS, Microprocessor without Interlocked Pipeline Stages.

```
        cmp     %a, %b
        ble     next
        nop
        add     %a, 1, %a
next:
```

would be translated in MIPS as

```
        slt     %b, %a, %t
        beq     %t, %g0, next
        nop
        addi    %a, 1, %a
next:
```

The beq and bneq instructions on MIPS compare the contents of two registers and must be used in conjunction with %g0 to provide the equivalent SPARC be and bne instructions. In the case of MIPS, the branch address is stored as a 16-bit signed word offset that is ored with the high four bits of the program counter to form the target address. Annulled branch instructions are also provided, but in the case of the MIPS architecture each annulled branch instruction is a separate instruction indicating that the branch is "likely." For example, the annulled form of the beq instruction is beql, which will annul the delay slot instruction if the branch is not taken.

The MIPS architecture supports the same load and store instructions with the exception of load and store double. The operands of the load and store instructions, however, are a register and/or a 16-bit sign-extended constant. An address formed from the sum of two registers, as in the SPARC architecture, is not possible.

The arithmetic instructions in MIPS include add, sub, mul, and div. These instructions are present in signed and unsigned forms; the signed forms cause a trap on overflow. The mul and div instructions are unusual, as they take many more cycles than one to execute, somewhat in contradiction to the RISC approach. These two instructions are, however, handled in much the same manner as the floating-point instruction are handled in the case of SPARC. Both instructions start and run to completion; as soon as they are started the machine continues to execute other instructions. If the results of the multiply or division are needed, the processor stalls until the instructions complete. Later forms of the SPARC architecture also support similar multiply and divide instructions. These instructions work in conjunction with two special machine registers, HI and LO. A subset of the logical instructions is present: and, xor, nor, and, or, as well as the three shift instructions.

A major difference occurs with the registers. There is no register file in the MIPS architecture.[3] Instead, there are only 32 general registers, which must be saved and restored by the programmer whenever subroutines are called.

The 32 general registers have the following assignment:

---

[3]The lack of a floating-point register file allows the memory management unit to be integrated onto the same chip in MIPS, reducing memory access time.

Rn	Name	Use
0	%g0	Always zero.
1	%at	Temporary for use by the set less instructions.
2,3	%o0, %o1	Return values from functions.
4–7	%i0–%i3	To pass the first four arguments to subroutines. Additional arguments are placed on the stack.
8–15	%t0–%t7	Temporary registers, not preserved over subroutine calls.
16–23	%l0–%l7	Local variables, preserved over subroutine calls.
24, 25	%t8, %t9	Several more temporary registers.
26, 27	%k0, %k1	Reserved for the operating system.
28	%g1	Global pointer register.
29	%sp	Stack pointer.
30	%l8	Another local variable register, preserved over subroutine calls.
31	%i7	Subroutine return address.

When a subroutine call is to be made any local registers, %l0–%l8, containing data that will be needed after the subroutine returns must be saved either by the caller or by the callee.[4] The convention is that a called program must save any of the local registers that it will use on subroutine entry to the stack. Before the return all the saved registers must be restored. This, of course, involves an st and an ld instruction for each register saved. Although this might appear to degrade the performance of the machine, one must bear in mind that when a context switch occurs, a SPARC machine must save the entire register file to the stack. The MIPS architecture does not support a frame pointer; instead, stack offsets must be handled relative to the stack pointer. The subroutine call places the return address into register 31, which must then be saved to the stack before another subroutine call.

The MIPS supports a separate floating-point coprocessor in the same manner as the SPARC architecture. The MIPS architecture provides instructions to move data between the integer unit registers and the floating-point registers, lacking in the SPARC architecture. Although data have to be moved from the integer unit to the floating-point unit via the stack in the SPARC architecture, such moves can normally be interleaved with floating-point instruction execution and thus do not involve any time penalty.

14.5   Summary

The SPARC architecture represents an evolution of computer architecture of almost 50 years. Much of this evolution has been driven by technological advances relating

---

[4]A compiler may use a technique called *interprocedural register allocation* to minimize the number of registers that must be saved.

to the relative cost and reliability of the various components of computers: registers, arithmetic logic units, and memory. We have seen the transition from vacuum tube technology through transistors to the VLSI chips of today, which embody an entire processor in a single device. Memory has similarly developed from magnetics to the solid-state memories of today. Concurrent with these advances have been developments in programming languages and operating systems. The hand-coded machine language programs of the first computers, occupying some few memory locations, have been replaced by high-level language-generated programs occupying megabytes of memory. Operating systems now allow for efficient execution of many programs simultaneously occupying memory and sharing common bulk storage. Current research is devoted to parallel machines in which large numbers of processing elements replace the single von Neumann machine.

In this chapter we have tried to trace the recent development that led to the SPARC architecture and to RISC architectures in general. We first discussed the PDP-11 computer, as it is a very clean architecture and was concurrent with the development of the C programming language. This machine transitioned into the VAX-11 to provide for virtual memory. The VAX-11 took advantage of microprogramming to provide an extensive instruction set. The RISC architecture was based on the development of compiler technology, which eliminated the need for complicated instructions, allowing for the efficient execution of the reduced resulting instruction set. RISC was also introduced at a time when the cost of memory was decreasing, eliminating the need to reduce the size of programs. Concurrent with the development of the SPARC architecture was the MIPS architecture. The two architectures are very similar, the principal difference being the elimination of the register file requiring the compiler to manage the allocation of variables to the available registers.

An understanding of machine architecture is necessary if one is to make intelligent use of the features provided by high-level languages. To understand a machine architecture it is necessary to understand its programming at the assembly language programming level. It is important to understand how various high-level program constructs translate into machine language to select control and data structures intelligently for efficient programming. Much emphasis is given to structured programming, a program must be efficient as well as correct, and this requires an understanding of a machine's architecture.

14.6 Exercises

14–1 Why is there no need to provide the separate condition-code-setting instructions of the SPARC architecture for the PDP-11?

14–2 Why is it difficult for assemblers to decide on byte, halfword, or word offsets when computing program counter relative addresses?

14–3 What is the difference between CISC and RISC processors?

Chapter 15

ULTRA SPARC

15.1 Introduction

In 1993 the SPARC International's Architecture Committee announced Version 9 of the SPARC architecture, which remains binary compatible with the existing SPARC architecture for user programs [28].

Most notably, the new architecture is *superscalar*, meaning that more than one instruction can be issued at a time for execution, and that the virtual address size is increased from 32 bits to 64 bits. These two architectural changes have implications which required a number of additions and modification to the instruction set. We will look at the increase in address size first and then discuss superscalar execution.

15.2 64-Bit Virtual Memory Addresses

It is said that the only mistake in computer design that is difficult to recover from is to get the address size wrong[19, 2]. This does not seem to have concerned the SPARC architects, who faced with the need to support a larger virtual memory address space, simply doubled the size of their integer registers from 32 bits to 64 bits and the deed was done. The Ultra SPARC has a 64-bit addressable virtual memory. Why so large? It is not that user programs have grown so large but that data sets have done so. Files and data sets are now frequently measured in gigabytes, and if they are to be mapped directly into memory, the virtual address size must increase accordingly.

When in the new architecture, byte, halfword, and word data are loaded into a register, they are now extended to 64 bits. All arithmetic is performed to 64-bit precision. It is also possible to manipulate 64-bit quantities directly and a new data type is defined for SPARC Version 9, signed extended and unsigned extended. For example, the Version 9 load instructions are

$$\begin{array}{lll}
\text{ldsb} & [\text{address}], \, \pmb{reg}_{rd} & \\
\text{ldsh} & [\text{address}], \, \pmb{reg}_{rd} & \\
\text{ldsw} & [\text{address}], \, \pmb{reg}_{rd} & \\
\text{ldub} & [\text{address}], \, \pmb{reg}_{rd} & \\
\text{lduh} & [\text{address}], \, \pmb{reg}_{rd} & \\
\text{lduw} & [\text{address}], \, \pmb{reg}_{rd} & \text{synonym ld} \\
\text{ldx} & [\text{address}], \, \pmb{reg}_{rd} &
\end{array}$$

Notice the addition of the `ldsw` instruction, which will load a 32-bit integer into a 64-bit register with sign extension. The `lduw` will load a 32-bit integer into a 64-bit register zero filling the 32 most significant bits. The `ldd` instruction, which loads two registers, still exists from Version 8 but is not recommended. The `ldx` instruction is new, loading a double word into a 64-bit register. Note that all memory addresses still have to be aligned. Similarly, there is a `stx` instruction for storing 64-bit data into memory. The `std` instruction, which stores the low 32 bits from two registers to two words in memory, is still present but no longer recommended.

The add and subtract instructions still exist, as do the 32-bit extended arithmetic instructions `addx` and `addxcc`, which have been renamed `addc` and `addccc` for Version 9. There is a slight problem with the `cc` instructions, which set the condition codes. Although the machine performs 64-bit arithmetic, many programs expect to be using 32-bit arithmetic. There is a difference in the condition codes. What is a signed overflow, if the operands are considered 32 bits long, is quite different when the operands are to be considered 64 bits long. To solve this problem, Version 9 defines two sets of condition codes, `%icc` and the new `%xcc`. When `cc` instructions are executed, bits of both sets of condition codes N, Z, V, and C bits are set and may be tested appropriately. Branching instructions have an additional operand, the condition code to be tested. For example, a branch greater instruction for word data would be written as

```
bg %icc, label
```

whereas for extended 64-bit data the instruction would be written as:

```
bg %xcc, label
```

In C programs, contrary to the philosophy that the `int` variable should be the same size as the register variable, the `int` variable remains a 32-bit quantity; the C long int variable on Ultra SPARC is now, however, 64 bits long, as are, of course, pointer variables. The char and short variables remain a byte and halfword, respectively.

Shifting instructions need to distinguish between 32 and 64-bit data. An arithmetic shift right for 32-bit data will replicate bit 31 as the data is shifted right, whereas for 64-bit data, bit 63 will be replicated.

```
sll    reg_rs1, reg_or_shcnt, reg_rd
srl    reg_rs1, reg_or_shcnt, reg_rd
sra    reg_rs1, reg_or_shcnt, reg_rd
sllx   reg_rs1, reg_or_shcnt, reg_rd
srlx   reg_rs1, reg_or_shcnt, reg_rd
srax   reg_rs1, reg_or_shcnt, reg_rd
```

SPARC Version 9 Architecture specifies an integer multiply and divide instruction:

```
mulx    reg_rs1, reg_or_imm, reg_rd
sdivx   reg_rs1, reg_or_imm, reg_rd
udivx   reg_rs1, reg_or_imm, reg_rd
```

The multiply instruction takes two 64-bit operands and computes a 64-bit result; the instruction is the same for both signed and unsigned data. The division instructions distinguishes between signed and unsigned data. The `mulscc` instruction is still there but no longer recommended.

Loading 64-bit constants is difficult as there is no 64-bit version of the `sethi` instruction. The `sethi` instruction does, however, set the high 32 bits of the register to zero as well as the low 10 bits. Thus to load a 32-bit constant into register %o0, we may write

```
sethi  %hi(const32), %o0
or     %o0, %lo(const32), %o0
```

However, if the 32-bit constant is negative, the code sequence above will leave the high 32 bits incorrectly zero. To propagate the sign bit, we may use an arithmetic shift instruction:

```
sethi  %hi(const32), %o0
or     %o0, %lo(const32), %o0
sra    %o0, %g0, %o0
```

which has been specialized to propagate the sign bit through the left half of the register.[1] The `setsw` synthetic instruction will generate such a code sequence, depending on whether the sign is positive or negative and will leave out the `sethi` or the `or` instructions, depending on the constant involved. Thus we might have written

```
setsw  const32, %o0
```

and have achieved the same result with a one- to three-long instruction sequence. Needless to say, `setsw` should not be used in a delay slot. The `setuw` synthetic

---

[1]Similarly, the srl instruction has also been specialized, so that with the second source operand 0, it will clear the upper 32 bits of the destination register.

instruction should be used to set 32-bit unsigned data into registers and is the same as the Version 8 set instruction.

To set a 64-bit constant into, say, %o0 using %o1 as a temporary register, we need the following sequence:

```
sethi   %uhi(const64), %o1
or      %o1, %ulo(const64), %o1
sllx    %o1, 32, %o1
sethi   %hi(const64), %o0
or      %o0, %o1, %o0
or      %o0, %lo(const64), %o0
```

Note that %uhi is an arithmetic operator that returns the high 22 bits of a 64-bit argument and that %ulo is an arithmetic operator that returns the low 10 bits of the upper 32 bits of its 64-bit argument. The synthetic instruction setx generates the sequence of code above leaving out any of the six possible instructions:

```
setx    const64, %o1, %o0
```

Handling 64-bit constants is an expensive operation.

15.3   Superscalar Execution

The original SPARC fetched instructions one by one. It was pipelined, which resulted in load delay slots (which the processor handled by stalling the pipeline if necessary) and branch delay slot instructions (handled by the programmer; see Section 2.5). Instructions were executed in the order in which they were fetched; however, floating-point instructions were passed off to the floating-point processor, allowing for parallel execution of integer and floating-point instructions. In a superscalar processor more than one instruction is fetched and executed simultaneously by a number of arithmetic logic units, ALUs. In a current version of the Ultra SPARC, two integer instructions and two floating-point instructions are executed at the same time. Future versions of SPARC contemplate issuing 16 instructions every cycle. Such a pipeline is shown in Figure 15.1.

The fetch unit fetches instructions, but now at a much greater rate. These instructions when fetched are decoded to add additional information to the instructions, which are then passed to the grouping logic unit . The grouping logic unit keeps a small number of instructions and tries to group them into sets of four instructions which may be executed together. Of these, two may be floating-point and two integer instructions. The reordering of instructions must be done in such a way that the result of execution does not differ from the execution of instructions, one after the other, in the order in which they were fetched. The result of the reordering must also not affect the results if an exception or an interrupt occurs. This is very difficult to do, but as it increases the effective instruction execution

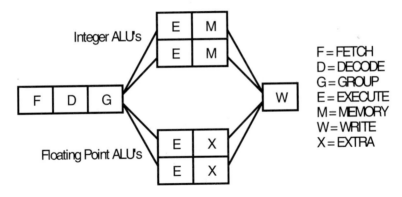

Figure 15.1: Ultra SPARC's Pipeline

rate, it is apparently worth doing.[2] If it is possible to form sets of instructions that may be executed together, the grouping logic unit then issues the instructions, one to each of the ALUs, of which there are two integer units and two floating-point units. The 4 instructions are then executed in parallel, effectively increasing the instruction execution rate by a factor of four. If there are no floating-point instruction to be executed, then of course, the instruction execution rate would only have been increased by a factor of 2. After the instructions have been executed, any exceptions are managed and the results written back to the register files, one for the integer unit and one for the floating-point unit.

While branching caused problems in pipelining, requiring the programmer to insert load and branch delay slot instructions, the situation is far more serious when a branch is encountered in a superscalar processor. All the instructions fetched and held in the grouping logic unit together with the instructions in execution must be flushed. If many branch instructions are encountered, our fourfold increase in instruction execution rate might begin to look more like a fourfold decrease in instruction execution rate. If we are to use superscalar execution, branches must at all costs be avoided or at least their effects mitigated. The new SPARC architecture addresses this problem directly in hardware by keeping track of branches and attempting to predict whether they will or will not be taken, so that instructions may be fetched in the correct order. The architecture also provides the programmer with three ways to help avoid flushing the pipeline: the supply of information regarding the likelihood of a branch being taken, the provision of multiple-condition-code registers, and the provision of conditional move instructions. We consider each in turn.

---

[2]One wonders where all the CISC computer architects went; it would appear that they are all now designing superscalar pipelines. The reader is referred to [26, 19] for a detailed treatment of this subject.

15.3.1   Branch Prediction

Consider the following code fragment, which is checking the range of a variable, theta, with the expectation that it is usually MIN < theta < MAX:

```
range = 1;
if (theta < MIN) {
  theta = MIN;
  range = 0;
  }
else if (theta > MAX) [
  theta = MAX;
  range = 0;
  }
```

and its translation into Version 8 code:

```
        mov     1, %range
        cmp     %theta, MIN
        bge,a   else
        cmp     %theta, MAX
        mov     MIN, %theta
        ba      done
        clr     %range
else:   ble     done
        nop
        mov     MAX, %theta
        clr     %range
```

which contains no less than two conditional branch instructions, both of which may be predicted to be taken. The unconditional branch instruction causes no problem, with the fetch unit directly fetching instructions from the new branch address after having fetched the delay slot instruction. In Version 9 branch instructions are followed, after a possible annulment flag, by either **pt** to indicate that the branch is predicted to be taken or by **pn** to indicate that the branch is predicted *not* to be taken.

Thus our corresponding Version 9 code would be

```
        mov      1, %range
        cmp      %theta, MIN
        bge,a,pt %icc, else
        cmp      %theta, MAX
        mov      MIN, %theta
        ba       done
        clr      %range
else:   ble,pt   %icc, done
        nop
        mov      MAX, %theta
        clr      %range
```

if neither pt or pn is specified the default pt is assumed. Note the additional argument to the branch instructions %icc, indicating that we are performing 32-bit arithmetic. With the conditional branch predicted the fetch unit will follow the prediction and fetch instructions from the branch address, assuming that the prediction is correct.

15.3.2   Branch on Integer Register

We are not quite out of the woods yet, however. There are two cmp instructions in the code above, both of which set the condition codes. Clearly, the second cmp instruction cannot be executed before the first branch has been executed. This is handled in two ways, one for integer instructions and one for floating-point instructions. In the case of integer instructions, the result of the compare instruction can be left in a register. Instead of using

```
subcc %theta, MIN, %g0
```

we can save the result of the comparison in a register, %o0 for example:

```
sub %theta, MIN, %o0
```

and then use a Version 9 "branch on integer register with prediction" instruction. These instructions are as follows:

brz{,a}{,pt|pn}	reg_{rs1}, label	branch if $[rs1] = 0$
brlez{,a}{,pt|pn}	reg_{rs1}, label	branch if $r[rs1] \leq 0$
brlz{,a}{,pt|pn}	reg_{rs1}, label	branch if $r[rs1] < 0$
brnz{,a}{,pt|pn}	reg_{rs1}, label	branch if $r[rs1] \neq 0$
brgz{,a}{,pt|pn}	reg_{rs1}, label	branch if $r[rs1] > 0$
brgez{,a}{,pt|pn}	reg_{rs1}, label	branch if $r[rs1] \geq 0$

where the contents of the first source register is tested and the branch taken or not, depending on whether the condition has been met. Thus we may rewrite our code without making use of the integer condition codes:

```
        mov         1, %range
        sub         %theta, MIN, %o0
        brgez,a,pt  %o0, else
        sub         %theta, MAX, %o1
        mov         MIN, %theta
        ba          done
        clr         %range
else:   brlez,pt    %o1, done
        nop
        mov         MAX, %theta
        clr         %range
done:
```

Notice that this code does not make use of the condition codes.[3]

15.3.3 Multiple Floating-Point Condition Codes

In the case of floating-point instructions, SPARC Version 9 architecture provides for four condition code registers: %fcc0, %fcc1, %fcc2, %fcc3, which must be specified in the floating compare instructions and in the branch instructions. For example, if our code segment was for double floating-point instructions, we would write

```
        mov         1, %range_r
        fcmpd       %fcc0, %theta_f, %min_f
        fbge,a,pt   %fcc0, else
        fcmpd       %fcc1, %theta_f, %max_f
        fmovd       %max_f, %theta_f
        ba          done
        clr         %range_r
else:   fble,pt     %fcc1, done
        nop
        fmovd       %max_f, %theta_f
        clr         %range_r
done:
```

Notice how there is no problem with the

```
        fbge,a,pt %fcc0, else
```

---

[3]Be careful. The branching condition for the bge instruction is NOT(N XOR V), which is correct even if the subtraction results in an overflow condition, whereas the branching condition for the brgez instruction is only NOT N. If there is any possibility that the comparison of two numbers might result in a 64-bit signed overflow condition, the branch with prediction instruction, bge, should be used not the branch on register instruction, which cannot test the overflow flag. Similar conditions exist when using unsigned arithmetic. However, as SPARC is performing 64-bit arithmetic, overflow for 32-bit quantities does not present a problem for the "branch on register condition" instructions.

instruction being executed before the

```
fcmpd     %fcc1, %theta_f, %max_f
```

is executed, as both instructions now refer to different condition code registers.

Notice also that in Version 9 all possible `mov` instructions are provided:

fmovs	$freg_{rs2}$, $freg_{rd}$	move
fmovd	$freg_{rs2}$, $freg_{rd}$	
fmovq	$freg_{rs2}$, $freg_{rd}$	
fnegs	$freg_{rs2}$, $freg_{rd}$	negate
fnegd	$freg_{rs2}$, $freg_{rd}$	
fnegq	$freg_{rs2}$, $freg_{rd}$	
fabss	$freg_{rs2}$, $freg_{rd}$	absolute value
fabsd	$freg_{rs2}$, $freg_{rd}$	
fabsq	$freg_{rs2}$, $freg_{rd}$	

15.3.4 Move Register on Condition

Considering our code segment there is really no need to branch at all; all that we are doing in this code segment is to store or not store data, depending on conditions. Realizing this, and the possibility of dramatically reducing the number of branch instructions, SPARC Version 9 includes a series of conditional move instructions.

The first set of instruction we consider are conditional move instructions based on the condition codes. These instructions test the integer condition codes, and if the condition is satisfied, the contents of the second source register, or the immediate constant, is moved to the destination register. Two sets of instructions exist for moving data between integer registers or between floating-point registers. The integer move instructions are

mova	$i\_or\_x\_cc$, $reg\_or\_imm_{11}$, reg_{rd}	
movn	$i\_or\_x\_cc$, $reg\_or\_imm_{11}$, reg_{rd}	
movne	$i\_or\_x\_cc$, $reg\_or\_imm_{11}$, reg_{rd}	synonym: movnz
move	$i\_or\_x\_cc$, $reg\_or\_imm_{11}$, reg_{rd}	synonym: movz
movg	$i\_or\_x\_cc$, $reg\_or\_imm_{11}$, reg_{rd}	
movle	$i\_or\_x\_cc$, $reg\_or\_imm_{11}$, reg_{rd}	
movge	$i\_or\_x\_cc$, $reg\_or\_imm_{11}$, reg_{rd}	
movl	$i\_or\_x\_cc$, $reg\_or\_imm_{11}$, reg_{rd}	
movgu	$i\_or\_x\_cc$, $reg\_or\_imm_{11}$, reg_{rd}	
movleu	$i\_or\_x\_cc$, $reg\_or\_imm_{11}$, reg_{rd}	
movcc	$i\_or\_x\_cc$, $reg\_or\_imm_{11}$, reg_{rd}	synonym: movgeu
movcs	$i\_or\_x\_cc$, $reg\_or\_imm_{11}$, reg_{rd}	synonym: movlu
movpos	$i\_or\_x\_cc$, $reg\_or\_imm_{11}$, reg_{rd}	
movneg	$i\_or\_x\_cc$, $reg\_or\_imm_{11}$, reg_{rd}	
movvc	$i\_or\_x\_cc$, $reg\_or\_imm_{11}$, reg_{rd}	
movvs	$i\_or\_x\_cc$, $reg\_or\_imm_{11}$, reg_{rd}	

Note that the signed immediate constant is reduced to 11 bits, due to the need to include the two bits to select the condition codes, %icc or %xcc. How do we use these instructions? Consider the integer code example shown above. This may be rewritten as follows, eliminating all branches:

```
mov      1, %range
cmp      %theta, MIN
movl     %icc, MIN, %theta
movl     %icc, 0, %range
cmp      %theta, MAX
movg     %icc, MAX, %theta
movg     %icc, 0, %range
```

If we are concerned about conflicts between setting and testing the single set of condition codes we may leave the result in a register and test it using the "move integer register on register condition" instructions. Here the contents of the first source resister are tested, and if the condition is met, the contents of the second source register or the immediate constant are moved into the destination register:

movrne	reg_{rs1}, *reg_or_imm*$_{10}$, reg_{rd}	$r[\text{rs1}] \neq 0$	synonym: movrnz
movre	reg_{rs1}, *reg_or_imm*$_{10}$, reg_{rd}	$r[\text{rs1}] = 0$	synonym: movrz
movrgez	reg_{rs1}, *reg_or_imm*$_{10}$, reg_{rd}	$r[\text{rs1}] \geq 0$	
movrlz	reg_{rs1}, *reg_or_imm*$_{10}$, reg_{rd}	$r[\text{rs1}] < 0$	
movrlez	reg_{rs1}, *reg_or_imm*$_{10}$, reg_{rd}	$r[\text{rs1}] \leq 0$	
movrgz	reg_{rs1}, *reg_or_imm*$_{10}$, reg_{rd}	$r[\text{rs1}] > 0$	

Again, overflow is not taken into consideration with these tests. Note also the small size of any immediate constant, 10 bits. Our code example rewritten using these instructions is

```
mov      1, %range
sub      %theta, MIN, %o0
movrlz   %o0, MIN, %theta
movrlz   %o0, 0, %range
sub      %theta, MAX, %o1
movrgz   %o1, MAX, %theta
movrgz   %o1, 0, %range
```

We can also move the contents of a floating-point register based on the integer condition codes or on the contents of an integer register:

fmov{s|d|q}a	$i\_or\_x\_cc$, $freg_{rs2}$, $freg_{rd}$	
fmov{s|d|q}n	$i\_or\_x\_cc$, $freg_{rs2}$, $freg_{rd}$	
fmov{s|d|q}ne	$i\_or\_x\_cc$, $freg_{rs2}$, $freg_{rd}$	synonym: fmovnz
fmov{s|d|q}e	$i\_or\_x\_cc$, $freg_{rs2}$, $freg_{rd}$	synonym: fmovz
fmov{s|d|q}g	$i\_or\_x\_cc$, $freg_{rs2}$, $freg_{rd}$	
fmov{s|d|q}le	$i\_or\_x\_cc$, $freg_{rs2}$, $freg_{rd}$	
fmov{s|d|q}ge	$i\_or\_x\_cc$, $freg_{rs2}$, $freg_{rd}$	
fmov{s|d|q}l	$i\_or\_x\_cc$, $freg_{rs2}$, $freg_{rd}$	
fmov{s|d|q}gu	$i\_or\_x\_cc$, $freg_{rs2}$, $freg_{rd}$	
fmov{s|d|q}leu	$i\_or\_x\_cc$, $freg_{rs2}$, $freg_{rd}$	
fmov{s|d|q}cc	$i\_or\_x\_cc$, $freg_{rs2}$, $freg_{rd}$	synonym: fmovgeu
fmov{s|d|q}cs	$i\_or\_x\_cc$, $freg_{rs2}$, $freg_{rd}$	synonym: fmovlu
fmov{s|d|q}pos	$i\_or\_x\_cc$, $freg_{rs2}$, $freg_{rd}$	
fmov{s|d|q}neg	$i\_or\_x\_cc$, $freg_{rs2}$, $freg_{rd}$	
fmov{s|d|q}vc	$i\_or\_x\_cc$, $freg_{rs2}$, $freg_{rd}$	
fmov{s|d|q}vs	$i\_or\_x\_cc$, $freg_{rs2}$, $freg_{rd}$	

fmovr{s|d|q}ne	reg_{rs1}, $freg_{rs2}$, $freg_{rd}$	$r[rs1] \neq 0$	synonym: fmovrnz
fmovr{s|d|q}e	reg_{rs1}, $freg_{rs2}$, $freg_{rd}$	$r[rs1] = 0$	synonym: fmovrz
fmovr{s|d|q}gez	reg_{rs1}, $freg_{rs2}$, $freg_{rd}$	$r[rs1] \geq 0$	
fmovr{s|d|q}lz	reg_{rs1}, $freg_{rs2}$, $freg_{rd}$	$r[rs1] < 0$	
fmovr{s|d|q}lez	reg_{rs1}, $freg_{rs2}$, $freg_{rd}$	$r[rs1] \leq 0$	
fmovr{s|d|q}gz	reg_{rs1}, $freg_{rs2}$, $freg_{rd}$	$r[rs1] > 0$	

Finally, we may move the contents of integer registers based on the floating-point condition codes:

mova	$\%fccn$, $reg\_or\_imm_{11}$, reg_{rd}	
movn	$\%fccn$, $reg\_or\_imm_{11}$, reg_{rd}	
movne	$\%fccn$, $reg\_or\_imm_{11}$, reg_{rd}	synonym: movnz
move	$\%fccn$, $reg\_or\_imm_{11}$, reg_{rd}	synonym: movz
movg	$\%fccn$, $reg\_or\_imm_{11}$, reg_{rd}	
movle	$\%fccn$, $reg\_or\_imm_{11}$, reg_{rd}	
movge	$\%fccn$, $reg\_or\_imm_{11}$, reg_{rd}	
movl	$\%fccn$, $reg\_or\_imm_{11}$, reg_{rd}	
movgu	$\%fccn$, $reg\_or\_imm_{11}$, reg_{rd}	
movleu	$\%fccn$, $reg\_or\_imm_{11}$, reg_{rd}	
movcc	$\%fccn$, $reg\_or\_imm_{11}$, reg_{rd}	synonym: movgeu
movcs	$\%fccn$, $reg\_or\_imm_{11}$, reg_{rd}	synonym: movlu
movpos	$\%fccn$, $reg\_or\_imm_{11}$, reg_{rd}	
movneg	$\%fccn$, $reg\_or\_imm_{11}$, reg_{rd}	
movvc	$\%fccn$, $reg\_or\_imm_{11}$, reg_{rd}	
movvs	$\%fccn$, $reg\_or\_imm_{11}$, reg_{rd}	

fmov{s|d|q}a	$\%fccn,\ freg_{rs2},\ freg_{rd}$	
fmov{s|d|q}n	$\%fccn,\ freg_{rs2},\ freg_{rd}$	
fmov{s|d|q}ne	$\%fccn,\ freg_{rs2},\ freg_{rd}$	synonym: fmovnz
fmov{s|d|q}e	$\%fccn,\ freg_{rs2},\ freg_{rd}$	synonym: fmovz
fmov{s|d|q}g	$\%fccn,\ freg_{rs2},\ freg_{rd}$	
fmov{s|d|q}le	$\%fccn,\ freg_{rs2},\ freg_{rd}$	
fmov{s|d|q}ge	$\%fccn,\ freg_{rs2},\ freg_{rd}$	
fmov{s|d|q}l	$\%fccn,\ freg_{rs2},\ freg_{rd}$	
fmov{s|d|q}gu	$\%fccn,\ freg_{rs2},\ freg_{rd}$	
fmov{s|d|q}leu	$\%fccn,\ freg_{rs2},\ freg_{rd}$	
fmov{s|d|q}cc	$\%fccn,\ freg_{rs2},\ freg_{rd}$	synonym: fmovgeu
fmov{s|d|q}cs	$\%fccn,\ freg_{rs2},\ freg_{rd}$	synonym: fmovlu
fmov{s|d|q}pos	$\%fccn,\ freg_{rs2},\ freg_{rd}$	
fmov{s|d|q}neg	$\%fccn,\ freg_{rs2},\ freg_{rd}$	
fmov{s|d|q}vc	$\%fccn,\ freg_{rs2},\ freg_{rd}$	
fmov{s|d|q}vs	$\%fccn,\ freg_{rs2},\ freg_{rd}$	

So that we may rewrite the floating-point version of our code as

```
mov      1, %range_r
fcmpd    %fcc0, %theta_f, %min_f
fmovdl   %fcc0, %min_f, %theta_f
movl     %fcc0, 0, %range_r
fcmpd    %fcc1, %theta_f, %max_f
fmovdg   %fcc1, %max_f,  %theta_f
movg     %fcc1, 0, %range_r
```

The Ultra SPARC architecture specifies an additional 32 registers. You may, as before, address the first 32 floating-point registers as single floating-point operands. You may also, as before, address the first 32 floating-point registers in pairs as double floating-point operands, %f0, %f2, %f4, ..., %f30, but now, in addition, you may address the new registers to provide for an additional 16 double floating-point registers, %f32, %f34, %f36, ..., %f62. Note that you may not address the upper floating-point registers to hold single floating-point operands. Finally, you may store 16 quad floating-point operands in %f0, %f4, %f8, ...,%f60.

15.4 Instruction and Data Prefetching

The Version 9 instruction set includes instructions for prefetching both instructions and data. Consider that you are about to branch to another part of your program. This will require instructions to be fetched from a different part of memory with the *strong* probability that the instructions will not be found in the cache memory. This can result in a number of lost machine cycles while the data is loaded into the cache from main memory. If you issue an "`iprefetch, label`" instruction somewhere before the branch, the cache will be loaded with instructions from the labeled location *before* you get to the branch, thus avoiding any delay when the branch instruction is executed.[4] Similarly, a `prefetch` instruction, with the same operands as a load instruction, will ensure that data from the addressed location is in the cache when it is needed. For example, in a loop where a load instruction is executed, using a register containing a pointer as the address, which will be incremented immediately after use to address the next data item, a prefetch instruction might well be executed to ensure that the data is in the cache when loop returns to the load instruction:

```
loop:   ldd   [%o0], %f4
        add   %f4, 8, %f4
        prefetch [%o0]
        . . .
```

15.5 Nonfaulting Loads

Before we discuss nonfaulting loads, we need to describe address spaces. When you use load and store instructions you are using address space USER_PRIMARY (80_{16}) by default. The address space specifier, a byte quantity, is added to a SPARC address to fully specify an address. If the machine is in little endian mode,[5] the default address space is USER_PRIMARY_LITTLE (88_{16}), which still addresses the same memory but reverses the byte ordering of data. Although alternate address spaces are used primarily by the operating system, they may also be used to change the machine addressing to a nonfaulting mode, in which case when an invalid address is supplied the machine returns zero and does not cause a fault. To use nonfaulting loads you need to load the %asi system register with the appropriate address space identifier and then use load and store alternate instructions. The nonfaulting load asi identifier is for big-endian data ASI_PRIMARY_NOFAULT (82_{16}) and ASI_PRIMARY_NOFAULT_LITTLE ($8A_{16}$) for little-endian data. The load and store alternate instructions are

---

[4]The iprefetch is a synthetic instruction resulting in a `bn,a,pt, label` instruction being generated.

[5]Data may be stored and accessed in either big endian order or in little endian order under Version 9 of the architecture.

```
        ldsba   [reg_plus_imm] %asi, reg_rd    load signed byte alternate
        ldsha   [reg_plus_imm] %asi, reg_rd    load signed halfword alternate
        ldswa   [reg_plus_imm] %asi, reg_rd    load signed word alternate
        lduba   [reg_plus_imm] %asi, reg_rd    load unsigned byte alternate
        lduha   [reg_plus_imm] %asi, reg_rd    load unsigned halfword alternate
        lduwa   [reg_plus_imm] %asi, reg_rd    load unsigned word alternate
        ldxa    [reg_plus_imm] %asi, reg_rd    load extended word alternate
        lda     [reg_plus_imm] %asi, freg_rd   load single floating-point alternate
        ldda    [reg_plus_imm] %asi, freg_rd   load double floating-point alternate
        ldqa    [reg_plus_imm] %asi, freg_rd   load quad floating-point alternate
```

and the corresponding store instructions:

```
        stba    reg_rd, [reg_plus_imm] %asi    store byte alternate
        stha    reg_rd, [reg_plus_imm] %asi    store halfword alternate
        stwa    reg_rd, [reg_plus_imm] %asi    store word alternate
        stxa    reg_rd, [reg_plus_imm] %asi    store extended word alternate
        sta     freg_rd, [reg_plus_imm] %asi   store single floating-point alternate
        stda    freg_rd, [reg_plus_imm] %asi   store double floating-point alternate
        stqa    freg_rd, [reg_plus_imm] %asi   store quad floating-point alternate
```

How would we use nonfaulting loads and stores? Consider the following C code:

```
while (ptr  && ptr -> val < x)
  ptr = ptr -> next;
```

and its straightforward translation into assembly language:

```
%sample8
loop: brz,pn    %ptr, done               !all done if ptr == 0
      nop
      ldd       [%ptr + cell_val], %ftmp !load value
      fcmpd     %fcc0,%ftmp, %x          !compare it to x, a stall
      fbl,a,pt %fcc0, loop               !good? branch back to loop
      ldx       [%ptr + cell_next], %ptr !load next pointer,
                                         !cause pipeline stall
                                         !at next instruction
                                         !at beginning of loop.
done:
```

is not very satisfactory, as each load instruction is followed immediately by a test of the contents of the register just loaded, resulting in a processor stall. If we use load alternate instructions, we may write code that separates the loading of a register as far as possible from the use of its contents:

```
          mov     0x82, %asi                    !nonfaulting big-endian
          mov     %ptr, %tmp                    !save ptr for loop exit
          ldda    [%ptr + cell_val], %ftmp      !nonfaulting load of value
   loop:  mov     %tmp, %ptr                    !save ptr value for loop exit
          brz,pn  %ptr, done                    !all done if ptr == 0
          ldxa    [%tmp + cell_next], %tmp      !load of next pointer
          fcmpd   %fcc0,%ftmp, %x               !finally compare value to x
          fbl,a,pt %fcc0, loop                  !good? branch back to loop
          ldda    [%tmp]0x82, %ftmp             !load next value
   done:
```

Note that when a load faults, its data is not used; its use is still protected by the test on the pointer, which now occurs after the attempt is made to load the data. When the pointer is valid, the data is in the register. When the pointer is invalid, the data is not there, but is not needed.

15.6 Changes to Supervisor Mode

Two fairly major changes to supervisor mode include the introduction of a hardware trap stack and the provision of an additional window overflow trap handler. The hardware trap stack enables the architecture to handle traps from within traps, which is not allowed under Version 8. The trap stack results in simplification of the system trap handling code.

The other change involves the saving of register windows when a process context switch occurs (see Section 13.5). Under Version 8 all active register windows had to be flushed to the stack before the memory context could be changed and new register windows brought in from memory. Under Version 9 the register sets do not have to be flushed to the stack before the memory context is changed, as the architecture provides for two window overflow traps, one to handle register windows belonging to the "other" context and one for the current context. Thus only one register window must be saved; as register window overflows occur the registers are flushed to the other memory context until all the register sets have been flushed. Register windows are then flushed to the current memory context. This is particularly useful when the context switch does not result in the need for many register sets.

These changes are detailed in the *SPARC Architecture Manual* and the interested reader is referred to [28].

15.7   Summary

There has always been a desire to make computers faster and to minimize the use of resources, circuits, and memory. Initially, this took the form of increasing the capability of instructions, as this would reduce the length of a program, resulting in faster program execution. Unfortunately, this also increased the complexity of the instruction execution. Translation of these instructions directly into hardware became increasingly difficult and expensive. The solution was to introduce a new micro architecture level below the instruction set level. Machine instructions would be translated into micro instructions for execution. The micro instructions were kept in a micro store to be fetched and executed to implement the now-higher-level machine instructions. This solved the problem of implementing a powerful instruction set, but did not solve the overall problem of maximizing performance while minimizing resources, as these machines tended to be slow in instruction execution. It also led to another problem, the proliferation of complex instructions. These instructions could be used to improve the performance of benchmark test programs but rarely found their way into compiler-generated code. It was also very difficult to write micro programs.

With memory becoming cheaper and the development of cache memory, the need for very capable instructions lessened; equivalent sequences of simpler instructions could be fetched at high rate and executed. This led to the development of RISC, of which SPARC is one of the best examples. The micro instruction level was abandoned and the simple instruction implemented directly in hardware. The initial SPARC architecture was very reminiscent of the earliest computer architectures, with the exception of pipelining and memory management.

The grouping logic of Ultra SPARC now performs the last pass of a traditional assembler: reordering instructions, renaming variables, creating new variables, predicting branch activity, etc. The programmer must now, however, be aware of the penalties of branching, making use of conditional move instructions whenever possible. The programmer should also specify instruction and data prefetching and make use of nonfaulting loads. With Ultra SPARC executing the same number of floating-point instructions as integer instructions each cycle, programs might be optimized, with respect to execution time, by re-typing some integer variables as floating double.[6]

Writing "good" assembly language programs is now becoming as difficult as writing micro programs for the old CISC machines. Efficient use of the new superscalar machines is heavily dependent on the availability of optimizing compilers tailored to the specific machine and task.

---

[6] All 32-bit integer data can be represented without loss of precision as floating double.

Appendix A

MACRO DEFINITIONS

```
divert(-1)    'To be found in file macro_defs.m'
'%%%%%%%%%%%%%%%%%%%%%%%%%%%%%%%%%%%%%%%%%%%%%%%%%%%%%%%%%%%%%%%%%'
'returns $1 aligned according to $2'
define('align_d', 'eval(((($1 + $2 - 1)/ $2) * $2))')
'%%%%%%%%%%%%%%%%%%%%%%%%%%%%%%%%%%%%%%%%%%%%%%%%%%%%%%%%%%%%%%%%%'
define('local_var', '!local variables define('last_sym', 0)')
define('var', 'define('last_sym',
eval((last_sym - ifelse($3,,$2,$3)) & -$2)) $1 = last_sym')

define('begin_main','.global    main
       .align  4
main:   save    %sp, eval(
           ( -92 ifdef('last_sym',' last_sym')) & -8), %sp')

define('end_main','mov  1, %g1
       ta       0')
'%%%%%%%%%%%%%%%%%%%%%%%%%%%%%%%%%%%%%%%%%%%%%%%%%%%%%%%%%%%%%%%%%'
'stack offset definitions'
define('struct_s', 64)
'define stack offset for the n th. argument, $1, starting at 1'
define(arg_d,'eval($1 * 4 + struct_s)')

'%%%%%%%%%%%%%%%%%%%%%%%%%%%%%%%%%%%%%%%%%%%%%%%%%%%%%%%%%%%%%%%%%'
'define which also prints an assembly language comment'
define('cdef','define('$1', '$2')!'$1 = $2 $3'')
define(comment)
```

395

```
'%%%%%%%%%%%%%%%%%%%%%%%%%%%%%%%%%%%%%%%%%%%%%%%%%%%%%%%%%%%%%%%'
'subroutine entry, $1 = subroutine name'
define(begin_fn,'.global         $1
        .align  4
$1:     save    %sp, eval( -92 ifdef('last_sym',' last_sym') & -8), %sp
undefine('last_sym')define('name_of_funct',$1)')


'subroutine end, return sequence,
 $1 = subroutine name, $2 = src1, $3 = src2 or imm, $4 = dst'
define(end_fn,'ifelse(
$1,name_of_funct,'ret
        restore' 'ifelse($2,,,  '$2, $3, $4')'
        .type   name_of_funct',' #function
        .size   name_of_funct',' . - name_of_funct''undefine(
                                        'name_of_funct')
,'errprint('     subroutine begin does not match end')')')
'%%%%%%%%%%%%%%%%%%%%%%%%%%%%%%%%%%%%%%%%%%%%%%%%%%%%%%%%%%%%%%%'
'begin defining the fields of a structure'
'$1 = struct name'
define(begin_struct, '!'define' structure $1
define('size_of_struct',0)define(
'name_of_struct',$1)define(
'align_of_struct', 0)')


'define a field of a struct'
'$1 = name of field, $2 = alignment, $3 if present number of bytes'
define(field, 'name_of_struct'_'$1 = align_d(
        size_of_struct,$2)define(
                'size_of_struct', eval(align_d(size_of_struct,$2)
  + ifelse($3,,$2,$3)))define(
  'align_of_struct', ifelse(
  eval($2 > align_of_struct),1,$2,align_of_struct))')


'end definition of a struct'
'$1 = name, defines size_of_$1 to be the size in bytes aligned to
align_of_struct'
define('end_struct', 'ifelse(
$1,name_of_struct,'define(
'size_of_$1',align_d(size_of_struct, align_of_struct)) define(
'align_of_$1',align_of_struct)
        !'align_of_$1', align_of_$1 bytes
        !'size_of_$1', size_of_$1 bytes','
errprint('     structure begin does not match end')')')')
```

```
'%%%%%%%%%%%%%%%%%%%%%%%%%%%%%%%%%%%%%%%%%%%%%%%%%%%%%%%%%%%%%%%'
'convert a decimal number into reverse binary, i.e. lsb as msb'
define(convert_d,'ifelse(eval($1/2),0,$1,
'eval($1 % 2)convert_d(eval($1 /2))')')

'generate code to multiply number in terms of shifts < and adds +'
define(translate_d,
'ifelse($1,,,substr($1,0,1),1,'+<translate_d(substr($1,1))',
'<translate_d(substr($1,1))')')

'detect where to apply booth_d recoding'
define(booth_d,
  'ifelse($1,,,
    'ifelse($1,<,,substr($1,0,4),+<+<,'-<<gobble_d(substr($1,4))',
                        'substr($1,0,1)booth_d(substr($1,1))')')')

'gobble_d up rest of string of <'s'
define(gobble_d,
  'ifelse($1,,+,
    'ifelse(substr($1,0,2),+<,'<gobble_d(substr($1,2))',
                        '+<booth_d(substr($1,1))')')')
'digits of a base 30 number system'
define(code_d,0123456789!@$%^&*=~|\/<>{}[]:;")

'translate_d <<< into counts'
define(compact_d,'ifelse($1,,,
 'ifelse(substr($1,0,1),<,'count_d($1,0)',
'substr($1,0,1)compact_d(substr($1,1))')')')

'counts strings of <<< in base 30'
define(count_d,
 'ifelse(substr($1,0,1),<,'count_d(substr($1,1),incr($2))',
'substr(code_d,$2,1)compact_d($1)')')

'%%%%%%%%%%%%%%%%%%%%%%%%%%%%%%%%%%%%%%%%%%%%%%%%%%%%%%%%%%%%%%%'
'cmul (1=multiplicand register, 2=constant multiplier,
       3=temp, 4 = product)'
define(cmul,
'ifelse($4,,'errprint(
'cmul usage: multiplicand reg, const mult, temp reg, prod reg')',
substr($2,0,1),-,'errprint('positive constants only')',
$1,$3,'errprint(
        'cmul: multiplicand and temp registers must be different')',
$3,$4,'errprint(
```

```
                    'cmul: temp and product registers must be different')',
index(0123456789, substr($2,0,1)),-1,'errprint(
'cmul: attempt to covert non numeric constant')',
'

                             !start open coded multiply for
                             !$4 = $1 * eval($2), using $3 as temp
            start_d($1,compact_d(booth_d(translate_d(convert_d(
                                             eval($2)))))),$3,$4)
                      ! 'end' open coded multiply
')')
'generates the beginning of multiply code'
'$1 = multiplicand, $2 = string, $3 = temp, $4 = prod'
define(start_d,
'ifelse($2,,'clr        $4',
$2,+,'ifelse($1,$4,,'mov         $1, $4')',
len($2),2,'sll   $1,   index(code_d,substr($2,0,1)), $4',
substr($2,1,1),+,'sll   $1,   index(code_d,substr($2,0,1)), $4
       sll     $4,   index(code_d,substr($2,2,1)), $3
generate_d(substr($2,3),$3,$4)',
substr($2,1,1),-,'sll   $1,   index(code_d, substr($2,0,1)), $4
       sll     $4,   index(code_d, substr($2,2,1)), $3
       sub     $3, $4, $4
generate_d(substr($2,4),$3,$4)',
substr($2,0,1),+,'ifelse(
substr($2,2,1),+,'sll   $1,   index(code_d,substr($2,1,1)), $3
       add     $3, $1, $4',
'sll    $1,   index(code_d,substr($2,1,1)), $3
       sub     $1, $3, $4')
generate_d(substr($2,3),$3,$4)',
'sll    $1,   index(code_d, substr($2,1,1)), $3
       sub     $3, $1, $4
generate_d(substr($2,3),$3,$4)')')


'generates tail of code'
'$1 = string, $2 = temp, $3 = prod'
define(generate_d,
'ifelse($1,,,
'ifelse(substr($1,0,1),+,'       add     $3, $2, $3
generate_d(substr($1,1),$2,$3)',
substr($1,0,1),-,'       sub     $3, $2, $3
generate_d(substr($1,1),$2,$3)',
'       sll     $2,   index(code_d,substr($1,0,1)), $2
generate_d(substr($1,1),$2,$3)')')')
divert dnl
```

Appendix B

REGISTER NAME MACRO DEFINITIONS

To be found in file `reg_defs.m`

```
.stabs "null",100,0,0,.LLtext0
.LLtext0:
.stabs "word:t1=r1;-2147483648;2147483647;",128,0,0,0
.stabs "byte:t2=r2;0;127;",128,0,0,0
.stabs "half:t8=r1;-32768;32767;",128,0,0,0
.stabs "single:t12=r1;4;0;",128,0,0,0
.stabs "double:t13=r1;8;0;",128,0,0,0
.stabs "void:t19=19",128,0,0,0
divert(-1)
'the above text must be included at the beginning of the .s file'
'%%%%%%%%%%%%%%%%%%%%%%%%%%%%%%%%%%%%%%%%%%%%%%%%%%%%%%%%%%%%%%%%%'
'defines registers, creates a stabs entry, and prints a comment'
'$1 = register name, $2 = SPARC register, $3 = type, $4 = comment '
define('def_reg','define('$1', '$2')
        .stabs "'$1':'r'ifelse(
$3,word,1,
$3,byte,2,
$3,half,8,
$3,single,12,
$3,double,13,19)"',64,0,0,'reg_to_n($2) !'$1 = %$2 $4'')

'converts a register name to the register number'
define('reg_to_n',
'ifelse(substr($1,0,1),g,'substr($1,1,1)',
substr($1,0,1),o,'eval(8+substr($1,1,1))',
```

```
substr($1,0,1),l,`eval(16+substr($1,1,1))',
substr($1,0,1),i,`eval(24+substr($1,1,1))',
substr($1,0,1),f,`eval(32+substr($1,1))',
$1,sp,14,$1,fp,30)')

divert dnl
```

Appendix C

MULTIPLICATION BY CONSTANTS

C.1   Introduction

In this appendix we develop macros to generate code to multiply by constants, required in multidimensional array access code. The multiplicand will be located in a register together with a temporary register that may be used to compute the product into a final register. The final register may be the same as the multiplicand register. The constant is small and positive. The product is generated by shifts, adds, and subtracts. We start by converting a multiplier into a binary representation of ones and zeros. We will then convert this to a string of <, indicating shifts, and + to indicate additions. Having done this, we perform the Booth recoding, introducing the symbol – to indicate subtraction. We then replace strings of <<< by a base 31 digit representing the count. Having generated this string, we will then generate the corresponding code, which would be simple apart from the initial conditions. This is a good test of our macro writing capabilities.

C.2   m4 Built-in Macros

To handle these strings of characters, we need to make use of a number of built-in macros of m4. We start with the string macros.

The macro processor **m4** provides macros for operations on strings.

The macro len returns the length, in characters, of its string argument:

```
len(how now brown cow)
```

returns 17.

A second macro substr(string, begin, length) returns a substring of the first string argument starting at the "begin" character, with the first character in the string at zeroth position, and of length "length":

```
substr(how now brown cow,8,5)
```

results in the string "brown." If the final argument is missing, the rest of the substring starting at the "begin" character position is returned:

```
substr(how now brown cow,8)
```

results in "brown cow."

One can also look for the occurrence of a substring in a string employing the macro index:

```
index(how now brown cow, brown)
```

returns 8. If the substring is not in the string, the index returns -1.

Finally, there is a transliteration built-in macro translit(string, from, to) in which any character in the string found in "string" is replaced by the character in "to," which has the same index as the character in "from." For example:

```
translit(how now brown cow, hnbc, HNBC)
```

results in "How Now BrowN Cow." Or

```
translit(how now brown cow, aeiou)
```

results in the elimination of all vowels from the string "hw nw brwn cw."

We will also need to sharpen our definition of ifelse. The complete form of **ifelse** is

```
ifelse( a1, a2, r1, a3, a4, r2, a5, a6, r3)
```

and evaluation is as follows:

> If the string a1 matches a2, the result is the string r1.
> If the match did not occur, a3 is checked to see if it matches a4; if it does, the result is r2.
> If a3 does not match a4, then a5 is checked against a6; if it matches, the result is r3.
> If the arguments come in triples, as described here, and no matches are detected, the result would be the null string.
> If one additional argument were supplied, and no matches occurred, the result would be the last string argument.

For example, if we were to add one additional argument to the ifelse above:

```
ifelse( a1, a2, r1, a3, a4, r2, a5, a6, r3, r4)
```

and no matches occurred, the result would be r4 instead of the null string. There is no limit to the number of arguments that are given to ifelse. We must remember that all the arguments to an ifelse are evaluated before the strings are compared to determine the value of the ifelse.

The built-in macro `eval` treats its argument as an arithmetic expression and returns a string corresponding to the evaluation of that expression. The arithmetic operators handled by eval are as follows:

unary + and -	
`** or ^`	exponentiation
`* /`	multiplication and division
`%`	modulus
`== != < <= > >=`	arithmetic relational operators
`!`	logical not
`&&`	logical and
`||`	logical or
`&`	bitwise and
`|`	bitwise or

Logical false is zero and true is one. Parentheses may be used to control the order of evaluation. For example:

```
eval(((5 && 1) * 2 ** 4  + 1) % 3)
```

has the value 2.

One additional arithmetic built-in function is **incr**, which adds one to its argument:

```
incr(100)
```

results in 101.

C.3   Conversion to Binary

Let us look at a macro to convert a decimal number to binary. We must make use of a recursive definition:

```
define(convert_d,'ifelse(eval($1/2),0,$1,
'convert_d(eval($1 / 2))eval($1 % 2)')')
```

If the division of the number by 2 is zero, there is only one digit and that digit is $1. Otherwise, we need to append the remainder of the number, divided by 2, to the conversion of the original number divided by 2. Consider the conversion of decimal 100 to binary. The first division by 2 results in a remainder of zero and a quotient of 50. As the quotient is not zero we need to append a zero (the first remainder) to the conversion of 50 to binary. The recursive call to convert results in another remainder of zero with a quotient of 25; thus we will need to append a zero (with the first zero appended to this) to the conversion of 25 to binary. The next recursive call to convert results in a remainder of 1 and a quotient of 12. Still the quotient is not zero, so that we must now append a 1 (with 00 to be appended) to the conversion of 12 to binary, and so on. The conversion, using the macro

```
convert_d(100)
```

results in 1100100.

It is easier to scan strings from the left with macros; we will reverse the binary conversion so that the least significant bit is in the most significant bit position. This requires a simple modification of convert_d shown above:

```
define(convert_d,'ifelse(eval($1/2),0,$1,
'eval($1 % 2)convert_d(eval($1 /2)))')')
```

Converting 100, convert_d(100), now results in 0010011, the reverse of the binary representation.

We will now translate this into a shift and add pattern, represented by a string consisting of the characters < to indicate a left shift and a + to indicate an addition:

```
define(translate_d,
'ifelse($1,,,
'ifelse(substr($1,0,1),1,+<,<)translate_d(substr($1,1)))')')
```

In this macro we have two nested ifelse's. The first tests to see if the string is null; if it is, the translation is complete. Otherwise, the first character is examined and is replaced by a +< if it is a one and by < if a zero. The macro then calls itself recursively with the remainder of the string. The evaluation of

```
translate_d(convert_d(100))
```

results in <<+<<<+<+<, the correct shifting and adding algorithm.

We could translate this string into machine instructions, but before we do we apply the Booth recoding to reduce the number of shifts and adds. The Booth recoding recognizes a sequence of shifts and adds and replaces it by an initial subtraction, followed by the same number of shifts, without adds, but followed finally by an addition. A sequence such as

```
+<+<+<+<+<+<
```

may be replaced by

```
-<<<<<<+
```

This encoding is performed by two macros, booth_d and gobble_d. Booth recognizes the beginning of a string of +<+ and gobble gobbles up the rest of the <+ strings:

```
'detect where to apply Booth recoding'
define(booth_d,
  'ifelse($1,,,
    'ifelse($1,<,,substr($1,0,4),+<+<,'-<<gobble_d(substr($1,4))',
                  'substr($1,0,1)booth_d(substr($1,1))')')')

'gobble up rest of string of <'s'
define(gobble_d,
  'ifelse($1,,+,
    'ifelse(substr($1,0,2),+<,'<gobble_d(substr($1,2))',
                    '+<booth_d(substr($1,1))')')')
```

so that while the output of:

```
translate_d(convert_d(63))
```

is +<+<+<+<+<+< the output of:

```
booth_d(translate_d(convert_d(63)))
```

is -<<<<<<+.

C.4 Conversion to a Base 31 Number

The string we have generated is the correct representation, but it will be more convenient to have the strings of <<< replaced by a single digit, representing the number of shifts. This will make code generation easier and will simplify pattern matching when we generate the initialization code. Unfortunately, there might be more than nine shifts, so we need symbols to represent 10, 11, 12, ... 31. These need to be nonalphabetic, as they might become concatenated to the beginning of a macro name. We pick the following symbols and define them as a string:

```
'digits of a base 31 number system'
define(code_d,0123456789!@$%^&*=~|\/<>{}[]:;")
```

In order to translate our string into a string consisting only of +-d, where d represents a base 31 digit, we make use of the following macros:

```
'translate <<< into counts.
find beginning of string and call count'
define(compact_d,'ifelse($1,,,
  'ifelse(substr($1,0,1),<,'count($1,0)',
'substr($1,0,1)compact_d(substr($1,1))')')')
```

```
'counts strings of <<< in base 31'
```

```
define(count_d,
 'ifelse(substr($1,0,1),<,'count_d(substr($1,1),incr($2))',
 'substr(code_d,$2,1)compact_d($1)')')
```

For example, the number 603 has the binary representation, 1001011011, and reverse binary representation, 1101101001. Applying the Booth recoding results in
-<<+<-<<+<+<<<+, and on calling compact, we obtain -2+1-2+1+3+.

C.5   Instruction Generation

Instruction generation consists of shifts, adds and subtracts. A macro generate
generates the instructions

```
'generates code'
'$1 = string, $2 = temp, $3 = prod'
define(generate_d,
'ifelse($1,,,
'ifelse(substr($1,0,1),+,'        add      $3, $2, $3
generate_d(substr($1,1),$2,$3)',
substr($1,0,1),-,'        sub      $3, $2, $3
generate_d(substr($1,1),$2,$3)',
'        sll      $2,    index(code_d,substr($1,0,1)), $2
generate_d(substr($1,1),$2,$3)')')')')
```

For example,the evaluation of

```
generate_d(compact_d(booth_d(translate_d(
                                convert_d(603)))), %g1, %r0)
```

results in

```
        sub      %r0, %g1, %r0
        sll      %g1,    2, %g1
        add      %r0, %g1, %r0
        sll      %g1,    1, %g1
        sub      %r0, %g1, %r0
        sll      %g1,    2, %g1
        add      %r0, %g1, %r0
        sll      %g1,    1, %g1
        add      %r0, %g1, %r0
        sll      %g1,    3, %g1
        add      %r0, %g1, %r0
```

This macro assumes that the product register has been cleared to zero and that
the multiplicand is in the temp register. To ensure that these conditions are met,
we need to define a macro to set up the initial conditions.

This time we start with the top-level routine, cmul:

```
'cmul (1=multiplicand register, 2=constant multiplier, 3=temp,
     4 = product)'
define(cmul,
'ifelse($4,,'errprint(
'cmul usage: multiplicand reg, const mult, temp reg, prod reg'
)', substr($2,0,1),-,'errprint('positive constants only')',
$1,$3,'errprint(
'multiplicand and temp registers must be different')',
'
                         !'start' open coded multiply for
                         !$4 = $1 * $2, using $3 as temp
  start_d($1,compact_d(booth_d(translate_d(convert_d($2)))),$3,$4)
                  ! 'end' open coded multiply
')')
```

The arguments to this macro are the register that contains the multiplicand; the positive, constant multiplier; a temporary register into which to place the shifted multiplicand; and finally, the register into which the product is to be placed. All this macro does is to perform some error checking and to call start_d with arguments: the multiplicand register, the shift-add-subtract string, the temporary register, and the product register.

The macro that cmul calls, start_d, handles the initialization. This macro recognizes the initial conditions given in the following table and distinguishes between the case where the multiplicand register %m is the same as the product register %p and when they are different. Shift counts are referred to by n and m. The temporary register is referred to as %t:

String	Code, %m == %p	Code, %m != %p
""	clr %p	clr %p
"+"	""	mov %m, %p
"n+"	sll %p, n, %p	sll %m, n, %p
"n+m..."	sll %p, n, %p	sll %m, n, %p
	sll %p, m, %t	sll %p, m, %t
"n-m+..."	sll %p, n, %p	sll %m, n, %p
	sll %p, m, %t	sll %p, m, %t
	sub %t, %p, %p	sub %t, %p, %p
"+n+..."	sll %m, n, %t	sll %m, n, %t
	add %t, %p, %p	add %t, %m, %p
"+n-..."	sll %m, n, %t	sll %m, n, %t
	sub %p, %t, %p	sub %m, %t, %p
"-n+..."	sll %m, n, %t	sll %m, n, %t
	sub %t, %p, %p	sub %t, %m, %p

The start_d macro encodes these states:

'generates the beginning of multiply code'

```
'$1 = multiplicand, $2 = string, $3 = temp, $4 = prod'
define(start_d,
'ifelse($2,,'clr          $4',
$2,+,'ifelse($1,$4,,'mov          $1, $4')',
len($2),2,'sll  $1,   index(code_d,substr($2,0,1)), $4',
substr($2,1,1),+,'sll    $1,   index(code_d,substr($2,0,1)), $4
        sll     $4,   index(code_d,substr($2,2,1)), $3
generate_d(substr($2,3),$3,$4)',
substr($2,1,1),-,'sll    $1,    index(code_d, substr($2,0,1)), $4
        sll     $4,   index(code_d, substr($2,2,1)), $3
        sub     $3, $4, $4
generate_d(substr($2,4),$3,$4)',
substr($2,0,1),+,'ifelse(
substr($2,2,1),+,'sll    $1,     index(code_d,substr($2,1,1)), $3
        add     $3, $1, $4',
'sll      $1,   index(code_d,substr($2,1,1)), $3
        sub     $1, $3, $4')
generate_d(substr($2,3),$3,$4)',
'sll      $1,   index(code_d, substr($2,1,1)), $3
        sub     $3, $1, $4
generate_d(substr($2,3),$3,$4)')')
```

There is an unpleasant number of initial cases, and the initialization code generation
is tricky if we are not to overwrite the contents of registers that we will need
subsequently, and are to avoid the use of unnecessary mov and **neg** instructions.

An example of the use of the cmul macro is:

```
mov     64, %o1
cmul(%o1, 100, %o0, %l0)
```

which expands to:

```
mov     64, %o1


                        !start open coded multiply for
                        !%l0 = %o1 * 100, using %o0 as temp
sll     %o1,    2, %l0
sll     %l0,    3, %o0
sub     %l0, %o0, %l0
sll     %o0,    2, %o0
add     %l0, %o0, %l0


                        ! end open coded multiply
```

Appendix D

USER MODE MACHINE INSTRUCTIONS

D.1 Syntax

Symbol	Definition	Comment
<n:m>		Bits n through m inclusive
r[n]	%g0 ... %o7	Integer register n
r[rd]		Destination register
r[rs1]		Source register
r[rs2]		Source register
f[n]	%f0 ... %f31	Floating-Point register n
const13	value	A signed constant that fits into 13 bits
const22	value	A constant that fits into 22 bits
const30	value	A constant that fits into 30 bits
regaddr	r[rs1] r[rs1] + r[rs2]	Address formed with the contents of registers only
address	r[rs1] + r[rs2] r[rs1] + const13 r[rs1] − const13 const13 + r[rs1] const13	Address formed from the contents of registers, immediate constant, or both

D.2   Arithmetic Instructions

Arithmetic addition and subtractions insctuctions including tagged arithmetic and extended arithmetic instructions.

add

10	rd	000000	rs1	i = 0	ignored	rs2

op2 = i == 0 ? r[rs2] : sign-extend(13 bit immediate);

10	rd	000000	rs1	i = 1	signed 13 bit immediate

1. **Purpose:** to perform integer addition

2. **Format: add**   rs1, op2, rd

3. **Operation:** r[rd] = r[rs1] + op2

4. **Condition Codes:** unaffected

5. **Description:** Performs the addition of r[rs1] and op2, using two's complement arithmetic, storing the result into r[rd]. The contents of r[rs1] and op2 are not affected.

addcc

10	rd	010000	rs1	i = 0	ignored	rs2

op2 = i == 0 ? r[rs2] : sign-extend(13 bit immediate);

10	rd	010000	rs1	i = 1	signed 13 bit immediate

1. **Purpose:** to perform integer addition, set condition codes

2. **Format: addcc**   rs1, op2, rd

3. **Operation:** r[rd] = r[rs1] + op2

4. **Condition Codes:**

```
N = r[rd]<31> == 1
Z = r[rd] == 0
V = (r[rs1]<31> & op2<31> &~r[rd]<31>) |
    (~r[rs1]<31> & ~op2<31> & r[rd]<31>)
C = (r[rs1]<31> & op2<31>) |
    (~r[rd]<31> & (r[rs1]<31> | op2<31>))
```

5. **Description:** Performs the addition of rs1 and op2, using two's complement arithmetic, storing the result into rd and setting condition codes. The contents of rs1 and op2 are not affected.

addx

10	rd	001000	rs1	i = 0	ignored	rs2

op2 = i == 0 ? r[rs2] : sign-extend(13 bit immediate);

10	rd	001000	rs1	i = 1	signed 13 bit immediate

1. **Purpose:** to perform extended precision integer addition

2. **Format:** addx   rs1, op2, rd

3. **Operation:** r[rd] = r[rs1] + op2 + C

4. **Condition Codes:** unaffected

5. **Description:** Used in multiple precision arithmetic to perform the addition of r[rs1] and op2, plus 1 if the carry bit is set, using two's complement arithmetic, storing the result into r[rd]. The contents of r[rs1] and op2 are not affected.

addxcc

10	rd	011000	rs1	i = 0	ignored	rs2

op2 = i == 0 ? r[rs2] : sign-extend(13 bit immediate);

10	rd	011000	rs1	i = 1	signed 13 bit immediate

1. **Purpose:** to perform extended precision integer addition, set condition codes

2. **Format:** addxcc   rs1, op2, rd

3. **Operation:** r[rd] = r[rs1] + op2 + C

```
N = r[rd]<31> == 1
Z = r[rd] == 0
V = (r[rs1]<31> & op2<31> &~r[rd]<31>) |
    (~r[rs1]<31> & ~op2<31> & r[rd]<31>)
C = (r[rs1]<31> & op2<31>) |
    (~r[rd]<31> & (r[rs1]<31> | op2<31>))
```

4. **Description:** Used in multiple precision arithmetic to perform the addition of rs1 and op2, plus 1 if the carry bit is set, using two's complement arithmetic, storing the result into rd and setting condition codes. The contents of rs1 and op2 are not affected.

taddcc

10	rd	100000	rs1	i = 0	ignored	rs2

op2 = i == 0 ? r[rs2] : sign-extend(13 bit immediate);

10	rd	100000	rs1	i = 1	signed 13 bit immediate

1. **Purpose:** to perform tagged integer addition, set condition codes

2. **Format:** taddcc   rs1, op2, rd

3. **Operation:** r[rd] = r[rs1] + op2

4. **Condition Codes:**

```
N = r[rd]<31> == 1
Z = r[rd] == 0
V = (r[rs1]<31> & op2<31> &~r[rd]<31>) |
    (~r[rs1]<31> & ~op2<31> & r[rd]<31>) |
    (r[rs1]<1:0> != 0 | op2<1:0> != 0)
C = (r[rs1]<31> & op2<31>) |
    (~r[rd]<31> & (r[rs1]<31> | op2<31>))
```

5. **Description:** Performs the addition of **rs1** and **op2**, using two's complement arithmetic, storing the result into **rd** and setting condition codes. The overflow flag is set if either of the source operands' low-order two bits are not zero. The contents of **rs1** and **op2** are not affected.

taddcctv

10	rd	100010	rs1	i = 0	ignored	rs2

op2 = i == 0 ? r[rs2] : sign-extend(13 bit immediate);

10	rd	100010	rs1	i = 1	signed 13 bit immediate

1. **Purpose:** to perform tagged integer addition, trap if either source operands' low-order two bits are not zero

2. **Format:** taddcctv rs1, op2, rd

3. **Operation:** r[rd] = r[rs1] + op2

4. **Condition Codes:** unaffected

5. **Description:** Performs the addition of **rs1** and **op2**, using two's complement arithmetic, storing the result into **rd**. Trap if either of the source operands' low-order two bits are not zero. The contents of **rs1** and **op2** are not affected.

sub

10	%rd	000100	%rs1	0	ignored	%rs2

op2 = i == 0 ? r[rs2] : sign-extend(13 bit immediate);

10	%rd	000100	%rs1	1	signed 13 bit immediate

1. **Purpose:** to perform integer two's complement subtraction

2. **Format:** sub   rs1, rs2, rd

3. **Operation:** r[rd] = r[rs1] - op2

4. **Condition Codes:** unaffected

5. **Description:** Performs the subtraction of the subtrahend operand from the minuend operand, using two's complement arithmetic, storing the result into the difference operand. The contents of the subtrahend and the minuend are not affected.

subcc

10	%rd	010100	%rs1	0	ignored	%rs2

op2 = i == 0 ? r[rs2] : sign-extend(13 bit immediate);

10	%rd	010100	%rs1	1	signed 13 bit immediate

1. **Purpose:** to perform integer subtraction and set condition codes

2. **Format:** subcc   rs1, rs2, rd

3. **Operation:** r[rd] = r[rs1] - op2

4. **Condition Codes:**

```
N = rd<31> == 1
Z = rd == 0
V = (rs1<31> & ~rs2<31> &~rd<31>) |
    (~rs1<31> & rs2<31> & rd<31>)
C = (~rs1<31> & rs2<31>) |
    (rd<31> & (~rs1<31> | rs2<31>))
```

5. **Description:** Performs the subtraction of the subtrahend operand from the minuend operand, using two's complement arithmetic, storing the result into the difference operand and setting the condition codes. The contents of the subtrahend and the minuend are not affected.

subx

10	rd	001100	rs1	i = 0	ignored	rs2

op2 = i == 0 ? r[rs2] : sign-extend(13 bit immediate);

10	rd	001100	rs1	i = 1	signed 13 bit immediate

1. **Purpose:** to perform extended precision integer subtraction

2. **Format:** subx   rs1, rs2, rd

3. **Operation:** r[rd] = r[rs1] - op2 - C

4. **Condition Codes:** unaffected

5. **Description:** Used in multiple precision arithmetic to perform the subtraction of the subtrahend operand from the minuend operand, minus 1 if the carry bit is set, using two's complement arithmetic, storing the result into the difference operand. The contents of the subtrahend and the minuend are not affected.

subxcc

10	rd	011100	rs1	i = 0	ignored	rs2

op2 = i == 0 ? r[rs2] : sign-extend(13 bit immediate);

10	rd	011100	rs1	i = 1	signed 13 bit immediate

1. **Purpose:** to perform extended precision integer subtraction, setting the condition codes

2. **Format:** subxcc   rs1, rs2, rd

3. **Operation:** r[rd] = r[rs1] - op2 - C

4. **Condition Codes:**

```
N = rd<31> == 1
Z = rd == 0
V = (rs1<31> & ~rs2<31> &~rd<31>) |
    (~rs1<31> & rs2<31> & rd<31>)
C = (~rs1<31> & rs2<31>) |
    (rd<31> & (~rs1<31> | rs2<31>))
```

5. **Description:** Used in multiple precision arithmetic to perform the subtraction of the subtrahend operand from the minuend operand, minus 1 if the carry bit is set, using two's complement arithmetic, storing the result into the difference operand setting the condition codes. The contents of the subtrahend and the minuend are not affected.

tsubcc

10	rd	100001	rs1	i = 0	ignored	rs2

`op2 = i == 0 ? r[rs2] : sign-extend(13 bit immediate);`

10	rd	100001	rs1	i = 1	signed 13 bit immediate

1. **Purpose:** to perform tagged integer subtraction, setting the condition codes

2. **Format:** `tsubcc    rs1, rs2, rd`

3. **Operation:** `r[rd] = r[rs1] - op2`

4. **Condition Codes:**

```
N = rd<31> == 1
Z = rd == 0
V = (rs1<31> & ~rs2<31> &~rd<31>) |
    (~rs1<31> & rs2<31> & rd<31>) |
    (r[rs1]<1:0> != 0 | op2<1:0> != 0)
C = (~rs1<31> & rs2<31>) |
    (rd<31> & (~rs1<31> | rs2<31>))
```

5. **Description:** Performs the subtraction of the subtrahend operand from the minuend operand, using two's complement arithmetic, storing the result into the difference operand and setting the condition codes. The overflow flag is set if either of the source operands low-order two bits are not zero. The contents of the subtrahend and the minuend are not affected.

tsubcctv

10	rd	100011	rs1	i = 0	ignored	rs2

`op2 = i == 0 ? r[rs2] : sign-extend(13 bit immediate);`

10	rd	100011	rs1	i = 1	signed 13 bit immediate

1. **Purpose:** to perform tagged integer subtraction, trap if either source operands' low-order two bits are not zero

2. **Format:** `tsubcctv  rs1, rs2, rd`

3. **Operation:** `r[rd] = r[rs1] - op2`

4. **Condition Codes:** unaffected

5. **Description:** Performs the subtraction of the subtrahend operand from the minuend operand, using two's complement arithmetic, storing the result into the difference operand and setting the condition codes. Trap if either of the source operands' low-order two bits are not zero. The contents of the subtrahend and the minuend are not affected.

mulscc

10	rd	100100	rs1	i = 0	ignored	rs2

10	rd	100100	rs1	i = 1	signed 13 bit immediate

1. **Purpose:** to perform one step of a multiply algorithm

2. **Format:** `mulscc     rs1, op2, rd`

3. **Operation:**

```
op1 = (N ^ V), r[rs1]<31:1>
op2 = Y<0> == 0 ? 0
         i == 0 ? r[rs2] : sign-extend(13 bit immediate)
r[rd] = op1 + op2
+Y = r[rs1]<0> Y<31:1>
```

4. **Condition Codes:**

```
N = r[rd]<31> == 1
Z = r[rd] == 0
V = (r[rs1]<31> & op2<31> &~r[rd]<31>) |
    (~r[rs1]<31> & ~op2<31> & r[rd]<31>)
C = (r[rs1]<31> & op2<31>) |
    (~r[rd]<31> & (r[rs1]<31> | op2<31>))
```

5. **Description:** Performs one step of the multiply algorithm: The contents of `r[res]` are right-shifted one with N ^ V being shifted in from the left to form op1. If the LSB of the Y register is a one, the contents of `op2` are added to op1 to form the result. The contents of the Y register are then left shifted one place with the bit shifted out of the right-hand side of `r[rs1]` being shifted in on the left. The condition codes are set.

rdy

10	rd	101000	ignored	ignored	ignored

1. **Purpose:** to read the contents of the Y register

2. **Format:** `rd        %y, rd`

3. **Operation:** `r[rd] = r[Y]`

4. **Condition Codes:** unaffected

5. **Description:** Reads the contents of the Y register. The contents of Y are not affected.

wry

10	ignored	110000	rs1	i = 0	ignored	rs2

op2 = i == 0 ? r[rs2] : sign-extend(13 bit immediate);

10	ignored	110000	rs1	i = 1	signed 13 bit immediate

1. **Purpose:** to write the contents of the Y register

2. **Format:** wr rs1, op2, rd

3. **Operation:** r[Y] = r[rs1] ^ op2

4. **Condition Codes:** unaffected

5. **Description:** Writes the contents of the Y register with the xor of r[rs1] and op2. The contents of rs1 and op2 are not affected.

D.3 Logical Instructions

Machine bitwise logical instructions.

and

10	rd	000001	rs1	i = 0	ignored	rs2

op2 = i == 0 ? r[rs2] : sign-extend(13 bit immediate);

10	rd	000001	rs1	i = 1	signed 13 bit immediate

1. **Purpose:** to perform bitwise and operation
2. **Format:** and rs1, op2, rd
3. **Operation:** r[rd] = r[rs1] & op2
4. **Condition Codes:** unaffected
5. **Description:** Performs the bitwise and of r[rs1] and op2, storing the result into r[rd]. The contents of r[rs1] and op2 are not affected.

andcc

10	rd	010001	rs1	i = 0	ignored	rs2

op2 = i == 0 ? r[rs2] : sign-extend(13 bit immediate);

10	rd	010001	rs1	i = 1	signed 13 bit immediate

1. **Purpose:** to perform bitwise and operation, set condition codes
2. **Format:** andcc rs1, op2, rd
3. **Operation:** r[rd] = r[rs1] & op2
4. **Condition Codes:**

```
N = r[rd]<31> == 1
Z = r[rd] == 0
V = 0
C = 0
```

5. **Description:** Performs the bitwise and of r[rs1] and op2, storing the result into r[rd] setting condition codes. The contents of r[rs1] and op2 are not affected.

andn

10	rd	000101	rs1	i = 0	ignored	rs2

op2 = i == 0 ? r[rs2] : sign-extend(13 bit immediate);

10	rd	000101	rs1	i = 1	signed 13 bit immediate

1. **Purpose:** to perform bitwise and operation with complement of op2
2. **Format:** andn rs1, op2, rd
3. **Operation:** r[rd] = r[rs1] & ~op2
4. **Condition Codes:** unaffected
5. **Description:** Performs the bitwise and of r[rs1] and complement of op2, storing the result into r[rd]. The contents of r[rs1] and op2 are not affected.

andncc

10	rd	010101	rs1	i = 0	ignored	rs2

op2 = i == 0 ? r[rs2] : sign-extend(13 bit immediate);

10	rd	010101	rs1	i = 1	signed 13 bit immediate

1. **Purpose:** to perform bitwise and operation with complement of op2 and set condition codes

2. **Format:** andn rs1, op2, rd

3. **Operation:** r[rd] = r[rs1] & ~op2

4. **Condition Codes:**

```
N = r[rd]<31> == 1
Z = r[rd] == 0
V = 0
C = 0
```

5. **Description:** Performs the bitwise and of r[rs1] and complement of op2, storing the result into r[rd] setting condition codes. The contents of r[rs1] and op2 are not affected.

or

10	rd	000010	rs1	i = 0	ignored	rs2

op2 = i == 0 ? r[rs2] : sign-extend(13 bit immediate);

10	rd	000010	rs1	i = 1	signed 13 bit immediate

1. **Purpose:** to perform bitwise or operation with op2

2. **Format:** or rs1, op2, rd

3. **Operation:** r[rd] = r[rs1] | op2

4. **Condition Codes:** unaffected

5. **Description:** Performs the bitwise or of r[rs1] and op2, storing the result into r[rd]. The contents of r[rs1] and op2 are not affected.

orcc

10	rd	010010	rs1	$i = 0$	ignored	rs2

op2 = i == 0 ? r[rs2] : sign-extend(13 bit immediate);

10	rd	010010	rs1	$i = 1$	signed 13 bit immediate

1. **Purpose:** to perform bitwise or operation with op2, set condition codes

2. **Format:** or rs1, op2, rd

3. **Operation:** r[rd] = r[rs1] | op2

4. **Condition Codes:**

```
N = r[rd]<31> == 1
Z = r[rd] == 0
V = 0
C = 0
```

5. **Description:** Performs the bitwise or of r[rs1] and op2, storing the result into r[rd], setting condition codes. The contents of r[rs1] and op2 are not affected.

orn

10	rd	000110	rs1	$i = 0$	ignored	rs2

op2 = i == 0 ? r[rs2] : sign-extend(13 bit immediate);

10	rd	000110	rs1	$i = 1$	signed 13 bit immediate

1. **Purpose:** to perform bitwise or operation with complement of op2

2. **Format:** orn rs1, op2, rd

3. **Operation:** r[rd] = r[rs1] | ~op2

4. **Condition Codes:** unaffected

5. **Description:** Performs the bitwise inclusive or of r[rs1] and complement of op2, storing the result into r[rd]. The contents of r[rs1] and op2 are not affected.

orncc

10	rd	010110	rs1	i = 0	ignored	rs2

op2 = i == 0 ? r[rs2] : sign-extend(13 bit immediate);

10	rd	010110	rs1	i = 1	signed 13 bit immediate

1. **Purpose:** to perform bitwise or operation with complement of op2, set condition codes

2. **Format:** orn rs1, op2, rd

3. **Operation:** r[rd] = r[rs1] | ~op2

4. **Condition Codes:**

   ```
   N = r[rd]<31> == 1
   Z = r[rd] == 0
   V = 0
   C = 0
   ```

5. **Description:** Performs the bitwise inclusive or of r[rs1] and complement of op2, storing the result into r[rd], setting condition codes. The contents of r[rs1] and op2 are not affected.

xor

10	rd	000011	rs1	i = 0	ignored	rs2

op2 = i == 0 ? r[rs2] : sign-extend(13 bit immediate);

10	rd	000011	rs1	i = 1	signed 13 bit immediate

1. **Purpose:** to perform bitwise xor operation with op2

2. **Format:** xor rs1, op2, rd

3. **Operation:** r[rd] = r[rs1] ^ op2

4. **Condition Codes:** unaffected

5. **Description:** Performs the bitwise exclusive or of r[rs1] and op2, storing the result into r[rd]. The contents of r[rs1] and op2 are not affected.

xorcc

10	rd	010011	rs1	i = 0	ignored	rs2

op2 = i == 0 ? r[rs2] : sign-extend(13 bit immediate);

10	rd	010011	rs1	i = 1	signed 13 bit immediate

1. **Purpose:** to perform bitwise xor operation with **op2**, set condition codes

2. **Format:** xor rs1, op2, rd

3. **Operation:** r[rd] = r[rs1] ^ op2

4. **Condition Codes:**

   ```
   N = r[rd]<31> == 1
   Z = r[rd] == 0
   V = 0
   C = 0
   ```

5. **Description:** Performs the bitwise exclusive or of r[rs1] and op2, storing the result into r[rd], setting condition codes. The contents of r[rs1] and op2 are not affected.

xnor

10	rd	000111	rs1	i = 0	ignored	rs2

op2 = i == 0 ? r[rs2] : sign-extend(13 bit immediate);

10	rd	000111	rs1	i = 1	signed 13 bit immediate

1. **Purpose:** to perform bitwise xnor operation with **op2**

2. **Format:** xnor rs1, op2, rd

3. **Operation:** r[rd] = ~(r[rs1] ^ op2)

4. **Condition Codes:** unaffected

5. **Description:** Performs the complement of the bitwise exclusive or of r[rs1] and op2, storing the result into r[rd]. The contents of r[rs1] and op2 are not affected.

xnorcc

10	rd	010111	rs1	i = 0	ignored	rs2

op2 = i == 0 ? r[rs2] : sign-extend(13 bit immediate);

10	rd	010111	rs1	i = 1	signed 13 bit immediate

1. **Purpose:** to perform bitwise xnor operation with op2, set condition codes

2. **Format:** xnor rs1, op2, rd

3. **Operation:** r[rd] = ~(r[rs1] ^ op2)

4. **Condition Codes:**

   ```
   N = r[rd]<31> == 1
   Z = r[rd] == 0
   V = 0
   C = 0
   ```

5. **Description:** Performs the complement of the bitwise exclusive or of r[rs1] and op2, storing the result into r[rd], setting condition codes. The contents of r[rs1] and op2 are not affected.

D.4   Shift Instructions

Machine shift instructions.

sll

10	rd	100101	rs1	i = 0	ignored	rs2

op2 = i == 0 ? r[rs2]<4:0> : shift count

10	rd	100101	rs1	i = 1	ignored	shift count

1. **Purpose:** to perform logical left-shift

2. **Format:** sll rs1, op2, rd

3. **Operation:** r[rd] = logical left-shift(r[rs1], op2)

4. **Condition Codes:** unaffected

5. **Description:** Shifts r[rs1] left logically (shifting in zeros from the right) op2 places, storing the result into r[rd]. The contents of r[rs1] and op2 are not affected.

srl

10	rd	100110	rs1	i = 0	ignored	rs2

op2 = i == 0 ? r[rs2]<4:0> : shift count

10	rd	100110	rs1	i = 1	ignored	shift count

1. **Purpose:** to perform logical right shift

2. **Format:** srl rs1, op2, rd

3. **Operation:** r[rd] = logical right shift(r[rs1], op2)

4. **Condition Codes:** unaffected

5. **Description:** Shifts r[rs1] right logically (shifting in zeros from the left) op2 places, storing the result into r[rd]. The contents of r[rs1] and op2 are not affected.

sra

10	rd	100111	rs1	i = 0	ignored	rs2

op2 = i == 0 ? r[rs2]<4:0> : shift count

10	rd	100111	rs1	i = 1	ignored	shift count

1. **Purpose:** to perform logical right arithmetic

2. **Format:** sra rs1, op2, rd

3. **Operation:** r[rd] = arithmetic right shift(r[rs1], op2)

4. **Condition Codes:** unaffected

5. **Description:** Shifts r[rs1] right logically (replicating the sign bit from the left) op2 places, storing the result into r[rd]. The contents of r[rs1] and op2 are not affected.

   Note: Arithmetic leftshift by one setting the condition may be implemented with and addcc instruction.

D.5 Load Instructions

Machine load instructions.

ldub

11	rd	000001	rs1	i = 0	asi	rs2

op2 = i == 0 ? r[rs2] : sign-extend(13 bit immediate);

11	rd	000001	rs1	i = 1	signed 13 bit immediate

1. **Purpose:** to load register with unsigned byte from memory

2. **Format:** ldub [rs1 + op2], rd

3. **Operation:** r[rd] = memory[r[rs1] + op2]

4. **Condition Codes:** unaffected

5. **Description:** Loads register with byte from memory; address is the sum of the contents of rs1 and op2. Either address operand may be missing. Zero fill r[rd]<31:8>.

ldsb

11	rd	001001	rs1	i = 0	asi	rs2

op2 = i == 0 ? r[rs2] : sign-extend(13 bit immediate);

11	rd	001001	rs1	i = 1	signed 13 bit immediate

1. **Purpose:** to load register with signed byte from memory

2. **Format:** ldsb [rs1 + op2], rd

3. **Operation:** r[rd] = memory[r[rs1] + op2]

4. **Condition Codes:** unaffected

5. **Description:** Loads register with byte from memory; address is the sum of the contents of rs1 and op2. Either address operand may be missing. sign-extend byte through r[rd]<31:8>.

lduh

11	rd	000010	rs1	i = 0	asi	rs2

op2 = i == 0 ? r[rs2] : sign-extend(13 bit immediate);

11	rd	000010	rs1	i = 1	signed 13 bit immediate

1. **Purpose:** to load register with unsigned halfword from memory

2. **Format:** lduh [rs1 + op2], rd

3. **Operation:** r[rd] = memory[r[rs1] + op2]

4. **Condition Codes:** unaffected

5. **Description:** Loads register with unsigned halfword from memory; address is the sum of the contents of rs1 and op2. Either address operand may be missing. Address must be halfword aligned. Zero fill r[rd]<31:16>.

ldsh

11	rd	001010	rs1	i = 0	asi	rs2

`op2 = i == 0 ? r[rs2] : sign-extend(13 bit immediate);`

11	rd	001010	rs1	i = 1	signed 13 bit immediate

1. **Purpose:** to load register with signed halfword from memory

2. **Format:** `ldsh [rs1 + op2], rd`

3. **Operation:** `r[rd] = memory[r[rs1] + op2]`

4. **Condition Codes:** unaffected

5. **Description:** Loads register with signed halfword from memory; address is the sum of the contents of `rs1` and `op2`. Either address operand may be missing. Address must be halfword aligned. sign-extend halfword through `r[rd]<31:16>`.

ld

11	rd	000000	rs1	i = 0	asi	rs2

`op2 = i == 0 ? r[rs2] : sign-extend(13 bit immediate);`

11	rd	000000	rs1	i = 1	signed 13 bit immediate

1. **Purpose:** to load register with word from memory

2. **Format:** `ld [rs1 + op2], rd`

3. **Operation:** `r[rd] = memory[r[rs1] + op2]`

4. **Condition Codes:** unaffected

5. **Description:** Loads register from memory; address is the sum of the contents of `rs1` and `op2`. Either address operand may be missing. Memory address must be word aligned.

ldd

11	rd	000011	rs1	i = 0	asi	rs2

`op2 = i == 0 ? r[rs2] : sign-extend(13 bit immediate);`

11	rd	000011	rs1	i = 1	signed 13 bit immediate

1. **Purpose:** to load two registers with a doubleword from memory

2. **Format:** `ld [rs1 + op2], rd`

3. **Operation:**

   ```
   r[rd] = memory[r[rs1] + op2]
   r[rd+1] = memory[r[rs1] + op2 + 4]
   ```

4. **Condition Codes:** unaffected

5. **Description:** Loads registers from memory; address is the sum of the contents of `rs1` and `op2`. Either address operand may be missing. Memory address must be doubleword aligned. Register number must be even; two registers are loaded.

D.6 Store Instructions

Machine store instructions.

stb

11	rd	000101	rs1	i = 0	asi	rs2
op2 = i == 0 ? r[rs2] : sign-extend(13 bit immediate);						
11	rd	000101	rs1	i = 1	signed 13 bit immediate	

1. **Purpose:** to store a low byte of register into memory

2. **Format:** stb rd, [rs1 + op2]

3. **Operation:** memory[r[rs1] + op2] = r[rd]

4. **Condition Codes:** unaffected

5. **Description:** Stores low byte of register into memory; address is the sum of the contents of **rs1** and **op2**. Either address operand may be missing.

sth

11	rd	000110	rs1	i = 0	asi	rs2
op2 = i == 0 ? r[rs2] : sign-extend(13 bit immediate);						
11	rd	000110	rs1	i = 1	signed 13 bit immediate	

1. **Purpose:** to store a low half of register into memory

2. **Format:** sth rd, [rs1 + op2]

3. **Operation:** memory[r[rs1] + op2] = r[rd]

4. **Condition Codes:** unaffected

5. **Description:** Stores low half of register into memory; address is the sum of the contents of **rs1** and **op2**. Either address operand may be missing. Memory address must be halfword aligned.

st

11	rd	000100	rs1	i = 0	asi	rs2
op2 = i == 0 ? r[rs2] : sign-extend(13 bit immediate);						
11	rd	000100	rs1	i = 1	signed 13 bit immediate	

1. **Purpose:** to store a register into memory

2. **Format:** st rd, [rs1 + op2]

3. **Operation:** memory[r[rs1] + op2] = r[rd]

4. **Condition Codes:** unaffected

5. **Description:** Stores register into memory; address is the sum of the contents of **rs1** and **op2**. Either address operand may be missing. Memory address must be word aligned.

std

11	rd	000111	rs1	i = 0	asi	rs2

op2 = i == 0 ? r[rs2] : sign-extend(13 bit immediate);

11	rd	000111	rs1	i = 1	signed 13 bit immediate

1. **Purpose:** to store two registers into memory

2. **Format:** std rd, [rs1 + op2]

3. **Operation:**

   ```
   memory[r[rs1] + op2] = r[rd]
   memory[r[rs1] + op2 + 4] = r[rd + 1]
   ```

4. **Condition Codes:** unaffected

5. **Description:** Stores two registers into memory; address is the sum of the contents of **rs1** and **op2**. Either address operand may be missing. Memory address must be doubleword aligned. Register number must be even; two registers are stored.

swap

11	rd	001111	rs1	i = 0	asi	rs2

op2 = i == 0 ? r[rs2] : sign-extend(13 bit immediate);

11	rd	001111	rs1	i = 1	signed 13 bit immediate

1. **Purpose:** to swap the contents of register with memory

2. **Format:** swap [rs1 + op2], rd

3. **Operation:** r[rd] ⇔ memory[r[rs1] + op2]

4. **Condition Codes:** unaffected

5. **Description:** Swaps the contents of a register with memory; address is the sum of the contents of **rs1** and **op2**. Either address operand may be missing. Memory address must be word aligned.

D.7 Integer Branch Instructions

Integer branch instructions.

ba

00	a	1000	010	disp22

1. **Purpose:** to branch always
2. **Format:** ba label
3. **Operation:**

```
r[pc] = r[npc];
r[npc] = r[pc] + sign_extend(disp22) << 2;
if (a == 1) annul next instruction;
```

4. **Condition Codes:** unaffected
5. **Description:** Branches always. Instruction operand is a label that is converted to a program counter relative address. The branch target address is stored as the number of words relative to the location of the branch instruction. If annulled, the next instruction in line is *not* executed.

bn

00	a	0000	010	disp22

1. **Purpose:** to branch never
2. **Format:** bn label
3. **Operation:**

```
r[pc] = r[npc];
r[npc] = r[npc] + 4;
if (a == 1) annul next instruction;
```

4. **Condition Codes:** unaffected
5. **Description:** Branches never. Instruction operand is a label that is converted to a program counter relative address. The branch target address is stored as the number of words relative to the location of the branch instruction. If annulled, the next instruction in line is *not* executed.

be

00	a	0001	010	disp22

1. **Purpose:** to branch on equal

2. **Format:** be label

3. **Operation:**

```
r[pc] = r[npc];
if (Z == 1)
  r[npc] = + sign_extend(disp22) << 2;
else{
  r[npc] = r[npc] + 4;
  if (a == 1) annul next instruction;}
```

4. **Condition Codes:** unaffected

5. **Description:** Branches on equal to zero. Instruction operand is a label that is converted to a program counter relative address. The branch target address is stored as the number of words relative to the location of the branch instruction. If the branch instruction is annulled and not taken, the next instruction in line is *not* executed.

bne

00	a	1001	010	disp22

1. **Purpose:** branch on not equal

2. **Format:** bne label

3. **Operation:**

```
r[pc] = r[npc];
if (Z == 0)
  r[npc] = + sign_extend(disp22) << 2;
else{
  r[npc] = r[npc] + 4;
  if (a == 1) annul next instruction;}
```

4. **Condition Codes:** unaffected

5. **Description:** Branches on not equal to zero. Instruction operand is a label that is converted to a program counter relative address. The branch target address is stored as the number of words relative to the location of the branch instruction. If the branch instruction is annulled and not taken, the next instruction in line is *not* executed.

bl

00	a	0011	010	disp22

1. **Purpose:** to branch on less

2. **Format:** bl label

3. **Operation:**

```
r[pc] = r[npc];
if ((N ^ V) == 1)
  r[npc] = + sign_extend(disp22) << 2;
else{
  r[npc] = r[npc] + 4;
  if (a == 1) annul next instruction;}
```

4. **Condition Codes:** unaffected

5. **Description:** Branches on less than zero. Instruction operand is a label that is converted to a program counter relative address. The branch target address is stored as the number of words relative to the location of the branch instruction. If the branch instruction is annulled and not taken, the next instruction in line is *not* executed.

ble

00	a	0010	010	disp22

1. **Purpose:** to branch on less or equal

2. **Format:** ble label

3. **Operation:**

```
r[pc] = r[npc];
if ((Z | N ^ V) == 1)
  r[npc] = + sign_extend(disp22) << 2;
else{
  r[npc] = r[npc] + 4;
  if (a == 1) annul next instruction;}
```

4. **Condition Codes:** unaffected

5. **Description:** Branches on less than or equal to zero. Instruction operand is a label that is converted to a program counter relative address. The branch target address is stored as the number of words relative to the location of the branch instruction. If the branch instruction is annulled and not taken, the next instruction in line is *not* executed.

bge

00	a	1011	010	disp22

1. **Purpose:** to branch on greater than or equal

2. **Format:** bge label

3. **Operation:**

```
r[pc] = r[npc];
if ((N ^ V) == 0)
  r[npc] = + sign_extend(disp22) << 2;
else{
  r[npc] = r[npc] + 4;
  if (a == 1) annul next instruction;}
```

4. **Condition Codes:** unaffected

5. **Description:** Branches on greater than or equal to zero. Instruction operand is a label that is converted to a program counter relative address. The branch target address is stored as the number of words relative to the location of the branch instruction. If the branch instruction is annulled and not taken, the next instruction in line is *not* executed.

bg

00	a	1010	010	disp22

1. **Purpose:** to branch on greater than

2. **Format:** bg label

3. **Operation:**

```
r[pc] = r[npc];
if ((Z | N ^ V) == 0)
  r[npc] = + sign_extend(disp22) << 2;
else{
  r[npc] = r[npc] + 4;
  if (a == 1) annul next instruction;}
```

4. **Condition Codes:** unaffected

5. **Description:** Branches on greater than zero. Instruction operand is a label that is converted to a program counter relative address. The branch target address is stored as the number of words relative to the location of the branch instruction. If the branch instruction is annulled and not taken, the next instruction in line is *not* executed.

blu

00	a	0101	010	disp22

1. **Purpose:** to branch on less, unsigned

2. **Format:** `blu label`

3. **Operation:**

```
r[pc] = r[npc];
if (C == 1)
  r[npc] = + sign_extend(disp22) << 2;
else{
  r[npc] = r[npc] + 4;
  if (a == 1) annul next instruction;}
```

4. **Condition Codes:** unaffected

5. **Description:** Branches on less than zero, unsigned. Identical to the `bcs` instruction. Instruction operand is a label that is converted to a program counter relative address. The branch target address is stored as the number of words relative to the location of the branch instruction. If the branch instruction is annulled and not taken, the next instruction in line is *not* executed.

bleu

00	a	0100	010	disp22

1. **Purpose:** to branch on less than or equal, unsigned

2. **Format:** `bleu label`

3. **Operation:**

```
r[pc] = r[npc];
if ((C | Z)  == 1)
  r[npc] = + sign_extend(disp22) << 2;
else{
  r[npc] = r[npc] + 4;
  if (a == 1) annul next instruction;}
```

4. **Condition Codes:** unaffected

5. **Description:** Branches on less than or equal to zero, unsigned. Instruction operand is a label that is converted to a program counter relative address. The branch target address is stored as the number of words relative to the location of the branch instruction. If the branch instruction is annulled and not taken, the next instruction in line is *not* executed.

bgeu

00	a	1101	010	disp22

1. **Purpose:** to branch on greater than or equal, unsigned

2. **Format:** `bgeu label`

3. **Operation:**

```
r[pc] = r[npc];
if (C == 0)
  r[npc] = + sign_extend(disp22) << 2;
else{
  r[npc] = r[npc] + 4;
  if (a == 1) annul next instruction;}
```

4. **Condition Codes:** unaffected

5. **Description:** Branches on greater than or equal to zero, unsigned. Identical to the `bcc` instruction. Instruction operand is a label that is converted to a program counter relative address. The branch target address is stored as the number of words relative to the location of the branch instruction. If the branch instruction is annulled and not taken, the next instruction in line is *not* executed.

bgu

00	a	1100	010	disp22

1. **Purpose:** to branch on greater than, unsigned

2. **Format:** `bgu label`

3. **Operation:**

```
r[pc] = r[npc];
if ((C | Z) == 0)
  r[npc] = + sign_extend(disp22) << 2;
else{
  r[npc] = r[npc] + 4;
  if (a == 1) annul next instruction;}
```

4. **Condition Codes:** unaffected

5. **Description:** Branches on greater than zero, unsigned. Instruction operand is a label that is converted to a program counter relative address. The branch target address is stored as the number of words relative to the location of the branch instruction. If the branch instruction is annulled and not taken, the next instruction in line is *not* executed.

bpos

00	a	1110	010	disp22

1. **Purpose:** to branch on positive

2. **Format:** bpos label

3. **Operation:**

```
r[pc] = r[npc];
if (N == 0)
  r[npc] = + sign_extend(disp22) << 2;
else{
  r[npc] = r[npc] + 4;
  if (a == 1) annul next instruction;}
```

4. **Condition Codes:** unaffected

5. **Description:** Branches on positive. Instruction operand is a label that is converted to a program counter relative address. The branch target address is stored as the number of words relative to the location of the branch instruction. If the branch instruction is annulled and not taken, the next instruction in line is *not* executed.

bneg

00	a	0110	010	disp22

1. **Purpose:** to branch on negative

2. **Format:** bneg label

3. **Operation:**

```
r[pc] = r[npc];
if (N == 1)
  r[npc] = + sign_extend(disp22) << 2;
else{
  r[npc] = r[npc] + 4;
  if (a == 1) annul next instruction;}
```

4. **Condition Codes:** unaffected

5. **Description:** Branches on negative. Instruction operand is a label that is converted to a program counter relative address. The branch target address is stored as the number of words relative to the location of the branch instruction. If the branch instruction is annulled and not taken, the next instruction in line is *not* executed.

bcs

00	a	0101	010	disp22

1. **Purpose:** to branch on C set

2. **Format:** `bcs label`

3. **Operation:**

```
r[pc] = r[npc];
if (C == 1)
  r[npc] = + sign_extend(disp22) << 2;
else{
  r[npc] = r[npc] + 4;
  if (a == 1) annul next instruction;}
```

4. **Condition Codes:** unaffected

5. **Description:** Branches on C bit set. Instruction operand is a label that is converted to a program counter relative address. The branch target address is stored as the number of words relative to the location of the branch instruction. If the branch instruction is annulled and not taken, the next instruction in line is *not* executed.

bcc

00	a	1101	010	disp22

1. **Purpose:** to branch on C clear

2. **Format:** `bcc label`

3. **Operation:**

```
r[pc] = r[npc];
if (C == 0)
  r[npc] = + sign_extend(disp22) << 2;
else{
  r[npc] = r[npc] + 4;
  if (a == 1) annul next instruction;}
```

4. **Condition Codes:** unaffected

5. **Description:** Branches on C bit clear. Instruction operand is a label that is converted to a program counter relative address. The branch target address is stored as the number of words relative to the location of the branch instruction. If the branch instruction is annulled and not taken, the next instruction in line is *not* executed.

bvs

00	a	0111	010	disp22

1. **Purpose:** to branch on signed overflow

2. **Format:** bvs label

3. **Operation:**

```
r[pc] = r[npc];
if (V == 1)
  r[npc] = + sign_extend(disp22) << 2;
else{
  r[npc] = r[npc] + 4;
  if (a == 1) annul next instruction;}
```

4. **Condition Codes:** unaffected

5. **Description:** Branches on signed overflow. Instruction operand is a label that is converted to a program counter relative address. The branch target address is stored as the number of words relative to the location of the branch instruction. If the branch instruction is annulled and not taken, the next instruction in line is *not* executed.

bvc

00	a	1111	010	disp22

1. **Purpose:** to branch on no signed overflow

2. **Format:** bvc label

3. **Operation:**

```
r[pc] = r[npc];
if (V == 0)
  r[npc] = + sign_extend(disp22) << 2;
else{
  r[npc] = r[npc] + 4;
  if (a == 1) annul next instruction;}
```

4. **Condition Codes:** unaffected

5. **Description:** Branches on no signed overflow. Instruction operand is a label that is converted to a program counter relative address. The branch target address is stored as the number of words relative to the location of the branch instruction. If the branch instruction is annulled and not taken, the next instruction in line is *not* executed.

D.8   Trap Instructions

Machine trap instructions.

ta

10	ignored	1000	111010	rs1	i = 0	ignored	rs2

`tt = 0x80 | (i == 0 ? r[rs2] : sign-extend(13 bit immediate)<6:0>);`

10	ignored	1000	111010	rs1	i = 1	signed 13 bit immediate

1. **Purpose:** to trap always
2. **Format:** `ta address`
3. **Operation:** to trap
4. **Condition Codes:** unaffected
5. **Description:** Traps always.

tn

10	ignored	0000	111010	rs1	i = 0	ignored	rs2

`tt = 0x80 | (i == 0 ? r[rs2] : sign-extend(13 bit immediate)<6:0>);`

10	ignored	0000	111010	rs1	i = 1	signed 13 bit immediate

1. **Purpose:** to trap never
2. **Format:** `tn address`
3. **Operation:** no operation
4. **Condition Codes:** unaffected
5. **Description:** Traps never.

te

10	ignored	0001	111010	rs1	i = 0	ignored	rs2

`tt = 0x80 | (i == 0 ? r[rs2] : sign-extend(13 bit immediate)<6:0>);`

10	ignored	0001	111010	rs1	i = 1	signed 13 bit immediate

1. **Purpose:** to trap on equal
2. **Format:** `te address`
3. **Operation:**

```
if (Z == 1)
  trap;
else{
  r[pc] = r[npc];
  r[npc] = r[npc] + 4;}
```

4. **Condition Codes:** unaffected
5. **Description:** Traps on equal to zero.

tne

10	ignored	1001	111010	rs1	i = 0	ignored	rs2

tt = 0x80 | (i == 0 ? r[rs2] : sign-extend(13 bit immediate)<6:0>);

10	ignored	1001	111010	rs1	i = 1	signed 13 bit immediate

1. **Purpose:** to trap on not equal

2. **Format:** tne address

3. **Operation:**

```
if (Z == 0)
  trap;
else{
  r[pc] = r[npc];
  r[npc] = r[npc] + 4;}
```

4. **Condition Codes:** unaffected

5. **Description:** Traps on not equal to zero.

tl

10	ignored	0011	111010	rs1	i = 0	ignored	rs2

tt = 0x80 | (i == 0 ? r[rs2] : sign-extend(13 bit immediate)<6:0>);

10	ignored	0011	111010	rs1	i = 1	signed 13 bit immediate

1. **Purpose:** to trap on less

2. **Format:** tl address

3. **Operation:**

```
if ((N ^ V) == 1)
  trap;
else{
  r[pc] = r[npc];
  r[npc] = r[npc] + 4;}
```

4. **Condition Codes:** unaffected

5. **Description:** Traps on less than zero.

tle

10	ignored	0010	111010	rs1	i = 0	ignored	rs2

tt = 0x80 | (i == 0 ? r[rs2] : sign-extend(13 bit immediate)<6:0>);

10	ignored	0010	111010	rs1	i = 1	signed 13 bit immediate

1. **Purpose:** to trap on less or equal
2. **Format:** tle address
3. **Operation:**

```
if ((Z | N ^ V) == 1)
   trap;
else{
   r[pc] = r[npc];
   r[npc] = r[npc] + 4;}
```

4. **Condition Codes:** unaffected
5. **Description:** Traps on less than or equal to zero.

tge

10	ignored	1011	111010	rs1	i = 0	ignored	rs2

tt = 0x80 | (i == 0 ? r[rs2] : sign-extend(13 bit immediate)<6:0>);

10	ignored	1011	111010	rs1	i = 1	signed 13 bit immediate

1. **Purpose:** to trap on greater than or equal
2. **Format:** tge address
3. **Operation:**

```
if ((N ^ V) == 0)
   trap;
else{
   r[pc] = r[npc];
   r[npc] = r[npc] + 4;}
```

4. **Condition Codes:** unaffected
5. **Description:** Traps on greater than or equal to zero.

tg

10	ignored	1010	111010	rs1	i = 0	ignored	rs2

`tt = 0x80 | (i == 0 ? r[rs2] : sign-extend(13 bit immediate)<6:0>);`

10	ignored	1010	111010	rs1	i = 1	signed 13 bit immediate

1. **Purpose:** to trap on greater than

2. **Format:** `tg address`

3. **Operation:**

```
if ((Z | N ^ V) == 0)
  trap;
else{
  r[pc] = r[npc];
  r[npc] = r[npc] + 4;}
```

4. **Condition Codes:** unaffected

5. **Description:** Traps on greater than zero.

tlu

10	ignored	0101	111010	rs1	i = 0	ignored	rs2

`tt = 0x80 | (i == 0 ? r[rs2] : sign-extend(13 bit immediate)<6:0>);`

10	ignored	0101	111010	rs1	i = 1	signed 13 bit immediate

1. **Purpose:** to trap on less, unsigned

2. **Format:** `tlu address`

3. **Operation:**

```
if (C == 1)
  trap;
else{
  r[pc] = r[npc];
  r[npc] = r[npc] + 4;}
```

4. **Condition Codes:** unaffected

5. **Description:** Traps on less than zero, unsigned. Identical to the `tcs` instruction.

tleu

10	ignored	0100	111010	rs1	i = 0	ignored	rs2

tt = 0x80 | (i == 0 ? r[rs2] : sign-extend(13 bit immediate)<6:0>);

10	ignored	0100	111010	rs1	i = 1	signed 13 bit immediate

1. **Purpose:** to trap on less than or equal, unsigned

2. **Format:** `tleu address`

3. **Operation:**

```
if ((C | Z)  == 0)
   trap;
else{
   r[pc] = r[npc];
   r[npc] = r[npc] + 4;}
```

4. **Condition Codes:** unaffected

5. **Description:** Traps on less than or equal to zero, unsigned.

tgeu

10	ignored	1101	111010	rs1	i = 0	ignored	rs2

tt = 0x80 | (i == 0 ? r[rs2] : sign-extend(13 bit immediate)<6:0>);

10	ignored	1101	111010	rs1	i = 1	signed 13 bit immediate

1. **Purpose:** to trap on greater than or equal, unsigned

2. **Format:** `tgeu address`

3. **Operation:**

```
if (C == 0)
   trap;
else{
   r[pc] = r[npc];
   r[npc] = r[npc] + 4;}
```

4. **Condition Codes:** unaffected

5. **Description:** Traps on greater than or equal to zero, unsigned. Identical to the `tcc` instruction.

tgu

10	ignored	1100	111010	rs1	i = 0	ignored	rs2
tt = 0x80 | (i == 0 ? r[rs2] : sign-extend(13 bit immediate)<6:0>);							
10	ignored	1100	111010	rs1	i = 1	signed 13 bit immediate	

1. **Purpose:** to trap on greater than, unsigned

2. **Format:** `tgu address`

3. **Operation:**

```
if ((C | Z) == 0)
  trap;
else{
  r[pc] = r[npc];
  r[npc] = r[npc] + 4;}
```

4. **Condition Codes:** unaffected

5. **Description:** Traps on greater than zero, unsigned.

tpos

10	ignored	1110	111010	rs1	i = 0	ignored	rs2
tt = 0x80 | (i == 0 ? r[rs2] : sign-extend(13 bit immediate)<6:0>);							
10	ignored	1110	111010	rs1	i = 1	signed 13 bit immediate	

1. **Purpose:** to trap on positive

2. **Format:** `tpos address`

3. **Operation:**

```
if (N == 0)
  trap;
else{
  r[pc] = r[npc];
  r[npc] = r[npc] + 4;}
```

4. **Condition Codes:** unaffected

5. **Description:** Traps on positive.

tneg

10	ignored	0110	111010	rs1	i = 0	ignored	rs2

tt = 0x80 | (i == 0 ? r[rs2] : sign-extend(13 bit immediate)<6:0>);

10	ignored	0110	111010	rs1	i = 1	signed 13 bit immediate

1. **Purpose:** to trap on negative

2. **Format:** tneg address

3. **Operation:**

```
if (N == 1)
  trap;
else{
  r[pc] = r[npc];
  r[npc] = r[npc] + 4;}
```

4. **Condition Codes:** unaffected

5. **Description:** Traps on negative.

tcs

10	ignored	0101	111010	rs1	i = 0	ignored	rs2

tt = 0x80 | (i == 0 ? r[rs2] : sign-extend(13 bit immediate)<6:0>);

10	ignored	0101	111010	rs1	i = 1	signed 13 bit immediate

1. **Purpose:** to trap on C set

2. **Format:** tcs address

3. **Operation:**

```
if (C == 1)
  trap;
else{
  r[pc] = r[npc];
  r[npc] = r[npc] + 4;}
```

4. **Condition Codes:** unaffected

5. **Description:** Traps on C bit set.

tcc

10	ignored	1101	111010	rs1	i = 0	ignored	rs2

`tt = 0x80 | (i == 0 ? r[rs2] : sign-extend(13 bit immediate)<6:0>);`

10	ignored	1101	111010	rs1	i = 1	signed 13 bit immediate

1. **Purpose:** to trap on C clear

2. **Format:** `tcc address`

3. **Operation:**

```
if (C == 0)
  trap;
else{
  r[pc] = r[npc];
  r[npc] = r[npc] + 4;}
```

4. **Condition Codes:** unaffected

5. **Description:** Traps on C bit clear.

tvs

10	ignored	0111	111010	rs1	i = 0	ignored	rs2

`tt = 0x80 | (i == 0 ? r[rs2] : sign-extend(13 bit immediate)<6:0>);`

10	ignored	0111	111010	rs1	i = 1	signed 13 bit immediate

1. **Purpose:** to trap on signed overflow

2. **Format:** `tvs address`

3. **Operation:**

```
  trap;
else{
  r[pc] = r[npc];
  r[npc] = r[npc] + 4;}
```

4. **Condition Codes:** unaffected

5. **Description:** Traps on signed overflow.

tvc

10	ignored	1111	rs1	i = 0	ignored	rs2	

tt = 0x80 | (i == 0 ? r[rs2] : sign-extend(13 bit immediate)<6:0>);

10	ignored	1111	111010	rs1	i = 1	signed 13 bit immediate

1. **Purpose:** to trap on no signed overflow

2. **Format:** tvc address

3. **Operation:**

```
if (V == 0)
   trap;
else{
   r[pc] = r[npc];
   r[npc] = r[npc] + 4;}
```

4. **Condition Codes:** unaffected

5. **Description:** Traps on no signed overflow.

D.9 Control Instructions

Machine control instructions.

call

01	disp30

1. **Purpose:** function call

2. **Format:** call label

3. **Operation:**

```
r[o7] = r[pc];  /* return address */
r[pc] = r[npc];
r[npc] = r[pc] + sign_extend(disp30) << 2;
```

4. **Condition Codes:** unaffected

5. **Description:** Call instruction causes an unconditional transfer to any address in memory. The current value of the program counter, which contains the address of the call instruction, is written into %o7. *Note*: If the target address is located in a register, use the jmpl instruction with rd = %o7.

jmpl

10	rd	111000	rs1	i = 0	ignored	rs2

`op2 = i == 0 ? r[rs2] : sign-extend(13 bit immediate);`

10	rd	111000	rs1	i = 1	signed 13 bit immediate

1. **Purpose:** unconditional, register-indirect control transfer

2. **Format:** jmpl address, rd

3. **Operation:**

```
r[rd] = r[pc];  /* return address */
r[pc] = r[npc];
r[npc] = r[rs1] + op2;
```

4. **Condition Codes:** unaffected

5. **Description:** jmpl instruction causes an unconditional, register-indirect delayed control transfer to r[rs1] + op2. The current value of the program counter, which contains the address of the jmpl instruction, is written into r[rd].

   Note 1: jmpl with rd = %g0 is used for a subroutine routine return, see synthetic instructions ret and retl.

   Note 2: jmpl with rd = %o7 is used as a register-indirect subroutine call.

rett

10	0	111001	rs1	i = 0	ignored	rs2

op2 = i == 0 ? r[rs2] : sign-extend(13 bit immediate);

10	0	111001	rs1	i = 1	signed 13 bit immediate

1. **Purpose:** to return from trap, and a register-indirect control transfer

2. **Format:** rett address

3. **Operation:**

```
increment CWP of PSR;            /*restore register set*/
r[pc] = r[npc];
r[npc] = r[rs1] + op2;           /*delayed control transfer*/
restore S field of PSR from PS;  /*previous mode*/
set ET field of PSR = 1;         /*enable traps*/
```

4. **Condition Codes:** unaffected

5. **Description:** The register set is restored; the rett instruction then causes an unconditional, register-indirect delayed control transfer to r[rs1] + op2. The supervisor/user state is restored from the PS field and then traps are enabled.

   Note 1: The instruction immediately before a rett must be a jump.

   Note 2: rett is a privileged instruction and is included here only for completeness.

sethi

00	rd	100	imm22

1. **Purpose:** to set high 22 bits of register

2. **Format:** sethi const22, r[rd]

3. **Operation:** r[rd] = (const22 << 10) & 0xffffff600;

4. **Condition Codes:** unaffected

5. **Description:** sethi zeros the least significant 10 bits of the destination register and replaces its high-order 22 bits with const22.

   sethi 0, %g0 is recommended as a nop instruction.

save

10	rd	111100	rs1	i = 0	ignored	rs2

op2 = i == 0 ? r[rs2] : sign-extend(13 bit immediate);

10	rd	111100	rs1	i = 1	signed 13 bit immediate

1. **Purpose:** to save caller's window

2. **Format:** save   rs1, op2, rd

3. **Operation:**

   ```
   save caller's register window
   r[rd] = r[rs1] + op2
   ```

4. **Condition Codes:** unaffected

5. **Description:** The save instruction decrements the cwp and compares it against the register invalid mask, wim. If the comparison indicates a register window overflow, a trap is generated; if not, the +cwp+ is updated and the active window becomes the previous window, thus saving the caller's register window. The instruction then behaves like an **add** instruction except that the source registers come from the old register set while the destination register is in the new register set.

restore

10	rd	111101	rs1	i = 0	ignored	rs2

op2 = i == 0 ? r[rs2] : sign-extend(13 bit immediate);

10	rd	111101	rs1	i = 1	signed 13 bit immediate

1. **Purpose:** to restore caller's window

2. **Format:** restore   rs1, op2, rd

3. **Operation:**

   ```
   restore caller's register window
   r[rd] = r[rs1] + op2
   ```

4. **Condition Codes:** unaffected

5. **Description:** The restore instruction increments the cwp and compares it against the register invalid mask, wim. If the comparison indicates a register window underflow, a trap is generated; if not, the +cwp+ is updated and the previous window becomes the active window, thus restoring the caller's register window. The instruction then behaves like an **add** instruction except that the source registers come from the old register set while the destination register is in the new register set.

D.10   Floating-Point Instructions

Machine floating-point instructions.

ldf

11	rd	100000	rs1	i = 0	ignored	rs2

op2 = i == 0 ? r[rs2] : sign-extend(13 bit immediate);

11	rd	100000	rs1	i = 1	signed 13 bit immediate	

1. **Purpose:** to load a floating-point register with a word from memory

2. **Format:** ld [rs1 + op2], rd

3. **Operation:** f[rd] = memory[r[rs1] + op2]

4. **Condition Codes:** unaffected

5. **Description:** Loads floating-point register from memory; address is the sum of the contents of rs1 and op2. Either address operand may be missing. Memory address must be word aligned.

lddf

11	rd	100011	rs1	i = 0	ignored	rs2

op2 = i == 0 ? r[rs2] : sign-extend(13 bit immediate);

11	rd	100011	rs1	i = 1	signed 13 bit immediate	

1. **Purpose:** to load two floating-point registers with a doubleword from memory

2. **Format:** lddf [rs1 + op2], rd

3. **Operation:**

   f[rd] = memory[r[rs1] + op2]
   f[rd+1] = memory[r[rs1] + op2 +4]

4. **Condition Codes:** unaffected

5. **Description:** Loads floating-point registers from memory; address is the sum of the contents of rs1 and op2. Either address operand may be missing. Memory address must be doubleword aligned. Register number must be even; two registers are loaded.

stf

11	rd	100100	rs1	i = 0	ignored	rs2

op2 = i == 0 ? r[rs2] : sign-extend(13 bit immediate);

11	rd	100100	rs1	i = 1	signed 13 bit immediate

1. **Purpose:** to store a floating-point register into memory

2. **Format:** stf rd, [rs1 + op2]

3. **Operation:** memory[r[rs1] + op2] = f[rd]

4. **Condition Codes:** unaffected

5. **Description:** Stores floating-point register into memory; address is the sum of the contents of rs1 and op2. Either address operand may be missing. Memory address must be word aligned.

stdf

11	rd	100111	rs1	i = 0	ignored	rs2

op2 = i == 0 ? r[rs2] : sign-extend(13 bit immediate);

11	rd	100111	rs1	i = 1	signed 13 bit immediate

1. **Purpose:** to store two floating-point registers into memory

2. **Format:** stdf rd, [rs1 + op2]

3. **Operation:**

   memory[r[rs1] + op2] = f[rd]
   memory[r[rs1] + op2 + 4] = f[rd + 1]

4. **Condition Codes:** unaffected

5. **Description:** Stores two floating-point registers into memory; address is the sum of the contents of rs1 and op2. Either address operand may be missing. Memory address must be doubleword aligned. Register number must be even; two registers are stored.

fitos

10	rd	110100	ignored	011000100	rs2

1. **Purpose:** to convert from integer to single precision floating-point

2. **Format:** fitos rs2, rd

3. **Operation:** f[rd] = (float) f[rs2];

4. **Condition Codes:** unaffected

5. **Description:** Converts 32-bit integer in floating-point register to single precision floating-point.

fitod

| 10 | rd | 110100 | ignored | 011001000 | rs2 |

1. **Purpose:** to convert from integer to double precision floating-point

2. **Format:** fitod rs2, rd

3. **Operation:**

   f[rd], f[rd + 1] = (double) f[rs2];

4. **Condition Codes:** unaffected

5. **Description:** Converts 32-bit integer in floating-point register to double precision floating-point. Destination register must be even.

fitoq

| 10 | rd | 110100 | ignored | 011001100 | rs2 |

1. **Purpose:** to convert from integer to extended precision floating-point

2. **Format:** fitoq rs2, rd

3. **Operation:**

   f[rd], f[rd + 1], f[rd + 2] , f[rd + 3]= (extended) f[rs2];

4. **Condition Codes:** unaffected

5. **Description:** Converts 32-bit integer in floating-point register to extended precision floating-point. Destination register number must be divisible by 4.

fstoi

| 10 | rd | 110100 | ignored | 011010001 | rs2 |

1. **Purpose:** to convert from single precision floating-point to integer and round

2. **Format:** fstoi rs2, rd

3. **Operation:** f[rd] = (int) f[rs2];

4. **Condition Codes:** unaffected

5. **Description:** Converts single precision floating-point to integer and round; 32-bit result in floating-point register.

fdtoi

10	rd	110100	ignored	011010010	rs2

1. **Purpose:** to convert from double precision floating-point to integer and round
2. **Format:** fdtoi rs2, rd
3. **Operation:** f[rd] = (int) f[rs2], f[rs2 + 1];
4. **Condition Codes:** unaffected
5. **Description:** Converts double precision floating-point to integer and round; 32-bit result in floating-point register. Source register must be even.

fqtoi

10	rd	110100	ignored	011010011	rs2

1. **Purpose:** to convert from extended precision floating-point to integer and round
2. **Format:** fqtoi rs2, rd
3. **Operation:**

   f[rd] = (int) f[rs2], f[rs2 + 1], f[rs2 + 2], f[rs2 + 3];
4. **Condition Codes:** unaffected
5. **Description:** Converts extended precision floating-point to integer and round. 32-bit result in floating-point register. Source register number must be divisible by 4.

fstod

10	rd	110100	ignored	011001001	rs2

1. **Purpose:** to convert from single precision floating-point to double precision floating-point
2. **Format:** fstod rs2, rd
3. **Operation:** f[rd], f[rd + 1] = (double) f[rs2];
4. **Condition Codes:** unaffected
5. **Description:** Converts single precision floating-point to double precision floating-point. Destination register must be even.

fstoq

10	rd	110100	ignored	011001101	rs2

1. **Purpose:** to convert from single precision floating-point to extended precision floating-point

2. **Format:** `fstoq rs2, rd`

3. **Operation:**

   `f[rd], f[rd + 1], f[rd + 2], f[rd + 3] = (extended) f[rs2];`

4. **Condition Codes:** unaffected

5. **Description:** Converts single precision floating-point to extended precision floating-point. Destination register number must be divisible by 4.

fdtoq

10	rd	110100	ignored	011001110	rs2

1. **Purpose:** to convert from double precision floating-point to extended precision floating-point

2. **Format:** `fdtoq rs2, rd`

3. **Operation:**

   `f[rd], f[rd + 1], f[rd + 2], f[rd + 3] =`
                           `(extended) f[rs2], f[rs2 + 1];`

4. **Condition Codes:** unaffected

5. **Description:** Converts double precision floating-point to extended precision floating-point. Source register must be even. Destination register number must be divisible by 4.

fdtos

10	rd	110100	ignored	011000110	rs2

1. **Purpose:** to convert from double precision floating-point to single precision floating-point and round

2. **Format:** `fdtos rs2, rd`

3. **Operation:**

   `f[rd] = (float) f[rs2], f[rs2 + 1];`

4. **Condition Codes:** unaffected

5. **Description:** Converts double precision floating-point to single precision floating-point. Source register must be even.

fqtod

| 10 | rd | 110100 | ignored | 011001011 | rs2 |

1. **Purpose:** to convert from extended precision floating-point to double precision floating-point and round

2. **Format:** fqtod rs2, rd

3. **Operation:**

   ```
   f[rd], f[rd + 1] =
             (double) f[rs2], f[rs2 + 1], f[rs2 + 2], f[rs2 + 3];
   ```

4. **Condition Codes:** unaffected

5. **Description:** Converts extended precision floating-point to double precision floating-point. Source register number must be divisible by 4. Destination register must be even.

fqtos

| 10 | rd | 110100 | ignored | 011000111 | rs2 |

1. **Purpose:** to convert from extended precision floating-point to single precision floating-point and round

2. **Format:** fqtos rs2, rd

3. **Operation:**

   ```
   f[rd] = (float) f[rs2], f[rs2 + 1], f[rs2 + 2], f[rs2 + 3];
   ```

4. **Condition Codes:** unaffected

5. **Description:** Converts extended precision floating-point to single precision floating-point. Source register number must be divisible by 4.

fmovs

| 10 | rd | 110100 | ignored | 000000001 | rs2 |

1. **Purpose:** to move a word from f[rs2] to f[rd]

2. **Format:** fmovs rs2, rd

3. **Operation:** f[rd] = f[rs2];

4. **Condition Codes:** unaffected

5. **Description:** Copies the contents of a floating-point register; multiple fmovs instructions are necessary to transfer multiple precision data.

fnegs

10	rd	110100	ignored	000000101	rs2

1. **Purpose:** to negate a word from f[rs2] to f[rd]
2. **Format:** fnegs rs2, rd
3. **Operation:** f[rd] = - f[rs2];
4. **Condition Codes:** unaffected
5. **Description:** Copies the contents of a floating-point register complementing the sign bit.

fabss

10	rd	110100	ignored	000001001	rs2

1. **Purpose:** to copy absolute value from f[rs2] to f[rd]
2. **Format:** fabss rs2, rd
3. **Operation:** f[rd] = | f[rs2] |;
4. **Condition Codes:** unaffected
5. **Description:** Copies the contents of a floating-point register clearing the sign bit.

fadds

10	rd	110100	rs1	001000001	rs2

1. **Purpose:** single precision floating-point add
2. **Format:** fadds rs1, rs2, rd
3. **Operation:** f[rd] = f[rs1] + f[rs2];
4. **Condition Codes:** unaffected
5. **Description:** Single precision floating-point add. Contents of rs1 and rs2 unaffected.

faddd

10	rd	110100	rs1	001000010	rs2

1. **Purpose:** double precision floating-point add
2. **Format:** faddd rs1, rs2, rd
3. **Operation:**
   f[rd], f[rd + 1] = f[rs1], f[rs1 + 1] + f[rs2], f[rs2 + 1];
4. **Condition Codes:** unaffected
5. **Description:** Double precision floating-point add. Contents of rs1 and rs2 unaffected. All registers must be even.

faddq

10	rd	110100	rs1	001000011	rs2

1. **Purpose:** extended precision floating-point add

2. **Format:** `faddq rs1, rs2, rd`

3. **Operation:**

   ```
   f[rd], f[rd + 1], f[rd + 2], f[rd + 3]  =
     f[rs1], f[rs1 + 1], f[rs1 + 2], f[rs1 + 3] +
     f[rs2], f[rs2 + 1], f[rs2 + 2], f[rs2 + 3];
   ```

4. **Condition Codes:** unaffected

5. **Description:** Extended precision floating-point add. Contents of rs1 and rs2 unaffected. All registers numbers must be divisible by 4.

fsubs

10	rd	110100	rs1	001000101	rs2

1. **Purpose:** single precision floating-point subtract

2. **Format:** `fsubs rs1, rs2, rd`

3. **Operation:** `f[rd] = f[rs1] - f[rs2];`

4. **Condition Codes:** unaffected

5. **Description:** Single precision floating-point subtract. Contents of rs1 and rs2 unaffected.

fsubd

10	rd	110100	rs1	001000110	rs2

1. **Purpose:** double precision floating-point subtract

2. **Format:** `fsubd rs1, rs2, rd`

3. **Operation:**

   ```
   f[rd], f[rd + 1] = f[rs1], f[rs1 + 1] - f[rs2], f[rs2 + 1];
   ```

4. **Condition Codes:** unaffected

5. **Description:** Double precision floating-point subtract. Contents of rs1 and rs2 unaffected. All registers must be even.

fsubq

10	rd	110100	rs1	001000111	rs2

1. **Purpose:** extended precision floating-point subtract

2. **Format:** fsubq rs1, rs2, rd

3. **Operation:**

   ```
   f[rd], f[rd + 1], f[rd + 2], f[rd + 3]  =
   f[rs1], f[rs1 + 1], f[rs1 + 2], f[rs1 + 3] -
   f[rs2], f[rs2 + 1], f[rs2 + 2], f[rs2 + 3];
   ```

4. **Condition Codes:** unaffected

5. **Description:** Extended precision floating-point subtract. Contents of rs1 and rs2 unaffected. All registers numbers must be divisible by 4.

fmuls

10	rd	110100	rs1	001001001	rs2

1. **Purpose:** single precision floating-point multiply

2. **Format:** fmuls rs1, rs2, rd

3. **Operation:** f[rd] = f[rs1] * f[rs2];

4. **Condition Codes:** unaffected

5. **Description:** Single precision floating-point multiply. Contents of rs1 and rs2 unaffected.

fmuld

10	rd	110100	rs1	001001010	rs2

1. **Purpose:** double precision floating-point multiply

2. **Format:** fmuld rs1, rs2, rd

3. **Operation:**

   ```
   f[rd], f[rd + 1] = f[rs1], f[rs1 + 1] * f[rs2], f[rs2 + 1];
   ```

4. **Condition Codes:** unaffected

5. **Description:** Double precision floating-point multiply. Contents of rs1 and rs2 unaffected. All registers must be even.

fmulq

| 10 | rd | 110100 | rs1 | 001001011 | rs2 |

1. **Purpose:** extended precision floating-point multiply

2. **Format:** fmulq rs1, rs2, rd

3. **Operation:**

   ```
   f[rd], f[rd + 1], f[rd + 2], f[rd + 3]  =
    f[rs1], f[rs1 + 1], f[rs1 + 2], f[rs1 + 3] *
    f[rs2], f[rs2 + 1], f[rs2 + 2], f[rs2 + 3];
   ```

4. **Condition Codes:** unaffected

5. **Description:** Extended precision floating-point multiply. Contents of rs1 and rs2 unaffected. All registers numbers must be divisible by 4.

fsmuld

| 10 | rd | 110100 | rs1 | 001101001 | rs2 |

1. **Purpose:** single precision to double precision floating-point multiply

2. **Format:** fsmuld rs1, rs2, rd ?

3. **Operation:** f[rd], f[rd + 1] = f[rs1] * f[rs2];

4. **Condition Codes:** unaffected

5. **Description:** Single precision to double precision floating-point multiply. Contents of rs1 and rs2 unaffected. Destination register must be even.

fdivs

| 10 | rd | 110100 | rs1 | 001001101 | rs2 |

1. **Purpose:** single precision floating-point division

2. **Format:** fdivs rs1, rs2, rd

3. **Operation:** f[rd] = f[rs1] / f[rs2];

4. **Condition Codes:** unaffected

5. **Description:** Single precision floating-point division. Contents of rs1 and rs2 unaffected.

fdivd

10	rd	110100	rs1	001001110	rs2

1. **Purpose:** double precision floating-point division

2. **Format:** `fdivd rs1, rs2, rd`

3. **Operation:**
   `f[rd], f[rd + 1] = f[rs1], f[rs1 + 1] / f[rs2], f[rs2 + 1];`

4. **Condition Codes:** unaffected

5. **Description:** Double precision floating-point division. Contents of rs1 and rs2 unaffected. All registers must be even.

fdviq

10	rd	110100	rs1	001001111	rs2

1. **Purpose:** extended precision floating-point division

2. **Format:** `fdviq rs1, rs2, rd`

3. **Operation:**

   ```
   f[rd], f[rd + 1], f[rd + 2], f[rd + 3]   =
   f[rs1], f[rs1 + 1], f[rs1 + 2], f[rs1 + 3] /
   f[rs2], f[rs2 + 1], f[rs2 + 2], f[rs2 + 3];
   ```

4. **Condition Codes:** unaffected

5. **Description:** Extended precision floating-point division. Contents of rs1 and rs2 unaffected. All registers numbers must be divisible by 4.

fsqrts

10	rd	110100	ignored	000101001	rs2

1. **Purpose:** single precision square root

2. **Format:** `fsqrts rs1, rs2, rd`

3. **Operation:** `f[rd] = sqrt(f[rs2]);`

4. **Condition Codes:** unaffected

5. **Description:** Single precision floating-point square root. Contents of rs2 unaffected.

fsqrtd

| 10 | rd | 110100 | ignored | 000101010 | rs2 |

1. **Purpose:** double precision square root
2. **Format:** fsqrtd rs1, rs2, rd
3. **Operation:** f[rd], f[rd + 1] = sqrt(f[rs2], f[rs2 + 1]);
4. **Condition Codes:** unaffected
5. **Description:** Double precision floating-point square root. Contents of rs2 unaffected.

fsqrtq

| 10 | rd | 110100 | ignored | 000101011 | rs2 |

1. **Purpose:** extended precision square root
2. **Format:** fsqrtq rs1, rs2, rd
3. **Operation:**

   f[rd], f[rd + 1], f[rd + 2], f[rd + 3] =
     sqrt(f[rs2], f[rs2 + 1], f[rs2 + 2], f[rs2 + 3]);

4. **Condition Codes:** unaffected
5. **Description:** Extended precision floating-point square root. Contents of rs2 unaffected.

fcmps

| 10 | ignored | 110101 | rs1 | 001010001 | rs2 |

1. **Purpose:** single precision compare, set floating condition codes
2. **Format:** fcmps rs1, rs2 ?
3. **Operation:** compare f[rs1] to f[rs2] and set floating condition codes
4. **Condition Codes:**

   E = f[rs1] == f[rs2]
   L = f[rs1] < f[rs2]
   G = f[rs1] > f[rs2]
   U = f[rs1] ? f[rs2]

5. **Description:** Compare single precision sources and set floating condition codes. Causes an exception if either source is a signaling NaN.

   Note: A non-floating-point instruction must be executed between a floating-point compare instruction and a floating-point branch instruction.

fcmpd

10	ignored	110101	rs1	001010010	rs2

1. **Purpose:** double precision compare, set floating condition codes
2. **Format:** `fcmpd rs1, rs2` ?
3. **Operation:** compare `f[rs1]` to `f[rs2]` and set floating condition codes
4. **Condition Codes:**

```
E = f[rs1], f[rs1 + 1] == f[rs2], f[rs2 + 1]
L = f[rs1], f[rs1 + 1] <  f[rs2], f[rs2 + 1]
G = f[rs1], f[rs1 + 1] >  f[rs2], f[rs2 + 1]
U = f[rs1], f[rs1 + 1] ?  f[rs2], f[rs2 + 1]
```

5. **Description:** Compare double precision sources and set floating condition codes. Causes an exception if either source is a signaling NaN.

   Note: A non-floating-point instruction must be executed between a floating-point compare instruction and a floating-point branch instruction.

fcmpq

10	ignored	110101	rs1	001010011	rs2

1. **Purpose:** extended precision compare, set floating condition codes
2. **Format:** `fcmpq rs1, rs2` ?
3. **Operation:** compare `f[rs1]` to `f[rs2]` and set floating condition codes
4. **Condition Codes:**

```
E = f[rs1], ... f[rs1 + 3] == f[rs2], ... f[rs2 + 3]
L = f[rs1], ... f[rs1 + 3] <  f[rs2], ... f[rs2 + 3]
G = f[rs1], ... f[rs1 + 3] >  f[rs2], ... f[rs2 + 3]
U = f[rs1], ... f[rs1 + 3] ?  f[rs2], ... f[rs2 + 3]
```

5. **Description:** Compare extended precision sources and set floating condition codes. Causes an exception if either source is a signaling NaN.

   Note: A non-floating-point instruction must be executed between a floating-point compare instruction and a floating-point branch instruction.

fcmpes

10	ignored	110101	rs1	001010101	rs2

1. **Purpose:** single precision compare, set floating condition codes, exception if unordered

2. **Format:** `fcmpes rs1, rs2` ?

3. **Operation:** compare `f[rs1]` to `f[rs2]` and set floating condition codes

4. **Condition Codes:**

   ```
   E = f[rs1] == f[rs2]
   L = f[rs1] <  f[rs2]
   G = f[rs1] >  f[rs2]
   U = f[rs1] ?  f[rs2]
   ```

5. **Description:** Compare single precision sources and set floating condition codes. Causes an exception if either source is a signaling or a quiet NaN.

   Note: A non-floating-point instruction must be executed between a floating-point compare instruction and a floating-point branch instruction.

fcmped

10	ignored	110101	rs1	001010110	rs2

1. **Purpose:** double precision compare, set floating condition code, exception if unordered

2. **Format:** `fcmped rs1, rs2` ?

3. **Operation:** compare `f[rs1]` to `f[rs2]` and set floating condition codes

4. **Condition Codes:**

   ```
   E = f[rs1], f[rs1 + 1] == f[rs2], f[rs2 + 1]
   L = f[rs1], f[rs1 + 1] <  f[rs2], f[rs2 + 1]
   G = f[rs1], f[rs1 + 1] >  f[rs2], f[rs2 + 1]
   U = f[rs1], f[rs1 + 1] ?  f[rs2], f[rs2 + 1]
   ```

5. **Description:** Compare double precision sources and set floating condition codes. Causes an exception if either source is a signaling or a quiet NaN.

   Note: A non-floating-point instruction must be executed between a floating-point compare instruction and a floating-point branch instruction.

fcmpeq

| 10 | ignored | 110101 | rs1 | 001010111 | rs2 |

1. **Purpose:** extended precision compare, set floating condition codes, exception if unordered

2. **Format:** `fcmpeq rs1, rs2` ?

3. **Operation:** compare `f[rs1]` to `f[rs2]` and set floating condition codes

4. **Condition Codes:**

```
E = f[rs1], ... f[rs1 + 3] == f[rs2], ... f[rs2 + 3]
L = f[rs1], ... f[rs1 + 3] <  f[rs2], ... f[rs2 + 3]
G = f[rs1], ... f[rs1 + 3] >  f[rs2], ... f[rs2 + 3]
U = f[rs1], ... f[rs1 + 3] ?  f[rs2], ... f[rs2 + 3]
```

5. **Description:** Compare extended precision sources and set floating condition codes. Causes an exception if either source is a signaling or a quiet NaN.

   Note: A non-floating-point instruction must be executed between a floating-point compare instruction and a floating-point branch instruction.

D.11 Floating-Point Branch Instructions

Machine floating-point branch instructions.

fba

00	a	1000	110	disp22

1. **Purpose:** floating branch always
2. **Format:** `fba label`
3. **Operation:**

   ```
   r[pc] = r[npc];
   r[npc] = r[pc] + sign_extend(disp22) << 2;
   if (a == 1) annul next instruction;
   ```

4. **Condition Codes:** unaffected
5. **Description:** Floating branch always. Instruction operand is a label that is converted to a program counter relative address. If annulled, the next instruction in line is *not* executed.

   Note: An integer instruction must be executed between a floating compare and a floating branch instruction.

fbn

00	a	0000	110	disp22

1. **Purpose:** floating branch never
2. **Format:** `fbn label`
3. **Operation:**

   ```
   r[pc] = r[npc];
   r[npc] = r[npc] + 4;
   if (a == 1) annul next instruction;
   ```

4. **Condition Codes:** unaffected
5. **Description:** Floating branch never. Instruction operand is a label that is converted to a program counter relative address. If annulled, the next instruction in line is *not* executed.

   Note: An integer instruction must be executed between a floating compare and a floating branch instruction.

fbu

00	a	0111	110	disp22

1. **Purpose:** branch on unordered

2. **Format:** `fbu label`

3. **Operation:**

```
r[pc] = r[npc];
if (U == 1)
  r[npc] = + sign_extend(disp22) << 2;
else{
  r[npc] = r[npc] + 4;
  if (a == 1) annul next instruction;}
```

4. **Condition Codes:** unaffected

5. **Description:** Branches on unordered. Instruction operand is a label that is converted to a program counter relative address. If the branch instruction is annulled and not taken, the next instruction in line is *not* executed.

   Note: An integer instruction must be executed between a floating compare and a floating branch instruction.

fbo

00	a	1111	110	disp22

1. **Purpose:** floating branch on ordered

2. **Format:** `fbo label`

3. **Operation:**

```
r[pc] = r[npc];
if ((E | L | G) == 1)
  r[npc] = + sign_extend(disp22) << 2;
else{
  r[npc] = r[npc] + 4;
  if (a == 1) annul next instruction;}
```

4. **Condition Codes:** unaffected

5. **Description:** Branches on ordered. Instruction operand is a label that is converted to a program counter relative address. If the branch instruction is annulled and not taken, the next instruction in line is *not* executed.

   Note: An integer instruction must be executed between a floating compare and a floating branch instruction.

fbe

00	a	1001	110	disp22

1. **Purpose:** floating branch on equal

2. **Format:** fbe label

3. **Operation:**

```
r[pc] = r[npc];
if (E == 1)
  r[npc] = + sign_extend(disp22) << 2;
else{
  r[npc] = r[npc] + 4;
  if (a == 1) annul next instruction;}
```

4. **Condition Codes:** unaffected

5. **Description:** Floating branch on equal to zero. Instruction operand is a label that is converted to a program counter relative address. If the branch instruction is annulled and not taken, the next instruction in line is *not* executed.

   Note: An integer instruction must be executed between a floating compare and a floating branch instruction.

fbue

00	a	1010	110	disp22

1. **Purpose:** floating branch on unordered or equal

2. **Format:** fbue label

3. **Operation:**

```
r[pc] = r[npc];
if ((E | U) == 1)
  r[npc] = + sign_extend(disp22) << 2;
else{
  r[npc] = r[npc] + 4;
  if (a == 1) annul next instruction;}
```

4. **Condition Codes:** unaffected

5. **Description:** Branches on unordered or equal. Instruction operand is a label that is converted to a program counter relative address. If the branch instruction is annulled and not taken, the next instruction in line is *not* executed.

   Note: An integer instruction must be executed between a floating compare and a floating branch instruction.

fbne

00	a	0001	110	disp22

1. **Purpose:** floating branch on not equal

2. **Format:** `fbne label`

3. **Operation:**

```
r[pc] = r[npc];
if ((L | G | U) == 1)
  r[npc] = + sign_extend(disp22) << 2;
else{
  r[npc] = r[npc] + 4;
  if (a == 1) annul next instruction;}
```

4. **Condition Codes:** unaffected

5. **Description:** Floating branch on not equal to zero. Instruction operand is a label that is converted to a program counter relative address. If the branch instruction is annulled and not taken, the next instruction in line is *not* executed.

   Note: An integer instruction must be executed between a floating compare and a floating branch instruction.

fblg

00	a	0010	110	disp22

1. **Purpose:** floating branch on less or greater

2. **Format:** `fblg label`

3. **Operation:**

```
r[pc] = r[npc];
if ((L | G) == 1)
  r[npc] = + sign_extend(disp22) << 2;
else{
  r[npc] = r[npc] + 4;
  if (a == 1) annul next instruction;}
```

4. **Condition Codes:** unaffected

5. **Description:** Floating branch on less than or equal to zero. Instruction operand is a label that is converted to a program counter relative address. If the branch instruction is annulled and not taken, the next instruction in line is *not* executed.

   Note: An integer instruction must be executed between a floating compare and a floating branch instruction.

fbl

00	a	0100	110	disp22

1. **Purpose:** floating branch on less

2. **Format:** fbl label

3. **Operation:**

```
r[pc] = r[npc];
if (L  == 1)
  r[npc] = + sign_extend(disp22) << 2;
else{
  r[npc] = r[npc] + 4;
  if (a == 1) annul next instruction;}
```

4. **Condition Codes:** unaffected

5. **Description:** Floating branch on less. Instruction operand is a label that is converted to a program counter relative address. If the branch instruction is annulled and not taken, the next instruction in line is *not* executed.

   Note: An integer instruction must be executed between a floating compare and a floating branch instruction.

fbul

00	a	0011	110	disp22

1. **Purpose:** branch on unordered or less

2. **Format:** fbul label

3. **Operation:**

```
r[pc] = r[npc];
if ((L | U) == 1)
  r[npc] = + sign_extend(disp22) << 2;
else{
  r[npc] = r[npc] + 4;
  if (a == 1) annul next instruction;}
```

4. **Condition Codes:** unaffected

5. **Description:** Floating branch on unordered or less than zero. Instruction operand is a label that is converted to a program counter relative address. If the branch instruction is annulled and not taken, the next instruction in line is *not* executed.

   Note: An integer instruction must be executed between a floating compare and a floating branch instruction.

fble

00	a	1101	110	disp22

1. **Purpose:** floating branch on less or equal

2. **Format:** `fble label`

3. **Operation:**

```
r[pc] = r[npc];
if ((E | L) == 1)
  r[npc] = + sign_extend(disp22) << 2;
else{
  r[npc] = r[npc] + 4;
  if (a == 1) annul next instruction;}
```

4. **Condition Codes:** unaffected

5. **Description:** Floating branch on less or equal to zero. Instruction operand is a label that is converted to a program counter relative address. If the branch instruction is annulled and not taken, the next instruction in line is *not* executed.

   Note: An integer instruction must be executed between a floating compare and a floating branch instruction.

fbule

00	a	1110	110	disp22

1. **Purpose:** floating branch on unordered, less or equal

2. **Format:** `fbule label`

3. **Operation:**

```
r[pc] = r[npc];
if ((E | L | U) == 1)
  r[npc] = + sign_extend(disp22) << 2;
else{
  r[npc] = r[npc] + 4;
  if (a == 1) annul next instruction;}
```

4. **Condition Codes:** unaffected

5. **Description:** Floating branch on unordered, less or equal. Instruction operand is a label that is converted to a program counter relative address. If the branch instruction is annulled and not taken, the next instruction in line is *not* executed.

   Note: An integer instruction must be executed between a floating compare and a floating branch instruction.

fbge

00	a	1011	110	disp22

1. **Purpose:** branch on greater than or equal

2. **Format:** `fbge label`

3. **Operation:**

```
r[pc] = r[npc];
if ((E | G) == 1)
  r[npc] = + sign_extend(disp22) << 2;
else{
  r[npc] = r[npc] + 4;
  if (a == 1) annul next instruction;}
```

4. **Condition Codes:** unaffected

5. **Description:** Branches on greater than or equal to zero. Instruction operand is a label that is converted to a program counter relative address. If the branch instruction is annulled and not taken, the next instruction in line is *not* executed.

   Note: An integer instruction must be executed between a floating compare and a floating branch instruction.

fbuge

00	a	1100	110	disp22

1. **Purpose:** floating branch on unordered, greater or equal

2. **Format:** `fbuge label`

3. **Operation:**

```
r[pc] = r[npc];
if ((E | G | U) == 1)
  r[npc] = + sign_extend(disp22) << 2;
else{
  r[npc] = r[npc] + 4;
  if (a == 1) annul next instruction;}
```

4. **Condition Codes:** unaffected

5. **Description:** Floating branch on unordered, greater or equal. Instruction operand is a label that is converted to a program counter relative address. If the branch instruction is annulled and not taken, the next instruction in line is *not* executed.

   Note: An integer instruction must be executed between a floating compare and a floating branch instruction.

fbg

00	a	0110	110	disp22

1. **Purpose:** floating branch on greater

2. **Format:** fbg label

3. **Operation:**

```
r[pc] = r[npc];
if (G == 1)
  r[npc] = + sign_extend(disp22) << 2;
else{
  r[npc] = r[npc] + 4;
  if (a == 1) annul next instruction;}
```

4. **Condition Codes:** unaffected

5. **Description:** Floating branch on greater. Instruction operand is a label that is converted to a program counter relative address. If the branch instruction is annulled and not taken, the next instruction in line is *not* executed.

   Note: An integer instruction must be executed between a floating compare and a floating branch instruction.

fbug

00	a	0101	110	disp22

1. **Purpose:** floating branch on unordered or greater

2. **Format:** fbug label

3. **Operation:**

```
r[pc] = r[npc];
if ((G | U) == 1)
  r[npc] = + sign_extend(disp22) << 2;
else{
  r[npc] = r[npc] + 4;
  if (a == 1) annul next instruction;}
```

4. **Condition Codes:** unaffected

5. **Description:** Floating branch on unordered or greater. Instruction operand is a label that is converted to a program counter relative address. If the branch instruction is annulled and not taken, the next instruction in line is *not* executed.

   Note: An integer instruction must be executed between a floating compare and a floating branch instruction.

Appendix E

SYNTHETIC INSTRUCTIONS AND PSEUDO-OPS

Synthetic Instruction		Instruction Generated		Comment
cmp	reg_{rs1}, reg_or_imm	subcc	reg_{rs1}, reg_or_imm, %g0	Compare
jmp	$address$	jmpl	$address$, %o7	Jump
call	reg_or_imm	jmpl	reg_or_imm, %o7	Call, pointer in register
tst	reg_{rs1}	orcc	reg_{rs1}, %g0, %g0	Test
ret		jmpl	%i7 + 8, %g0	Return from subroutine
retl		jmpl	%o7 + 8, %g0	Return from leaf subroutine

Synthetic Instruction	Instruction Generated	Comment
set $value$, reg_{rd}	or %g0, $value$, reg_{rd}	If -4096 $\leq$value$\leq$ 4095
set $value$, reg_{rd}	sethi %hi($value$), reg_{rd}	If ((value & 0x1ff) == 0)
set $value$, reg_{rd}	sethi %hi($value$), reg_{rd}; or reg_{rd}, %lo($value$), reg_{rd}	Otherwise *Warning*: Do not use *set* in an instruction's delay slot.
not reg_{rs1}, reg_{rd}	xnor reg_{rs1}, %g0, reg_{rd}	One's complement
not reg_{rd}	xnor reg_{rd}, %g0, reg_{rd}	One's complement
neg reg_{rs2}, reg_{rd}	sub %g0, reg_{rs2}, reg_{rd}	Two's complement
neg reg_{rd}	sub %g0, reg_{rd}, reg_{rd}	Two's complement
inc reg_{rd}	add reg_{rd}, 1, reg_{rd}	Increment by 1
inc $const_{13}$, reg_{rd}	add reg_{rd}, $const_{13}$, reg_{rd}	Increment by $const_{13}$
inccc reg_{rd}	addcc reg_{rd}, 1, reg_{rd}	Increment by 1 and set icc
inccc $const_{13}$, reg_{rd}	addcc reg_{rd}, $const_{13}$, reg_{rd}	Increment by $const_{13}$ and set icc

Synthetic Instruction		Instruction Generated		Comment
dec	reg_{rd}	sub	reg_{rd},1, reg_{rd}	Decrement by 1
dec	$const_{13}$, reg_{rd}	sub	reg_{rd}, $const_{13}$, reg_{rd}	Decrement by $const_{13}$
deccc	reg_{rd}	subcc	reg_{rd},1, reg_{rd}	Decrement by 1 and set icc
deccc	$const_{13}$, reg_{rd}	subcc	reg_{rd}, $const_{13}$, reg_{rd}	Decrement by $const_{13}$ and set icc
btst	reg_or_imm, reg_{rs1}	andcc	reg_{rs1}, reg_or_imm, %g0	Bit test
bset	reg_or_imm, reg_{rd}	or	reg_{rd}, reg_or_imm, reg_{rd}	Bit set
bclr	reg_or_imm, reg_{rd}	andn	reg_{rd}, reg_or_imm, reg_{rd}	Bit clear
btog	reg_or_imm, reg_{rd}	xor	reg_{rd}, reg_or_imm, reg_{rd}	Bit toggle
clr	reg_{rd}	or	%g0, %g0, reg_{rd}	Clear register
clrb	[$address$]	stb	%g0, [$address$]	Clear byte
clrh	[$address$]	sth	%g0, [$address$]	Clear halfword
clr	[$address$]	st	%g0, [$address$]	Clear word
mov	reg_or_imm, reg_{rd}	or	%g0, reg_or_imm, reg_{rd}	
mov	%y, reg_{rs1}	rd	%y, reg_{rs1}	
mov	reg_or_imm, %y	wr	%g0, reg_or_imm, %y	

Mnemonic	Arguments	Description
.ascii	"string" [,"string"]*	Generates the given sequence of ASCII character bytes.
.asciz	"string" [,"string"]*	Generates the given sequence of ASCII character bytes, each string terminated by null byte.
.text	"string"	Changes the current segment to text, and sets the location counter to the location of the next available byte in that segment. The default segment at the beginning of assembly is text.
.data	"string"	Changes the current segment to data, and sets the location counter to the location of the next available byte in that segment.
.bss	"string"	Changes the current segment to bss, and sets the location counter to the location of the next available byte in that segment.
.skip	n	Increments the location counter by n, which allocates n bytes of empty space in the current segment.
.align	boundary	Aligns the location counter on a 0-mod-*boundary* boundary; *boundary* may be 1 (which has no effect), 2, 4, or 8.
.byte	8bitval [,8bitval]*	Generates (a sequence of) initialized bytes in the current segment.
.half	16 bitval [,16bitval]*	Generates (a sequence of) initialized halfwords in the current segment. The location counter must already be aligned on a halfword boundary (use .align 2).
.word	32bitval [,32bitval]*	Generates (a sequence of) initialized words in the current segment. The location counter must already be aligned on a word boundary (use .align 4).

Mnemonic	Arguments	Description
.single	Orfloatval [,Orfloatval]*	Generates (a sequence of) intiialized single precision floating-point values in the current segment. The location counter must already be aligned on a word boundary (use .align 4).
.double	Orfloatval [,Orfloatval]*	Generates (a sequence of) initialized double precision floating-point values in the current segment. The location counter must already be aligned on a doubleword boundary (use .align 8).
.quad	Orfloatval [,Orfloatval]*	Generates (a sequence of) initialized quad precision floating-point values in the current segment (.quad currently generates quad precision values with only *double precision* significance). The location counter must already be aligned on a doubleword boundary (use .align 8).
.global	symbol, size [,symbol]	Marks the (list of) user symbols as "global." Note that when a symbol is both declared to be global and defined (i.e., used as a label, used as the left operand of an = pseudo-op, the .global must appear *before* the definition.
.common	symbol_name, size	Declares the name and size (in bytes) of a FORTRAN-style NAMED COMMON area.
.empty		Used in the delay slot of a control transfer instruction (CTI), this suppresses assembler complaints about the next instruction's presence in a delay slot. Some instructions should not be in the delay slot of a CTI.

INSTRUCTIONS SORTED ALPHABETICALLY

Appendix G

POWERS OF 2

Powers of 2 in Hexadecimal, Decimal, and Pages

n	$2^n{}_{16}$	$(2^{32} - 2^n)_{16}$	$2^n{}_{10}$		
1	2	fffffffe	2		
2	4	fffffffc	4		
3	8	fffffff8	8		
4	10	fffffff0	16		
5	20	ffffffe0	32		
6	40	ffffffc0	64		
7	80	ffffff80	128		
8	100	ffffff00	256		
9	200	fffffe00	512		
10	400	fffffc00	1024	1Kb	
11	800	fffff800	2048	2Kb	
12	1000	fffff000	4096	4Kb	1 page
13	2000	ffffe000	8192	8Kb	2 pages
14	4000	ffffc000	16384	16Kb	4 pages
15	8000	ffff8000	32768	32Kb	8 pages
16	10000	ffff0000	65536	64Kb	16 pages
17	20000	fffe0000	131072	128Kb	32 pages
18	40000	fffc0000	262144	256Kb	1 segment
19	80000	fff80000	524288	512Kb	2 segments
20	100000	fff00000	1048576	1Mb	4 segments
21	200000	ffe00000	2097152	2Mb	8 segments
22	400000	ffc00000	4194304	4Mb	16 segments
23	800000	ff800000	8388608	8Mb	32 segments
24	1000000	ff000000	16777216	16Mb	1 region
25	2000000	fe000000	33554432	32Mb	2 regions
26	4000000	fc000000	67108864	64Mb	4 regions
27	8000000	f8000000	134217728	128Mb	8 regions
28	10000000	f0000000	268435456	256Mb	16 regions
29	20000000	e0000000	536870912	512Mb	32 regions
30	40000000	c0000000	1073741824	1Gb	64 regions
31	80000000	80000000	2147483648	2Gb	128 regions
32	100000000		4294967296	4Gb	1 context
33	200000000		8589934592	8Gb	2 contexts
34	400000000		17179869184	16Gb	4 contexts
35	800000000		34359738368	32Gb	8 contexts
36	1000000000		68719476736	64Gb	16 contexts

Appendix H

MACRO LANGUAGE PROCESSOR m4

NAME

m4 – macro language processor

SYNOPSIS

m4 [*filename*] ...

SYSTEM V SYNOPSIS

/usr/5bin/m4 [**–es**] [**–B***int*] [**–H***int*] [**–S***int*] [**–T***int*] [**–D***name=val*] [**–U***name*] [*filename*]...

AVAILABILITY

The System V version of this command is available with the *System V* software installation option. Refer to *Installing SunOS 4.1* for information on how to install optional software.

DESCRIPTION

m4 is a macro processor intended as a front end for Ratfor, C, and other languages. Each of the argument files is processed in order; if there are no files, or if a file name is '–', the standard input is read. The processed text is written on the standard output.

Macro calls have the form:

name(*argument1*[, *argument2*, ...,] *argumentn*)

The '(' must immediately follow the name of the macro. If the name of a defined macro is not followed by a '(', it is interpreted as a call of the macro with no arguments. Potential macro names consist of letters, digits, and '_', (underscores) where the first character is not a digit.

Leading unquoted SPACE, TAB, and NEWLINE characters are ignored while collecting arguments. Left and right single quotes (' ') are used to quote strings. The value of a quoted string is the string stripped of the quotes.

When a macro name is recognized, the arguments are collected by searching for a matching right parenthesis. If fewer arguments are supplied than are in the macro definition, the trailing arguments are taken to be NULL. Macro evaluation proceeds normally during the collection of the arguments, and any commas or right parentheses which happen to turn up within the value of a nested call are as effective as those in the original input text. After argument collection, the value of the macro is pushed back onto the input stream and rescanned.

SYSTEM V OPTIONS

The options and their effects are as follows:

–e   Operate interactively. Interrupts are ignored and the output is unbuffered.

–s   Enable line sync output for the C preprocessor (#line ...)

–B*int*   Change the size of the push-back and argument collection buffers from the default of 4,096.

–H*int*   Change the size of the symbol table hash array from the default of 199. The size should be prime.

–S*int*   Change the size of the call stack from the default of 100 slots. Macros take three slots, and non-macro arguments take one.

–T*int*   Change the size of the token buffer from the default of 512 bytes.

To be effective, these flags must appear before any file names and before any **–D** or **–U** flags:

–D*name*[*=val*]
         Define *filename* to be **val** or to be NULL in *val*'s absence.

–U*name*
         Undefine *name*.

USAGE

Built-In Macros

487

m4 makes available the following built-in macros. They may be redefined, but once this is done the original meaning is lost. Their values are NULL unless otherwise stated.

define   The second argument is installed as the value of the macro whose name is the first argument. Each occurrence of $n in the replacement text, where n is a digit, is replaced by the n'th argument. Argument 0 is the name of the macro; missing arguments are replaced by the NULL string.

undefine   Remove the definition of the macro named in the argument.

ifdef   If the first argument is defined, the value is the second argument, otherwise the third. If there is no third argument, the value is NULL. The word *unix* is predefined.

changequote Change quote characters to the first and second arguments. **changequote** without arguments restores the original values (that is, ' ').

divert   **m4** maintains 10 output streams, numbered 0-9. The final output is the concatenation of the streams in numerical order; initially stream 0 is the current stream. The *divert* macro changes the current output stream to the (digit-string) argument. Output diverted to a stream other than 0 through 9 is discarded.

undivert   Display immediate output of text from diversions named as arguments, or all diversions if no argument. Text may be undiverted into another diversion. Undiverting discards the diverted text.

divnum   Return the value of the current output stream.

dnl   Read and discard characters up to and including the next NEWLINE.

ifelse   Has three or more arguments. If the first argument is the same string as the second, then the value is the third argument. If not, and if there are more than four arguments, the process is repeated with arguments 4, 5, 6, 7 and so on. Otherwise, the value is either the last string not used by the above process, or, if it is not present, NULL.

incr   Return the value of the argument incremented by 1. The value of the argument is calculated by interpreting an initial digit-string as a decimal number.

eval   Evaluate the argument as an arithmetic expression, using 32-bit arithmetic. Operators include +, −, *, /, %, ^ (exponentiation); relationals; parentheses.

len   Return the number of characters in the argument.

index   Return the position in the first argument where the second argument begins (zero origin), or −1 if the second argument does not occur.

substr   Return a substring of the first argument. The second argument is a zero origin number selecting the first character; the third argument indicates the length of the substring. A missing third argument is taken to be large enough to extend to the end of the first string.

translit   Transliterate the characters in the first argument from the set given by the second argument to the set given by the third. No abbreviations are permitted.

include   Return the contents of the file named in the argument.

sinclude   Is similar to **include**, except that it says nothing if the file is inaccessible.

syscmd   Execute the system command given in the first argument. No value is returned.

maketemp   Fill in a string of XXXXX in the argument with the current process ID.

errprint   Print the argument on the diagnostic output file.

dumpdef   Print current names and definitions, for the named items, or for all if no arguments are given.

SYSTEM V USAGE

In the System V version of **m4**, the following built-in macros have added capabilities.

Built-In Macros

define　　'$#' is replaced by the number of arguments; $* is replaced by a list of all the arguments separated by commas; $@ is like '$*', but each argument is quoted (with the current quotes).

changequote　　Change quote symbols to the first and second arguments. The symbols may be up to five characters long.

eval　　Additional operators include bitwise '**&**', '|', '^' and '~'. Octal, decimal and hex numbers may be specified as in C. The second argument specifies the radix for the result; the default is 10. The third argument may be used to specify the minimum number of digits in the result.

The System V version of **m4** makes available the following additional built-in macros.

defn　　Return the quoted definition of the argument(s). It is useful for renaming macros, especially built-ins.

pushdef　　Like **define**, but saves any previous definition.

popdef　　Remove current definition of the argument(s), exposing the previous one, if any.

shift　　Return all but the first argument. The other arguments are quoted and pushed back with commas in between. The quoting nullifies the effect of the extra scan that will subsequently be performed.

changecom　　Change left and right comment markers from the default # and NEWLINE. With no arguments, the comment mechanism is effectively disabled. With one argument, the left marker becomes the argument and the right marker becomes NEWLINE. With two arguments, both markers are affected. Comment markers may be up to five characters long.

decr　　Return the value of the argument decremented by 1.

sysval　　Return code from the last call to **syscmd**.

m4exit　　Exit immediately from **m4**. Argument 1, if given, is the exit code; the default is 0.

m4wrap　　Argument 1 will be pushed back at final EOF. For example, '**m4wrap("cleanup()")**'.

traceon　　With no arguments, turn on tracing for all macros (including built-ins). Otherwise, turn on tracing for named macros.

traceoff　　Turn off trace globally and for any macros specified. Macros specifically traced by **traceon** can be untraced only by specific calls to **traceoff**.

SEE ALSO

cc(1V)

m4 — A Macro Processor, in *Programming Utilities and Libraries*

NOTES

While the compiler allows 8-bit strings and comments, 8-bits are not allowed anywhere else. The **cc**(1V) command does not generate or support 8-bit symbol names because, until ANSI C, non-ASCII support was not expected. The ANSI C specification now suggests that string literals and comments can contain any characters from any character code set.

Bibliography

[1] R. S. Barton. A new approach to the functional design of a computer. In *Proc. Western Joint Computer Conf.*, pages 393–396, 1961.

[2] C. G. Bell and W. D. Strecker. Computer structures: What have we learned from the pdp-11. In *Proc. Third Annual Symposium on Computer Architecture*, pages 1–14, 1976.

[3] A. W. Burks, H. H. Goldstine, and J. von Neumann. Preliminary discussion of the logical design of an electronic computing instrument. In W. Aspray and A. Burks, editors, *Papers of John von Neumann*, pages 97 – 146. MIT Press, Cambridge, Mass., 1987.

[4] Blue Sky Research. *Textures User's Guide*. Blue Sky Research, Portland Oreg., 1988.

[5] Digital. *pdp11 Processor Handbook*. Digital Equipment Corporation, Maynard, Mass., 1975.

[6] Digital. *vax11 Processor Handbook*. Digital Equipment Corporation, Maynard, Mass., 1981.

[7] Ralph E. Gorin. *Introduction to Decsystem-20*. Digital Equipment Corporation, Maynard, Mass., 1981.

[8] Joe Heinrich. *MIPS R4000 User's Manual*. Prentice Hall, Upper Saddle River, N.J., 1993.

[9] Hewlett-Packard. *HP-15C Owner's Handbook*. Hewlett-Packard Company, Palo Alto, Calif., 1982.

[10] Kathleen Jensen and Niklaus Wirth. *Pascal User Manual and Report*. Prentice Hall, Upper Saddle River, N.J., 3rd edition, 1985.

[11] Brian W. Kernighan and Dennis M. Ritchie. *The C Programming Language*. Prentice Hall, Upper Saddle River, N.J., 2nd edition, 1988.

[12] Donald E. Knuth. *The Art of Computer Programming*. Addison-Wesley, Reading, Mass., 2nd edition, 1973.

[13] Leslie Lamport. *LATEX: A Document Preparation System, User's Guide and Reference Manual*. Addison-Wesley, Reading, Mass., 1986.

[14] Henry M. Levy and Richard H. Eckhouse, Jr. *Computer Programming and Architecture: The VAX-11*. Digital Press, Woburn, Mass., 1980.

[15] M. Morris Mano. *Computer System Architecture*. Prentice Hall, Upper Saddle River, N.J., 1993.

[16] John McCarthy. Recursive functions of symbolic expressions and their computation by machine. *Communications of the ACM*, 1960.

[17] John McCarthy, Paul W. Abrahams, Daniel J. Edwards, Timothy P. Hart, and Michael I. Levin. *LISP 1.5 Programmer's Manual*. MIT Press, Cambridge, Mass., 1960.

[18] Jon Meyer and Troy Downing. *JAVA Virtual Machine*. O'Reilly, Sebastopol, Calif., 1997.

[19] David A. Patterson and John L. Hennessy. *Computer Architecture: A Quantitative Approach*. Morgan Kaufmann, San Francisco, 1990.

[20] Norman R. Scott. *Computer Number Systems and Arithmetic*. Prentice Hall, Upper Saddle River, N.J., 1985.

[21] SIGPLAN Notices. IEEE standard for binary floating-point arithmetic. Technical Report 22:2, IEEE, New York, 1985.

[22] SPARC International Inc. *The SPARC Architecture Manual*. Prentice Hall, Upper Saddle River, N.J., 1992.

[23] Richard M. Stallman. *Gnu emacs Manual*. Technical report, Free Software Foundation, 1985.

[24] Richard M. Stallman. *Debugging with GDB: The GNU Source-Level Debugger*. Technical report, Free Software Foundation, 1998.

[25] Sun Microsystems. Sun-4 assembly language reference manual. Technical Report 800-3086-10, Sun Microsystems, 1990.

[26] Andrew S. Tanenbaum. *Structured Computer Organization*. Prentice Hall, Upper Saddle River, N.J., 4th edition, 1990.

[27] University of California, Berkeley. *UNIX Programmer's Manual, Supplementary Documents*. USENIX Association, Berkeley, Calif., 1984.

[28] David L. Weaver and Tom Germond. *The SPARC Architecture Manual, Version 9.* Prentice Hall, Upper Saddle River, N.J., 1994.

[29] M. Wilkes, D. J. Wheeler, and S. Gill. *The Preparation of Programs for an Electronic Digital Computer.* Addison-Wesley, Reading, Mass., 1951.

[30] M. V. Wilkes. *Memoirs of a Computer Pioneer.* MIT Press, Cambridge, Mass., 1985.

INDEX